THE NEW ENCYCLOPEDIA OF
SNAKES

THE NEW ENCYCLOPEDIA OF
SNAKES

CHRIS MATTISON

Princeton University Press
Princeton and Oxford

CONTENTS

To my parents,
Ron and Rose Mattison, who nurtured
my interest in animals and books.

Published in the United States, Canada, and the Philippine
Islands by Princeton University Press, 41 William Street,
Princeton, New Jersey 08540

First published in the UK 1995 by Blandford
Revised and updated edition published in the UK in 2007
by Cassell Illustrated, a division of
Octopus Publishing Group Ltd.

Library of Congress Control Number 2007922951

ISBN-13: 978-0-691-13295-2
ISBN-10: 0-691-13295-X

nathist.press.princeton.edu

Designed by Jon Wainwright
Commissioning Editor Laura Price
Art Director Philip Gilderdale
Illustrations by Alan Rollason
Map illustrations by Jon Wainwright

Printed in China

10 9 8 7 6 5 4 3 2 1

Page 1: A medieval bronze belt buckle in the form of a stylised adder, excavated
from a field in East Anglia, England.

INTRODUCTION

In this book I have set out to describe and explain,
in a readable way, the lives of snakes. In doing so, I
hope that it will introduce the reader to the same sense
of fascination and wonderment that I have felt when
watching and studying them, whether in the field
or in captivity.

The information has been obtained in a number of
ways. Although I have drawn on personal experiences
where I felt it appropriate, a book of this type is not the
place for original observations. Rather, it is a means of
communicating information that numerous professional
and amateur herpetologists have accumulated over the
years. Many such observations have appeared in scientific
journals and society publications that are not widely
read by the general public and so the information they
contain is often overlooked; I have attempted to extract
those pieces of knowledge that are most likely to be of
interest to amateur herpetologists, as well as to general
naturalists who may wish to know more about snakes.
In doing so, I acknowledge the massive contribution that
has been made by innumerable researchers and writers
upon whose efforts I have relied and whose findings
I have plundered. I have given references in places,
but only where a specific piece of information has been
used or where I have drawn heavily from major review
articles. I feel that the insertion of too many references
disrupts the text to an unacceptable degree and often
serves no useful purpose in a book of this type.

Some of the material consists of interesting 'snippets'
relating to some of the more unusual or spectacular
species or to their behaviour. Most of it, though,
concerns underlying principles and generalisations that
apply to all snakes, bearing in mind that it is not always
possible to give simple, hard-and-fast rules about how
snakes live; this reflects their diversity as well as the
lack of knowledge about certain aspects of their lives.

Throughout the book, I have tried to adopt an
evolutionary approach. Snakes have been moulded
by natural selection.

The array of shapes, sizes, colours and behaviour
patterns that we see are the end products of this process
and I believe that it is not possible to produce an account
of them without continual reference to evolutionary
forces and pressures; understanding these allows us to
answer many of the questions about why snakes look and
behave the way they do. I apologise in advance if some of

this material seems complicated, although I have tried to present it in simple terms wherever possible.

Natural selection is the driving force behind evolution. Organisms evolve in response to changes in their physical environment as well as interactions with other organisms, of the same or different species, with which they share their environment. Most environmental changes are gradual and evolution keeps pace with them to produce ever-more efficient answers to new problems.

Often, one species' loss is another one's gain. More recently, the human species has brought about far-reaching changes, the speed of which easily outstrips evolution. Organisms that have taken millions of years to become good at what they do, have no response to these changes. They are not able to adapt to new conditions in the space of a few generations and many of them, including snakes, are becoming rare or extinct.

Our reaction to this problem seems to vary with the type of animal concerned. Because snakes are among the most secretive and overlooked components of the biological diversity with which we share our world, relatively little attention has been paid to their conservation in the past – it is hard to love something you can't see!

Furthermore, there is an ingrained distrust of snakes, fuelled largely by ignorance, even though most are harmless and many are useful and beautiful to look at. There is some evidence that attitudes towards snakes, along with other aspects of nature, are changing. I hope that this book will continue this trend by contributing towards a greater understanding of them and, through this, a greater appreciation.

Since writing the first edition of this book a large number of changes have taken place, resulting in the need for this revised edition. Broadly speaking, these have come about through three far-reaching developments.

Firstly, in research. In the laboratory, advances in DNA technology and other methods of biochemical analysis have helped to clarify the similarities and differences between species, genera and families. This has resulted in numerous taxonomic changes at every level, including three (or possibly four) new families since the first edition, raising the number from 15 to 18 – a 20 per cent increase! Many species have been reclassified, including

several familiar groups such as the rat snakes, and new names have to be learned. Over 400 new species have been added. In the field, miniaturisation of electronics and advances in the science and techniques of telemetry have enabled scientists to study individual and social behaviour of secretive animals such as snakes on a far greater scale than was ever possible in the past. Because of this, we are only now beginning to appreciate that these are not fundamentally mindless creatures that lead random, happenchance lives, but ones which have effective and sophisticated strategies to ensure their survival and procreation.

The second important change is the way in which knowledge is shared, through the internet. Information is far easier to access and communication between researchers is faster. The first edition took two years to research and replies to enquiries sometimes took several months to arrive, especially if the people concerned were away on field work. The internet has speeded up the process but, at the same time, it has led to the proliferation of inaccurate and spurious information in the public domain. Separating the wheat from the chaff has become more important than it was previously.

Finally, concerns about habitat destruction, which were arguably uppermost in the thoughts of most conservationists in the 1980s and 1990s, have been supplemented, or eclipsed, with concerns over global climate change. Some scientists predict that up to one third of the earth's species may become extinct in the next century. Many of these will be snakes, lost as a result of desertification, rising sea levels and increasing pressure on land that will be required to feed and house a burgeoning human population in a period of diminishing resources.

Even now, many naturalists, myself included, will be noticing changes on a local level. The days when one could find a dozen or more adders during the course of a casual walk on the heaths of southern England are long gone, while populations of tropical species in seemingly pristine habitats such as the rain forests of Borneo or Costa Rica seem to be shrinking for no apparent reason. Urgent attention is needed if these trends are to be halted or reversed.

Chris Mattison

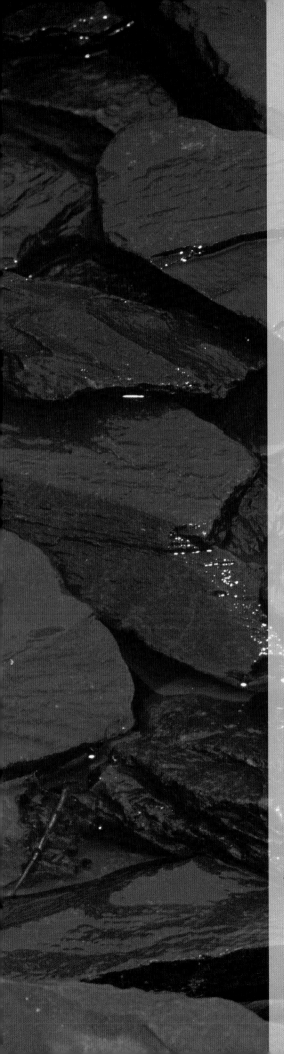

CHAPTER 1

THE ORIGINS AND EVOLUTION OF SNAKES

Snakes are reptiles. In other words, they belong to the order Reptilia, which also includes the turtles and tortoises, the crocodilians, a pair of odd lizard-like creatures from New Zealand called the tuataras, the lizards and the amphisbaenians. All these groups of animals are related, but some are more related than others. The most important assemblage, as far as snakes are concerned, is the order Squamata. This order is divided into three suborders: Ophidia, containing the snakes, Sauria, containing the lizards, and the Amphisbaenia. (Outside the tropics, the amphisbaenians, sometimes known as worm lizards, are not well known: the 165 or so species are restricted to warmer parts of the world where they spend the greater part of their lives burrowing beneath the surface of the ground.)

A typical snake: moderately slender with an almost cylindrical body and a head that is distinct from its neck. The scales are arranged regularly on the body and, in this species, a black-necked garter snake, *Thamnophis cyrtopsis*, they are also arranged in a regular fashion on the top of the head. Members of some families may have many small scales covering the head instead.

DEFINING SNAKES

WHAT MAKES A SNAKE DIFFERENT FROM AMPHISBAENIANS AND LIZARDS? THIS IS NOT QUITE SUCH A RIDICULOUS QUESTION AS IT MAY SEEM. IN FACT, IT IS NOT TOO EASY TO COME UP WITH A DEFINITION THAT INCLUDES ALL THE SNAKES BUT EXCLUDES OTHER MEMBERS OF THE SQUAMATA. FIRSTLY, SNAKES HAVE NO LEGS – BUT NEITHER DO MANY LIZARDS NOR MOST AMPHISBAENIANS. SNAKES HAVE NO EYELIDS BUT, AGAIN, NEITHER DO SOME LIZARDS NOR ANY OF THE AMPHISBAENIANS. SNAKES HAVE NO EXTERNAL EAR OPENINGS – AGAIN, NEITHER DO SOME LIZARDS NOR ANY AMPHISBAENIANS.

We can, however, use a combination of characteristics that will get pretty close to defining snakes. All snakes have a backbone (i.e. they are vertebrates) but lack limbs, eyelids and external ear openings. In addition, most snakes have a specialised row of scales along the underside of their bodies, the ventrals, whereas lizards have various patterns of scales but never a single row. The scales of amphisbaenians are peculiar in that they are arranged in rings around the body, so that small species superficially resemble earthworms. On the question of legs, even those lizards that have lost their legs retain vestiges of the limb girdles, as do the amphisbaenians, although some families of snakes do retain vestigial pelvic girdles, none of them have pectoral girdles. Finally, most snakes have unique skulls – the bones of their upper jaws are not united at the snout but are free to move away from one another, so allowing the passage of larger prey items than would otherwise be the case. This arrangement is not found in lizards or amphisbaenians. In the hand, snakes are supple and muscular whereas legless lizards tend to be more rigid.

IS IT A SNAKE?

Snakes are long, slender vertebrates without legs. This definition is not enough to separate snakes from some other groups of animals, though. Eels, for instance, are also long and slender and have no legs, but their scales are very small and they breathe through gills, which can plainly be seen just behind the head.

It is not so easy to separate legless lizards and amphisbaenians, from snakes. All are reptiles, their bodies are covered with scales and they all breathe through lungs. All these reptiles evolved limblessness for the same reason – to help them crawl quickly through dense vegetation or to burrow in loose soil. Limbs would get in the way.

All the amphisbaenians, except for three species in the genus *Bipes* are limbless (and *Bipes* only have front limbs). Limbless lizards, or lizards in which the limbs have been reduced to such a degree that they are all but absent, are found in seven families. The chart below will help to distinguish between snakes and other limbless reptiles, but by far the easiest way to differentiate them is to become familiar with species living in your area – the glass lizards of North America, for instance, do not look similar to any of the snakes found in the same region, nor does the European slow worm. The only likely source of confusion could be the case of three flap-footed lizards from Australia, which are thought to be mimics of certain juvenile brown snakes of the genus *Demansia*.

▲ Although they look superficially like snakes, legless lizards, such as the European slowworm, *Anguis fragilis*, differ from them in several ways, including the presence of eyelids and a different arrangement of scales on their undersides.

▲ Most amphisbaenians also lack legs but the arrangement of their scales into regular rings immediately distinguishes them from both snakes and lizards. *Blanus cinereus*, from Spain.

▲ The Texas thread snake and its close relatives do not have the wide ventral scales characteristic of more advanced snakes but they lack eyelids and the rows of scales on their back overlap each other.

Snake, lizard or amphisbaenian?

1 Animal has four legs ⟶ **Lizard**
Animal has no legs ⟶ Go to 2

2 Scales arranged in rings around body ⟶ **Amphisbaenian**
Scales overlapping and tile-like ⟶ Go to 3

3 Eyelids present ⟶ **Legless lizard**
Eyelids absent ⟶ Go to 4

4 Single row of wide ventral scales ⟶ **Snake**
Several row of small ventral scales ⟶ **Legless lizard**
Ventral scales, same as other scales, cylindrical body ⟶ **Blind snake**

THE ORIGINS AND EVOLUTION OF SNAKES

AN UNDERSTANDING OF THE ORIGIN AND EVOLUTION OF SNAKES IS AN IMPORTANT ASPECT OF THE CLASSIFICATION OF THE LIVING SPECIES INTO GENERA, FAMILIES AND SO ON. PREVIOUSLY, BIOLOGICAL CLASSIFICATION WAS BASED MORE ON THE OUTWARD APPEARANCE OF ORGANISMS WITH LITTLE REGARD TO THEIR EVOLUTIONARY HISTORY. (THIS WOULD BE RATHER LIKE SORTING LIBRARY BOOKS BY THE COLOUR OF THEIR JACKETS RATHER THAN THEIR SUBJECT MATTER AND IS OBVIOUSLY A LESS USEFUL SYSTEM.) MODERN CLASSIFICATION IS INTENDED TO REFLECT THE RELATIONSHIPS BETWEEN SPECIES, GENERA AND FAMILIES.

There is a common assumption that snakes evolved from their closest relatives, the lizards. Members of seven families of lizards, including the Australian snake-lizards (Pygopodidae), the skinks (Scincidae) and the anguids (Anguidae), demonstrate a tendency for their legs to become smaller and many species have lost them altogether. Leglessness has therefore evolved independently in several unrelated lizard families and is likely to have occurred several more times during the course of evolution. Snakes are thought to be derived from such a family of lizards, although the actual link is unknown. Current scientific opinion favours a lineage that includes the monitor lizards (Varanidae) as the one from which snakes evolved, although there are several possible alternatives. (As it happens, there are currently no legless monitors but this does not exclude the possibility that they existed at some time in the past.)

If we assume that all snakes arose from a common ancestor, it should be possible, in an ideal world, to work back, through the fossil record, and develop a 'pedigree chart' showing the relationship between all the species and their ancestors. Unfortunately, the fossil record, owing to its chancy and indiscriminate nature, is far too incomplete to enable this type of analysis to take place and so the results of much careful research are very often inconclusive.

A number of different characteristics are used to classify snakes. These include general morphology; the arrangement of bones in the skull and other parts of the skeleton, especially the presence or absence of a pelvic girdle, of hypapophyses (spike-like projections pointing downwards from the vertebrae), or of a coronoid bone (a small bone in the lower jaw); the structure of the hemipenes (the paired copulatory organs of male snakes) and microscopic and biochemical material such as the chromosome arrangement (karyotype) and protein analyses. Obviously, only a very small proportion of these tools is available to palaeontologists.

Most fossil snake material consists of vertebrae. Although the structures of vertebrae may differ between groups of snakes, it is rarely possible to distinguish between closely related forms from this type of material alone.

Fossil skulls are more useful and are found from time to time but, even so, the absence of soft parts of extinct snakes will always make their relationships with living forms open to debate. Other problems include the small size, and therefore delicate bones, of some of the more primitive snakes, such as the blind snakes and thread snakes which, though undoubtedly present in ancient times, rarely show up in the fossil record.

From what we do know, it seems that snakes first appeared between 100 and 150 million years ago, during the early Cretaceous period. Between then and now, they evolved into the 2,880 or so species currently recognised as well as an inestimable number of other forms that became extinct in the meantime.

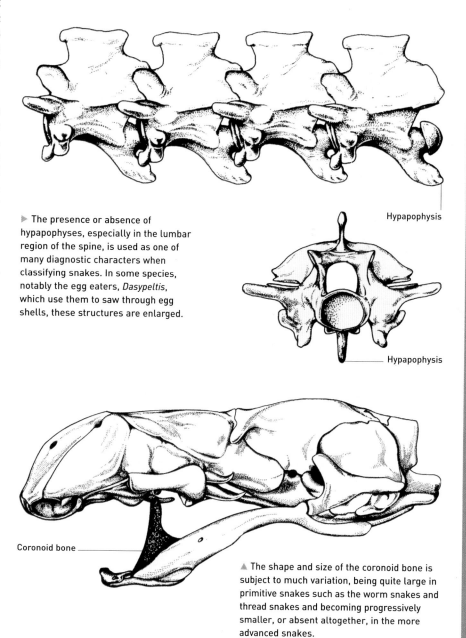

▶ The presence or absence of hypapophyses, especially in the lumbar region of the spine, is used as one of many diagnostic characters when classifying snakes. In some species, notably the egg eaters, *Dasypeltis*, which use them to saw through egg shells, these structures are enlarged.

Hypapophysis

Hypapophysis

Coronoid bone

▲ The shape and size of the coronoid bone is subject to much variation, being quite large in primitive snakes such as the worm snakes and thread snakes and becoming progressively smaller, or absent altogether, in the more advanced snakes.

The earliest known snake is *Lapparentophis defrennei*. It shows no link with earlier snake-like reptiles and so its origin is a mystery at present. Its fossils have been found in what is now North Africa and it was a terrestrial snake. The next oldest remains are those of a marine species, *Simoliophis*, found in areas of Europe and North Africa that previously formed part of the sea bed. This species first appeared at the beginning of the late Cretaceous period (100 million years ago). By the end of the Cretaceous period (65 million years ago), however, the families to which *Lapparentophis* and *Simoliophis* belonged had already become extinct, but many more snakes had evolved, including

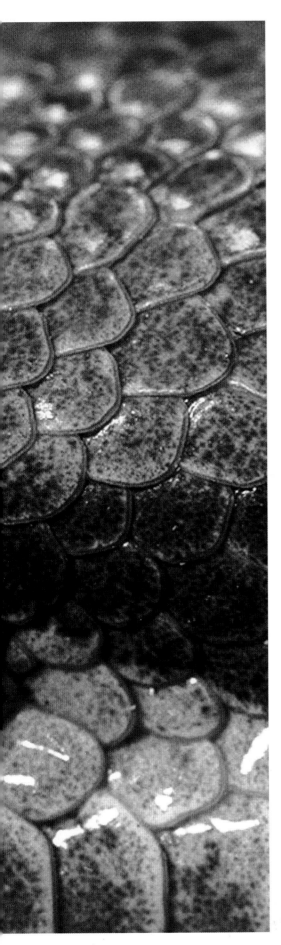

◄ All snakes lack eyelids. Instead, all except members of the most primitive families have a single transparent scale, known as a brille, covering each eye. The outer layer of this is shed periodically, with the rest of the epidermis.

▼ Members of certain primitive families retain vestiges of the pelvic girdle. In boas, pythons and a few other families, its presence is associated with small claws or spurs located on either side of the vent. Male boas and pythons use their spurs to stimulate the females during courtship.

representatives of at least two more families that later became extinct and at least two that still survive (the pipe snakes, Aniliidae, and the boas, Boidae). Fossil snakes from this era have been found in most parts of the world, showing that, by the time the dinosaurs became extinct, snakes had already diversified and become widespread.

After the Cretaceous period, snakes were in the ascendant: at least seven families were present, including the boas, which appear to have reached the peak of their speciation around this time and formed perhaps the dominant family. Colubrid snakes, which make up by far the largest number of species today, did not appear until the end of the Eocene period or the beginning of the Oligocene (36 million years ago) and began to diversify rapidly into numerous species during the Miocene period (22.5 to 5.5 million years ago). Their diversification coincided with the disappearance of several of the more ancient lineages of snakes, perhaps because the latter were unable to compete with the better adapted species that were evolving. The number of boids was also reduced at this time. Also appearing during the Miocene period were representatives of two other important families, the Viperidae (vipers) and the Elapidae (cobras and their relatives) and a smaller family, the Acrochordidae (file snakes).

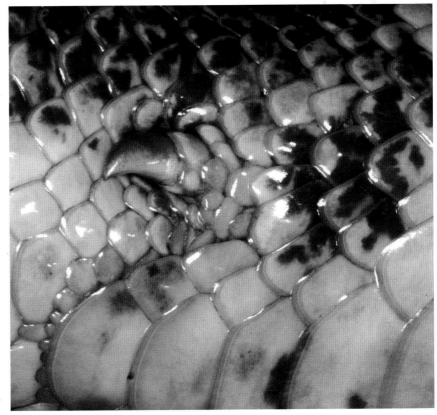

MODERN SNAKE CLASSIFICATION

THE SNAKES LIVING TODAY, THEN, OWE THEIR EXISTENCE TO A RATHER COMPLICATED HISTORY OF EVOLUTION, SPECIATION AND EXTINCTION GOING BACK OVER 100 MILLION YEARS. DURING THAT TIME THE SHAPE OF THE LANDMASSES HAS CHANGED ENORMOUSLY. THE PRESENT DISTRIBUTION OF THE SURVIVING FAMILIES IS DEPENDENT, TO SOME EXTENT, ON THE TIME AT WHICH THEY EVOLVED: OLD FAMILIES TEND TO HAVE A WORLDWIDE DISTRIBUTION WHEREAS NEWER FAMILIES HAVE OFTEN FAILED TO REACH PARTS OF THE WORLD THAT BECAME ISOLATED AS A RESULT OF THE BREAKING UP OF THE LANDMASSES, A PROCESS THAT HAD ALREADY BEGUN WHEN THEY FIRST PUT IN AN APPEARANCE AND WHICH CONTINUES TO THIS DAY. CHAPTER 4 DEALS IN MORE DETAIL WITH THE GLOBAL DISTRIBUTION OF SNAKES.

The classification of surviving snakes, though strongly linked to, and dependent on, their evolution, is somewhat easier than that of extinct snakes. It is not straightforward, though, because many species are imperfectly known while others seem to have conflicting characteristics, making it difficult to assign them to one family or another. Again, different degrees of importance are assigned to various characteristics by different researchers. Many arrangements have been put forward over the years, some of them differing only slightly from previous classifications, while others are more radical.

Most experts now accept 18 or 19 families of snakes but the 2950 or so species are not equally divided between them. Two families, the Aniliidae and the Loxocemidae, contain a single species; three or four others, the Anomochilidae, Xenopeltidae and the Bolyeriidae, each contain two species (although one member of the Bolyeriidae is almost certainly extinct), while the Acrochordidae contains three. Thus six families (one-third of the total) account for just 11 species (0.37% of all snakes). At the opposite extreme, the largest family, the Colubridae, currently has over 1880 species assigned to it. This family is certainly derived from a number of ancestral lines and future research will undoubtedly divide it into a number of smaller families. At present, it is

broken down into subfamilies, some of which are better defined than others. A more thorough account of the families and their genera is given in Chapter 10.

A major division is made between some very primitive snakes and the more advanced ones. The most primitive species are all small burrowing snakes with rudimentary eyes, smooth, shiny scales and undifferentiated belly scales. They are placed in the families Anomalepidae (early blind snakes), Typhlopidae (worm snakes) and Leptotyphlopidae (thread snakes) and differ so widely from other snakes that they are grouped together in an infra-order called the Scolecophidia ('blind snakes'). They feed mainly on the larvae and eggs of termites and ants and their jaws are rigid. They have few teeth, sometimes none on the upper or lower jaw, depending on the family.

All other families of snakes are grouped together in the second infra-order, the Alethinophidia ('true snakes'). The arrangement of these families, the order in which they evolved and how they are related to each other has not been finally resolved and a few families have been moved back and forth as new evidence and new theories appear. The first six families can be called 'early true snakes'. They are primitive but not as primitive as the blind snakes. Members of these families – the Anomochilidae (the dwarf pipe snakes), Aniliidae (South American pipe snake), Cylindrophiidae (Asian pipe snakes), Uropeltidae (shield-tails), Xenopeltidae (sunbeam snakes) and the Loxocemidae (Central American burrowing snake) are all burrowers, their jaws are rigid or capable of only a small amount of movement and their ventral scales are narrow. They have smooth, shiny scales and are sometimes known informally as the 'glossy snakes'. They contain only about 50 species between them, mostly in the Uropeltidae.

The dwarf pipe snakes are from Southeast Asia. These two species, *Anomochilus leonardi* and *Anomochilus weberi*, used to be classified with the Asian pipe snakes, *Cylindrophis* and are sometimes included in another primitive family, the Uropeltidae (see below). They are now regarded as intermediate between the blind snakes and the rest of the alethinophidians and have been removed from all past associations and given their own family.

The Uropeltidae was for many years a catch-all family for a variety of small primitive snakes but it is now restricted to a group of burrowing snakes from southern India and Sri Lanka, often known as shield-

tailed snakes. The pipe snakes belonging to the genus *Cylindrophis* have been given their own family, the Cylindrophiidae, containing ten species. The single member of the Aniliidae, the South American Pipe Snake, *Anilius scytale*, lives in northern South America but it also bears a superficial resemblance to species from Southeast Asia and, like the dwarf pipe snakes, it was included with the Asian pipe snakes, *Cylindrophis*, previously part of the Uropeltidae.

Next come two small families, the Loxocemidae (Central American burrowing snake) and the Xenopeltidae (sunbeam snakes) with one and two species respectively, that seem to be intermediate between the primitive true snakes and the more advanced snakes. Their jaws have some degree of flexibility and they are also burrowers, although much larger than members of the previous families. The Central American burrowing snake, *Loxocemus bicolor*, was thought for a long time to belong with the pythons. It has also been classified with the *Xenopeltis* species, which it superficially resembles in some ways. Now it is considered sufficiently different from all other snakes to be given a family of its own. The Xenopeltidae, with two species, *Xenopeltis unicolor* and *Xenopeltis hainanensis*, occurs in Southeast Asia and southern China. The sunbeam snakes have smooth, iridescent scales and lead burrowing lives.

All the remaining snakes, i.e. the vast majority, have jaws that are loosely articulated and that can be distended and they are therefore able to swallow larger prey. These species also have wide ventral scales. They are sometimes called the macrostomata or 'large-mouthed snakes'.

We are more familiar with members of the Boidae and Pythonidae than with any of the snake mentioned so far. These two families include all the giant snakes – boas, pythons, anacondas and so on – as well as a number of small to medium-sized species. (There is a case for regarding the pythons as part of the Boidae but it is more usual nowadays to consider each as a separate family.) Boas occur in North, Central and South America, in Africa, Southeast Europe, Madagascar and the Pacific region. Most are arboreal or terrestrial but the anacondas are semi-aquatic and a well-defined group of small to medium sized species, are semi-fossorial. These include the sand boas, and are placed in a separate subfamily, the Erycinae. The pythons are exclusively Old World in distribution and occur in Africa, Asia and Australia. They may be terrestrial, arboreal or semi-aquatic but

AN EVOLUTIONARY TREE OF THE LIVING FAMILIES OF SNAKES

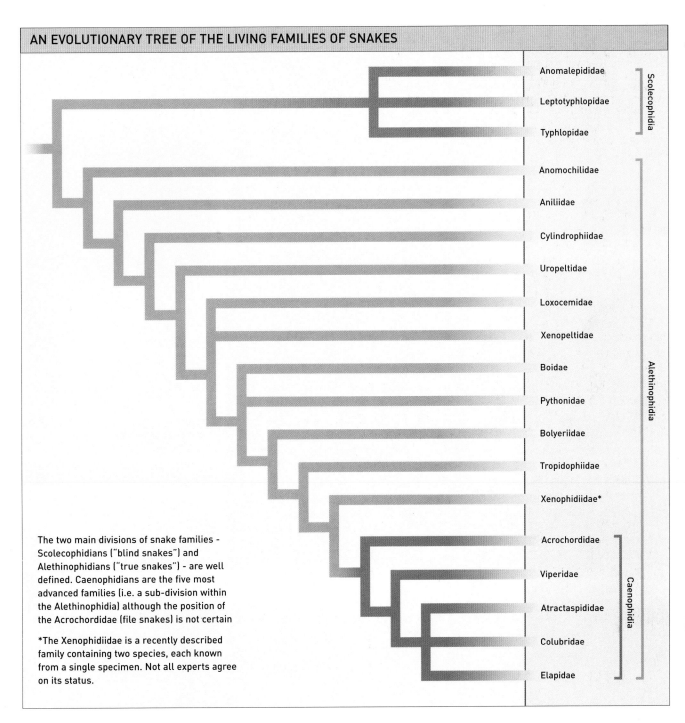

The two main divisions of snake families -
Scolecophidians ("blind snakes") and
Alethinophidians ("true snakes") - are well
defined. Caenophidians are the five most
advanced families (i.e. a sub-division within
the Alethinophidia) although the position of
the Acrochordidae (file snakes) is not certain

*The Xenophidiidae is a recently described
family containing two species, each known
from a single specimen. Not all experts agree
on its status.

there are no out-and-out burrowing species.
An important difference between boas and
pythons is that the former (with one
exception) give birth to live young whereas
the pythons lay eggs. Some boas and pythons
have rows of heat-sensitive organs situated
amongst the scales bordering their jaws. Boas
and pythons are typically powerful
constrictors, eating mostly warm-blooded
prey including domestic animals and, on rare
occasions, humans.

The West Indian boas constitute a separate
family, the Tropidophiidae, restricted to the
Caribbean region and, to a limited extent,
South America. They should not be confused
with the true boas and it might be less
confusing if they were known by their
alternative name, 'wood snakes'. They are
viviparous. The Round Island boas,
Bolyeriidae, are, as their name suggests,
restricted to Round Island, in the Indian
Ocean. One member of this family, *Bolyeria
multocarinata*, is probably extinct and nothing
is known of its reproduction but the surviving
species is oviparous.

Two species of strange snakes, *Xenophidion
acanthognathus* and *X. schaeferi*, known as
Malaysian spine-jawed snakes, have been the
subject of much taxonomic debate since their
discovery in 1987 and 1988 respectively. They
were initially placed in the Colubridae until
subsequent studies disproved this, then they
were moved to the Tropidophiidae, and
affinities have also been pointed out between
them and the Bolyeridae (Round Island
Boas). It was finally decided that they should
be given a family of their own (the
Xenophidiidae), but neither snake has been
collected again since their discovery, and are
represented by a single preserved specimen
each, so they are still very much an unknown
quantity. See also page 215.

Moving on to the most advanced families, sometimes known as the Caenophidia, we have five families that share several advanced features. The Acrochordidae, or file snakes, are difficult to place. The three species are completely aquatic, living in coastal waters, estuaries and inland lakes. Their scales are unlike those of other snakes and they have several other peculiarities that may be due to their ancestry but that may also result from their unusual lifestyle. They lack hind limb girdles but have other characteristics that suggest a primitive origin and so, for the time being at least, they are placed in an intermediate position between the primitive families and the more advanced ones.

All the remaining families tend to be larger, more widespread and more numerous. They are considered to be more recently evolved: unlike the families dealt with so far, except the file snakes, their hind limb girdles have disappeared, and nor do they have a coronoid bone. The Atractaspididae, is a relatively small family of burrowing snakes restricted to Africa (with one species in the Middle East) sometimes called burrowing asps. Some members of the family, placed in the genus *Atractaspis*, have enormous hinged fangs at the front of their upper jaws but few other teeth. These are called stiletto snakes and were once thought to be vipers. They are now recognised as a genus that has become highly adapted to living and feeding below ground. Other species in the Atractaspididae have small grooved fangs in the front or rear of their mouths, but are effectively harmless to humans. The family contains a wide diversity of species, many of which are poorly known.

The Colubridae is, by far, the largest family of living snakes. Its 1,880 or so species have moved into almost every possible ecological niche and diversified accordingly. Only in Australia are its members not the dominant component of the snake fauna. Colubrids are found in trees, on the ground, beneath the ground and in the water (although there are no exclusively marine species). Colubrid snakes are typical in having more or less slender, elongated bodies, large scales covering their heads and large eyes. A wide variety of food is taken by the various species, some specialising in certain prey, e.g. snails, eggs, etc., while others are generalists and eat almost anything small enough to be swallowed. A number of species are venomous but their methods of delivering the venom are not as well developed as in the cobras or the vipers; only a few are dangerous to man. Their reproductive habits are also varied, with some species laying eggs and others giving birth to live young.

The cobras and their relatives are placed in the family Elapidae. This is usually taken to include the sea snakes, baits, mambas, coral snakes and a host of Australian species that have evolved to fill all the niches made available by the scarcity of colubrids and the lack of vipers on that continent. Elapids are the main family of snakes in Australia, which has the dubious honour of being inhabited by more venomous snakes than harmless ones (although not all of them are dangerous to man). The cobra family is characterised by hollow venom fangs fixed at the front of their upper jaws and specialised ducts that carry the venom from the venom glands to the tip of the fangs. Cobras may be aquatic, terrestrial, burrowing or climbing in habit and may lay eggs or give birth to live young.

Some authorities treat the sea snakes, together with the Australian terrestrial elapids as a separate family, the Hydrophiidae and yet others place only the sea snakes into the this family and give the sea kraits, *Laticauda*, their own family, the Laticaudidae. More conservatively, though, these are regarded as subfamilies and this is the course I have followed here.

The vipers, Viperidae, have the most highly evolved venom-delivery service of any snakes. They have not spread to Australasia, perhaps appearing in the region after this landmass had broken away from the rest of the world (and thereby leaving the door open for snakes from other families to fill their niche). Apart from this, they are widespread, and occur further north and further south than any other snakes and at higher altitudes (in the Himalayas). Their fangs are relatively long and are hinged so that they can be folded back when not in use. One distinctive group of vipers, known as pit vipers due to a pair of heat-sensitive pits between their eyes and nostrils, first appeared in Asia and then spread to North, Central and South America, moving across the land bridge that occupied the region where the Bering Straits are now. The pits themselves are structurally different from those found in some boas and pythons and have evolved independently. The pit vipers are placed in a subfamily, the Crotalinae, and some of its members are among the most easily recognised snakes in the world; they have a unique characteristic in the form of a rattle on the end of their tail.

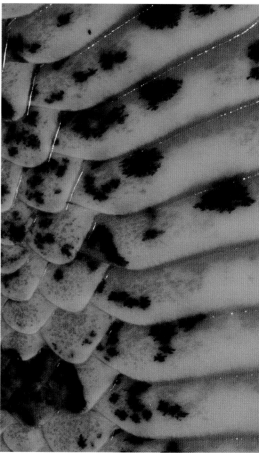

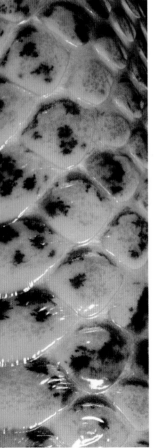

▲ (top left) The pit vipers, such as this white-lipped pit viper, *Trimeresurus albolabris*, with heat-sensitive pits and a sophisticated method of venom delivery, represent the pinnacle of snake evolution, even though they are not necessarily the last family to have appeared.

◀ (left) Except for members of the most primitive families, and a few specialised kinds such as sea snakes, all snakes have a row of wide ventral scales beneath their bodies.

▲ (top right) Snakes are thought to have evolved from a group of lizards similar to the monitors, Varanidae, although this is by no means conclusive. This is a Bengal monitor, from Sri Lanka.

▲ (above) Most (but not all) lizards have heterogeneous scales, with different shapes on different parts of their bodies, as on this male chameleon, *Chamaeleo hoehnelii*.

CHAPTER 2
MORPHOLOGY AND FUNCTION

Although snakes are all long, slender animals lacking limbs, external ears and eyelids, there is considerable variation between them, enough in fact for over 2,950 species to be recognised on superficial characteristics alone. Animals of all kinds look the way they do, not by accident, but for a reason. Their size, shape, colours and markings suit them to the tasks they have to perform in order to survive and reproduce. Snakes are no exception.

A Leopard snake easily scales a vertical tree trunk in a temperate forest.

THE LIFE OF A SNAKE

In order to live long enough to pass on their genes, snakes need to achieve certain goals. They must feed so that they can grow to maturity but, at the same time, they must avoid being eaten by other animals. In order to do either of these things, it will be necessary to move around, and so some form of locomotion must be developed. Depending on the habitat they find themselves in, locomotion may involve swimming, climbing or burrowing as well as straightforward crawling across the ground.

If our snake finds enough food and avoids all its predators long enough to reach maturity, it is then faced with the more esoteric problem of finding a member of the same species but of the opposite sex, and achieving a form of sexual union in order to bring spermatozoa and ova together.

All the functions outlined so far are behavioural. Feeding, locomotion, defence, reproduction and so on all require the snake to make an action or a sequence of actions.

Other functions take place beneath the skin. Finding, subduing and swallowing prey, for instance, must be followed by digestion and assimilation if it is to have any purpose. Such functions depend on internal anatomy and biochemistry.

These actions, of course, will be made easier if the snake is well equipped at the outset and this in turn depends upon genetic programming. This, then, is how evolution operates — animals that are well equipped tend to survive while those that are not tend not to. We have to assume that, after thousands of generations, each species has reached a point in its evolution that works well — if it did not, it would have died out. We do not, however, need to assume that each evolutionary line has reached its pinnacle — snakes will probably go on evolving into more efficient organisms for as long as there is somewhere for them to live.

Our basic assumption, then, is that each species of snake is the size, shape and colour it is because it has arrived at a good (but not necessarily perfect) design. Now we can look in more detail at each facet of that design, bearing in mind the evolutionary principles that control them.

SIZE AND SHAPE

SIZE AND SHAPE, TOGETHER WITH COLOUR AND MARKINGS, HELP TO GIVE EACH SNAKE ITS IDENTITY. THEY MAY ALSO HOLD IMPORTANT CLUES TO THE LIFESTYLE OF THE SNAKE BECAUSE CERTAIN HABITATS AND CONDITIONS TEND TO LIMIT OR ENCOURAGE THE WAY IN WHICH SNAKES EVOLVE.

Size

The statistic that is of most interest to the layman is that of length. Few zoological facts are in as much contention as those regarding the lengths of snakes: the exaggerations of fishermen are nothing compared with the stories of pythons and 'boa constrictors' measuring 15–18 metres (50–60 feet) told by what would otherwise be regarded as fairly reliable explorers and biologists of the nineteenth century.

There is no denying that the lengths of snakes are notoriously difficult to estimate. Few of them stretch out straight in order to allow themselves to be measured accurately. Indeed, few of them could be expected to keep still while this was carried out. Portions of large snakes seen slithering away, glimpsed through gaps in the dense vegetation in which they often live, can be misleading, even to careful observers. Snakes that are killed are often too large and heavy to be transported from the place of their death to a place where

their size can be measured accurately. In any case, snake carcasses and skins can be stretched by anything up to 20 per cent, perhaps more, either deliberately or inadvertently.

The 'big six'

Altogether, there are six species that may be loosely termed 'giant snakes'. Two of these live in South America, there are another two in Asia, while Africa and Australasia have one each. Tall stories of legendary snakes are divided between the species although the two large snakes found in South America seem to have more than their fair share.

The anaconda, *Eunectes murinus*

On the grounds of weight alone, there is almost no doubt that the South American anaconda is the world's largest snake. Length seems more important to the record breakers, however, and it is in this department that controversy occurs.

The largest anaconda ever reported was 18.9 m long (62 ft) killed by Colonel Percy Fawcett, of the Royal Artillery, in Brazil in 1907. This gigantic snake was shot while trying to escape up a riverbank. There is considerable doubt surrounding the episode, though, not least because it has been estimated that a snake of this huge size would be unable to support its own bulk (although this in itself is inconclusive because the anaconda is a semi-aquatic species that is buoyed up by water when swimming).

Other gigantic anacondas include one shot in 1910 by Lange along the Jivari River in Peru and claimed by him to have measured

▼ The anaconda, *Eunectes murinus*, the largest snake in the world.

16.5 m (54 ft) in length. Another one, reputedly of similar size, was seen, but not killed, by the explorer de Graff in 1927.

A more down-to-earth report concerns a specimen of 11.4 m (37 ft 6 in) in length, shot in Colombia in 1944, and this record was accepted for many years. Like several others, it has been repeated by successive authors, thereby gaining some degree of credibility. This particular specimen was killed by a prospecting party led by a geologist, Roberto Lamon. When the party returned to photograph and skin the snake (having eaten their lunch in the mean time!) they found it had gone. Presumably it had recovered and crawled or swum away. Another record is that of 11.6 m (38 ft), killed by Indians during an expedition by the Brazilian General Rondon (who later lent his name to Rondonia, a large region of Amazonian Brazil).

Reports of specimens in the 9–10.7 m (30–35 ft) size range are more plentiful and include several that cannot be easily dismissed because they have involved scientists whose reputations for reliability are otherwise unchallenged. For instance, a 10.4 m (34 ft) anaconda was shot in British Guiana by Vincent Roth, director of the national museum. Mr R. Mole, a naturalist who made many important contributions to the natural history of Trinidad, reported a 10 m (33 ft) example there in 1924 and Dr F. Medem, from Colombia University, reported a specimen measuring 10.26 m (33 ft 8 in) killed in the Guaviare River.

It is worth noting that, compared with the reticulated python, the anaconda makes a poor captive, being bad tempered and often failing to feed adequately. For this reason it is not so often displayed in zoological gardens, despite its obvious attractions.

The reticulated python,
Python reticulatus
The reticulated python has a wide range over much of Southeast Asia. It could well be the longest snake in the world, although it is much more slender than the anaconda. Strangely, there are far fewer dubious stories concerning the length of this species than the anaconda, and they tend to concentrate more on its appetite for human prey rather than its size.

Oliver mentions a specimen of 10 m (33 ft) that was killed by locals in Celebes and measured accurately by a civil engineer, but there was no evidence. A number of captive specimens have approached 9 m (30 ft), and there are several authenticated reports of reticulated pythons of around the 8.5 m (28 ft)

AN EASY WAY OF MEASURING SNAKES

Measuring snakes presents various problems, not least of which is that of keeping them still. The following method can be used to good effect. First place the snake on a thick pad of foam rubber and gently lay a piece of glass over the foam, trapping the snake. Using a marker pen, draw a line on the glass, starting at the snake's snout and following its midline all the way to the tip of the tail. Now release the snake and return it to the wild (or to its cage).

You can measure the length of the line in one of two ways: either use one of the small gadgets sold for measuring distances on maps or, if this is not available, lay a piece of string along the line and measure it after it has been straightened out again.

The advantages of using this 'squeeze box' method are twofold. Firstly, the snake will not have been stretched, as sometimes happens when attempting to straighten out a snake and, secondly, the snake is less likely to be stressed. If the snake is a poisonous or bad-tempered individual, the operator is also less likely to be stressed! Unfortunately, although the method works well with the great majority of species, it can only be used with medium-sized snakes, up to 1 m or 1.5 m (4 or 5 ft) in length.

Snakes that have been photographed in the field can be measured without using a squeeze box. Photograph the snake alongside an object of known length – a ruler, field guide, etc., then release the snake. If you are using slide film, project the processed transparency on to a large piece of board or paper, moving it backwards and forwards until the object of known length is the correct size. Now draw a line along the length of the snake, on the paper. Measure in the same way as the line on the squeeze box. If you are using print film you will have to compare the length of the object to its image on the film and correct for scale after you have measured the snake (or project the negative).

The shed skins of snakes should not be used to obtain a measurement as they will be, on average, 10 per cent longer than the snake they came from. A series of skins from the same snake as it grows, together with the dates on which the snake produced them, can provide a good indication of its growth rate, however, and makes an interesting project for young snake keepers.

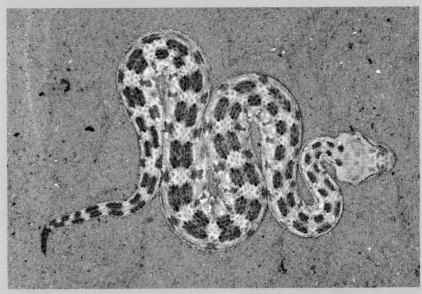

▲ The reticulated python, *Python reticulatus*, is probably the longest snake and the largest Old World species.

mark. These include a live specimen of that size in the possession of an animal dealer, John Hagenbeck, in 1905, reported by Colonel Frank Wall in his book *Snakes of Ceylon*. This snake weighed 113.4 kg (250 lb). Another one, measuring 7.6 m (25 ft) and weighing 138.3 kg (305 lb) was the largest snake ever displayed at the National Zoo, Washington, and is now in the United States National Museum. The discrepancy between the weights of this and the Hagenbeck specimen could easily be accounted for by the relative condition of the two snakes or by sexual dimorphism, female snakes normally being bulkier than males of a similar length.

The Indian python, *Python molurus*

This species occurs in two forms, *Python molurus molurus* and *P. m. hivittatus*, the latter subspecies being the Burmese python. A third form, *P. m. pimbura*, is restricted to the island of Sri Lanka although it is not always recognized as a distinct subspecies. It seems that any of the three forms can grow into giants and, although the average adult size for this species is probably around 3.7 m (12 ft), there are a number of reliable records giving details of specimens approaching 6 m (20 ft).

For instance, Wall, in the book mentioned above, states that 'specimens of 18 feet [5.5 m] are not very uncommon', and goes on to list several well-documented specimens exceeding this size, from the Indian mainland and from Sri Lanka. These include a specimen in the collection of the Bombay Natural History Society measuring 5.84 m (19 ft 2 in) and weighing 90.7 kg (200 lb), shot by the Maharajah of Cooch Behar in Assam, and two of 5.8 m (19 ft) shot in Sri Lanka. Other, slightly less easily verified, accounts mention specimens of 6.7 m (22 ft) and 7.6 m (25 ft) although there is always the danger, when dealing with this species, that confusion between it and the reticulated python may occur as their ranges overlap in places.

The African python, *Python sebae*

The African python, sometimes also known as the rock python, is the only really large snake present on the African continent. Although its size has been stated as 7.6 m (25 ft), FitzSimons in his *Snakes of Southern Africa*[2] states that '. . . it is most unusual nowadays to find a snake exceeding 20 feet [6.1 m], while the average length of adults can be put at 13 to 15 feet [4-4.6 m]...' He goes on to record that 4.6-4.9 m (15-16 ft) captive specimens can weigh up to 54.4 kg (120 lb). There could be confusion here due to the fact that *Python sebae* is now considered to be two separate species, *P. sebae* to the north and *P. natalensis* to the south, so it is difficult to be sure to which form FitzSimons was referring.

▼ The African python, *Python sebae*, is the largest African snake.

▶ The Indian python, *Python molurus*, can grow to almost 6 m (20 ft).

The Kinghorn's, or scrub, python, *Morelia kinghorni*

This Australasian species presents something of an enigma. Although adults average only 3-3.7 m (10-12 ft) or less, there are a few reports of specimens far exceeding this size. These include one of 8.5 m (28 ft) killed at Greenhill, Cairns and measured by L. Robichaux in 1948. This snake was reported by Worrell,[3] while another, more modest one, of 7.2 m (23 ft 8 in), was measured by S. Dean and reported by Pope.[4] Since these records were made, a new species of giant python, the Oenpelli python, *Morelia oenpelliensis*, has been described from Arnhem Land, Australia, to further add to the confusion. Kinghorn's python used to be known as the amethystine, or scrub python, *Morelia amethistina*, but this name now describes snakes from Indonesia only, the Australia population having been renamed *M. kinghorni* in 2000. The maximum size of *M. amethistina* has not been reported.

The common boa, *Boa constrictor*

The common boa is not, and never has been, regarded as the largest species of snake except perhaps in the public imagination via the media. At the same time, no other snake has captured the public imagination to quite the same extent, and the tales of returning nineteenth-century explorers were considered incomplete unless they included an account of a close encounter with one of these gigantic serpents.

Just how big *does* the 'boa constrictor' grow? Until recently, the record size of this species was widely accepted as being 5.64 m (18 ft 6 in). This length was attributed to a specimen killed in Trinidad sometime during the Second World War by a malaria control work party under the command of a Mr Colin Pittendrigh. Unfortunately, and as is so often the case, the carcass of the huge snake could not be preserved under the prevailing conditions, although the record was widely accepted and reported, initially by Oliver[5] and, subsequently, by many more authors.

In a recent article, Hans Boos, a notable Trinidadian herpetologist, has thrown light on this episode, and casts some doubt, not on the size of the snake killed by Mr Pittendrigh, but on its identification.[6] It appears that Mr Pittendrigh had excluded the possibility that this snake was an anaconda, *Eunectes murinus*, on the grounds of inappropriate habitat. Hans Boos has found a number of anacondas near to where the Pittendrigh snake was killed. Furthermore, eyewitness accounts have given retrospective descriptions of the snake that seem to be more in keeping with the colorations of the anaconda.

On balance, then, it would appear that the snake in question could well have been a large anaconda rather than a common boa. This likelihood is made all the more feasible when it is considered that the next largest boa constrictor found on the island measured only 3.35 m (11 ft) (and would therefore have weighed probably less than half Pittendrigh's specimen) whereas on the adjacent mainland (Venezuela) the maximum recorded size, given by Rose (1966),[7] is 4.2 m: this translates to just over 13 ft 6 in, a mere bootlace compared with any of the other 'big six'. Only one other record is larger than this (disregarding all the reports that can probably be traced back to the Trinidadian specimen) and this is one of 4.5 m (just over 14 ft 6 in), given by Amaral as the maximum size the species attains in Brazil.[8]

Several conclusions can be drawn from these varied and scattered records concerning

The common boa, *Boa constrictor*, is fairly well down the league table of giants, rarely exceeding a length of 4 m (13 ft) and usually remaining significantly shorter than this.

The amethystine python, *Morelia amethistina*, from New Guinea, where it is the largest snake.

large snakes. Firstly, it appears that, as expected, many of the reports concerning the largest specimens are unsubstantiated and fail to stand up to careful scrutiny. This much is to be expected, human nature being what it is. Furthermore, all these large species, with the exception of the amethystine python, are bulky animals, with a proportionately large girth compared with other, more familiar species. A coiled snake, with a girth the size of a man's thigh, for instance, could quite easily be estimated to measure ten metres or more when in reality it may measure less than six,

especially if it is a gravid female or an individual that has recently fed.

A slightly worrying aspect is the amount of time that has elapsed since any very large snakes have been reported. Recent books and articles have been unable to improve on records provided by authors such as Wall and Oliver: their statistics are often repeated, but rarely exceeded, by later authors. Does this mean that snake slayers of today are more honest or more careful in their measurements, or have all the large snakes disappeared during the last 50 years or so? The truth is probably a combination of both. Early observers from uncharted jungles had nothing much on which to base their reports, so a large snake may just as well have measured 18 m (60 ft) as 9 m (30 ft) if its body was not available for inspection.

On the other hand, some of the more reliable records of the first half of this century still stand. Authors such as FitzSimons state

that 'it is most unusual *nowadays* to find snakes exceeding 20 feet [6.1 m]', suggesting that at one time snakes of this size may have been more commonplace. There can be no doubt that human pressures act in several ways against the chances of snakes reaching large sizes. Mainly, there are fewer remote areas left. Snakes encountered during the course of road building, prospecting or other pioneering activities are likely to be killed on sight, preventing them from reaching their full size – and, of course, the bigger they are, the less chance that they will escape notice.

It may be, then, that we will never see wild snakes the like of those killed by Fawcett, Lange, Lamon, and the Maharajah of Cooch Behar (even allowing for any exaggerations they may have made). It does seem likely, though, that a captive snake will eventually reach the 9 m (30 ft) target. As conditions in zoos and private collections have improved, the maximum sizes of several of the smaller species of snakes have been easily exceeded by captive specimens. This probably stems from a better and more reliable feeding regime coupled with protection from natural diseases, parasites and predators.

Costs and benefits of large size

Being large confers a number of advantages, not least the ability to avoid predation and to eat a wider variety of prey. At the same time, large snakes need to eat more than small ones. Even though snakes can survive on remarkably small amounts of food, finding enough prey to keep a 130 kg (300 lb) body and soul together is no easy task, especially for an animal that is not very mobile and must, to a great extent, sit and wait for its meals to come blundering by before pouncing. Large snakes, then, must ensure they live in areas where suitable food is relatively abundant.

In addition, their large bodies take longer to warm up than small ones and, being cold-blooded, they cannot become fully active unless their body temperature is raised to a suitable level. For this reason, they are restricted to warm parts of the world. In practice, the regions where both these requirements are met fall within the tropics. Here, the ambient temperature is suitable and there is a reasonable chance of finding food every few days.

▲ The tropical Central and South American snakes belonging to the genus *Imantodes* are among the most slender species: this is *I. lentiferus.*

Of our 'big six', the anaconda and the reticulated python are more or less restricted to tropical rainforest regions. The Indian python is also largely a forest species although it may also be found in open country, especially around farms and villages. The huge distribution of the boa constrictor falls within rainforest in South and Central America, but it also ranges north into deciduous forests and even semi-desert thorn scrub habitat in parts of northern Mexico. The African python and the amethystine python are generalists. They may be found in grasslands, scrub, along river courses and in forests.

The 'dwarfs'

Going to the other extreme, the smallest species of snake measures about 10 cm (4 in) and belongs to the family Typhlopidae, or blind snakes. It is hard to say exactly which species of blind snake is the smallest because several are about the same size and, in any case, it would be difficult to know if any of the measured animals were fully grown when they were measured – blind snakes are secretive, burrowing snakes of which only a tiny proportion of each species is likely to be available for sampling. There are many other species of snake in the 10-30 cm (4-12 in) size range.

◀ An undescribed worm snake, *Typhlops* species, from Sri Lanka. All worm and thread snakes are diminutive. The smallest snake belongs to one of these families but its exact identity is difficult to establish because some are known from only a few specimens.

Shape

Just as snakes vary in size, so they vary in shape. Compared to most other animals, all are long and thin of course, but some are longer and thinner than others. There is some degree of correlation with habitat here as arboreal species tend to be more slender, have longer tails, and are therefore lighter relative to their length. Examples include the long-nosed tree snake, *Ahaetulla nasuta*, the twig or bird snake, *Thelotornis capensis* and, especially, the blunt-headed tree snake, *Imantodes cenchoa* and its relatives. The two arboreal boids, *Corallus canina* and *Morelia viridis*, may not seem to fit into this pattern, being more stoutly built than most arboreal snakes, until they are compared with the other boids, when it will be seen that they have evolved a fair way towards the long-and-slender model. Certain terrestrial species are also long and slender. These include the active, fast-moving hunters, often diurnal species such as the whipsnakes, *Coluber* and *Masticophis*, and the sand snakes, *Psammophis*. Other terrestrial species may be short and stout, however. These consist of the sit-and-wait predators such as several vipers, notably the Gaboon viper and puff adder, *Bitis gabonica* and *Bitis arietans*, some Australian elapids, especially the death adders, *Acanthophis* species, and five pythons, *Python regius*, *P. anchietae* and, most notably, three species of short-tailed pythons, *P. breitensteini*, *P. brongersmai* and *P. curtus*, from Southeast Asia.

There is also variation in the shape of snakes' cross-sections. Burrowing snakes tend to be cylindrical whereas terrestrial species are more or less flattened on their ventral surface – this gives them an increased area over which to grip and push against the ground when they move. Arboreal snakes, apart from being slender, may be flattened from side to side (e.g. *Corallus*), as are aquatic species, especially the most highly adapted forms such as the sea snakes. A few species, such as the African file snakes (*Mehelya* species) the kraits (*Bungarus* species) and, to a lesser extent, the American indigo snake (*Drymarchon corais*), are triangular in cross-section with their dorsal midline forming a prominent ridge along the length of their bodies. The purpose of this body shape is unknown.

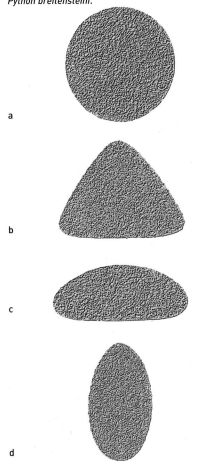

▲ Heavy bodied snakes are found mainly among the vipers, boas and pythons. This is a Borneo short-tailed python, *Python breitensteini*.

▶ Variations in the cross-sectional shapes of snakes: (a) cylindrical, as found in many burrowing and semi-burrowing species; (b) triangular, a shape whose function is uncertain but which is found in several widely separated species such as the African file snakes, *Mehelya* and the American indigo snake, *Drymarchon corais*; (c) dorsally flattened, a shaped found in many heavy-bodied species, such as the larger vipers, and which is often exaggerated when these and other species bask; (d) laterally flattened, as found in many arboreal snakes, such as the tree boas, *Corallus*, and others, and also in aquatic species such as the sea snakes.

a

b

c

d

COLOUR

SNAKES COME IN ALMOST EVERY COLOUR. SOME SPECIES, SUCH AS THE NORTH AMERICAN GREEN SNAKES, *OPHEODRYS* AND *LIOCHLOROPHIS*, ARE UNIFORM IN THEIR COLORATIONS WHEREAS THE PATTERN OF OTHERS, SUCH AS THE GABOON VIPER, *BITIS GABONICA*, ARE UNBELIEVABLY INTRICATE.

Many diurnal snakes are striped, whereas many nocturnal or crepuscular species tend to be banded. Some vary from one individual to another, even when they are from the same clutch of eggs, and a few start off one colour and then change as they grow. These colour schemes, convenient though they are for identification, are not there for the benefit of herpetologists. Each has a role to play in helping the snake to survive. Furthermore, their role in survival may be primarily defensive, as in camouflage, or physiological, in increasing the absorption of heat or protecting vital organs from excessive radiation.

How colour is produced

Colours, as we perceive them, may be caused in three different ways. Two of them are due to structural factors – the physical properties of the surface – and the other is due to pigments in the scales and is therefore chemical in nature. The cells that are responsible for colours are known collectively as chromatophores.

Pigments

Pigmentary colour is caused by groups of chromatophores containing coloured chemicals, situated within the scales. They lie mainly at the junction of the dermis and the epidermis. This is the most familiar form of colorations and gives a wide rage of hues. A number of different pigments have been isolated from snakes, some being more common than others. Melanin is almost universal in occurrence and gives rise to several different colours: black or dark brown (eumelanin), light brown and yellow (phaeomelanin), or grey. The cells containing melanin (melanophores) are irregularly branched, with arms reaching out in all directions. The arm of one melanophore will overlap with those of many of its neighbours, forming a complicated matrix. The pigment itself is in the form of granules and these may be spread throughout each cell, in which case

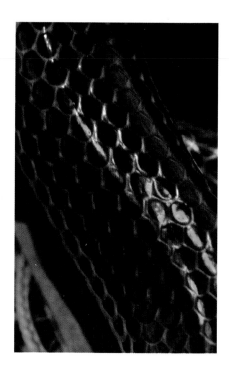

▲ Snakes' scales are often highly iridescent, as in the aptly named sunbeam snake, *Xenopeltis unicolor*, from Southeast Asia.

▼ Another brilliantly iridescent species is the rainbow boa, from South America; this is the Brazilian subspecies, *Epicrates cenchria cenchria*.

the area will appear light. Other pigments may be present; some yellows, reds and oranges are produced by carotenoids, and white is produced by guanine, a pigment that is a metabolic by-product. Combinations of different pigments can clearly give an almost infinite palette of shades and hues.

Interference colour (iridescence)

Iridescence is a feature of many species. It is not caused by pigments but by the physical properties of light. The outer layer of a snake's scale is thin and transparent. When light strikes it from an angle, it is split into its spectral components and each wavelength produces a different colour. Depending on the nature of the surface, and of the underlying colours, this produces an iridescent effect. As the snake moves, or as the observer's position moves, the colours appear to change. All snakes with smooth scales are, to some extent, iridescent, but some are more so than others. Iridescence is most noticeable in black or dark coloured snakes. The species that are best known for this type of colorations include the Asian

sunbeam snake, *Xenopeltis unicolor*, the rainbow boa, *Epicrates cenchria*, and several other boids.

Tyndall scattering

This type of colorations is quite common throughout the animal kingdom. It owes its effect to the scattering of light by small particles, known as iridophores. These consist of stacks of purine crystals embedded in cells, which reflect and refract light in a particular way. Short wavelengths of light, at the blue end of the spectrum, are affected more than the others and so the colour produced is blue. (The sky appears blue for exactly the same reason.) In certain species of snakes, a layer of cells containing small reflecting particles is found well below the surface of the scales. If the effect they produced worked alone, the snake would be blue and there are a few blue snakes, notably among the South American pit vipers belonging to the genera *Bothriopsis* and *Bothriechis*. Usually, however, the blue effect is combined with a layer of yellow chromatophores, known specifically as xanthophores. These cells overlie the cells

▲ Where mutations occur a variety of colour variants are possible. In this example, a San Diego gopher snake, *Pituophis catenifer annectans*, all the black pigment is missing but the underlying orange pigment, normally obscured, is still present.

containing the iridophores and, together, they produce green (holding a piece of yellow cellophane up to the blue sky produces the same effect). Green is a much more common colour in snakes than blue because it helps to camouflage those snakes that live among vegetation. Green snakes are found in many families and many parts of the world and include the emerald boa, *Coarrallus caninus*, the green tree python, *Morelia viridis*, several arboreal pit vipers, such as *Trimeresurus* species and a great many colubrids that are mainly arboreal species.

Patterns of snakes

Although some snakes are uniform in colour, many have markings consisting of spots, blotches, stripes and bands of different colours of shades. These are created by different patches of scales taking on the various colours and can be caused by groupings of different pigments. This is most easily understood by studying the colorations of the many colour mutants that are widely bred in captivity. In amelanistic corn snakes, for instance, the black pigment is missing and the full red areas can be easily seen. Furthermore, the red saddles on the back of these snakes are much brighter than they are on normally coloured individuals because the red areas are usually overlain with a diffuse layer of black pigment (melanin). In anerythristic individuals on the other hand, it is the red pigment that is missing and the extent of the black areas can be better appreciated. To take just one more example, the albino form of the black ratsnake, *Pantherophis obsoletus obsoletus*, retains light red or pink blotches along its back, even though normal adults are plain black; this is evidence that the black pigment, melanin, does not replace but obscures other pigments as the snake matures.

The patterns of many species need not only be caused by a combination of pigmentary colours but can result from structural and pigmentary colorations. Many species have a superimposed iridescent sheen overlying their deeper, more solid colours, and even in uniformly coloured snakes, such as the green species referred to above, the exact shade of green varies according to how much or how little melanin overlies the iridophores and xanthophores.

Genetic control of colour

Colour, like other characteristics, is under the control of genes. These behave in the usual Mendelian fashion, whereby a gene may be dominant or recessive and the quota of dominant and recessive genes will control the colour. This applies to cases where species exist in more than one colour form as well as to artificially selected mutant strains. When a normally coloured snake is carrying a recessive gene for amelanism, for instance, its condition is known as heterozygous. There is no way of telling, superficially, that it carries the mutant gene because that gene's opposite number is normal. An amelanistic snake, on the other hand, must carry two mutant recessive genes (otherwise it would not look amelanistic).

Genes programme for the formation of xanthophores as well as pigments. Since the xanthophores change the blue colorations to green by filtering the light coming back from iridophores, the absence of xanthophores results in blue snakes. These

▲ Colour patterns of snakes are made up of a mosaic of pigments, some of which are not obvious. Here, small spots of black pigment, melanin, are distributed locally on the otherwise pale green scales of and emerald boa, *Corallus caninus*. This produces a fringe of darker green scales surrounding the white dorsal markings.

are not common but have been recorded in the green python, *Morelia viridis*.

Colour changes

Snakes may change their colours in two ways. A few species are capable of limited colour change throughout a fairly short period of time. This aspect is not very well documented but a few examples can be mentioned. A small form of common boa, popularly known as the Hog Island boa, can change the tone of its colorations quite significantly. This usually occurs at night when the snake becomes paler with a more washed-out pattern. A similar situation exists in the Oenpelli python from northern Australia, which is brown during the day and pale silvery grey at night. The Round island boa, *Casarea dussumieri*, the Pacific boa, *Candoia carinata*, and several of the small West Indian *Tropidophis* species are also capable of limited colour change, always from dark during the day to light at night.

Female Madagascan tree boas, *Sanzinia madagascariensis* become darker when they are pregnant, presumably to optimise the absorption of radiation and thus speed up the development of their embryos. In a similar vein, there is some evidence that other species of snakes become darker

during cooler weather, including the Australian taipans, *Oxyuranus*, and the brownsnakes, *Pseudonaja*, also from Australia. All these examples concern dark or light coloration and therefore melanin is the pigment involved. It can be surmised, then, that the colour changes are brought about by melanin granules being mobilised within the melanophores, as is the case with animals in other groups that are well known for colour changes, such as chameleons, fishes and cephalopods.

Colour change on a longer time scale is rather better known. There are a great many species in which the juveniles are differently coloured or marked from adults if the same species. In its simplest form this transition involves an overall darkening of the colours. The milksnakes, *Lampropeltis triangulum*, are good examples, where the brightly coloured hatchlings gradually become duller as they grow, and they eventually turn almost uniform black in some subspecies, for example, *L. t. andesiana*. Here, the melanin production must continue throughout the life of the snake, gradually suffusing its surface with black and obscuring the underlying pattern. The various subspecies of the North American rat snakes, *Pantherophis obsoletus*, also undergo colour changes as they mature. All subspecies start off grey or light tan with a number of darker saddles running along the length of their backs. As they grow, the saddles become less obvious and eventually fade altogether. Depending on the subspecies, other markings may develop and the overall colorations may change. The one exception is the grey rat snake, *P. o. spiloides*, in which the saddles are retained throughout the life of the snake and the colour and markings of juveniles are much the same as those of the adults. Other rat snakes, including a European species, *Elaphe quatuorlineata*, also undergo changes in which juveniles are blotched but adult are uniformly coloured or striped.

There are several other, more dramatic examples of colour change. The best known are those for the emerald tree boa, *Corallus caninus*, and the green tree python, *Morelia viridis*. These two species show a remarkable degree of convergence in their appearance and behaviour (a topic discussed in more detail elsewhere) and even extend this to colour change. Both species are bright green as adults but juvenile pythons are usually bright sulphur yellow, occasionally brick red or brown whereas juvenile emerald boas are usually orange but may also be yellow or brown. The change in appearance usually occurs quite quickly, usually within the first year, and is presumably the result of the production of new pigments due to unknown triggers. Juvenile Madagascan tree boas, *Sanzinia madagascariensis*, are also red at birth and change to the normal greenish colorations before they reach one year of age. No totally satisfactory explanation had been proposed for this remarkable convergence, involving as it does species from South America, Australasia and Madagascar. Each of the species concerned is arboreal, but each is rather bulkier than most other arboreal snakes. The most likely explanation is that the colour change corresponds to a change in habit, with young snakes perhaps occupying different positions within the forest canopy.

PRODUCING NORMAL OFFSPRING FROM ALBINO PARENTS

Although colour is controlled by genes, there need not be a single gene controlling each colour: in fact, this is almost never the case. Pigments such as melanin are the end result of a chain of biochemical reactions in which there are several intermediate products. Chemicals act on each of these intermediate products in turn, transforming them to the next product in the chain. Genetic defects can affect any of the steps in the chain. Amelanism, for example, can be caused in several ways, with the process being blocked at one of several stages. So, if we take two amelanistic snakes that have different defective genes and breed them together, the resultant offspring will be normal.

To explain this more easily, let us assume that a chemical, Y, is responsible for converting a pigment precursor, A, to a second precursor, B. Then a second chemical, S, is responsible for converting B to the end product, pigment C (melanin in our example). Now, the first snake has the gene for manufacturing chemical Y but the gene for producing chemical Z is defective. The second snake has the gene for manufacturing chemical X but the one for producing chemical Y is defective. There is a breakdown in the biochemical pathway in both snakes and so they appear amelanistic.

If they breed together, however, the first snake will supply their offspring with the gene for producing chemical Y and the second snake will supply them with the gene for producing chemical Z. The offspring will have functioning genes for producing both chemicals and the bio-chemical pathway has been restored – two amelanistic snakes have bred together to produce normal-looking offspring.

In 'real life' the pathway will not be as simple as this. there may be many steps in the process of producing a pigment, but the general principle is the same.

▶ Albinism in these two types of albino Queretaro kingsnakes, *Lampropeltis ruthveni*, is controlled by different genes. If they are bred together, they will produce normal-looking offspring, although each offspring will carry a recessive gene for one or other type of albino.

Natural populations with aberrant coloration

Because colorations is under genetic control, it is always possible that mutations will arise. Under normal circumstances, these would soon fall prey to predators and the frequency of such mutant genes would be kept at a low level within populations. In certain situations, however, the mutation can provide a benefit that outweighs the disadvantages.

Melanism

Most mutation examples concern melanistic populations, especially of snakes living in abnormally cold conditions. Thus certain populations of some European viper species, including adders, *Vipera berus*, asps, *V. aspis* and Spanish vipers, *V. seoanei*, have a tendency towards melanism, as do some populations of the eastern garter snake, *Thamnophis sirtalis sirtalis*, in several localities around Lake Erie in Ontario, Canada, and elsewhere in the more northern parts of the subspecies' range. All these snakes live in cool regions, either by virtue of their distribution at northerly latitudes or because they inhabit mountains. A similar situation exists within populations of the tiger snake, *Notechis scutatus*, in Tasmania. These snakes show great variation in their colour and markings, but uniform black individuals are more frequent in the cooler west, southwest and montane parts of the island. Black populations, sometimes regarded as a separate species, *N. ater*, also occur on some of the small islands in the Bass Straits. In other cases, melanism has become fixed in variable, or polymorphic, species. These include the eastern hognose snake, *Heterodon platyrhinos*, which may have dark spots on a yellow, brown or reddish background but which also occurs as a plain black form. Similarly, in the aptly named variable kingsnake, *Lampropeltis mexicana thayeri*, there is a variety of colour patterns, one of which is plain black.

Albinism

Albinism is rather more difficult to live with than melanism: whereas melanistic snakes may not be quite as well camouflaged as normally coloured individuals, pure white ones are definitely not. Although the occasional adult albino does crop up, the majority of them must perish long before they reach the stage where they can reproduce and pass on their albino genes. In fact, there is just a single known example of a naturally occurring albino population. This is in Japan, where there is an entire population of albino rat snakes, *Elaphe climacophora*, living

in and around the city of Iwakuni. The snakes are protected by the Japanese government as a national monument and a captive breeding programme has been initiated so that the population, which is declining due to habitat destruction, can be maintained.

In captivity, of course, the risks of predation are non-existent and so colour mutations are able to survive, provided they are healthy in other respects. In this way large captive populations of selected colour forms have been built up by snake breeder, and these include strains in which one or more pigment is lacking altogether, e.g. amelanistic (lacking black pigment), anerythristic (lacking red pigment) as well as total albinos, which lack all pigment. Where all the pigment is lacking but the xanthophores are present, the snake will take on a yellowish colorations, as in some strains of pythons.

Other colour variations

Other variations in colour and pattern within a species fall into the categories of polymorphism, where two or more types of colorations are present in a population, and sexual dimorphism, where males and females are differently coloured or marked. These phenomena are dealt with elsewhere under defence (page 125) and sexual dimorphism (page 163).

▼ Snakes' scales are formed from thickened areas of skin and are therefore integral with it, unlike fishes' scales, which can be scraped off. Here the skin is stretched, pulling the scales apart so that they do not form a continuous covering.

THE SKIN AND SCALES

SNAKES' SKIN IS COMPLETELY COVERED WITH SCALES OF VARIOUS TYPES. THE SKIN AND SCALES TOGETHER FORM THE INTEGUMENT. THIS MUST PERFORM A NUMBER OF FUNCTIONS.

The skin

Although snakes are covered with scales, part of their integument consists of skin. When the snake's body is distended, after a large meal, for instance, this interstitial skin can be easily seen and, indeed, it is the areas of skin between the scales that gives the snake's body its flexibility. Other than this important function, snakes' interstitial skin is unremarkable, except in a few cases where it is coloured differently from the scales and is used in displays to intimidate predators. The twig snake, *Thelotornis capensis*, for example, inflates its neck when annoyed, exposing a large black marking on its interstitial skin. The boomslang, *Dispholidus typus* in which the interstitial skin may be blue, has a similar display as do some of the bronzeback snakes, *Dendrelaphis*, from Southeast Asia.

The scales

Reptile scales are formed from thickened areas of the epidermis. In this respect, they are unlike the scales of fishes, which can be removed individually without damaging the skin.

◀ *Malpolon moilensis* from Egypt.

SCALE POLISHING

Snakes of a few species 'polish' their scales with a secretion that they obtain from their nostrils. Species in which this type of behaviour has been observed include the Montpellier snake, *Malpolon monspessulanus*, from southern Europe, its close relative *M. moilensis* from North Africa, and four species of sand snakes, *Psammophis*, from Africa and the Middle East.

In *Malpolon* the oily fluid is secreted via a small aperture on the outside of the nasal flap. Polishing is carried out by moving the head up and down over its flanks and its ventral scales, about 100 times, moving progressively along its body as it goes. In this way, the secretion is applied in a continuous zig-zag line along almost the entire length of the ventral surface, with the snake turning its body over slightly to allow contact between its snout and its underside. Each side of the head is used in alternative sequences.

During warm weather, *Malpolon monspessulanus* polishes itself regularly, throughout the day. During cool weather, polishing seems to be restricted to the periods immediately after shedding its skin, and just after it has eaten.

The hissing sand snake, *Psammophis sibilans*, polishes itself in a similar manner although its movements are more complicated. The head passes over the back of the snake to polish the scales on the opposite side of its body, i.e. the right nostril comes into contact with scales on the snake's left flank, wipes the scales backwards and forwards and then moves over to the other side. As it works its way down the body, the scales on the ventral surface and on the flanks, on both sides of its body, are covered. At the same time, each section of its body is raised in turn to allow the nostril to contact the snake's underside.

The other species of sand snakes in which polishing has been observed are *P. condanarus*, *P. schokari* and *P. subtaeniatus*. Their methods and movements are similar to those of *P. sibilans*, but with minor variations. The purpose of this behaviour is not known with certainty but it may help to reduce water loss. The permeability of snakes' scales is partly dependent on the amount of lipids secreted, because these oily substances help to seal the scales and prevent the passage of water across their surface.

On the other hand, scale polishing might be concerned with chemical communication; the aromatic substances produced in the nasal glands are smeared over the body so that the snake marks the ground over which it crawls.

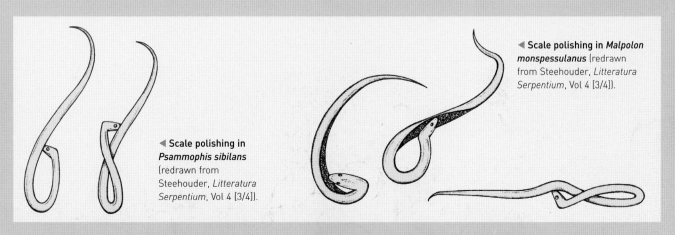

◀ Scale polishing in *Psammophis sibilans* (redrawn from Steehouder, *Litteratura Serpentium*, Vol 4 [3/4]).

◀ Scale polishing in *Malpolon monspessulanus* (redrawn from Steehouder, *Litteratura Serpentium*, Vol 4 [3/4]).

All snakes are covered in scales, but their shapes, textures and arrangements vary greatly. They fulfil several purposes. They form a good degree of physical protection from general wear and tear when the snake moves across rough surfaces, etc. At the same time, the use of small units of armour allows greater flexibility than would large bony plates and snakes depend heavily on flexibility during locomotion and when subduing their prey. Elasticity is also important when swallowing.

Certain scales are used in locomotion, when their edges are hooked over irregularities in the surface (see Locomotion, later in this chapter).

The scales of most snakes also contain the cells that give the snake its characteristic colour and markings, which are especially important in defence, such as camouflage, warning colorations.

Permeability of the skin

Although scales must help to prevent dehydration, this may be a less important function than was formerly believed; desert species have a high degree of resistance to desiccation, but rainforest species do not – even though both types are covered in broadly similar arrangements of scales. This would seem to indicate that other mechanisms are of greater importance in this function.

Permeability may also alter throughout the snake's active season. This is thought to be due to the secretion of lipids, which reduce permeability. Permeability may be under the physiological control of the snake to some extent, although this has not been proved. Of the species tested, the most permeable skin was that of the little file snake, *Acrochordus granulatus*, which is ten times more permeable than that of diamondback rattlesnakes, for instance. This is thought to help prevent the snake from drying out if it becomes stranded on the mud at low tide. The skin attracts water which moves through the small channels between its granular scales, forming a kind of water jacket. (Lillywhite and Sanmartino, 1993).[9]

Another species with a very permeable skin is the semi-aquatic queen snake, *Regina septemvittata*. Snakes from dry environments tend to have less permeable skin, as would be expected, although habitat does not always correlate exactly with skin permeability. The skins of different species of sea snakes, for instance, have differing permeabilities, which is unusual as they all inhabit marine environments (Dunson and Freda, 1985).[10]

▲ On Isla Fernandina, in the Galapagos, a colubrid snake has used a rock and some vegetation to help it to crawl out of its old skin.

Shedding the skin

Snakes' scales consist of two layers, an outer one that is presented to the outside world and an inner one which forms continually beneath the outer layer and which will take its place when the outer layer is shed. Between these two layers is a thin layer of clear cells that enable the other two layers to separate during shedding. Prior to shedding, the snake secretes an oily substance into this space in order to facilitate shedding; its markings become obscure and the eyes appear opaque or blue. The epidermis is normally shed in one piece, with the snake starting the process by rubbing its snout on a rough object then removing its old skin by crawling through vegetation or against a rock, bark or other rough surface. Once the skin has been shed, the old inner layer becomes the new outer layer and a new inner layer begins to develop.

The pigment cells are not contained in the epidermis but in the dermis, a layer of connective tissue that lies beneath the epidermis. Therefore, the shed skin is not coloured, although it may contain traces of the pattern in the form of faint dark markings. Because the new skin has not been subjected to the wear that the old one was, the colours of the snake are often much brighter than they were prior to shedding. In species in which the colour changes throughout the life of the snake, these changes are often more noticeable directly after shedding, even though they actually occur gradually.

Frequency of shedding depends on many factors. As shedding is to some extent dependent on growth. young snakes tend to shed more often than adults because they grow more quickly. As their growth rate slows down, so does the frequency of shedding. All snakes shed occasionally, however, even those that have all but stopped growing. In temperate species that go through a resting period, or hibernation, during the winter, shedding often takes place early in the spring almost as soon as they become active. Sexual activity is often heightened during the days immediately following this 'vernal' shed.

Female snakes often shed their skins just before laying eggs or giving birth to live young. This 'pre-laying' shed takes place at a predetermined time before laying, eight to ten days in most rat snakes and kingsnakes, for example, and is therefore very useful in predicting the date of egg laying. In other species, such as pythons, there is an identifiable pre-laying shed but the timing may not be as constant. Females go through another shed shortly after laying, the post-laying shed.

Snakes that have been injured often shed frequently, sometimes shedding several times in rapid succession even though they have not eaten between sheds. This is presumably under hormonal control and serves to speed up the rate of healing.

The shed skin of a snake is moist and supple immediately after shedding, due to the oily substance present, and the new skin of the snake may be similarly slightly tacky. After a few hours, however, this wears off and the shed skin becomes brittle. Shed skins are appreciably longer than the snakes from which they have come away, by up to 20 per cent.

The rattlesnake's rattle

The rattle on the tail of rattlesnakes, genera *Crotalus* and *Sistrurus*, is formed from the successive remains of the scale covering the extreme tip of the tail. In most snakes, this scale is conical and the epidermis covering it comes away with the rest of the shed skin. In rattlesnakes, however, the terminal scale is shaped like an hour-glass, with a constriction somewhere around its centre line. After the first shed, the skin around this terminal scale becomes thicker than normal. When the young snake sheds for the second time, this scale is torn away from the old skin, because it is held in place by the constriction. Now a new skin is formed around the tip of the tail but it shrinks away from the piece of old skin so that it is attached only loosely. When the snake sheds again, the second layer is prevented from coming away, the tail has two segments, one inside the other, and the cycle starts over again. Eventually, a number of segments are built up, the oldest towards the end of the tail and the freshest towards its base. Each segment, then, represents a shed skin, but, although the snake may shed four or more times each year, rattles that consist of more than six or seven segments

▲ Prior to shedding their skin, snakes secrete an oily substance between the old outer layer of epidermis and the new inner one. This substance is opaque, causing the snake's markings to become dull and its eyes to appear milky. The snake is a Central American rat snake, *Pseudoelaphe flavirufa*.

▲ The rattlesnake's rattle consist of sections of thickened skin, left behind each time they shed and articulating loosely on each other.

▲ The outer layer of skin of a common boa is rolled back from left to right as the snake crawls out of it. Snakes usually shed their epidermis in one piece.

▲ The horns over the eyes of the North African desert horned viper, *Cerastes cerastes*, are modified scales. Their function is uncertain but some other desert vipers also have horns or raised scales over their eyes.

◄ Hognose snakes, of which this is the southern species, *Heterodon simus*, have a modified rostral scale that they use for digging.

are rare because the material is brittle and the tip, including the button, is usually broken off, leaving only the most recently formed rings. The purpose of the rattle is discussed in Chapter 6.

Types of scales

Snakes' scales are not all of the same type. There is variation between species and between different parts of the same species. In some families of snakes, notably the colubrids and elapids, large plate-like scales cover the head and these are arranged in a more or less consistent pattern and are easily identifiable. They are therefore of value in helping to identify species.

These head scales are given names by which they can be recognized. The diagram shows the position of these for a typical example. One of the most conspicuous is the rostral scale; this is a single large scale positioned on the end of the snout and in many species it is enlarged or modified to provide a tool for burrowing, as in the shovel-nosed snakes, *Chionactis*, and the hognose snakes, *Heterodon*. Other specialised scales found on the head of snakes include the horns over the eyes of some species. These may comprise a single, thorn-like scale as in the African desert horned viper, *Cerastes cerastes*, and the horned adder, *Bitis caudalis*, a cluster of pointed scales as in the many-horned adder, *Bitis cornuta*, and the eyelash viper, *Bothriechis schlegelii*, or they may be formed from a single raised scale, as in the American sidewinder, *Crotalus cerastes*, or a group of them, as in *Pseudocerastes*, from the Middle East.

Other species, most notably the rhinoceros viper, *Bitis nasicornis*, have a cluster of enlarged, pointed scales on their snouts, while in other species, the snout is extended into an upturned rostral appendage, or nose horn comprising numerous small scales over a bony or fleshy protuberance; this feature is especially frequent among, but not restricted to, the vipers, notably the European nose-horned viper, *Vipera ammodytes*, and its relatives. The fishing snake, *Erpeton tentaculatum*, of Southeast Asia is unique in possessing a pair of 'tentacles' attached to the end of its snout. For many years these were thought to perform as lures since the snake is aquatic and feeds exclusively on fish. It has since been shown, however, that the structures could not be wriggled about in the way that would be necessary for a successful lure. Neither can they be used as organs of touch as they have no nerve endings.

► The arrangement of the scales on the heads of snakes tends to be fairly constant within species and can be used as an aid to identification.

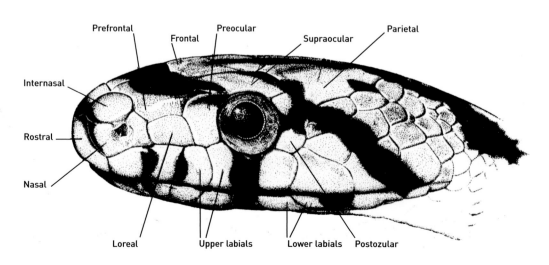

Prefrontal

Frontal

Preocular

Supraocular

Parietal

Internasal

Rostral

Nasal

Loreal

Upper labials

Lower labials

Postozular

▶ The eyelash viper, *Bothriechis schlegelii*, from Central America, has a cluster of spine-like scales over each eye. A few other species share this characteristic, including the eyelash boa, *Trachyboa boulengeri*, which comes from the same part of the world.

▼ The rhinoceros viper, *Bitis nasicornis*, has an elaborate cluster of raised scales on its snout.

▼ (below left) The nose-horned viper, *Vipera ammodytes*, has a fleshy 'horn' on its snout. Some other vipers also have upturned snouts but rarely as pronounced as this.

▼ (below right) The horns or 'tentacles' of the fishing snake, *Erpeton tentaculatum*, probably serve to break up the snake's outline.

It seems likely that they serve the rather more mundane purpose of disguising the outline of the snake's head when it is waiting motionless to ambush its prey. The cryptic longitudinal markings on the body of the snake, and its colorations, further support this theory.

Other strange nasal projections are seen in the three Madagascan snakes belonging to the genus *Langaha*. These single organs are also thought to enhance crypsis as the snakes are long and slender and frequently rest motionless among vines and thin branches. Unaccountably, in *L. alluaudi* only females are so adorned, while in *L. nasuta* the males have a straightforward soft fleshy spike on the end of their snouts whereas the females have a more elaborate affair in which the projection is modified into a series of lobes and serrations.

Snakes' tails can be long or short, pointed or blunt or, in a few cases, they may end in other structures. Rattlesnakes' rattle are described on page 35. Some species, such as worm snakes, *Typhlopidae*, have tails that end in a small spine, which they use to push against the substrate when burrowing. When they are held in the hand they use the spine to push against the skin, probably in an attempt to push themselves forward rather than to cause harm, as some authors have suggested. A few colubrids, such as the well-named sharp-tailed Snake, *Contia tenuis*, from western North America, has a short tail ending in a pointed terminal scale.

Uropeltids have the strangest tails of all, though. Members of the genus *Uropeltis* have obliquely truncated tails, like a banana that has been sliced at an angle of about 45°. The resulting oval, flat surface is covered in rough, heavily keeled keeled or tuberculate scales. Other species in the family have abruptly flattened tails in two or four small spines or,

▲ The scales of the hairy bushviper, *Atheris hispida*, are elongated and pointed, with their tips raised, giving the snake a rough, hairy appearance.

▼ The scales of many snakes have keels, or ridges, running down their centres. They may be very obvious, as in this puff adder, or hardly visible, or absent altogether, depending on the species.

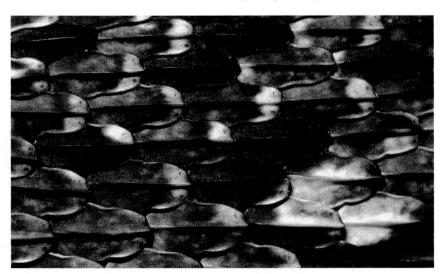

as in the *Rhinophis* species, in a single rounded conical scale covered with granular tubercles and lacking pigment. All these devices probably give the snake something to push against when it is burrowing and the bullet-shaped terminal scale of *Rhinophis* species may act as a plug, blocking the progress of pursuing predatory snakes.

Scales on the dorsal surface of the bodies of most species tend to be diamond shaped and overlap like the tiles of a roof. They are organised into regular rows that can be counted and used as an aid to identification. Their tips may be rounded, as in the *Typhlops* species, or more pointed. The hairy bush viper, *Atheris hispida*, where the apices of the scales are drawn out into raised, spiky tips, is an extreme example of pointed scales. Further variation in the scales is provided by keels. These structures run along the mid-line of the scales and may be prominent, slight or absent altogether. There tends to be some degree of consistency within closely related species although some genera contain species with keeled scales and others with smooth ones. Keeled scales probably help to improve traction under certain circum-stances and they are commonly found among the semi-aquatic natricine colubrids and the fishing snake, *Erpeton*, for instance. Other aquatic species, however, lack keels.

In the saw-scaled vipers, *Echis*, and the desert vipers belonging to the genus *Cerastes*, the large keels are modified so that they can be rubbed together to produce a rasping sound and this behaviour is mimicked, with similar results, in some of the egg-eating snakes, for example, *Dasypeltis* (see Chapter 6, page 131).

Snakes with smooth scales may be able to move more rapidly through vegetation, loose sand, etc., as their polished surfaces produce less drag. This type of scalation is commonly seen in burrowing or semi-burrowing snakes, although species from other habitats may also have smooth scales.

The three species of snakes belonging to the family Acrochordidae are unusual in having small granular scales. This is thought to be an adaptation to the totally aquatic lifestyle of these strange but interesting species, and may help them to hold slippery fish, which form their main prey, in their coils. Algae frequently grows over the surface of these scales and this undoubtedly enhances their camouflage.

The scales covering the belly of all snakes, except blind snakes, are arranged in a single row, a feature that separates them from lizards. These ventral scales usually correspond to the position and number of ribs and commonly number more in females than in males of the same species. They are not always constant, however, and the ventral scale counts are usually given as a range, or two ranges (one for males and one for females) for each species. The ventral scale immediately in front of the cloaca is known as the pre-anal scale and it may be single or divided, depending on the species. Similarly, the scales beneath the tail, known as the subcaudals, may also be single or divided. Even in species with divided subcaudals, it is not unusual to find one or more single subcaudals scattered among the more typical ones.

LOCOMOTION

IN THE LOCOMOTION DEPARTMENT, SNAKES HAVE A FAIRLY OBVIOUS HANDICAP – THEIR LACK OF LEGS. IN THIS THEY ARE ALMOST UNIQUE AMONG THE TERRESTRIAL VERTEBRATES. CONSIDERING THE RANGE OF HABITATS IN WHICH THEY ARE FOUND, HOWEVER, THE PROBLEM OF LEGLESSNESS APPEARS NOT TO HAVE PLACED TOO MANY RESTRICTIONS ON THEIR ABILITY TO MOVE AROUND.

In practice, snakes have evolved a number of distinct types of movement, the method used sometimes depending on the size of the snake and sometimes on the substrate over or through which it is moving. Most species can switch from one type of locomotion to another as the circumstances demand, but others are more specialised and only perform efficiently in their own particular environment.

Serpentine crawling
The most common form of snake locomotion is that seen when a small or medium sized snake is travelling across rough ground. It consists of a side-to-side wriggling, sometimes known as lateral undulation. An identical form of movement is used when moving quickly through dense undergrowth or branches. Simply speaking, the snake uses the sides of its body to push against small irregularities in the surface of the substrate. At any given time, various points along the body of the snake are pushing simultaneously against a number of fixed points. As the snake moves forward, new parts of the body are continuously coming into contact with the same points and so all parts of the body follow the same line and the snake moves forward steadily with an almost fluid grace. During swimming, the same sequence of events takes place but the body of the snake pushes against the resistance of the water.

Concertina locomotion
Concertina locomotion is most often seen in burrowing snakes but can also be observed when a more typical species is crawling through a tube or along a narrow space between two immovable objects. First, the head and the front part of the body are extended forward, while the back half is curved several times to provide an anchor. In a burrow, for instance, this brings a number of points to bear on the sides of the burrow. Once the head and front part of the body are fully extended they, in turn, are used to gain purchase on the surface in the same way so that the back part of the body and the tail can be drawn up. The sequence is repeated as many times as is necessary.

▶ **(a)** Typical serpentine locomotion, in which the body is wriggled from side to side, is used by snakes crossing an uneven surface. Successive loops of the body push against small irregularities.
(b) A similar method is used to crawl over rough surfaces except that large objects such as rocks, etc. are used to provide the anchor points.
(c) Arboreal snakes use branches to give purchase and are often capable of spanning large gaps due to their body shape.

a   b   c

▲ In concertina locomotion the snake uses the back half of its body to provide an anchor point while the front half is thrust forward. Then the front half grips the surface while the back half is drawn up, and so on.

◄ The body of some species, notably the rat snakes is an effective compromise between their terrestrial and arboreal habits. The edges of the ventral scales are strongly keeled, providing a ridge that is useful in gripping the bark of trees when climbing.

▲ When moving along existing underground tunnels, snakes use a method of locomotion that is similar to concertina locomotion, except that the sides of the tunnel provide purchase for one section of the body while the rest moves forward.

▽ In rectilinear crawling, alternative sections of the ventral skin and scales are moved forward relative to the rest of its body. The snake progresses in a more or less straight line (like a caterpillar). This method is used mainly by large, heavy-bodied species such as pythons, boas and some vipers.

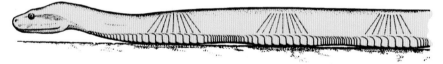

▲ Sidewinding is used by a number of snake species that live on loose sand and soil. The snake moves sideways in a series of looping movements and leaves a characteristic track. Many sidewinding species are specialists that use it almost exclusively but sometimes other species may revert to a type of sidewinding when circumstances dictate.

A similar type of movement is used for climbing rough surfaces, such as the bark of trees. In order to increase their efficiency, some species, such as the North American rat snakes have a pair of ridges running along their bodies near the edge of their ventral scales and this ridge provides additional grip.

Yet another variation of the technique is used by the burrowing snakes belonging to the family Uropeltidae (shield tails). In these species, parts of the vertebral column can be bent into a series of curves while the sides of the body remain parallel. This causes the body to become shorter and thicker, so the snake can jam itself between the walls of its burrow with one part of its body while another part is thrust forward or drawn along behind.

Rectilinear crawling

Some heavy-bodied snakes, especially boas, pythons and vipers, abandon the usual serpentine method altogether and use the edges of the scales on their undersides as anchor points to pull themselves forward. Smaller snakes may also use this method if they are unable to get enough purchase to thrust diagonally against the substrate, as in serpentine locomotion. During the final stages of stalking their prey, many snakes edge forwards in a more or less straight line, using a variation of rectilinear locomotion so as not to alert their intended victim.

The operation consists of stretching forward and hooking the edges of the scales over small irregularities, then pulling the body up to this point. Alternate parts of the body will be stretching and pulling at the same time, and the muscles then relax and contract in a series of smooth waves running along the length of the snake. The animal moves in a straight line with none of the characteristic sideways wriggling usually associated with snake locomotion.

Sidewinding locomotion

Sidewinding is a specialised form of locomotion usually associated with a particular group of snakes. It is used by species, notably vipers, that live in areas of loose, windblown sand. There are snakes in North America, South America, North Africa, southern Africa and central Asia that sidewind, showing that the technique has evolved independently on several occasions.

Sidewinding is rather like concertina locomotion in that one part of the body acts as an anchor while another part is moved forward. Starting from a resting position, the head and neck are raised off the ground and thrown sideways, while the rest of the body provides purchase. Once the head, back and fore part of the body are on the ground again they in turn act as an anchor while the other parts of the body catch up. Almost as this is happening, though, the head and neck are flung sideways again, resulting in a continuous and remarkably effective looping movement across the sand. The snake moves at about 45° to the direction in which it is pointing and leaves a trail of characteristic markings in the sand.

Speed of movement

Speed of movement is related to method but is not totally dependent on it. Basically, snakes move as fast as they need to. Thus, active diurnal hunters move rapidly, using a serpentine crawling method of locomotion, whereas large heavy-bodied vipers, which tend to ambush their prey, are often slow and sluggish and may use rectilinear crawling to move around.

The speed at which a snake can travel is open to debate and, like the length of snakes, it is often exaggerated. The green mamba is often quoted as one of the fastest snakes; it has been accurately timed at 7 miles (11 km) per hour. It seems likely that several other species, such as whipsnakes and racers, *Coluber*, coachwhips, *Masticophis*, Australian whipsnakes, *Demansia*, and the sand snakes, *Psammophis*, can equal this speed, at least over short distances. Even so, the possibility that any snake could chase and overtake a reasonably fit human is highly unlikely.

▼ The arrangement of loosely interlocking wing-like processes on snakes' vertebrae prevent extreme twisting of the vertebral column and the spinal cord.

Structures associated with locomotion

Locomotion is achieved with the help of a series of muscles, arranged diagonally along each side of the snake. The ends of these muscles are attached to ribs, sometimes joining adjacent ribs but mostly joining ribs that are some distance apart. It is the particular pattern of contraction and relaxation of these muscles that controls the type of locomotion. For instance, if muscles on one side of the snake are contracted at the same time as the equivalent muscles on the other side are relaxed, the body will bend. If, on the other hand, opposite sets of muscles are contracted and relaxed in time with one another, the snake's body will remain more or less straight.

Since snakes have so many ribs, over 400 pairs in some cases, the coordination of these muscles can become very complex with, sometimes, one part of the body doing one thing while another part does something entirely different.

In order for the snake to be able to bend and coil its body, the vertebrae (equivalent to the number of ribs) must be capable of a high degree of sideways flexibility and a simple ball and socket arrangement allows this to occur. On the other hand, the amount of twisting movement must be limited because the spinal cord runs through a canal near the top of each vertebra and must be protected: if the vertebrae had complete freedom to spin independently of one another, the nerves inside the spinal column would be wrung like a piece of cloth. For this reason, each vertebra has a number of wing-like processes that interlock loosely with the corresponding processes on the adjacent vertebrae. This limits the amount of twisting.

THE SENSES

ANIMALS INTERACT WITH THEIR SURROUNDINGS BY PROCESSING INFORMATION AND ACTING UPON IT. THE INFORMATION ARRIVES IN VARIOUS FORMS AND SO THE KEENER THE SENSES OF THE ANIMAL, THE MORE QUICKLY AND EFFICIENTLY IT WILL BE ABLE TO RESPOND. SNAKES ARE NO EXCEPTION TO THIS BUT DIFFER FROM OTHER VERTEBRATES IN THE WAY IN WHICH THEY RELY ON THEIR VARIOUS SENSES. SEVERAL NOVEL SENSES ARE FOUND UNIQUELY IN THE SNAKES AND THESE MAY HAVE EVOLVED AS A RESULT OF THEIR POOR EYESIGHT.

Sight

Although all snakes are predators, their organs of sight are not very efficient, This anomaly may stem from their origins as primitive burrowing reptiles, evolved from burrowing lizards. Burrowing animals have little use for eyes and they tend to degenerate over a long period of time – various insects, amphibians and fish that live in caves and other totally dark conditions demonstrate very well how this may come about. Similarly, primitive burrowing snakes, such as those belonging to the Typhlopidae and Leptotyphlopidae, which spend the greater part of their lives beneath the surface, have only rudimentary eyes, covered with a scale and, at most, capable only of distinguishing light from dark.

Having returned to the surface at a later date in their history, the more advanced snakes had to reinvent the eye and, although this was achieved, many of the more sophisticated features had been lost forever. In particular, it appears that members of only one genus of snakes, *Ahaetulla*, are able to focus by changing the shape of their lens: all other species must focus by moving the lens backwards and forwards, as in a camera. This ponderous method provides a more limited degree of focusing ability. In addition, the cells that line the retina, known as rods and cones, and which enable vision to take place under a range of light intensities, are not as well organised in snakes as they are in most other vertebrates, and many snakes lack one or other of these types of cells altogether. The net outcome is an inability to see detail and, in particular, the inability to notice stationary

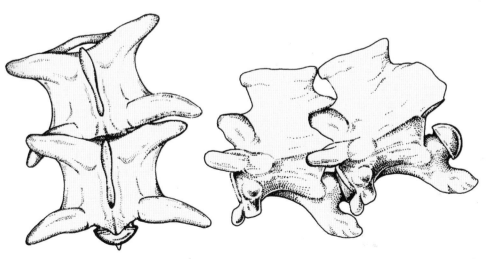

SNAKE EYES

Whereas the eyes of most snakes have simple, rounded pupils if they are diurnal, and horizontally elliptical pupils if they are nocturnal, there are some specialisations. Asian vine snakes, *Ahaetulla*, have elongated pupils and 'wrap-around' eyes that enable them to judge distance accurately. The boomslang, a diurnal hunter, has large eyes with teardrop shaped pupils with a small extension towards the front and perhaps this serves the same purpose. Nocturnal hunters have sensitive eyes and shut down their pupils in response to light, perhaps none more so than the montane slug-eating snake, *Asthenodipsas vertebralis*, from Malaysia.

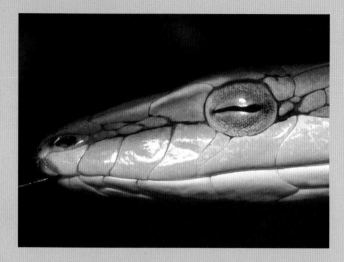

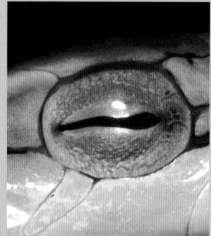

◀ Vine snakes belonging to the genus *Ahaetulla* have elongated horizontal pupils. This is the common vine snake, *A. nasuta*, from Southeast Asia.

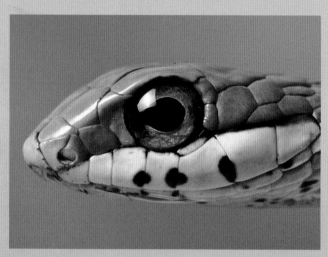

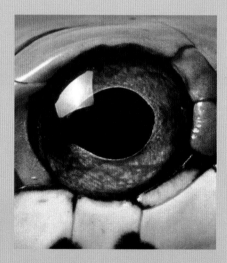

◀ The boomslang, *Dispholidus typus*, a diurnal, arboreal snake, has teardrop-shaped pupils.

◀ The montane slug-eating snake, *Asthenodipsas vertebralis*, is a strictly nocturnal species with vertical pupils that close down to a small oval point in daylight.

▲ The scale covering the eye, the brille, is a specialised scale found in all but the most primitive snakes. It is shed periodically with the rest of the epidermis. This western sand snake, *Psammophis trigrammus* from southern Africa, has just begun the shedding process.

objects. Sensitivity to movement is enhanced, however, and the wide field of view, provided by the position of the eyes on either side of the head, allows snakes to notice activity that may indicate danger or a potential meal. The eyes of snakes have limited mobility except for a few species, notably the vine snakes belonging to the genus *Oxybelis*, which can swivel their eyes to search for prey, danger, etc., while still maintaining a motionless position. Others, including short-tailed pythons, also swivel their eyes but to a lesser extent.

Predictably, the species that have evolved the most efficient visual equipment are diurnal hunters, such as the whipsnakes and garter snakes. Diurnal hunters such as these are usually recognisable by means of their large circular pupils. Nocturnal hunters, such as the lyre snakes, *Trimorphodon*, and the cat snakes, *Telescopus*, also have large

eyes, but with vertically elliptical pupils that close down to narrow slits during the day.

A few species, notably the long-nosed tree snakes, *Ahaetulla*, of which there are eight species in Asia, and the twig snakes, *Thelotornis*, (three species in Africa) have large eyes and horizontally elliptical, or keyhole-shaped, pupils. This arrangement has evolved to give the snakes a high degree of binocular vision and is associated with a long narrow snout along which the snake can look in order to judge distances. They may further enhance their binocular vision by swaying from side to side when lining up their prey. These snakes are active by day and stalk their agile lizard prey by sight. They need to judge distances carefully and strike accurately because they are unlikely to get a second chance.

In addition to their inefficient eyes, snakes lack eyelids, a feature that separates

them from all but a few lizards. Instead, most species have a single large scale covering the eye, sometimes known as the brille or spectacle. This protects the eye from damage and is shed at intervals along with the rest of the scales. Some primitive snakes lack a brille and the eye is covered by one or more conventional scales.

Hearing

Snakes are popularly thought to be deaf. This is not strictly true because, although they lack external signs of ears, they do retain the vestiges of the sound-transmitting equipment in the form of a small bone, the stapes. This bone is in contact with the quadrate bone, which in turn articulates with the lower jaw. As the lower jaw is often in contact with the ground, sensitivity to vibrations must be extremely acute. In addition, low frequency airborne sounds may also set up vibrations and these can probably also be detected by snakes.

One of the implications of a lack of hearing is that vocal communication between individuals is not possible, as it is in frogs and toads, for instance. Therefore, the sounds that certain snakes do produce – hisses and rattles – have evolved in order to communicate with other kinds of animals, as warnings, and not with each other.

Smell

The lack of keen sight and sensitive hearing has led to the development of other, more specialised sense organs in snakes. One of these is the Jacobson's organ, found only in snakes and in some groups of lizards. The Jacobson's organ works in conjunction with, and in addition to, the nostrils and the olfactory part of the brain. It consists of a pair of sacs lined with sensory cells, situated in the front of the palate. The sacs open to the roof of the mouth via a pair of narrow ducts and their inner ends are connected to a separate branch of the olfactory nerve.

When a snake wants to investigate its surroundings, it flicks its tongue out, through a notch in the upper jaw known as the lingual fossa. The tongue picks up scents in the form of airborne molecules and is then withdrawn into the mouth. Here the twin tips of the forked tongue are inserted into the opening ducts of the Jacobson's organ, the molecules are identified, and the information is passed to the brain. Active snakes use their tongues constantly and probably rely on their Jacobson's organ as much as, if not more than, their nostrils. When not in use, the tongue rests in a fleshy sheath on the floor of the mouth.

Heat-sensitive pits

The senses already described are present to some extent in all snakes. Certain groups, however, have evolved additional sense organs that are unique in the animal kingdom. These are specialised heat-sensitive pits found in the boas, pythons and pit vipers. Pit vipers belong to the subfamily Crotalinae, and include the rattlesnakes, *Crotalus* and *Sistrurus*, as well as members of several other genera. Due to the distant relationships between boids and vipers, and the differences in the structure of their pits, they must have evolved independently.

The structure of the pits was first described as long ago as the early nineteenth century, although the first experiments to establish their purpose were made in the 1930s, first on a pit viper by Noble in 1934,[12] then on a

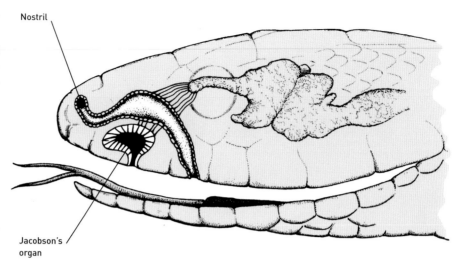

Nostril

Jacobson's organ

▲ Jacobson's organ is situated in the front of the head and opens on to the roof of the mouth where the tips of the tongue can be inserted into its opening. Nerves from the organ connect it to the olfactory lobe of the brain.

▲ When activated, the tongue is extended for some considerable distance and flickered around in the air to pick up scent molecules. This snake is a Southern Pacific rattlesnake, *Crotalus viridis helleri*.

◄ Snakes' tongues can be extended even when their mouths are closed, through a notch in the upper jaw known as the lingual fossa.

python by Ros in 1935, then on pit vipers again by Noble and Schmidt in 1937.[13]

Basically, the pits are lined with a layer of epithelial cells containing a number of thermoreceptors. Nerves from these receptors link the pits with the brain. The pits of the pit vipers are rather more sophisticated than those of boas and pythons. They consist of two compartments, an inner one and an outer one, divided by a membrane. The inner one is connected to the outside through a narrow pore-like channel that opens just in front of the eye. This serves to equalise the air pressure on either side of the membrane and also records the ambient temperature of the air. Heat originating from a warm-blooded animal is detected only by the outer surface of the membrane, and the snake is thus able to differentiate between convected warm air, such as a warm breeze, and a radiant object.

A hunting pit viper is therefore well equipped to detect prey. Vibrations may alert it first, then identification is made using the tongue and Jacobson's organ. At closer range the pits provide the necessary information to enable it to strike accurately, even in total darkness. A blind rattlesnake, for instance, scored direct hits on its prey 48 out of 49 times, a success rate that was comparable to that of rattlesnakes that could see. When its pits were covered, however, its success rate fell to

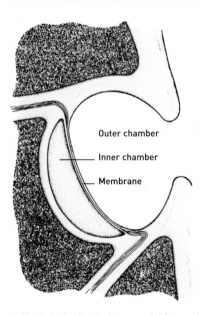

▲ Heat pits in the pit vipers are fairly simple structures. The base of the chamber is lined with a thin, sensitive membrane that detects temperature differences. These are then relayed to the brain by nerves, which are accommodated in channels in the maxillary bone. By moving the head, the amount of heat detected in each pit can be balanced so that an accurate strike can be made, even in total darkness.

Outer chamber
Inner chamber
Membrane

FACIAL PITS IN VIPERS

The pit vipers have evolved the most effective pits. In these species, found in North, Central and South America and in Asia, the heat-sensitive pits take the form of a single large organ on each side of the head, roughly situated just below a line between the eye and the nostril and slightly nearer the nostril.

▲ The Milos viper, *Macrovipera schweizeri*, is a typical viper, without pits.

The pits are edged with small scales and directed forwards. They were originally thought to be ears, then additional nostrils – pit vipers are still known as *cuatro narices* (four nostrils) in parts of Latin America.

Experiments have shown that at least some species are sensitive to changes in temperature of as little as 0.001°C (0.002°F). Using these organs, the location of prey, or enemies, can be accurately assessed, even in total darkness. This implies that messages obtained by each pit can be compared and that the snake can use this information to judge not only the position of the prey but also its range, rather in the same way that animals with binocular vision can judge distances.

▲ The way in which the pits are directed forward can be seen in this San Lucas rattlesnake, *Crotalus ruber lucasensis*, from Baja California.

◄ (top) Emerald boa, *Corallus caninus*, showing large heat pits between its rostral and labial scales.

◄ (bottom left) The rosy boa, *Charina trivirgata*, has no heat pits.

◄ (bottom right) Children's python, *Antaresia childreni*, has shallow heat pits in some of its lower labial scales.

▼ Diamond python, *Morelia spilota*, showing large heat pits in its rostral and labial scales.

FACIAL PITS IN BOAS AND PYTHONS

Among the boas, facial pits are found in three genera: *Corallus*, *Epicrates* and *Sanzinia*. When present they are located between the labial scales and they may be large and extensive, as in *Corallus*, or there may be just a few shallow pits, as in *Epicrates*. Species that feed on warm-blooded prey – mammals and birds – tend to be better equipped than those that feed on lizards and frogs, although the common boa, *Boa constrictor*, is an exception because it lacks pits even though it feeds mainly on warm-blooded prey. The Pacific boas, *Candoia*, also lack pits as do all the members of the subfamily Erycinae – the sand boas, *Eryx* and *Gongylophis*, the Calabar boa, *Calabaria*, and the rosy boa and rubber boa, both *Charina*. Lack of pits in these species is probably due to their early separation from the main boa stock before heat-sensitive pits evolved. In any case, they are burrowing snakes in which pits would become clogged with sand and soil.

In pythons the pits are found within the labial and, sometimes, the rostral scales. Once more, though, heat pits are not universal among the genera. Members of *Morelia* and *Python* are well-endowed whereas others, such as *Antaresia* and *Liasis*, have only a small series of shallow pits. The two species of *Aspidites*, lack pits altogether; they feed largely on cold-blooded prey and so pits would perhaps be of limited use to them.

4 out of 15 attempts. Furthermore, when prey was hit accurately, the more vulnerable head or thorax were the areas most likely to be penetrated by the fangs.[14] This gives a good indication of the accuracy with which pit vipers can strike, using only their facial pits.

Before leaving this subject, it is worth noting that experiments conducted by Breiderbach (1990) have shown that warm objects can also be detected by vipers without facial pits. They were able to differentiate between warm and cold objects and struck at warm objects.[15] It is not known how this is achieved, nor how their accuracy compares with that of the pit vipers. One would suspect that their abilities are far more limited.

Scale tubercles and pits

In snakes, and in most families of lizards, there are certain scales with areas where the cuticle is thinner. Because nerve endings are concentrated in the region immediately under these areas, it seems almost certain that they are sense organs of some description. Their purpose, however, is still largely unknown although we can make certain theoretical assumptions. Two types of organs are recognisable: tubercles and pits.

Tubercles are very small, 1-2 mm in diameter, and each consists of a rounded elevation, or pimple, surrounded by a circular depression. Beneath the tubercle, the epidermis is raised to fit into its underside and the nerve ending lies just below the epidermis. Pits are larger than tubercles, up to 3 mm in diameter and may be oval rather than circular. The cuticle is thinner at the bottom of the pit and this is the area where nerve endings are situated.

Tubercles

Tubercles are the most common, both in terms of the numbers of snakes on which they are found and also in terms of numbers of scales that have them. So far they have been found on every snake examined for them but they are not equally numerous on all of them. On the primitive snakes, Typhlopidae, Leptotyphlopidae and Anomalepidae, they are found only on the forward parts of the head, with hardly any traces on the body or tail. Some of the other primitive snakes have plenty of tubercles, however. *Xenopeltis* and *Loxocemus* have them on the head, body and tail, as do the members of the Uropeltidae, the shield-tailed snakes, which also have large numbers on the specialised rough scale on the end of their tails. Among the boas and pythons, there is more variability, with some species having many tubercles while others have them

▲ Small tubercles occur on certain scales of many snakes, especially those around the head, and may play a tactile role. They are more obvious in this Pacific ground boa, *Candoia carinata*, than in many species.

only in certain areas: in *Epicrates*, for instance, they are found only on the head. In the higher snakes – colubrids, elapids and vipers – tubercles are found on the head, especially on the rostral and labial scales. They may extend on to the dorsal and ventral scales but are usually less numerous here than on the head.

The general assumption is that tubercles are more numerous in areas of the body that come into contact with objects as the snake moves around. Unless this is coincidental, it would appear to lead to the conclusion that the tubercles are organs of touch.

Similar structures were found on scales near the vent of male rough earth snakes, *Virginia striatula*. Because they are confined to males, these secondary sex characteristics are thought to help the male to locate the female's vent during courtship and mating. Ridges and bumps have also been noted in the same area of male snakes belonging to a variety of other species, including garter snakes, water snakes and a coral snake, and their function is presumably similar.

Pits

Unlike tubercles, pits have been found only on the higher snakes. They are not found in all species, however, and appear to be absent in elapids, for instance. Caution is required in this area, though, because anatomists have often failed to realise the importance of pits (and tubercles) and they have only been looked for in a small proportion of snakes. Where they do occur, pits are more numerous on the head, especially around the snout, than they are on other parts of the

body. Furthermore, where pits and tubercles are found on the same scales, they tend to be found on different parts of these scales. On the body, pits are found mainly on the tips (apices) of the scales and, for this reason, are sometimes known as apical pits.

Even less is known about the function of the pits than of the tubercles. One theory is that they are light sensitive. Evidence for this is that they tend to be absent in burrowing forms.

Other researchers have proposed that the pores, and other thin areas on the scale, allow an oily substance to exude on to the outer surface of the scales; this would then act as a barrier to water. Alternatively, the pits may exude substances which play a part in chemical communication, helping snakes to find and identify one another and, possibly, to mark territories.

▲ Small pits, known as apical pits, sometimes occur on the tips of the scales covering snakes' bodies. Here, pairs of apical pits are plainly visible on the scales of a Baird's rat snake, *Pantherophis bairdi*.

INTERNAL ANATOMY

THE INTERNAL ANATOMY OF SNAKES IS LITTLE DIFFERENT, IN EFFECT, FROM THAT OF OTHER VERTEBRATES. THE EMPHASIS IN THIS SECTION WILL THEREFORE CONCENTRATE ON THE AREAS IN WHICH SNAKES DIFFER FROM TYPICAL VERTEBRATES, AND HOW THE ORGANS ARE ARRANGED IN SUCH ELONGATED ANIMALS.

As in other animals, the organs can be unravelled, figuratively speaking, into a number of sets, each set constituting one of the basic anatomical systems.

Digestive system

The digestive system starts with the mouth and it is here that most of the modifications have taken place. The oral glands, that secrete a cocktail of substances to enable the snake to swallow its food more easily and to begin the process of digestion, are well developed. They consist of glands in the tongue, below the tongue and in the lips. The latter, more correctly known as labial or parotid glands, are especially large in some species and the substances they secrete contain strong digestive juices.

Certain colubrid snakes are, to some extent, venomous. Their venom is delivered to enlarged teeth towards the rear of their mouth and so they are commonly known as rear-fanged species. The venom in these species is produced in the Duvernoy's gland, which is a modified salivary gland but rather different in structure from the venom glands of vipers and elapids. The gland, which varies in size from species to species, empties into a central duct. This duct opens near the rear fangs, in a fold between the base of the teeth and the lips. The teeth of some species have grooves running along their lengths and the saliva, or venom, is drawn along these by capillary action.

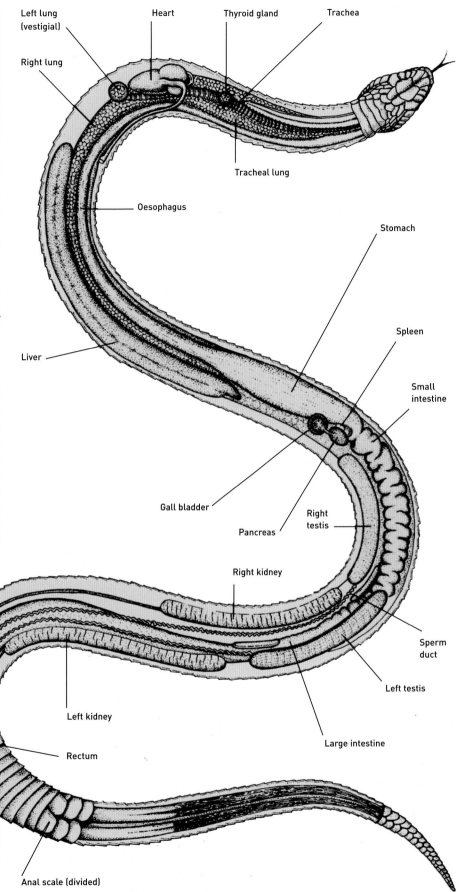

▶ Internal anatomy of a snake (simplified)

The composition of the modified saliva varies. It may secrete only mucous cells, in which case there is no venom whatsoever: species producing this type of secretion do not have enlarged rear fangs. On the other hand, it may contain enzymes that help to break down proteins and, depending on their strength, snakes producing this type of secretion may be classed as venomous. They include the boomslang, *Dispholidus typus*, twig snakes, *Thelotornis*, and an Asian species, *Rhabdophis tigrinus*, all of which have caused fatalities in humans, as well as numerous other colubrids that may produce mild symptoms in man but which are more effective against their normal prey.

In some of the higher snakes, the elapids and vipers, the digestive secretions have evolved into a powerful form of venom. Venom glands, when present, originate from the upper labial glands and open by means of a narrow duct into the grooves or cavities of the poison fangs. The venom glands may be greatly enlarged and, in some species, extend for a considerable distance along the body of the snake. They are surrounded by muscles known as the masseter muscles, which are used to squeeze the venom gland, forcing the venom that is stored there through the venom ducts to the fangs. In this way they differ from the fangs of rear-fanged snakes and the poisonous lizards, *Heloderma*, in which the venom is drawn along the fang by capillary action. Also, in *Heloderma* the poison fangs are in the lower jaw.

The tongue of snakes is not used in swallowing. Its function has been altered to that of an aid to smell, and it is used in conjunction with the Jacobson's organ, which has already been described.

The throat and oesophagus of snakes are highly muscular, for forcing food items down towards the stomach, and greatly distendable, in order to accommodate large prey. The oesophagus becomes gradually wider about one-third of the way along the body of the snake until it opens out to the stomach. This consists of a wider, muscular section of the gut where additional secretions attack the food. The pancreas and gall bladder are situated at the further end of the stomach. The lower intestine is slightly coiled, but not as much as in animals with a more conventional shape; this is possible because all snakes are carnivorous and so they do not require the long and convoluted gut found in herbivorous or omnivorous animals. The lower intestine merges into the rectum, which finally opens to the cloaca and finally the vent, where the remains of undigested food are voided.

Respiratory system

Although respiration in snakes is fundamentally the same as in other air-breathing vertebrates, a high degree of modification has been necessary in order to enable the necessary apparatus to fit into their bodies. In the vast majority of species the left lung is either very small or absent altogether, with only the Boidae having a sizeable left lung. The right lung, on the other hand, is greatly extended backwards and may, in aquatic species, extend for almost the entire length of the body; in these species, the far end of the lung, known as the saccular lung, has only limited ability to extract oxygen but is used instead for air storage and as a buoyancy organ.

An additional organ is found around the windpipe of some snakes, where the vascular lining of the lung extends forwards. This structure, known as the tracheal lung, gives

▼ The bull snake, *Pituophis catenifer sayi*, is capable of producing especially loud hisses, which tend to intimidate wary potential predators (and humans).

additional capacity. This can be important not only for aquatic species but also where feeding behaviour prevents breathing. The snail-eating snakes belonging to the genera *Dipsas* and *Sibon*, for instance, have large tracheal lungs. These species specialise in eating snails, a habit that involves burying their heads in the shells while they extract the soft parts. Tracheal lungs may also help other snakes to continue breathing when large items of prey are swallowed. As the food passes down the body, parts of the lung are compressed and do not function well; by extending its length, the tracheal lung ensures that at least one part of the lung can be expanded normally at all times.

Also connected with the need to continue breathing when large items of food are being swallowed, the opening of the windpipe, the glottis, takes the form of a muscular tube that can be thrust forward from the floor of the mouth and held open despite the pressure exerted by the food.

Snakes do not have a true voice but may produce a hiss by expelling the air rapidly

from their lung. This sound can be especially loud and startling in some species, such as the American gopher snakes, *Pituophis*, and hognose snakes, *Heterodon*. This sound is produced when air rushes across a special membrane in the glottis, causing vibration.

Circulatory system

The circulatory system is similar to that of other animals except that the heart has three chambers, not four as in mammals (or crocodilians). The pulmonary part of the system, taking blood to the lungs for gaseous exchange, is more important in reptiles than it is in amphibians, for instance, which rely, to a large extent, on gaseous exchange across the surface of their skin. The arrangement of the aorta, the large artery leaving the heart, is modified in snakes and may be variable throughout the families.

Excretory system

The main modifications here concern the lack of a bladder and the placement of the kidneys. Snakes do not excrete urea in the form of urine. As an aid to water conservation, especially important to those species that live in an arid environment, snakes reclaim almost all the fluid from their system and excrete their nitrogenous waste material in the form of uric acid, a semi-solid white material that contains the minimum amount of fluid necessary to carry it out of the body.

The kidneys are greatly elongated and staggered within the body cavity, so that the left kidney is significantly more forward than the right one.

Nervous system

The nervous system serves the sense organs, as described earlier in this chapter. Peculiarities in the system are confined to the organs that are not present in most other animals, such as the branch of the olfactory nerve that goes to the Jacobson's organ and to the heat-sensitive pits in those species that have them. Additional nerve endings are found immediately below the scale pits and tubercles, so far found only in snakes, and of which the exact functions are unknown.

Otherwise the system is more or less conventional. The spinal cord extends the whole length of the backbone. The system as a whole is somewhat less complex than it is in higher animals, as snakes lack many of the appendages that would normally be served by the nervous system. Having said this, some of the more primitive species have a network of nerves that would normally go to the hind limbs if they had them – good evidence that the ancestors of snakes had legs.

Reproductive system

The most important step that enabled reptiles to move away from the water was the development of a shelled egg, and some species later evolved viviparity to further their adaptation to the terrestrial environment. Either method of reproduction requires internal fertilisation and, although some amphibians practise a simple form of this, in reptiles it is well developed, with the evolution of a paired copulatory organ in males, the hemipenes, and of a shell gland in the females of those species that lay eggs.

The female reproductive system

Female snakes normally have a pair of ovaries, staggered like the kidneys so that they can be accommodated into the elongated body. In some snakes the left oviduct is missing. Snake eggs are large because they contain enough yolk to nourish the developing embryo until it hatches as a fully formed juvenile. The eggs mature in the ovary, where yolk is produced. Yolking, or vitellogenesis, is dependent on the condition of the female – if she is underweight it will not occur and the eggs will develop no further. The eggs mature simultaneously and break through the wall of the ovary into the body cavity. Here they are collected by the funnel-shaped end of the oviduct (the infundibulum) and then move into the oviduct. Fertilisation takes place here, either by sperm introduced while the mature ova are waiting in the oviduct or by sperm stored from a previous mating, possibly several months previously. A specialised structure or chamber, the seminal receptacle, situated towards the posterior end of the oviduct, is used to store the sperm. In oviparous species, the shell is formed in the lower part of the oviduct, just before the eggs are laid.

The male reproductive system

Male snakes have paired testes, staggered like the ovaries and the other paired organs. Long coiled tubes, the seminiferous tubules, lead from the testes, carrying sperm to the ureter, where they are stored in a bladder-like structure. The ureter opens into the cloaca where another structure, the papilla urogenitalis is situated. A groove transports the sperm from this structure to the base of the hemipenes. Each hemipenis lies at the base of the tail, normally inverted and forming a thick area that may be used to visually determine the sex of the snake. The hemipenes can also be everted in living snakes by applying upward pressure at the base of the tail. In addition, the opening of the inverted hemipenes can be seen beneath the pre-anal scale and its length can be probed with a narrow instrument.

At copulation, blood is forced into the hemipenes and, at the same time, a muscle pulls the hemipenes out of the tail. Only one hemipenis is used to copulate – individual snakes appear to favour either the left or right organ although either can, theoretically, be used.

The hemipenes have no enclosed sperm duct but rather an external groove that ends in a lip surrounded by a fleshy rim. When the hemipenis is inserted into the cloaca of the female, the groove forms a channel along which the sperm can travel. The surface of the hemipenis is covered with spines and projections, often arranged in rosettes. These are thought to help the male snake to locate the cloacal opening of the female and to fix the hemipenis in place once copulation has begun. The hemipenes of some species are branched and in these species the female's cloaca is also branched. Similarly, if the hemipenes are covered with spines, the female's cloaca has a thicker wall than in those species in which spines are reduced or absent. Dissection of females has shown that in every case the internal shape of the cloaca corresponds closely to the shape of the hemipenes of males of the same species. The system therefore forms an isolating mechanism, preventing unrelated species from mating and the shape and structure of the hemipenes are of considerable interest to taxonomists as they form part of a 'lock-and-key' mechanism. Although males can only usually mate effectively with females of the same species, the mechanism is not as effective as it was once thought to be as hybrid snakes are not uncommon under the artificial conditions of captivity, and naturally occurring hybrids are also found from time to time.

In tropical snakes the testes are probably active throughout the year, but in temperate snake species they usually produce sperm during the height of the active season, in summer and early autumn. The snakes then enter hibernation with plenty of stored sperm which is used the following spring during the breeding season. There are a limited few exceptions to this arrangement, however, where the males produce the majority of their sperm in the spring, store it and use it later in the same year. This system has only been shown for a few species, although it may be more widespread.

The skull and skeleton

The skeletons and skulls of snakes have been extremely modified, especially in the more advanced families and it is possible, to some extent, to trace the evolution of the suborder by examining their progressive modifications.

The skull

Compared with their closest relatives, the lizards, the skulls of snakes are far more delicate and loosely articulated. This comes as a result of their feeding habits. Whereas most lizards have rigid jaws that can chew and dismember their prey, snakes swallow it whole, without chewing. This would restrict them to eating small animals were it not for the elasticity of the jaws and the skin around them. Not all snakes are capable of stretching their jaws to great dimensions, however. The thread snakes, Leptotyphlopidae, have reduced mouths and very short lower jawbones. The jaws of the other blind snakes, the pipe snakes, shield tails and the sunbeam snakes, are capable of only a little more movement. In more advanced snakes, the bones of the skull are capable of more independent movement and the mouth can be opened much wider in order to accommodate prey that has a diameter far greater than the snake's head.

This is possible because the bones of the upper and lower jaws are loosely connected, rather than being fused to one another and to the cranium, or braincase. This allows them to move outwards as well as backwards and forwards, independently of the rest of the skull or of each other, helping them to pull prey into the mouth while at the same time moving out of the way so that it can be swallowed. To avoid damage to the brain when large prey is forced through the mouth, the bones on the roof of the mouth are extended and strengthened. The two halves of the lower jaw are not connected at the front (chin) but are joined by an elastic ligament, allowing them to move away from one another, further increasing the capacity of the mouth.

The teeth

The number and arrangement of snakes' teeth vary greatly according to the species; some have practically no teeth at all while others have numerous teeth as well as teeth of several different types. Typically, snakes have teeth along the ridge of the lower jaw, the maxilla (the outer portion of the upper jaw), the palatine bones (long bones that run along the roof of the mouth inside the maxillary bones) and the pterygoid bones (paired bones that are fixed to the palate at the front and the quadrate bones at the back).

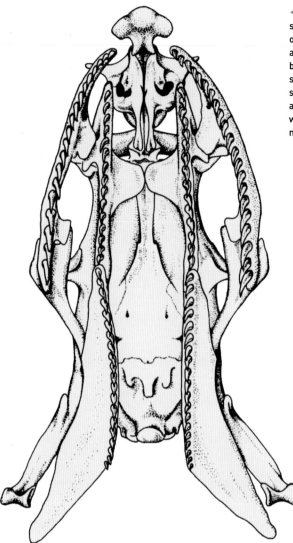

◄ The structure of the skull showing tooth-bearing bones of the upper jaw. The exact arrangement of the tooth-bearing bones varies from snake to snake (and a few species lack teeth) but snakes are typically well endowed with teeth on both their maxillary and palatine bones.

Their teeth are of the pleurodont type. This means that they are attached to the inner edges of the jawbones, rather than on top of them. They are replaced throughout the life of the snake: replacement teeth develop at the bases of the existing ones, ready to be swung upwards and sideways when the old tooth is shed. Shed teeth are often swallowed, sometimes because they have become embedded in prey, and can be found in the snake's faeces.

Many typical snakes, i.e. most colubrids, have teeth that are more or less equal in size and shape. This type of dentition is known as aglyphous (without fangs). Others, though, have specialised dentition. Opisthoglyphous snakes have one or two pairs of enlarged teeth towards the back of their mouths and are commonly known as rear-fanged. All rear-fanged snakes are colubrids or atractaspids, and the fangs are associated with the presence of Duvernoy's glands, described on page 115.

Because of the position of these fangs, and the usually low potency of the venom, they are not normally regarded as dangerous to humans, although a few species have caused deaths. Where enlarged fangs are present in the back of the mouth, there is invariably a gap in front of them. This is known as the diastema and allows the enlarged fangs to be deeply embedded in the prey.

Some species of colubrids, usually referred to the subfamily Xenodontinae (meaning strange teeth), have an unusual arrangement whereby two rear fangs are attached to the back of the upper jaw. When the mouth is closed, the teeth are positioned horizontally, but when the mouth is opened wide the upper jaw swings into a more vertical position, and the teeth are brought into play. These snakes, which include the well-known hognose snakes, *Heterodon*, of North America as well as the lesser known genera *Lystrophis*, *Waglerophis* and *Xenodon* from Central and

South America, feed largely on toads, which often inflate their bodies when faced with a predator, so the purpose of the enlarged teeth may be to puncture the bodies of the toads, making them easier to swallow. If the fangs were permanently erect, the snake would be unable to close its mouth without injuring itself.

Other snakes have modified teeth at the front of their jaws. The members of the Elapidae, comprising the cobras, mambas, kraits, coral snakes and related species, have short venom fangs attached to the maxillary bones. These fangs are hollow, with an inlet at the base and an outlet near the tip. During envenomation, venom is ducted to the inlet and forced through the small hole at the tip of the fang. The only exceptions are the spitting cobras belonging to the genera *Naja* and *Hemachatus*, in which the outlet is situated in the front of the fang, somewhat above its tip, so that when pressure is applied to the venom gland the venom is forced through it at high speed.

The fangs of the vipers are even more highly modified. They are hollow, like those of the elapids, but tend to be longer, allowing the venom to be injected further into the prey. In order to accommodate them in the mouth when it is closed, the maxilla, to which they are attached, is hinged in such a way that the fangs are folded backwards, along the roof of the mouth, when not in use (see page 52). Both the elapids and the vipers have a diastema immediately behind their venom fangs.

▲ The Cuban whipsnake, *Alsophis cantherigerus*, is a member of the Xenodontinae and therefore has the strange hinged jaw arrangement of these snakes.

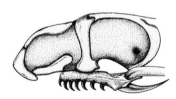

▼ Xenodontine snakes have a hinged arrangement in their jaws, shown diagrammatically here. Their enlarged rear fangs can be swung forward and may be used to puncture their prey or to give a better grip. In general, these snakes are not regarded as dangerous although they may possess a Duvernoy's gland.

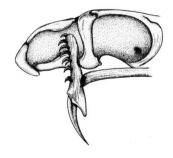

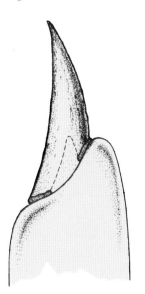

▲ The teeth of snakes are of the pleurodont type – they do not rest in a socket but are attached to the angled top of the jawbone on which they are set.

Snakes of the family Atractaspididae have a variety of fang arrangements. In *Atractaspis*, which is the largest genus, the fangs are attached to the maxilla. The maxilla, prefrontal and frontal bones all interlock in a unique manner and the fangs have only a limited degree of movement. They can be swung sideways and are used with a stabbing motion, without the necessity of opening the mouth fully. This is thought to be an adaptation to hunting while in underground tunnels and burrows. *Atractaspis* has lost all the other teeth in its upper jaw and those in the lower jaw are greatly reduced. Related species have fangs at the back of their mouths while others have fixed fangs at the front.

When snakes' teeth are examined microscopically, they are found to have a pair of ridges running along their length. In some species that eat reptile eggs, such as *Oligodon*, these are very pronounced and are thought to be used for cutting through the eggshells. *Oligodon* species are popularly known as 'kukri' snakes in recognition of their knife-like teeth. Certain other species have additional shallow ridges, fluting, or striations along the length of some of their teeth, with the deepest grooves being towards the base of the teeth. These structures are found mainly in aquatic and semi-aquatic, fish-eating species, such as the file snakes, *Acrochordus*, and the homalopsine colubrids such as *Enhydris*, and are thought to help the snakes to penetrate the hard scales and therefore grasp their prey

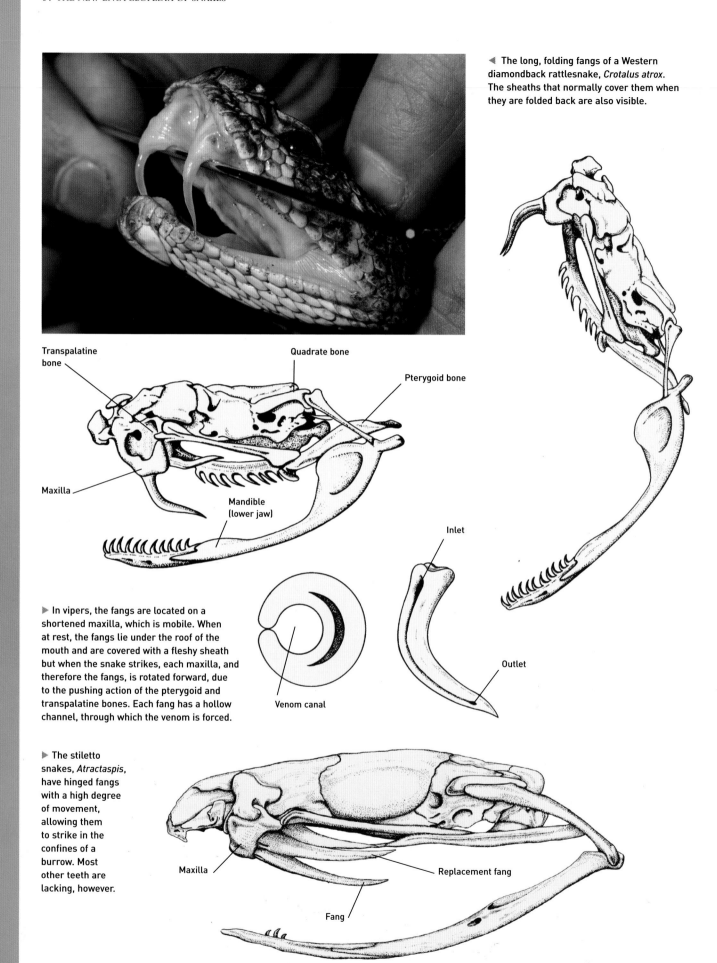

◄ The long, folding fangs of a Western diamondback rattlesnake, *Crotalus atrox*. The sheaths that normally cover them when they are folded back are also visible.

Transpalatine bone

Quadrate bone

Pterygoid bone

Maxilla

Mandible (lower jaw)

Inlet

Outlet

Venom canal

► In vipers, the fangs are located on a shortened maxilla, which is mobile. When at rest, the fangs lie under the roof of the mouth and are covered with a fleshy sheath but when the snake strikes, each maxilla, and therefore the fangs, is rotated forward, due to the pushing action of the pterygoid and transpalatine bones. Each fang has a hollow channel, through which the venom is forced.

► The stiletto snakes, *Atractaspis*, have hinged fangs with a high degree of movement, allowing them to strike in the confines of a burrow. Most other teeth are lacking, however.

Maxilla

Replacement fang

Fang

more firmly. Similar structures have been found on the teeth of snakes that eat earthworms and molluscs, where they may also aid penetration (Vaeth, Rossman and Shoop, 1985).[16]

The teeth of *Xenopeltis unicolor* and *Scaphiodontophis annulatus* teeth are attached by ligaments that act as hinges, allowing slippery prey such as skinks to slide past them in one direction but snagging them if they try to wriggle back the other way.

The skeleton

Snakes' skeletons consist very simply of a skull and a number of precaudal and caudal vertebrae. The precaudal vertebrae each bear a rib but there is no breast bone, or sternum, and so the free ends of the ribs are connected to each other, and to the dorsal and ventral scales, by muscles. These are important in locomotion and in constriction. The vertebrae themselves are numerous, sometimes numbering over 400 and the number is slightly variable, even within species.

Each vertebra has a central portion, or centrum, which is shaped like a short cylinder with one convex and one concave end. These ends articulate on the corresponding ends of the centra that adjoin them. Above the centrum is a neural arch, an arch of bone through which the spinal cord runs. A number of spines or processes jut out from this basic structure, and these also articulate with their counterparts on neighbouring

vertebrae. The hypapophyses, which are downwardly projecting processes, are not found throughout the suborder – they are absent altogether in the Typhlopidae and Leptotyphlopidae, for instance, and are often missing from burrowing species in other families. They are invariably present in aquatic snakes, however, although their exact function is not clear. In the egg-eating snakes, *Dasypeltis*, the hypapophyses on the first few vertebrae extend down into the throat and are used to break through the shell of birds' eggs on which these species feed.

The caudal vertebrae, which make up the tail, are simplified and do not have ribs attached to them. In a few snakes, belonging to the genera *Scaphiodontophis* and *Coluber*, the vertebrae of the tail may break as a defensive mechanism, although they may lack the fracture plane running across the vertebrae that is found in many families of lizards.

No snakes have pectoral girdles but members of some of the more primitive families, such as the thread and worm snakes, pipe snakes, boas and pythons, have pelvic girdles. Male boas and pythons also have vestigial hind limbs, in the form of spurs, attached to the girdles.

▼ Snakes' skeletons, consisting of a large number of articulating vertebrae and ribs that are not joined by a breastbone, create body forms that are extremely supple, as here, in a Baird's rat snake, *Pantherophis bairdi*, from northern Mexico.

NOTES
1. Wall. Frank (1921), Ophidia Taprobanica or the Snakes of Ceylon. H. R. Cottle, Government Printer, Colombo, Ceylon (Sri Lanka).
2. FitzSimons, V. F. M. (1962), Snakes of Southern Africa. Purnell and Sons Ltd., Cape Town.
3. Worrell. E. (1958), Song of the Snake. Angus and Robertson, London.
4. Pope, C. H. (1961), The Giant Snakes. Routledge and Kegan Paul, London.
5. Oliver, J. A. (1958), Snakes in Fact and Fiction. The Macmillan Company, New York.
6. Boos, (1992), 'A note on the 18,5 ft Boa Constrictor from Trinidad', Bulletin of the British Herpetological Society, 40:15-17.
7. Rose, J. A. (1966), La Taxonomia y Zoogeografia de los Ofidios en Venezuela. Universidad Central de Venezuela, Caracas.
8. Amaral, A. do (1978), Serpentes do Brasil. Ministry of Education and Culture, Sao Paulo, Brazil, 1977.
9. Lillywhite, H. B. and Sanmartino, V. (1993), 'Permeability and water relations of the hygroscopic skin of the file snake, Acrochordus granulatus', Copela, 1993(1):99-103.
10. Dunson, W. A. and Freda J. (1985), 'Water permeability of the skin of the amphibious snake Agkistrodon pisclvorous', Journal of Herpetology, 19 (1):93-98.
11. Ros, M. (1935), 'Die Lippengruben der Pythonen als Temperaturorgane', Jenaisch. Zeit. fur Natuerwiss, 70:1-32.
12. Noble, G. K. (1934), 'The structure of the facial pit of pit vipers and its probable function', Anat. Rec., 58, supp. p. 4.
13. Noble, G. K. and Schmidt, A. (1937), 'The structure and function of the facial and labial pits of snakes', Proc. Am. Phllos. Soc., 77(3):263-288.
14. Kardong, K. V. and Mackessy, S. P. (1991), 'The strike behaviour of a congenitally blind rattlesnake', Journal of Herpetology, 25(2): 208-211.
15. Breiderbach, C. A. (1990), 'Thermal cues influence strikes in pitless vipers', Journal of Herpetology, 24(4):448-450.
16. Vaeth, R. H., Rossman, D. A. and Shoop, W. (1985). 'Observations of tooth surface morphology in snakes', Journal of Herpetology, 19 (1):20-26.

CHAPTER 3
HOW SNAKES LIVE

Snakes, like other organisms, do not live their lives in isolation. They have to interact with other animals, which may be of the same species, in which case they could be mates or rivals, or of other species, in which case they could be potential prey or predators. These are biological factors, to be dealt with in the next section. They also interact with the physical environment – factors such as heat and cold, wet and dry, light and dark. These are dealt with first.

Most garter snakes are closely associated with water and many are semi-aquatic in their behaviour. Their habitats range from streams and riversides to ponds and the margins of lakes.

THE PHYSICAL ENVIRONMENT

SNAKES' SENSES MONITOR BOTH BIOLOGICAL AND PHYSICAL ENVIRONMENTS, AND THE SNAKE REACTS AS NECESSARY, USING INVOLUNTARY OR VOLUNTARY ACTIONS. INVOLUNTARY ACTIONS CONSIST OF THE PHYSIOLOGICAL PROCESSES THAT OPERATE TO MAINTAIN THE STATUS QUO, OR HOMEOSTASIS, WITHIN THE BODY AND MAY BE SUPPLEMENTED BY BEHAVIOURAL ACTIVITIES SUCH AS MOVING FROM ONE PLACE TO ANOTHER. VOLUNTARY ACTIONS COMPRISE BEHAVIOURAL RESPONSES – MOVEMENT, ALTERING THE BODY SHAPE OR POSTURE AND BRINGING ADDITIONAL SENSE ORGANS INTO PLAY.

Thermoregulation

Reptiles are unable to produce much of their body heat internally, as can the birds and mammals, but rely almost entirely on external sources, a system known as ectothermy (as opposed to endothermy). For many species, especially those from cooler climates, this dominates their daily and seasonal activity patterns and is the key to understanding how snakes live.

Even though they are commonly labelled 'cold blooded', snakes, like other organisms, need to attain certain body temperatures in order that the natural processes of muscle activity, nerve activity, digestion, spermatogenesis and so on can take place. Snakes regulate their body temperature by a combination of behavioural and physiological responses. The behavioural responses are by far the more important, however, and the physiological ones act more as fine tuning.

Despite their reliance on external sources of heat, most snakes are not completely at the mercy of their environment, as is sometimes thought. Research has consistently shown that snakes' body temperatures are frequently higher than those of their surroundings, especially at the beginning of the day when they are warming up, but that they may also be cooler than their surroundings should these become dangerously hot. Many species are able to keep their body temperatures within very narrow 'operating bands' during their active periods, often within 1°C (2°F) of their preferred body temperature.

Furthermore, they are able to do this despite the fact that their long, slender bodies, which are not covered with fur, feathers or other insulating material, are not ideally suited to retaining heat.

Operating temperatures

Snakes attempt to maintain their preferred body temperature through behavioural activities. If the temperature falls too low the snake will freeze to death (lethal minimum) and if it gets too high the snake will die from heat exhaustion (lethal maximum). Other important values are the critical minimum and maximum temperatures – these occur when the snake loses the power of locomotion and is therefore unable to move to a more favourable location. The precise temperatures vary according to the species and, possibly, other factors such as whether the snake has fed recently, if it is reproductively active, or if it is about to shed its skin. Within a wide-ranging species it can often be shown that individuals from the cooler parts of the range can tolerate lower temperatures than those from warmer parts of the range, although their preferred body temperatures may be identical.

In the past, two methods have been used to establish the preferred body temperature for a snake. Active snakes can have their temperature taken in the field when they are found fortuitously, or they can be kept under controlled conditions in which they are offered a choice of temperatures. Both these methods are useful but they have the drawback that it is necessary to disturb the snake, and therefore to subject it to stress, in order to obtain results. More recently, telemetry systems have been used.

These work by implanting a miniature electronic radio transmitter into the body of the snake, then using a receiver to monitor its signal. With the right equipment, the system can be used to give a continual readout of the snake's body temperature, as well as its whereabouts, over a long period of time. Body temperatures for resting as well as active snakes can then be obtained without undue disturbance.

The results produced by pooling all these methods seem to show that snakes of most species prefer to keep their body temperatures at or around 30°C (86°F) – rather warmer than is often thought. Their activity range is wide, however, with temperatures as low as 10°C (50°F) and as high as 40°C 104°F) having been recorded from active snakes. The pattern that emerges from these figures is that snakes can become active well before their bodies have warmed up to their preferred, or ideal, level – this makes sense, of course, because resting snakes in shaded underground retreats, for instance, would otherwise remain where they were and never get the chance to warm their bodies up. Having become active, they then try to reach their ideal body temperature as quickly as possible and, having done so, ensure that it does not rise more than a few degrees above this. Lethal high temperatures are much closer to the preferred temperatures than are the lethal low ones and so avoidance of extremely hot conditions is always more urgent than avoidance of cold ones.

Although snakes are not ideally designed to conserve heat, being without fur or feathers, they can improve the efficiency with which they absorb and retain heat by using a number of strategies. Their long, slender bodies have a high surface-to-weight ratio and, since heat is

▼ Temperature 'landmarks' in thermoregulation of a typical snake. The stippled area covers the normal activity range, the preferred temperatures are those between which the snake tries to maintain its body temperature, the critical minimum and maximum are the temperatures at which it loses the power of locomotion (and hence the option of retreating to somewhere more suitable) and the lethal minimum and maximum are the temperatures at which it dies.

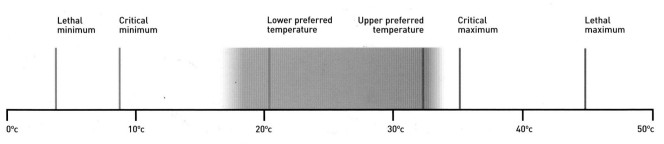

| Lethal minimum | Critical minimum | | Lower preferred temperature | Upper preferred temperature | Critical maximum | Lethal maximum |

0°c   10°c   20°c   30°c   40°c   50°c

▲ In order to warm up quickly, snakes may flatten their bodies against a warm substrate, as this Milos viper, *Macrovipera schweizeri*, is doing.

absorbed over their surface, they can increase heat uptake by stretching out. By flattening their bodies they will improve the surface-to-weight ratio even more, and at the same time they allow radiant heat (i.e. from the sun) to fall on a greater proportion of their skin. The underside of their bodies will also be in closer contact with the substrate and this, too, may increase heat absorption by conduction.

Basking snakes do not always expose themselves to full view and many bask out of sight by lying beneath flat rocks (or, in artificial situations, under pieces of tin and other debris) where they can absorb warmth without running the risks of predation.

Nocturnal snakes often bask early on during their period of activity by flattening themselves against a rock or warm sand. Where surfaced roads pass through their habitat, snakes may bask on the road, often to their cost (but also to the benefit of herpetologists, who frequently use this fact to sample the snakes in a large area quickly and easily).

Conversely, heat can be retained by reducing the surface-to-weight ratio. This is achieved by coiling, the tightness of the coils acting as an accurate mechanism to regulate heat loss. In extreme cases, snakes may coil into an almost spherical mass and by doing so they reduce the surface-to-weight ratio to its lowest possible value and keep heat loss to an absolute minimum. Taking this a stage further, a large number of snakes, coiled up together, would be able to conserve heat more efficiently by

forming a coiled mass: their aggregate surface-to-weight ratio would be relatively smaller than if each one coiled separately. This does seem to happen under certain circumstances, particularly during temporary periods of cold conditions, when snakes may be found coiled around one another.

Evidence that aggregations of snakes are the result of a desire to conserve heat is largely circumstantial. For instance, only northern species of rattlesnakes congregate in large numbers in dens while pythons and boas tend to be found together only in cooler parts of their ranges. Saving heat by aggregating would, of course, be only a temporary advantage because over a long period of time, as in hibernation, all the heat would be lost anyway. In the early spring,

though, the inhabitants of a rattlesnake den may emerge to bask for short periods each day and, by aggregating during the following night, they could prevent their temperature from falling too low, so enabling them to be active earlier the next day. The more individuals that were involved, the greater would be the effect and therefore benefit. It is worth noting that the members of such an opportunistic aggregation need not all be the same species and, indeed, large numbers of snakes, comprising three or four different species, have been discovered on a fairly regular basis (although heat conservation is not always necessarily the prime motive for these aggregations – see under 'Water balance', page 65).

Colour also plays a part in heat absorption. It is well known that black objects absorb heat much better than light coloured ones and so snakes living in cooler climates have a tendency to be dark in colour. In Australia, for instance, two of the most characteristic southern genera, the copperheads, *Austrelaps*, and the tiger snakes, *Notechis*, both of which are represented on Tasmania, have darker than average species, often black, in the southern portions of their ranges.

This difference is not restricted to entire species, however; sometimes individuals from temperate parts of the range are darker in colour than those from warmer areas, where a species has a wide range. For instance, black

▼ The black tiger snake, *Notechis ater*, comes from southeastern Australia, where its black colour helps it to absorb heat more quickly, a distinct advantage in the relatively cool places in which it lives.

examples of the common garter snake, *Thamnophis sirtalis*, are found in isolated colonies towards the northern limits of the species' range, in Canada and northern United States, and European adders, *Vipera berus* have a similar tendency to be darker in the more northern parts of the species' range, especially in Scandinavia and northern Britain. (Populations living on islands may also contain a high proportion of black individuals; this can also be for other reasons.)

There is growing evidence that snakes living in regions with distinct warm and cool seasons may even change colour slightly in order to improve heat absorption during cool weather and also to prevent overheating during hot weather. So far, only Australian snakes belonging to the Elapidae have been shown to do this but it is possible that snakes in other parts of the world have evolved similar mechanisms.

Still on the subject of colour, an unusually high number of snakes have black heads. These snakes expose their heads while keeping the rest of their bodies under cover. The dark pigmentation will help the head to

◀ Mole snakes from the south of their range are more likely to be black than those from further north of the continent. This one is on the Cape Peninsula, South Africa.

▼ Snakes with black heads, such as Gould's black-headed snake, *Unechis gouldii*, can expose only their heads when they begin to bask. This ensures that warmth reaches their brain and sense organ quickly, making them less vulnerable to predators.

absorb heat, which can then be shunted, via the blood, to the rest of the body. The advantages of this system would be that the brain and the sense organs, practically all restricted to the head, would be the first parts of the body to begin operating efficiently, so the snake could be alert to danger before it took the risk of exposing itself completely. Black-headed species are found in many parts of the world: to take just a few examples at random there are several Australian species, such as the black-headed python, *Aspidites melanocephalus*, and Gould's black-headed snake, *Unechis gouldii*, as well as the American black-headed snakes, *Tantilla* species, the almost indistinguishable Middle Eastern species *Rhynchocalamus melanocephalus*, and, to a lesser extent, the European smooth snakes, *Coronella* species and hooded snake, *Macroprotodon cucullatus*.

Conversely, snakes living under hot conditions are often pale in colour in order to reflect heat (although this may also result from camouflage). Because they move about in close contact with the substrate, which is often extremely hot, their undersides are also pale in colour and this may also help to prevent them from overheating, allowing them to remain active longer than they would if they had dark undersides. For species that hunt diurnal lizards, for instance, this is an important consideration.

Despite the efficiency with which snakes are able to regulate their body temperatures, it is inevitable that some fluctuations will occur. These take two forms.

Daily thermoregulatory patterns
Firstly, there will be a daily pattern, and the degree to which this swings up and down will depend on whether the snake comes from a tropical or temperate region. If it comes from a temperate region, the amount of fluctuation will depend on the time of year – in early spring and late autumn there will be greater fluctuations than during midsummer and midwinter because the day/night temperature differences will be greater. Superimposed upon these daily fluctuations will be the overall seasonal fluctuations; again, these will be greater for species from temperate regions and some tropical species may be able to maintain fairly constant temperatures throughout the year.

The actual process of gaining heat from the surroundings varies with the species and with the season (in temperate species, at least). It is simplest to first consider a typical diurnal species, such as a garter snake, *Thamnophis*, or a European grass snake, *Natrix*. Tricks used by these species to raise the body temperature include stretching out the body while flattening and tilting it towards the source of heat (usually the sun), in order to expose as much surface area as possible. These snakes tend to be black or dark in colour and this helps them to absorb radiant heat more effectively. Heat-gaining activities take place in the morning, the exact time depending on the season – in early spring the snakes may not emerge until midday and retreat again a few hours later. On overcast days they may not emerge at all. By midsummer, though, they may be able to gain enough heat by basking for just a few minutes early in the morning. Basking snakes may begin by exposing only their heads.

Having attained the ideal body temperature, the snake will then go about its usual activities, including foraging for food, searching for a mate and so on. If these activities take it into cooler places, it may bask again later in the day in order to 'top up' its body temperature. As evening falls, the snake will seek shelter, often underground, and by coiling its body it will reduce the surface-to-volume ratio so that heat loss is kept to a minimum. In this way, its body temperature next morning may be only slightly below its preferred level, even though the ambient temperature may have fallen quite drastically.

Nocturnal, crepuscular or secretive species are not able to bask in the sun. Instead, they may flatten their bodies against a material such as rock, which retains heat. This will extend their period of activity into the night,

even though the ambient temperature may already have fallen below their preferred level. They will need to seek shelter again before their bodies cool down to the critical temperature so that they are not exposed to possibly lethal temperatures during the coldest parts of the night.

In a way, comparing the thermoregulatory behaviour of diurnal and nocturnal snakes is putting the cart before the horse. More often than not, the activity pattern of the snake is controlled by the prevailing temperature in the place that it lives. Thus in cold regions snakes are likely to be diurnal, whereas in hot places they are more likely to be nocturnal or crepuscular. Very often nocturnal species are active at night *because* of temperature considerations: they live in areas where daytime temperatures would be lethal for them.

In tropical regions, where daily temperature fluctuations are smaller, snakes may not need to gear their periods of activity so closely to periods of suitable temperature. The availability of their food, and the time when it is most easily found, may be more important. Even in the tropics, however, ambient temperatures at ground level, under the forest canopy, can often be appreciably lower than the preferred temperatures of the snakes that live there and so it is wrong to assume that these species have higher preferred temperatures than temperate ones. On the other hand, they will almost certainly be less tolerant of cold temperatures (because they have not needed to evolve a system for coping with them) and so the critical and lethal minimum temperatures are likely to be rather higher than those of temperate snakes.

Seasonal thermoregulatory patterns

In places where there are significant temperature differences from season to season, snakes' activity patterns may also change. So, whereas diurnal snakes are rarely active at night, so-called nocturnal snakes are often active during the day at certain times of the year. During cooler parts of the year, they may be more active at dawn and dusk, i.e., they become crepuscular, or even during the middle part of the day, i.e., they become diurnal. Western diamondback rattlesnakes, *Crotalus atrox*, for instance, are usually found at night but during the spring they become active in the late afternoon and forage during daylight hours, returning to their retreat early in order to escape from the cold night-time temperatures. These shifts in their activity patterns are in response solely to temperature considerations.

As the days become shorter and cooler, snakes may be active for only a short spell each day and on especially cold days they may not emerge at all. Whenever there is a prolonged cold season, they will cease to be active altogether. They enter a period of dormancy, sometimes known as hibernation, although this is not the same as hibernation in

mammals since they may well become active for short periods throughout the winter if conditions permit.

Some snakes prefer to hibernate in damp situations, possibly to avoid the dangers of desiccation during cold weather. Groups of hibernating snakes have been found in flooded burrows and in old farm wells, for

◄ A western diamondback rattlesnake, *Crotalus atrox*, in a typical ambush situation in the late afternoon of a sunny April day. This species is mainly nocturnal but is active during the day early in the year, when the nights are too cold for it to hunt.

instance, and there are cases where snakes have become completely frozen. Some species are well adapted to cope with extremely cold spells of weather and, even if they do become frozen, most will recover once they have warmed up again.

Cool season behaviour varies with species and the places they live. Species from areas with cold winters retreat to hibernation sites, where they may congregate with other snakes of the same or different species. These dens are commonplace among rattlesnakes in the northern latitudes of North America and with the European adder, *Vipera berus*, and certain other members of the same genus, whereas other species of these same genera, living in warmer places, hibernate individually or in small groups. The dens may be located within the normal activity range of the individual snakes, or they may be some distance away, forcing the snakes to migrate to and from the dens in the autumn and spring. Other species of snakes hibernate individually, usually within their home range. Individual hibernation sites include cavities in rocks, old rodent burrows and holes at the base of trees. Some small species are often found in abandoned ants' nests, either singly or with other snakes. In warmer areas, snakes may only need to shelter temporarily, during short cold spells of weather, and are active between these periods.

Increasing temperatures in the spring will eventually penetrate their hibernacula and arouse them. Many species emerge from communal dens to bask in its vicinity for a few hours each day. Mating may occur at this time, with the males using sperm that was produced during the previous summer and stored over the winter. As the weather warms up the snakes gradually disperse and their daily thermoregulatory patterns take over once more.

Limitations

So far, we have considered snakes that have some degree of choice as to where they go and what they do – they can bask, coil, shelter or disappear down a deep, cool burrow. There are groups of snakes, however, that do not have all these options. They include many fossorial species such as the

LIFE IN THE COLD

Animals living in extremely cold environments need to evolve some means of surviving subzero temperatures. Birds and mammals, being endotherms, manage by producing heat internally, maintaining their body temperatures at a suitable level regardless of the prevailing conditions. Cold-blooded animals, however, do not have this option and must evolve an alternative strategy, or die.

Throughout the animal kingdom, two such strategies have evolved: 'supercooling' and 'freezing tolerance'. Supercooling allows the body fluids to fall below their freezing point without the formation of ice; freezing tolerance is an ability to withstand formation of ice in the body.

In supercooling, substances in the system, known as cryoprotectants, act as antifreeze to prevent the formation of ice within the body's cells: in other words, they lower the freezing point of the body fluids. One of the most common cryoprotectants is glycerol and related substances, found in many species of insects and fishes that inhabit waters that regularly freeze.

Freezing tolerance is an adaptive ability that allows the formation of ice in the body's cells without lethal consequences. It is an alternative to supercooling but may also work in conjunction with it.

Because the body fluids contain dissolved salts along with water, their normal freezing point is below 0°C (32°F), but only just: experiments have shown that reptiles' body fluids have a freezing point of -0.6°C (30.9°F). Snakes living at the extremes of their range may experience sudden temperature drops to values below this and so they would die if they did not have some mechanism to counteract it. One such species is the red-sided garter snake, *Thamnophis sirtalis parietalis*, which is the most northerly occurring species in North America and is found up to 60°N in parts of Canada. This species hibernates in communal dens, sometimes numbering several hundred individuals.

In a series of experiments to establish the tolerance of this species to cold, T. A. Churchill and K. B. Storey lowered the body temperatures of the snakes to freezing point and below (*Can. J. of Zoology*, 71(7):99-105). They found that, in the autumn, garter snakes could survive short periods at -5.5°C (22.1°F) and longer periods, up to three hours, at -2.5°C (27.5°F). During this time, their body fluids contained up to 40 per cent of ice. After 10 hours, their body fluids had an ice content of over 50 per cent and only about half survived: after 24 and 48 hours, the ice content had risen to 70 per cent of their total body fluids and none survived. In the middle of winter, however, their results were somewhat different: they could only survive temperatures down to -1.2°C (29.8°F).

In order to find out which strategy the snakes were using to counteract freezing, they investigated samples from the organs of the frozen snakes. They did not find glycerol in any of the organs they checked, but they did find increased levels of glucose in the liver and increased levels of lactate in the heart. Otherwise, there was no sign of these or other common cryoprotectants in the snakes' organs. What they did find was abnormally high traces of an amino acid, taurine, which is known to have a role in freeze-tolerant molluscs.

From these results, it seems likely that red-sided garter snakes can withstand freezing conditions due to their ability to tolerate the formation of ice in the body fluids for short periods. This ability is greatly enhanced in the autumn, but by midwinter it no longer exists. The implications of this study are that this species has evolved a strategy for surviving short-term freezing by a combination of supercooling and freezing tolerance in the autumn, when it may be caught out by sudden frosts while it is still active above ground, but its survival during hibernation is dependent on finding suitable sites below ground that protect it from long-term freezing.

blind snakes and the thread snakes, and freshwater and marine water snakes. All these species have very limited opportunities to regulate their body temperatures. Burrowing snakes may be able to move up and down through the substrate to allow a limited amount of thermoregulation to take place, but there is no evidence that they actually do this. Similarly, water and sea snakes could move through the layers of water in order to thermoregulate, but, again, they appear not to. The colour of some sea snakes may help them to absorb radiation more quickly and therefore elevate their body temperature above that of the seas they live in and this has been shown for at least one species, *Pelamis platurus*, which spends its time at the surface of the water and has a dark dorsal surface. Most other sea snakes live at deeper levels, however, and so their coloration is likely to be controlled by factors other than thermoregulation.

How do burrowing and aquatic snakes regulate their body temperatures, then? The probable answer is that they do not. All the species studied so far had body temperatures about the same as their surroundings. This restricts them to parts of the world where ambient temperatures approach their preferred body temperatures: strictly burrowing and aquatic snakes are found only in tropical regions or are restricted to pockets of land outside the tropics where temperatures are relatively warm and stable.

The advantages of ectothermy

It is worth making the point here that, although ectothermy is often looked upon as a limitation, or as evidence of a primitive, poorly developed life style, nothing could be further from the truth. Indeed, reptiles owe their success in many parts of the world, where they are the dominant group of vertebrates, to ectothermy. Warm-blooded, or endothermic, animals such as mammals and birds rely heavily on heat produced via their metabolic processes. In other words, a large proportion of their food (perhaps as much as 90 per cent) is diverted away from growth, maintenance and reproduction, and channelled into heat production. For this reason, they need to feed frequently and so are restricted to places where they can be sure of a regular food supply. Reptiles on the other hand, require food only to maintain themselves and to grow and reproduce if possible. This enables them to survive on a small fraction of the food that would normally be required by a bird or mammal of the same body weight.

▲ Aquatic marine snakes, such as the yellow-bellied sea snake, *Pelamis platurus*, have limited opportunities to thermoregulate. For this reason, they are only found in warmer parts of the world.

The desert is the most obvious example of an environment where food is scarce and there are advantages to be gained from being able to survive on very little. Reptiles are often the most numerous form of vertebrate life in such places and many species are so well adapted to life in the desert that they have evolved specialised methods of survival.

The disadvantages of ectothermy

Despite the above, ectothermy does have certain drawbacks. Firstly, it restricts reptiles to parts of the world where the daily temperatures reach fairly high levels for at least part of the day. Species living close to the Arctic Circle, in Scandinavia and Canada, have very limited periods of activity, often only three or four months of the year. They may take many years to attain sexual maturity and females may breed only every two, three or four years, using the 'fallow' years to build up enough fat to produce offspring. Because large bodies take longer to warm up than small ones, snakes living in cold environments cannot grow too big: all the larger species of snakes are found in or near the tropics.

Although snakes' low metabolic rates help them to survive on very little food, there is a trade-off in terms of energy. Endotherms, with their high metabolic rates are able to sustain work over a long period because their breathing and heart rates can continually supply oxygen to the muscles. Only after a relatively long period of exertion do the muscles build up, an oxygen debt. Snakes, on the other hand, with their low metabolic rates, build up an oxygen debt very quickly. Although they can continue to operate by breaking down stored chemicals in the muscle cells (anaerobic metabolism) this will also be of limited duration because there is only a limited amount of material that can be processed. For this reason, they may be capable of short bursts of activity, when chasing prey or escaping from predators for instance, but they soon 'burn out' and must rest until they have replenished their systems.

In practice, snakes overcome this problem by rarely venturing far from their retreats and, in particular, only the most active species are seen out in the open, away from suitable cover.

Physiological thermoregulation

Although behaviour is by far the most important means that snakes use to thermoregulate, there are occasions when physiological processes help to maintain, or even raise, their body temperatures. The most familiar example of this is that of brooding pythons. It has been known for many years that female pythons coil around their eggs during incubation. Although this behaviour also serves to protect their eggs, thermoregulation is at least as important. In the Indian python, *Python molurus*, temperatures taken within the coils are usually noticeably higher than those of the surrounding air. Brooding females tighten or loosen their coils in response to ambient temperature. They also twitch or shiver regularly while coiled around their eggs and these muscle contractions generate enough metabolic heat to raise their body temperature, and therefore that of the eggs, above that of the surrounding air temperature. As the temperature falls, especially at night, so the frequency of shivering increases. During brooding females can lose up to 15 per cent of their body weight due to metabolic cost of shivering. Although other pythons also shiver during brooding, temperature rises have only been definitely established for the one species. Some species manage to warm their eggs by leaving them to bask, then returning to transfer warmth from their bodies to the eggs – this, of course, is a behavioural rather than a physiological activity.

Apart from in brooding pythons, physiological thermoregulation in snakes has not been thoroughly investigated. The general feeling is that such mechanisms would be of little use to small species because they lose heat to their surroundings too quickly. In large species, however, the metabolic rate and the heart rate have been shown to change according to the conditions. These changes could help the snake to warm up quickly and then to retain its body heat longer. In this way, it would increase the time it could be active, both at the beginning and end of its activity period.

Respiration

Respiration in snakes is, in most ways, similar to respiration in birds and mammals, including ourselves. There are a few modifications and practical differences, however.

The lungs

Generally speaking, the reptile lung is an improvement on the amphibian lung – it has to be because amphibians can also breathe through their skin whereas reptiles cannot.

Because of their elongation, the left lung of snakes is either greatly reduced or effectively absent. The capacity of the right lung may be increased to compensate and, in some species, there is an additional 'tracheal lung' formed from a forward extension of the right lung.

The actual process of breathing – getting air in and out of the lungs – is done simply by expanding the rib cage, as in mammals, so that air is pulled into the lungs by suction and pumped out again when the muscles operating the ribs relax. Snakes can often be seen moving the throat up and down as though they were pumping air. Although amphibians use this technique to get air into the lungs, snakes seem to use it only to draw air into the nostrils and so enhance their sense of smell.

Gaseous exchange

Compared with mammals, there are basic differences in the biochemical processes, brought about by the slower metabolism of snakes and their shape. The lungs are not as efficient as those of birds and mammals, and, in particular, they are not good at eliminating carbon dioxide, the main waste product of respiration. The excess carbon dioxide left in the poorly ventilated lung enters the bloodstream and combines with water to form carbonic acid. This then breaks down to bicarbonate ions. Because of their inefficient lungs, reptiles have needed to adapt to a higher concentration of bicarbonate ions in their bloodstream.

Gaseous exchange is also affected by temperature – at higher temperatures oxygen is absorbed much more quickly. The effect of this is that snakes breathe very occasionally, and use very little oxygen, when they are cold. As they warm up, so does their respiration rate. Even so, snakes and other reptiles use much less oxygen than would a bird or mammal of equivalent size and, in extreme cases, snakes can survive without oxygen for several hours.

In ectothermic animals, metabolism, and therefore the rate at which oxygen is used up, is also dependent on activity. As one would expect, sleeping and resting snakes breathe less often than ones that are looking for food or are otherwise active.

The sea snakes are a special case. They need to avoid having to spend too much time repeatedly coming up to the surface in order to breathe. Studies have shown that most species come to the surface to breathe every half hour or so, but that they may stay submerged, voluntarily, for up to two hours. Although their basic anatomy is the same as that of terrestrial snakes, sea snakes' lungs have a greater capacity. There is a large tracheal lung, extending well forward. The part of the lung extending backwards (the saccular lung) is not functional but forms a large air store. Its wall is thick and muscular, unlike the saccular lung of other snakes, and so the air can be forced forwards into the functional part of the lung (bronchial lung) where its oxygen can be extracted.

Sea snakes are also unusual in the amount of gaseous exchange that can take place across the surface of their skin. Despite the scaly covering, some species are able to absorb up to one-fifth of their oxygen requirement in this way, a far greater proportion than any land-dwelling species.

Although the aquatic wart or file snakes, *Acrochordus*, are not related to the true sea snakes, they also have extended saccular and tracheal lungs to increase their capacity and they can also absorb oxygen through their skin. In addition, the granulated file snake, *A. granulatus*, has a greater volume of blood, relative to its size, than other snakes.

Water balance

All reptiles are covered with scales and this was one of the factors that helped them to leave the aquatic environment to which amphibians are still more or less tied. Reptiles' skins are not completely waterproof, however, and about two-thirds of their water loss takes place through the skin. It is interesting that the scales themselves are not significantly better at retaining water than the skin between them – a few mutant snakes lack scales altogether and these specimens have been shown, experimentally, to be just as good at retaining water as normal, scaled, individuals.

Because of the relative impermeability of their skins, snakes are not capable of soaking up water in the same way that amphibians do. Therefore they must drink from time to time or obtain water from their food. Freshwater aquatic and semi-aquatic species and rainforest species have a ready and abundant supply of drinking water. At the other extreme, desert species are often unable to drink for long periods of time and so water obtained from food is most important for them. Similarly, sea snakes do not have access to fresh water, although species belonging to the subfamily Laticaudinae come ashore occasionally and have been observed drinking from rainwater pools that form in rocky crevices during rain and from drops of rainwater on foliage.

After their scaly skins, the most important weapon in snakes' battle to conserve water is their excretory system. Unlike mammals, snakes convert their nitrogenous waste products to uric acid. This is a crystalline substance that can be excreted as a white paste-like substance containing almost no water. This greatly helps species from arid or marine environments to survive with little water.

Behaviourally, snakes may reduce the rate at which they lose water from their bodies by coiling. As in heat retention, this reduces the amount of surface area they expose and, thereby, the area over which evaporation can take place. In addition, if a number of snakes coil together, each individual will reduce its exposed surface area even further. Large aggregations of small, temperate snakes such as the red-bellied snake, *Storeria occipitomaculata*, are thought to have this purpose, while as long ago as 1936 Noble and Clasen showed that DeKay's snake, *Storeria dekayi*, and Butler's garter snake, *Thamnophis butleri*, lost less weight when coiled together than when they were separate, the difference being due to differences in water loss.

Not all snakes are equally good at saving water and their efficiency depends very much on their natural habitat – it has been estimated that rainforest species lose water about 100 times more quickly than desert ones. This, of course, is a function of evolution – mechanisms for saving water only evolve where there is a need.

Salt balance

The bodies of animals need salt to carry out their various functions. The most important salts are sodium and potassium although there are smaller quantities of a number of other salts, all obtained through the diet. The amount of salts in the system must be regulated and this is normally performed by the kidneys. The kidneys work to remove salt when there is too much and to conserve it when there is too little. In this respect, snakes are no different from other animals, although the actual concentrations of salts obviously varies.

Snakes living in the sea, however, are faced with a tricky problem; the salts in their bodies are at a lower concentration than in their surroundings, i.e. the sea in which they live. Through osmosis, there will be a tendency for water to flow out of their bodies until the concentrations are equalised. This would cause them to dehydrate and so must be prevented. The problem is most simply dealt with by making the skin as impermeable to water as possible and, as expected, marine snakes have much less permeable skins than other snakes.

▲ The three species of acrochordids, such as the Arafura file snake, *Acrochordus arafurae*, have several adaptations that suit them to a totally aquatic lifestyle, including a larger lung capacity than other snakes.

◄ Colubrids belonging to the subfamily Homalopsinae frequently enter brackish or salt water and they have a gland for removing excess salt from their systems. It is situated in the roof of their mouth and therefore differs from the salt glands of the true sea snakes. The bockadam, *Cerberus rynchops*, is a typical homalopsine snake and is found in mangrove swamps and estuarine waters along the northern coast of Australia.

Sea snakes' food, consisting almost entirely of marine fish, is salty, and excess salt is therefore bound to accumulate in their systems. This must be excreted in some way, but, unlike its mammalian counterpart, the reptilian kidney is not able to secrete salts at a higher concentration than is present in the blood. An alternative method must be found to dispose of the excess salt and this has evolved in the form of specialised glands, not found in other snakes. In the sea snakes, sea kraits and wart snakes, this gland is situated under the tongue, and is therefore known as the sublingual gland. A duct leads from the gland to the sheath that surrounds the tongue so that every time it is pushed out of the mouth a small quantity of highly salty water is pushed out first.

The homalopsine water snakes (which are members of the Colubridae) do not have a sublingual salt gland but have independently evolved a salt gland in the roof of their mouths. The one or two species of natricine water snakes that enter brackish water, notably *Nerodia fasciata compressicauda*, seem not to have evolved a salt gland at all and they presumably live within their bodies' salt tolerance by only entering pure sea water for short periods of time and by drinking plenty of fresh water.

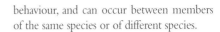

THE BIOLOGICAL ENVIRONMENT

THE BIOLOGICAL ENVIRONMENT COMPRISES THE ORGANISMS THAT LIVE IN THE SAME PLACE AND WHICH HAVE SOME BEARING ON THE SNAKE'S LIFE. BECAUSE PLANTS DO NOT FIGURE IN THE DIET OF SNAKES, THEY HAVE LESS OF AN IMPACT THAN THEY DO IN HERBIVOROUS GROUPS OF ANIMALS. PLANTS ARE IMPORTANT, HOWEVER, IN PROVIDING COVER FOR SNAKES OF ALL SIZES, AND PILES OF DEAD VEGETATION ARE VERY OFTEN USED BY SNAKES AS EGG-LAYING SITES. PLANTS, INCLUDING TREES, HARBOUR THE ANIMALS THAT SNAKES PREY ON AND SO THEY ARE IMPORTANT, INDIRECTLY, IN THIS RESPECT. FINALLY, PLANTS BUFFER PHYSICAL ENVIRONMENTAL FACTORS, SUCH AS TEMPERATURE AND HUMIDITY, BY PROVIDING SHADE, ABSORBING WATER AND SO ON.

Some aspects of the biological environment are dealt with elsewhere: animals that may form the prey of snakes are discussed in Chapter 5, those that may in turn prey upon them are dealt with in Chapter 6, and those of the same species, that may be mates or rivals, are covered in Chapter 7.

Interactions that do not involve eating, being eaten, or mating, may be termed social behaviour, and can occur between members of the same species or of different species.

Social behaviour

Social behaviour is about interactions between individuals in the species – how they space themselves in the environment, how and why they communicate with one another and whether they live as individuals or in groups.

Studying the social behaviour of secretive animals such as snakes obviously presents many problems to researchers. Whereas birds and mammals can be observed from a distance, these methods are not generally available for snakes. Furthermore, snakes do not communicate with each other by sound, nor by visual display, at least as far as we know. The social behaviour of snakes is limited, therefore, and such information as we have often arrives fortuitously, as when pairs of mating or fighting snakes are happened upon by chance or when an aggregation of snakes is uncovered accidentally.

It is generally accepted, then, that snakes are not social animals. They are almost unique in the vertebrate kingdom in not showing any regular form of grouping, and of being essentially non-territorial. Aggregations of snakes appear to be incidental; they are formed in places where the environment is particularly favourable for one reason or another or they huddle together to conserve heat or water, as mentioned earlier. These are not really social activities because the groups may contain snakes of various ages, sexes and species and may occur at almost any time of the year: they do not show any consistent patterns. There appear to be few if any interactions between the individuals of such aggregations although they must obviously tolerate one another at close quarters.

Mating aggregations have been observed in certain species. These are often, though not always, species in which large numbers of individuals hibernate *en masse* and the best known example is probably that of red-sided garter snakes, *Thamnophis sirtalis parietalis*, in Manitoba, where huge numbers of individuals have been found in 'mating balls' immediately after their emergence from hibernacula. Other examples concern species that do not hibernate: small groups of male diamond pythons may remain with a female for about four to six weeks during

◀ **Red-sided garter snakes congregate in huge numbers immediately after emerging from their hibernacula.**

the breeding season, for instance. Other observations seem to indicate that one or more males will track down and follow a 'ripe' female for several days or even weeks and that these animals can often be found in close proximity to one another at this time.

Hibernacula, or dens, normally contain members of the same species, although mixed aggregations of snakes are not uncommon. Where good sites are hard to find, all the snakes from the surrounding areas may converge on them. Lang (1969) found that abandoned ant mounds are widely used as hibernacula in Minnesota, and, over a two-year period, eleven ant nests yielded 2,019 red-bellied snakes, *Storeria occipitomaculata*, 276 smooth green snakes, *Liochlorophis vernalis*, and 131 eastern garter snakes, *Thamnophis sirtalis*. A single mound contained a total of 299 snakes, including all three species. Snakes from these sites were estimated to have travelled 150-300 m (160-320 yds) from the areas where they were active in the summer. In another survey, Carpenter (1953)[2] dug out ant mounds in Michigan, and up to seven species of snakes were found in a single mound. These included two species of garter snakes, *Thamnophis sirtalis* and *T. butleri,* ribbon snakes, *T. sauritus*, water snakes, *Nerodia sipedon*, smooth green snakes, *Liochlorophis vernalis*, red-bellied snakes, *Storeria occipitomaculata*, and a De Kay's snake, *Storeria dekayi*.

Other snakes may occasionally co-habit with other types of reptiles, as in the case of the Florida indigo snake, *Drymarchon corais couperi*, which is often associated with the burrows of gopher tortoises, especially in the winter months when cool weather may drive it underground for a few days at a time.

Other types of aggregation involve the movement of snakes to particular areas for purposes other than hibernation or mating. Examples of these are rather scarce, although it has been noted that females of some species are found close to one another immediately before laying eggs or giving birth. Reichenbach (1982),[3] for example, described an aggregation of about 150 pregnant female garter snakes, *Thamnophis sirtalis*, in a small area at an abandoned brick factory in Ohio. The snakes were found under pieces of corrugated metal sheet scattered over the site and these are thought to have attracted the

▶ Hatchling snakes usually disperse as soon as they hatch, although adverse weather may cause them to remain in the vicinity of their clutch mates for a short time.

snakes because they provided good basking sites. Males were present but in much smaller numbers. In another case, Graves and Duvall (1993)[4] discovered that female prairie rattlesnakes, *Crotalus v. viridis*, in Wyoming moved to specific areas when they were pregnant. These 'rookeries' were always in rocky places and may have enabled the females to warm themselves more easily.

It is safest to assume, in the absence of more evidence, that aggregations such as these occur when suitable basking or egg-laying sites are in short supply or when they are concentrated in a fairly small area. With egg-laying species, the correct soil type, or soil with the right moisture content, may attract gravid snakes.

Populations

The structure of snake populations has been studied in only a small number of species. Certain deductions can be made from these studies, however.

Mortality

Most population studies have shown that mortality among medium-sized, temperate species is highest during the snake's first year. This is because small snakes are more prone to predation; because they are not large enough to store sufficient food to see them through long periods of starvation; because they dehydrate more easily than large snakes (due to a larger relative surface area); and because they are generally less experienced at coping with the trials of life. Once they approach sexual maturity their prospects improve and

mortality among adult snakes may account for only a small part of the population each year.

Abundance

Like many other aspects of their biology, the density of snake populations is hard to measure, due to their secretive habits. The proportions of males, females and juveniles within a population is even more difficult to establish for the same reason.

High densities of snakes often occur seasonally, due to their gravitation towards or away from hibernation or aggregation sites. At other times, there appears to be little or no pattern to the way in which they space themselves out in the environment; densities fluctuate from time to time and from place to place as they move hither and thither.

Estimates of population numbers can sometimes be made by mark and recapture methods, where a number of snakes are captured and marked. Some idea of numbers can be obtained by calculating the proportion of marked individuals that crop up in subsequent collections. Unfortunately, for this method to be accurate, a relatively large number of snakes need to be marked, and there must be a good number of recaptures. Other precautions need to be taken in order to avoid errors in the calculation and better results are obtained if the study is conducted over a long period of time.

Using this technique, population densities as high as 1,849 snakes per hectare (748 per acre) have been established for the ring-neck snake, *Diadophis punctatus* (Fitch, 1975),[5] 1,289 snakes per hectare (522 per

acre) for the striped swamp snake, *Regina alleni* (Godley, 1980),[6] and 729 snakes per hectare (295 per acre) for the worm snake, *Carphophis amoenus* (Clark, 1970).[7] It is worth pointing out that these are all relatively small snakes, two of which are secretive and feed largely on worms and other soft-bodied invertebrates (which are usually in plentiful supply), and the other (*R. alleni*) is a semi-aquatic species in which populations are necessarily concentrated in suitable habitat. The vast majority of mark and recapture studies have shown populations to be much less dense than these figures, very often less than one snake per hectare. Furthermore, hardly any tropical snakes have been studied in this way. When the same species has been studied at different times in different places, widely different results may be obtained. This serves to illustrate the problems associated with population studies of this kind.

Population numbers probably fluctuate from year to year, according to the amount of food available and, subsequently, on the reproductive success of the adults. Some species are relatively short-lived, sometimes only surviving for a year or two, and their populations are more likely to change drastically in response to environmental factors than those of long-lived species. Whereas fluctuations in population numbers may mirror fluctuations in food supply, steady declines can often be attributed to habitat changes, usually due to human activities such as construction. These, too, are difficult to measure but can often be noticed even by casual observers. Increases in population may also be due to habitat changes and have been noted in a few cases, as, for instance, when species colonise areas that have become irrigated, or when introduced species thrive in a new environment.

Sex ratios

Apart from population numbers, it is interesting to look at the proportion of males and females within a population. The flowerpot snake, *Ramphotyphlops braminus*, is a female-only species (see page 149, Chapter 7) and can be ignored here. Otherwise, male and female snakes would be expected to occur in equal numbers at hatching. Since they are usually of similar size, there is no advantage in producing a higher proportion of one sex over another.

This seems to be the case in all the species that have been studied, with just a few exceptions. Four involve species in which males predominate: the copperhead,

THE IDEAL SEX RATIO

Except in a few unusual cases, the sex ratio among most species of snakes is found to be roughly 50:50. Since male snakes do not help the female to raise the young, they do not need to form pair bonds and are therefore free to mate with as many females as they can find. So, because a single male can mate with any number of females, it may seem that a system that favoured a large number of females and a few males would be more sensible. Furthermore, in many mating systems, dominant males mate with several females whereas small or subordinate males never get to mate at all and so they are effectively 'wasted'. Why should such a system have evolved?

R. A. Fisher offered the explanation in his 1930 book *The Genetical Theory of Natural Selection* (Clarendon, Oxford). The key to understanding this problem is to realise that animals do not act 'for the good of the species' but for the good of themselves. More accurately, their *genes* act for the good of themselves: each gene within an animal's system wants to find itself duplicated in as many of that animal's offspring as possible.

Consider a hypothetical population where females outnumber males by 10 to one. Each female breeds for 10 years and produces 10 eggs: her reproductive potential is 100 offspring, each of which shares half of her genes and half of their father's. Each male, however, will mate with 10 females, on average and so his reproductive potential is 1,000 offspring, each of which will contain half of his genes: males will be 10 times more successful at proliferating their genes. The best strategy now would be for each female to produce more male offspring (because this would give them the largest possible number of grandchildren). The sex ratio will begin to swing towards a 50:50 split until, eventually, the population will contain an equal number of males and females.

Since males are so valuable in terms of producing grandchildren, will the sex ratio become biased towards males? The answer is no, because if there is a surplus of males, not all of them will get the chance to mate. All the females will produce young every breeding season, all other things being equal, but some of the males will not. If the pendulum swings too far in favour of males, there will be advantages in producing females.

In practice, populations do not oscillate between abundances of males and females: the selective pressures of producing one sex or the other are equally balanced and, over time, a stable system will have arisen.

Although there are exceptions to this rule, in social animals, and in species in which the sexes are different sizes, these do not seem to apply to snakes. Of the 2,950 or so snake species, the two sexes occur in roughly equal numbers. Skewed sex ratios, in which one sex or the other predominates, have been established in only five species, and the differences are only slight in some of them. *Apparent* skewed ratios sometimes show up when male and female snakes have different habits: males may be more active than females, for instance, or they may be more brightly coloured, as in some vipers, and then are more likely to be caught. Again, some batches of newborn or newly hatched snakes may contain more of one sex than another but this is invariably due to chance: if a large enough sample was available, the sex ratio would correct itself.

▲ The Japanese rat snake, *Elaphe climacophora*, is unusual because populations seem to contain more females than males, for no apparent reason.

Agkistrodon contortrix (in which there are twice as many males at birth as there are females); the four-striped rat snake, *Elaphe quadrivirgata*; the Australian mainland tiger snake, *Notechis scutatus*; and the gopher snake, *Pituophis catenifer*. The fifth exception is the Japanese rat snake, *Elaphe climacophora*, in which females predominate at hatching. There are no obvious explanations.

In later life, sex ratios can differ from those that are found at hatching or birth, due to sampling error, dispersal of one sex or another, or differential mortality, where one sex is more likely to die early in life than the other.

Rarity

The opposite of abundance is, of course, rarity. The term 'rare' can have several meanings, depending on its context. It can be applied to snakes that have a restricted range such as a small island, or those that have a much larger range over which they are thinly scattered.

At the same time, rarity can be an artifact of human powers of observation – species that 'rarely' interact with mankind or which live in inaccessible places. Many tropical snakes, for instance, are known from only a handful of specimens; this does not necessarily mean that they are rare because, very often, they

live in regions that are little visited by herpetologists. It is possible that the maps that show their distribution have more to do with the distribution of herpetologists than with the snakes. This is a major problem because the areas where there are lots of snakes – Amazonia, Central Africa, Southeast Asia – tend to have very few herpetologists. Ironically, areas where there are many herpetologists tend to have fewer snakes.

It is also important to distinguish between total rarity and local rarity. Most species become rare towards the edges of their range, though they may be common elsewhere. In Britain, for instance, the smooth snake, *Coronella austriaca*, is extremely rare, although it is quite common over much of continental Europe.

There are three other reasons for snakes to be naturally rare. Firstly, all animals that operate towards the top of the food chain are likely to be rare. As energy flows up the food chain, about 90 per cent of it is lost at each level. By the time it reaches the higher levels, there is precious little left to support the animals that forage there. Snakes may be positioned at various stages in the food chain. Many species are small and feed on small animals, such as invertebrates, which are plentiful. These snakes are likely to be common (though often overlooked because they are small and secretive). Larger species, however, operate much closer to the top of the food chain and one would expect them to be rarer.

Secondly, some species are so highly specialised, in terms of their food preferences or some other requirement, that there will always be an upper limit to their population densities. Examples include: the African egg eaters, Dasypeltis; species that only eat amphisbaenians or centipedes; and species that lay their eggs in termite nests, and many others.

Thirdly, the species that have evolved in isolation are likely to be rare. This applies especially to island species, such as the many endangered snakes of the West Indies and other island groups throughout the world (see Chapter 4). It also applies to species that evolve on ecological 'islands', such as isolated mountain ranges. A similar situation prevails among species whose ranges have become fragmented through the appearance of a physical barrier to dispersal, either natural or man made. Since snakes have very limited abilities to cross hostile habitats, their opportunities to break out of restricted habitats are few. Not only is their habitat limited, but the colonies may be founded by few individuals, leading to a lack of genetic variation which itself makes them vulnerable. For instance, the Golden Lancehead, *Bothrops insularis*, from the small Brazilian island of Queimada Grande, may be dying out due to the appearance in the population of a lethal gene. This gene causes some snakes to be intersexes – they have characteristics of both males and females and are sterile. Without the opportunity to

RARE SNAKES

A number of snakes are known only from very few specimens, but they are not necessarily rare – some live in areas that have been little visited and others are very secretive species. Some species, however, are on the verge of extinction, usually because they have very limited distributions, often islands, and have suffered greatly from habitat destruction.

The following examples are a few of the species that are considered rare, for various reasons.

Australian thread snakes Four species are known from single specimens: *Ramphotyphlops margaretae*, *R. micromma*, *R. troglodytes* and *R. yampiensis*. A fifth species, *R. kimberleyensis*, is known from two specimens. Four of the five come from the northwestern region of Australia, the 'Kimberley', which is difficult to explore and where many interesting animals have been discovered in recent years. The other species, *R. margaretae*, is from the arid interior of Australia. Thread snakes are small, secretive burrowing species that are easily overlooked.

The rough-scaled carpet python This species, *Morelia carinata*, was described in 1981 from a specimen collected ten years previously, in 1971. It also lives in the Kimberley region of Australia. A second specimen was found in 1987 and a third in 1993. To date, about ten have been found.

▲ Rough-scaled python, *Morelia carinata*.

Cropan's tree boa *Corallus cropanii*, sometimes included in the genus *Corallus*, was first described in 1954 from southeastern Brazil. Only three specimens are known.

Tropidophis fuscus This species, which has no common name, was described in 1992 from two specimens, found in Cuba. No further specimens have been found to date.

Round Island boa *Casarea dussumeri* is found only on Round Island, which has an area of only about 1 sq km (250 acres). In 1983 it was estimated that only 75 individuals remained and it is probably the world's rarest snake. A captive breeding programme has been instigated to try to increase its numbers with a view to reintroducing it at a later date.

outbreed, they could be doomed to extinction through inbreeding.

If we look at communities of snakes, most of them seem to consist of a relatively small number of very common species and a larger number of rare ones. Allowing for the somewhat selective nature by which snakes are found, the most reasonable explanation for this is that common species are well adapted to the environment and are usually found to be generalists, especially with regard to their food requirements. The rare species, on the other hand, are often specialists, with limited resources available to them. The habitat, and the resources it contains, have been divided up, over time, between a number of species, but it has not been divided equally. Specialists scratch a living by eating items that the common species either overlook or are not equipped to deal with. In addition, species that occur in low densities are less likely to attract the attention of predators than abundant species. The predators will not only form search images of the more common species but may also acquire behavioural and morphological adaptations that are aimed at those species. Certain species exploit this system by being polymorphic: they are trying, in effect, to become two or more rare species instead of one common one. (Polymorphism is discussed in Chapter 6.)

Although there is no evidence that the species richness of snake communities is controlled by predators, there are precedents in other branches of biology. It is well known that grazing, which is a form of predation (on grass), produces a rich community of plants that often includes many rare species. Among animals, it has been found that when predatory starfish were removed from a community, the number of species in the community fell from 15 to eight. Predators of snakes may 'make room' for some of the rarer species by controlling the numbers of the more common ones.

NOTES
1. Lang, J. W. (1969), 'Hibernation and movements of *Storcria occipitomaculata* in Northern Minnesota', Contributed papers to the 12th annual meeting of the SSAR, in *Journal of Herpetology*, 3(3-4):196-197.
2. Carpenter, C. C. (1953), 'A study of hibernacula and hibernating associations of snakes and amphibians in Michigan', *Ecology*, 34(1):74-80.
3. Reichenbach, N. G. (1982), 'An aggregation of female garter snakes under corrugated metal sheets', *Journal of Herpetology*, 17(4):412-413.
4. Graves, B. M. and Duvall. D. (1993), 'Reproduction, rookery use, and thermoregulation in free-ranging, pregnant *Crotalus p. viridis*', *Journal of Herpetology*, 27(1):33-41.
5. Fitch, H. S. (1975). 'A demographic study of the ringneck snake (*Diadophis punctatus*) in Kansas', *Univ. Kans. Mus. Nat. Hist. Misc. Publ.*, 62:1-53.
6. Godley, J. S. (1980), 'Foraging ecology of the striped swamp snake, *Regina alleni*, in southern Florida', *Ecol. Monogr.*, 50:411-436.
7. Clark, D. R. (1970), 'Ecological study of the worm snake. *Carphophis amoenus*', *Univ. Kans. Publ. Mus. Nat. Hist.*, 19:85-194.

CHAPTER 4
WHERE SNAKES LIVE

The distribution of snakes can be looked at on two scales. Global patterns of distribution are interesting because they tell us about the evolution and spread of the major families and also, incidentally, add to our knowledge of the geological history of the earth's landmasses. On a smaller scale, it is plain to see that different snakes tend to live in different habitats. These two viewpoints are not exclusive, and the distribution of a particular species will depend on an interplay between the global distribution of its near relatives and the availability of a suitable habitat.

A European asp, *Vipera aspis*, basks in early spring within sight of snow-capped peaks in northern Italy.

HABITATS

SNAKES ARE FOUND IN MOST TYPES OF HABITATS. WHERE THEY ARE NOT FOUND, THE CLIMATE IS NORMALLY THE LIMITING FACTOR – VERY COLD PLACES, SUCH AS TUNDRA, THE POLAR ICE CAPS AND VERY HIGH MOUNTAINS LACK SNAKES BECAUSE THEY ARE UNTENABLE FOR LARGE ECTOTHERMS REQUIRING A RELATIVELY HIGH BODY TEMPERATURE IN ORDER TO OPERATE.

With regard to habitat type, snakes can either be classed as generalists (those species that are found throughout a region within a number of different habitat types) and specialists (those species that are invariably found in a particular type of habitat). The distinction is not clear cut, though, and species may show differing degrees of specialisation.

Tropical forests

Tropical forests are found in Central America and the Caribbean region, South America, Africa, Madagascar, India, Southeast Asia and northern Australia. The threats to their existence, through logging, agricultural development, pollution, etc., have been well publicised and need no further comment here. It is estimated that removal of large expanses of tropical forests had eliminated, or critically depleted, about half of the world's species of plants and animals, including snakes, by the end of the twentieth century.

Ecologists recognise several different types or subdivisions of tropical forests, depending on altitude, amount of rainfall and plant types. The distribution of snakes within these categories has not been thoroughly established and the habitat will be dealt with in its entirety.

Tropical forests are well known for the richness of their flora and fauna. Snakes fit this pattern, attaining their greatest diversity in tropical forests. A number of factors contribute to this. Firstly, temperature is rarely a problem because most tropical regions remain at a fairly constant, moderately high temperature throughout the year, despite the closed canopy. They offer a wide scope of microhabitats, including a range of niches for arboreal, terrestrial, semi-aquatic and burrowing snakes. Some of these niches are only available because of the prevailing, near optimum temperatures, allowing snakes to be active even though they have limited or no opportunities to bask.

Tropical forests offer abundant cover, both for secretive species that hide among or under vegetation and forest debris, and for cryptic species that 'hide in full view',

▼ Tropical rainforests provide plenty of niches for a variety of snakes, including large ones like this reticulated python in Borneo.

▶ Rubber boas live in wooded areas, including conifer forests, in parts of their range in western North America. They are the hardiest of the boas and also the smallest.

especially some of the green arboreal species. Prey is not normally a problem either, with an abundance of other animals to eat, ranging from the smallest invertebrates up to medium-sized mammals and including amphibians, birds, bats and other reptiles. Several snakes from this habitat have developed specialised diets, such as land molluscs, and have evolved appropriate adaptations. In addition, many tropical forest species feed on smaller snakes.

Contrary to popular belief, snakes are not easily found in large numbers in tropical forests. Collections often show a great species diversity but actual numbers of each species may be very low. For example, in an expedition to Belize in Central America, Stafford (1991)[1] recorded 12 species but, of these, six records consist of single specimens, two records consist of two specimens and another consists of three specimens. Only one species, *Mastigodryas melanolomus*, was classed as common. This almost certainly reflects the difficulty of finding snakes in this type of habitat – during clearance operations, such as road building and logging, snakes are often found to be incredibly numerous.

Of the 18 currently recognised snake families, all are represented in tropical forests except two: the Bolyeriidae and the Acrochordidae.

Temperate forests

In contrast to tropical forests, temperate forests are not rich in snakes, either in terms of species or numbers. The cool climate of temperate regions is compounded by the canopy cover and such species that are found in this type of habitat are usually restricted to lightly wooded areas, forest fringes and clearings.

Black rat snakes, *Pantherophis o. obsoletus*, for example, are found around the edges of forests in temperate parts of North America. This habitat preference appears to be correlated with birds' nesting habits, which provide a favoured source of food for the snakes. Owing to agricultural practices, the amount of this habitat is decreasing, leading to a reduction in the numbers of the snakes.

Deserts

Deserts are found in North and South America, Africa, Asia and Australia. The largest expanse includes the Sahara and a series of other deserts extending eastwards across the Arabian peninsula and into central Asia. In North America, deserts cover much of the southwestern United States and northern Mexico. Altogether, arid and semi-arid regions cover about 30 per cent of the earth's surface. Although they are defined as areas in which there is a deficiency of water, their characteristics vary from place to place, according to temperature and altitude. Thus there are the sand deserts, such as the Sahara, the Atacama and the Namib, characterised by dunes, and stony deserts like the Sonoran and Chihuahuan Deserts. Each of these presents peculiar problems to the plants and animals that have colonised them. Not all deserts are hot places: most have wide temperature fluctuations from day to nigh and some experience severely cold winters.

Deserts are among the best habitats in which to find and observe snakes. The species richness and numbers of individuals are in sharp contrast to the situation for other groups of animals, especially birds and mammals. The reason that they are so successful here is partly related to their ectothermy; because they do not use any part of their food intake to produce heat, snakes can exist on much less food than a bird or a mammal of equivalent size, about one-fiftieth of the amount, according to

▲ Deserts are the home of many species of snakes which are ideally suited to withstand their low productivity. Different types of deserts attract different species and communities: the gravel desert of the Sonoran complex is home to a large number of rattlesnakes as well as diurnal and nocturnal colubrids, a boa, an elapid and a thread snake.

◄ Dunes provide a different type of desert environment for another set of species. Extensive dune systems are found in several parts of the world: these form part of the Namib Desert.

▶ The American sidewinder, *Crotalus cerastes*, which is perfectly adapted to deserts containing substantial areas of windblown sand, through its locomotion and coloration.

some estimates, and they can survive long periods without any food. This is obviously helpful in areas where the food supply is limited and unreliable.

The lack of water that characterises deserts is overcome partly by snakes' scaly skins, which help to limit the amount of water lost, and partly by their excretory systems, which produces waste in the form of uric acid, a semi-solid requiring very little water to carry it out of the body. In addition, their relatively small size and long, slender shape (in most cases) are beneficial when it comes to avoiding lethally high temperatures (and lethally low temperatures) as they can easily crawl into small crevices among rocks or down rodent burrows, where temperatures are tolerable. Their low food requirement, and therefore their need to forage only occasionally, allows them to shelter from the heat or cold for as long as is necessary. Furthermore, their well-developed sensory systems, especially their ability to detect vibration, the tongue and Jacobson's organ, and the heat-sensitive pits of several species, make them well adapted to nocturnal foraging when necessary.

Desert species may be found among a number of snake families, especially the Colubridae and the Viperidae, and including, to a lesser extent, members of the Boidae, the Elapidae and even the Leptotyphlopidae.

Grasslands and savannah

Grasslands are distributed throughout the mid latitudes, often known under local terms such as steppe (Asia), prairie (North America), veld (South Africa) and pampas (Argentina). Many of them cover vast areas and some have been created, or enlarged, by human activity or by natural fires, destroying the forest cover. Savannah is the term used for tropical areas of low vegetation, including grasses, and may form a link between deserts and tropical forests. Grassland and savannah covers about one-quarter of the world's surface.

Many grasslands are extensively cultivated or grazed by livestock and this is not beneficial to reptile life. Periodic fires, either natural or due to human intervention, hinder the establishment of viable populations of snakes, either directly or by eliminating their food supply, as does spraying with pesticides. It seems likely, however, that snakes have never fully exploited open grasslands in the same way that they have other habitats, although the reasons for this are not altogether clear. Overall temperatures may not be high enough in many of these regions and food supply may be sparse, while lack of cover may increase the chances of predation, especially from birds of prey.

Although snakes are not widely found in this type of habitat, there are exceptions, especially in Africa, where the African rock python, *Python sebae*, for example, is almost limited to open situations, although only where rock outcrops provide satisfactory cover. In North America, species such as the hognose snakes, *Heterodon*, one or two species of rattlesnakes, *Crotalus*, and some forms of the gopher snake, *Pituophis melanoleucus*, are found in prairies although they are not limited to them. European grasslands are not extensive like those in other parts of the world, often being divided into fields and meadows by hedges and walls, providing some cover and protection from extremes of temperature. Several species of *Vipera* may be found in such areas, as may the rat snakes, *Elaphe*, and various whipsnakes. All of these species tend to be generalists, rather than grassland specialists.

Swamps and marshes

Swamps and marshes may be found throughout the world wherever the water table is close to the surface. They may be permanent, as in the Florida Everglades, or temporary, either drying out seasonally or becoming inundated with water, as in the Pantanal. In addition, the fringes of lakes,

ponds, rivers and streams often provide a significant amount of semi-aquatic or marsh-like habitat. Mangrove swamps form a particular type of habitat, associated with coasts and estuaries in favourable tropical regions.

These types of habitats are widely used by snakes. One of their main prey types, amphibian, dwells there, and fish are also available more often than not. Tropical and subtropical swamps are more heavily utilised than temperate marshes, due simply to the benefits of higher temperatures. The natricine colubrids, such as the European *Natrix* and the North American *Nerodia* species are especially associated with damp habitats,

▲ The Serengeti is just part of the huge savannah that comprises a vast swathe across East and southern Africa.

▼ Only specialised snakes, such as the sea kraits, are completely at home in a tropical marine environment.

▲ Cypress swamp, Florida. Wetlands, swamps and marshes provide homes for a variety of aquatic, semi-aquatic and arboreal snakes. Many feed on fish and amphibians.

but very many tropical snakes may also be found in damp situations. Mangrove swamps are inhabited by a number of rather specialised snakes, including a species of file snake, *Acrochordus javanicus*, and some marine snakes, which forage around them at high tide. Certain natricine snakes that feed on crustaceans are also found here.

Aquatic habitats

Aquatic habitats may be freshwater or marine. Purely aquatic snakes are more or less confined to the tropics because water acts as a heat sink, preventing snakes from maintaining body temperatures very much higher than the water surrounding them. Most aquatic snakes feed, naturally enough, on fish, although some also eat fish eggs and invertebrate.

The homalopsine colubrids (possibly forming a separate snake family, the Homalopsidae) all come from Southeast Asia, and are totally aquatic in habits, living in fresh-water ponds and lakes. Some of them may enter the sea occasionally. Of the three species belonging to the Acrochordidae, or file snakes, two live in fresh water and the other in brackish coastal or estuarine waters.

The most highly adapted aquatic species are the sea snakes and sea kraits. The 47 sea snakes have the widest distribution, covering the coastal waters from southeastern Africa, across India and Southeast Asia to the northern coasts of Australia. A single species, the yellow-bellied sea snake, extends this range to the west coast of Central and South America as it is pelagic, drifting in the upper layers of the ocean, often in large shoals or 'slicks'

▼ Although several species of boas and pythons are associated with wet habitats, none is more at home in them than the water python, *Liasis fuscus*, from Australia.

THE EFFECTS OF CHANGING HABITATS

Even subtle changes in habitat can lead to changes in the species found in a given area. In a survey undertaken in 1987 and 1989, Mendelson and Jennings looked at the effects of habitat alteration in southeastern Arizona and adjacent southwestern New Mexico (*Journal of Herpetology*, 26[1]:38-45). They compared their findings with those of a survey which took place about 30 years previously.

The area comprises a mixture of semi-desert grassland and desert scrub but, since the first survey was carried out, much of the grassland has been replaced with scrub, altering the relative proportions of the two types of habitat. In addition, large numbers of cattle watering troughs have been installed in the area.

Altogether, 23 species of snakes were found, although many of these occurred in very low numbers. The most significant species were two species of rattlesnakes, the western diamondback and the Mojave, *Crotalus atrox* and *C. scutulatus*, the gopher snake, *Pituophis catenifer* and the chequered garter snake, *Thamnophis marcianus*.

By comparing the numbers of each species found, as a percentage of the total number of snakes, it was possible to show how the snake community had altered; the garter snake had become much more common (9.7 per cent of the total snakes found compared to 1.1 per cent in the previous survey), almost certainly due to the presence of the cattle troughs, which attract breeding amphibian such as spadefoot toads, *Scaphiopus*, on which the garter snakes feed. Western diamond back rattle-snakes had increased slightly, from 15.0 per cent to 18.4 per cent of total snakes found but the Mojave rattle-snake had declined dramatically, from 45.5 per cent to 17.5 per cent. The gopher snake had increased slightly, from 14.1 per cent to 16.9 per cent.

These figures show that, as the semi-desert grassland gives way to desert scrub, the western diamondback rattlesnake benefits at the expense of the Mojave species. The garter snake, and perhaps the gopher snake, on the other hand, probably benefit from increased ranching activity.

▼ Western diamondback rattlesnake, *Crotalus atrox*.

of snakes, while at the opposite extreme, another species, the Lake Taal snake, *Hydrophis semperi*, lives only in a freshwater lake on Luzon Island, Philippines.

The sea kraits live in coastal waters around Southeast Asia and islands in the southwestern Pacific region. One species, Crocker's sea krait, *Laticauda crockeri*, lives in a land-locked freshwater crater lake on Rennell Island, in the Solomons group. Sea kraits are less well adapted to an aquatic lifestyle than the sea snakes as they need to come ashore to lay their eggs and some species drag their food ashore before eating it.

Mountains
Montane environments occur throughout the world, often surrounded by other types of habitat such as forest, desert or grasslands and therefore becoming ecological islands. They present snakes with the serious problem of dealing with low temperatures, either seasonally or permanently. Tropical mountains are usually covered with forests, such as cloud forest, and a few of the species from lower altitudes may find their way into moderately high altitudes here on occasion, but mountain tops above the tree line at any latitude are not very heavily populated by snakes.

Of all the snakes, the vipers have most exploited the montane habitat. *Gloydius himalayanus* has been reported at an altitude of 4,900 m (16,000 ft) in the Himalayas, the highest recorded for any species of snake, although it is more commonly found between 1,500 and 3,000 m (5,000 and 10,000 ft). *G. strauchi* lives at elevations of up to 4,267 m (14,000 ft) in Tibet and *G. montirola* is found between 3,600 and 4,000 m (12,000 and 13,000 ft) in Szechwan, China. *G. halys* goes up to at least 4,000 m (13,000 ft) in central Asia and *G. intermedius* to at least 3,000 m (10,000 ft) in the desolate Lar Valley of Iran (now flooded), along with *Vipera latifi*. Three Vipera species from Europe, *V. berus*, *V. aspis* and *V. ursinii*, may reach up to 2,900 m (9,500 ft) in parts of their range.

In North America, the highest ranging species is the Mexican dusky rattlesnake, *Crotalus triseriatus*, recorded at more than 4,300 m (14,100 ft) in central Mexico. Several other rattlesnakes can be found at altitudes exceeding 3,000 m (10,000 ft), including the Pacific rattlesnake, *C. viridis*, in California and Arizona, the cross-banded mountain rattlesnake, *C. transversus*, the twin-spot rattlesnake, *C. pricei*, the rock rattlesnake, *C. lepidus*, and the small-headed rattlesnake, *C. intermedius*, in Mexico. Willard's ridge-nosed rattlesnake, *C. willardi*, and the blacktailed rattlesnake, *C. molossus*, reach almost to 3,000 m (10,000 ft) in Arizona and adjacent parts of Mexico.

In Africa yet another viper, the berg adder, *Bitis atropos*, is found up to 3,000 m (10,000 ft). Other species may reach similar altitudes in the mountains of central and East Africa but these areas are poorly explored herpetologically. Similarly, in the South American Andes, altitudinal records are poorly documented but, again, it would seem that vipers fill the montane niches with *Bothriopsis pulchra* occurring at around 3,000 m (10,000 ft) in Ecuador.

Urban and disturbed habitats
Although the encroachment of the human species in all its forms is nearly always disastrous to wildlife, including snakes, some man-made habitats can, in exceptional circumstances benefit certain species. Vermin, in the form of rodents which accompany human development, provide a ready source of food for some of the larger snakes. Harmless snakes are tolerated in some parts of the world for this reason. Other commensals, such as insects, attract small

▶ Mountains present a number of problems for snakes, including cold conditions for much of the year. Nevertheless, there are many specialised montane species, several of which live among the jumbled rocks of American talus slides (scree) here in the Chiricahua Mountains of Arizona.

lizards, especially geckos, and these, in turn, are preyed on by numbers of snakes.

Agricultural development in the developed world is usually accompanied by the use of chemical pesticides and herbicides which do nothing to enhance the habitat as far as snakes are concerned, but in developing countries, where low-tech agriculture is still carried out, snakes may again be tolerated or even encouraged by farmers due to their beneficial effects on rodent populations.

Judging by the numbers that are often found in them, abandoned dwellings often provide good refuges for snakes living in otherwise featureless habitats. They may be attracted by the cover afforded by the structures themselves or, again, by populations of rodents that live in such places. Flooded quarries and gravel pits can provide additional habitats for aquatic and semi-aquatic snakes, and at least one population of the queen snake, *Regina septemvittata*, has moved into an abandoned quarry on one of the islands in Lake Erie following an increase in the numbers of crayfish since the quarrying stopped. In Britain, many abandoned gravel pits, often stocked with fish for the benefit of anglers, have healthy populations of grass snakes, *Natrix natrix*.

▶ (above) Coconut and other plantations are good places to find snakes, which benefit from the influx of small rodents and may use piles of fallen palm fronds in which to hide. The species that move into these places, however, may not be the same ones that lived there before the plantation replaced natural forest.

▶ (below) Deserts are especially prone to habitat destruction and there is less chance of regeneration than there is in rainforests, for instance. Agriculture, involving irrigation, spraying, road building and human settlements, is one of the main threats.

ADAPTATIONS TO HABITATS

EACH TYPE OF ENVIRONMENT CAN BE REGARDED AS A SET OF CIRCUMSTANCES, OR PROBLEMS, THAT MUST BE FACED. NATURAL SELECTION IS THE PROCESS THROUGH WHICH ANIMALS ARRIVE AT A DESIGN AND FUNCTION THAT BEST SUITS THEM TO THE VARIOUS CIRCUMSTANCES THEY FIND THEMSELVES IN. UNDER A GIVEN SET OF CONDITIONS, INDIVIDUALS WITH QUALITIES THAT ARE BEST SUITED TO THOSE CONDITIONS ARE THE MOST LIKELY TO SURVIVE AND PASS ON THEIR GENES. THIS IS THE DRIVING FORCE BEHIND EVOLUTION, IN WHICH EACH POPULATION GRADUALLY CHANGES IN MANY SUBTLE WAYS UNTIL IT RESEMBLES ITS ANCESTORS LESS AND LESS. IT ADAPTS TO ITS SURROUNDINGS.

Habitats, then, tend to shape the animals that live in them. The size, shape, colour and other anatomical and behavioural modifications become the 'signature' of snakes from a particular type of habitat. The reason for this is quite simple. Two species of snakes, faced with identical problems, are quite likely to solve them in the same way, regardless of which part of the world they live in or what family they belong to. They come to share certain characteristics and may even look like one another. Where this produces very close similarities between unrelated species, the term 'convergent evolution' is used.

There is a corollary to this, of course. Where closely related populations find themselves in differing conditions, they will each eventually adapt to their own circumstances. Over a period of time and successive generations,they will begin to look different from one another and at some stage these differences will have reached the point where they could be classed as different species. This process is known as 'adaptive radiation'.

Although many snakes show very few extreme modifications, there are certain characteristics that can be identified as being more frequently seen in snakes from a certain type of habitat.

Snakes in trees

Arboreal snakes are most common in tropical and subtropical countries where over half of the species may live in trees. Here, temperatures are suitable for snakes even in the shade and, in addition, the high rainfall favours a dense growth of tall vegetation, giving arboreal animals plenty of scope.

In the rain forests of Southeast Asia five fascinating species of flying snakes, *Chrysopelea*, can launch themselves from high branches by suddenly straightening their body from an S-shaped position. As they fall they spread their ribs, causing their underside to become concave, and this allows them to parachute gracefully down to the ground or lower vegetation, covering a significant horizontal distance in the process. As a matter of interest,

▲ The ornate flying snake, *Chrysopelea ornata*, is one of five flying snakes that live in the rainforests of Southeast Asia.

other flying reptiles – nearly 30 species of flying dragons, *Draco* species, and six flying geckos, *Ptychozoon* – also live in the same rainforests but they have no counterparts in South or Central America. The more open structure of Asian forests, with well-spaced, tall trees with few branches below the canopy, seems to lend itself better to semi-controlled flight than the more luxuriant, crowded nature of Neotropical forests, hence this evolutionary quirk.

▼ Tall forest trees with wide gaps between them are suitable for use by reptiles that can glide long horizontal distances.

Arboreal species are found mainly among the Colubridae, Viperidae, Boidae and the Pythonidae and in some regions they may account for 50 per cent or more of the snake fauna. There is no obvious explanation for the lack of elapids (with exception of the mambas) among arboreal snakes, in spite of their close relationship with, and similarity to, the colubrids.

The most highly modified species are those that are totally arboreal, or nearly so. Many other species which spend differing amounts of time in trees and bushes may show certain of the characteristics of arboreal snakes, or may show the characteristics in less obvious ways.

Highly arboreal snakes have long, thin bodies, and long tails that are usually prehensile. Their bodies are often flattened from side to side; this gives them extra rigidity in the vertical plane, allowing them to cantilever out to bridge gaps between branches. Their heads are often long, with pointed snouts. Some of the tree snakes that are bulkier than average, such as the boas, pythons and some vipers, are nevertheless thin compared with their close relatives. Lightness of weight is an important consideration, especially for species that may need to crawl along thin branches in order to reach their food, and also helps the snake in stretching from one branch to another. The slender shape also helps some species to remain hidden when resting among vines, twigs and thin branches. The main disadvantages of a long, thin shape are the inability to store food or to produce large clutches of eggs. The tropical distribution minimises these problems, however, because food is usually abundant throughout the year in the tropics and breeding may take place for all, or most of, the year.

Nearly all arboreal snakes are green or brown in colour to escape detection, by predators or prey, or both. In most, the underside is lighter in colour than the dorsal surface, a pattern known as counter shading, also seen in fishes. The principle behind this is that light will fall on the dorsal surface, making it appear lighter, whereas the underside will be in shadow, making it appear darker; when viewed from the side, the expected three-dimensional image will be hard to discern. Many species have longitudinal lines, especially through the eye, in order to enhance their camouflage, and some of

CONVERGENT EVOLUTION AND PARALLEL EVOLUTION

Snakes living in different parts of the world are often very similar to one another, or they may share certain unusual characteristics. These characteristics may be related to defence, feeding, reproduction, or to other facets of their lives, and their similarities may be limited to one or two features – the pattern of their markings, the shape of their snout, their method of reproduction, etc. In other cases, the similarity may encompass several aspects of the snakes, to the extent that unrelated species from different parts of the world can be difficult to tell apart without close examination.

Species that look alike usually live in similar habitats, and have similar life-styles: they have similar ecological requirements. Each species has had to solve the same problems in order to survive, and each has arrived at the same solution.

Where the species are descended from a common ancestor they may have many shared genes, retained in the population because they are valuable; the term 'parallel evolution' is often used for pairs or groups of species of this type.

If groups of species come to resemble each other more closely than their ancestors did, however, the term used is 'convergent evolution'. Species that show convergent evolution do not share the same genes: their characteristics have evolved independently. Convergence can sometimes pose problems in the field of classification because similarities in appearance, or in certain characteristics, do not necessarily imply that the species that have them are closely related.

There are many examples of convergent evolution among snakes but it is perhaps best illustrated by the emerald tree boa, *Corallus caninus*, from South America, and the green tree python, *Morelia viridis*, from Australasia. These species look like one another and are about the same size. They also behave in a similar fashion, draping themselves over horizontal branches and hanging their heads down in order to ambush their food. The young of both species have different colours from the adults.

▼ The emerald boa, *Corallus caninus* (below left), and the green tree python, *Morelia viridis* (below right).

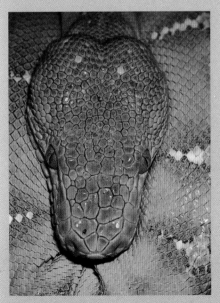 

▲ Snakes of the genus *Ahaetulla* have elongated, horizontal pupils and, hence, binocular vision. This allows them to judge distances accurately, a useful asset when climbing and striking at their prey.

the more spectacular ones have patterns simulating lichen-covered branches.

The eyes of arboreal snakes are typically large with vertical pupils, characteristic of nocturnal hunters. Those belonging to the genera *Ahaetulla* and *Thelotornis*, however, have horizontal keyhole shaped pupils that help them to judge distances well (see Chapter 2, pages 42, 43). Because prey can easily be lost if it is not firmly grasped, many arboreal snakes have long teeth, especially useful for penetrating the plumage of birds, while others are venomous species, either front- or rear-fanged, that hold their prey while their fast-acting venom takes effect.

Of the 'occasional' arboreal snakes, the rat snakes show a further adaptation. Some species, those more inclined to climb, have a well-defined ridge at the junction of their ventral and dorsal scales, so that each ventral scale has a corner on each side. This is used to gain purchase on rough vertical surfaces such as the bark of trees. A similar arrangement exists in the arboreal boas and pythons, *Corallus* and *Morelia*, which have laterally flattened bodies so that the ventral scales are narrow and also form ridges, although not as well defined as those of the rat snakes.

Burrowing snakes

Snakes that burrow are found mainly in tropical and subtropical regions because, like arboreal species, their opportunities to raise their body temperature above that of their surroundings are limited. Burrowing snakes are found in every family except the Tropidophiidae and the Acrochordidae. Several families, such as the Anomalepidae, Leptotyphlopidae, Typhlopidae, Aniliidae and Uropeltidae, contain *only* burrowing species. The degree to which they burrow, and therefore the degree to which they have evolved morphological adaptations, vary. Many species are exclusively burrowers – they spend all or most of their lives beneath the ground. Other species, however, burrow only on occasions and may regularly be found on the surface.

These species burrow to avoid danger or extremes of heat to lay their eggs or to find their prey, and so their adaptations to burrowing may not be obvious from their outward appearance. The type of substrate in which they live also plays its part in the direction in which adaptations occur. Species that burrow in loose, drifting sand, for example, will look rather different from those that tunnel through harder soils.

The confirmed burrowers, or tunnellers, are those species that spend their whole lives underground, only occasionally emerging on to the surface. They can be characterised by a number of anatomical features. Their heads are not well defined from their bodies and either their eyes are small or they may be very simple and covered with scales. Their bodies are cylindrical in cross-section and their scales are smooth and shiny. Their tails are short and, in some species, end in a short spine or more elaborately modified scales. The three most primitive families of snakes, the Anomalepididae, Typhlopidae and Leptotyphlopidae, show all these characteristics, as do members of the Uropeltidae, in which the tails of some species end in an oblique plate-like scale covered with small spines. All the snakes in these four families have skulls that are heavily built and which are more rigid than those of most other snakes, to help them to force their way through the substrate. This limits the size of food they can engulf, although this is not normally a problem as they all eat invertebrate, mainly ants and termites in the case of members of the three primitive families, and earthworms in the case of the shield-tails. Both *Xenopeltis* species, and *Loxocemus bicolor*, which is the sole member of its family, have cylindrical bodies, small eyes

◄ *Typhlops diardi*, from Asia, is a member of a family containing only burrowing snakes. Its eyes are rudimentary, it has smooth, shiny scales and a cylindrical body.

and smooth, shiny scales, especially *Xenopeltis*, which are beautifully iridescent when seen in sunlight.

Burrowing members of other families show varying degrees of adaptation. The burrowing boids all belong to the subfamily Erycinae, and include the rubber and rosy boas, *Charina bottae*, in North America, and the sand boas, *Eryx* and *Gongylophis*, in Africa, Asia and Europe. These species follow the typical pattern for burrowing snakes (smooth shiny scales, short blunt tail, wedge-shaped snout, small eyes).

Examples of burrowing snakes among the Colubridae are not so easily categorised. A number of them dig or burrow for their food and they may show slight modifications to the shape of their snouts; hognose snakes, both American and Madagascan, *Heterodon* and *Leioheterodon*, leaf-nosed snake, *Phyllorhynchus*, patch-nosed snakes, *Salvadora*, and long-nosed snakes, are all examples in which their common names reflect the salient features. Other species 'swim' through sand, moving effortlessly through loose particles in a typical serpentine manner. These species, which include the North American shovel-nosed snakes, *Chionactis*, and sand snakes, *Chilomeniscus*, and the African shovel-snouted snakes, *Prosymna*, have wedge-shaped snouts, underslung jaws and ingeniously designed nostrils that can be closed by valves to prevent sand from getting into places where it's not wanted. Members of the cobra family, including the African garter snakes, *Elapsoidea*, and the Australian *Simoselaps* (several of which are also called shovel-nosed snakes) parallel these adaptations across the continents, and some of them are practically identical to look at.

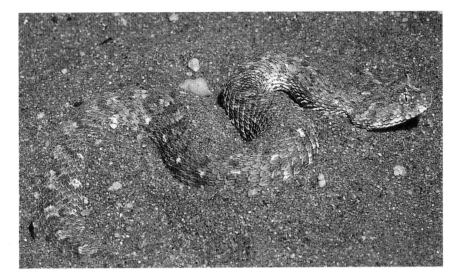

▲ Like several species that live in sandy or dusty places, the Namaqua dwarf adder, *Bitis schneideri*, hides itself by shuffling beneath the surface.

Other burrowing elapids include the coral snakes from South America, which use burrows to hunt their food which, in most species, consists almost exclusively of other burrowing reptile. As a rule, they do not form their own burrows but simply pursue their prey along tunnels that are already formed. Their adaptations to a subterranean life, therefore, are limited to the smooth, shiny scales, small eyes and cylindrical bodies.

The burrowing asps, or atractaspidids, are all burrowing species but, again, it seems probable that many of them move through the burrows that were made by their prey. Some species have a unique adaptation connected with their feeding habits: their fangs can be moved laterally and projected from the side of their mouth when it is closed. This enables them to stab their prey without opening their mouths, useful when in a burrow.

Snakes from sandy places often use a different type of burrowing. They are 'shufflers', working their way below the surface by rocking their bodies to and fro.

A different type of burrowing is undertaken by a number of desert species, especially those from sandy areas. These species are 'shufflers', working their way down below the surface by rocking their bodies to and fro. For this to be effective, the body must be flattened, or capable of being made so by spreading the ribs. The flanks are then drawn into a sharp edge, and are easily pushed into the substrate, which eventually covers them. Unlike most burrowing snakes, these species have keeled scales and are to be found almost entirely within the Viperidae, and include the sidewinder, *Crotalus cerastes*, from North America, the desert horned vipers, *Cerastes* species, from North Africa and the Middle East and the carpet, or saw scaled vipers, *Echis*, from Africa, the Middle East and western Asia. Burrowing in these species serves the purpose of concealment, as they rest with just their eyes, and horns if they have them, showing on the surface. From this position they are well placed to ambush their prey. A similar strategy is used by some sand boas, notably the Arabian sand boa, *Eryx jayakari*, which has upwardly directed eyes.

Aquatic snakes

Most snakes (including arboreal and burrowing forms) can swim quite well but some are totally aquatic or almost so. These include all three species of file snakes (Acrochordidae), certain colubrids, especially those belonging to the

▶ The snout of the shovel-nosed snake, *Chilomeniscus stramineus*, is modified for sand-swimming.

subfamilies Homalopsinae and, to a lesser extent, the Natricinae, and the sea snakes and sea kraits, Hydropheinae and Laticaudinae, which are either classified with the elapids or placed in families of their own. Only one viper, the cottonmouth, *Agkistrodon piscivorus*, is normally associated with water.

Adaptations seen, to a greater or lesser extent, in aquatic species, include the placement of the eyes and nostrils towards the top of the head, and a laterally flattened body and, especially, tail. The purposes of these modifications are fairly obvious: the nostrils enable the snake to breathe without breaking the surface, the upward pointing eyes enable it to watch for predators from above and the flattened tail helps to propel it quickly through the water.

Other adaptations include keeled scales (although these are not confined to aquatic and semi-aquatic species), which may help them to swim more easily. Heavily keeled scales are especially characteristic of the natricine colubrids, many of which are semi-aquatic, but are not always present in aquatic snakes. The scales of the file snakes are rough and granular, and are thought to help them to grasp fish when they coil around them.

The aquatic marine species have salt glands, either beneath the tongue (in the file snakes and the marine elapids) or up in the roof of the mouth (in the homalopsine colubrids).

Other adaptations are less obvious and are concerned with the mechanics of diving. Because these species remain submerged for considerable amounts of time, the capacity of the lungs has increased. In addition, part of the lung functions as an organ of buoyancy. In the case of a file snake, *Acrochordus granulatus*, an abnormally large amount of blood circulates, further adding to its diving efficiency. It has roughly twice as much blood as a land snake of similar size and the blood can hold more oxygen than that of other species of snakes. This is of great value because it allows the file snake to remain submerged for longer and, in particular, to remain hidden in underwater burrows during the day, when it is inactive. Furthermore, the file snake may be unique among marine species in being a 'sit and wait' predator, so its ability to remain motionless underwater for extended periods is of special importance.

WORLD PATTERNS OF DISTRIBUTION

EVEN WHERE SUITABLE HABITATS EXIST, SNAKES MAY BE ABSENT ALTOGETHER, OR CERTAIN FAMILIES MAY BE FOUND WHEREAS OTHERS ARE NOT. IN OTHER PLACES, SEVERAL FAMILIES ARE REPRESENTED. THEN AGAIN, CLOSELY RELATED SPECIES MAY BE SEPARATED BY SEVERAL THOUSAND MILES (OF OCEAN FOR INSTANCE). THE DISTRIBUTION OF SNAKES, AND THE WAYS IN WHICH THEY HAVE DISPERSED AND SPECIATED, ARE POTENTIALLY AMONG THE MOST FASCINATING ASPECTS OF THEIR BIOLOGY.

On a local level, species owe their distribution to their urge to spread into neighbouring areas as their population grows. A growing population is accompanied by an expanding range. A shrinking population, in contrast, often goes hand in hand with a contracting or fragmenting range. During successful periods, populations grow until they become overcrowded and this forces some animals into fresh areas. During less successful periods, areas are vacated, but these are not always the most recently populated ones. In this way, the range of a population changes almost imperceptibly and often in tune with changing environmental conditions. Some species adapt to new conditions better than others and they become widespread, often at the cost of more specialised species. The ranges of some species may become smaller and smaller until they disappear altogether – they become extinct.

Obviously, the spread of populations will, sooner or later, be stopped at physical barriers such as oceans, deserts, mountains, etc. Barriers for one species, however, may be dispersal corridors for others, depending on their habitat preferences. Over long periods of time, barriers and corridors change position as a result of geological activity. For example, snakes reached Madagascar from the African mainland before the Mozambique Channel was formed. Similarly, North and South America were

once separated and so the opportunities to disperse up and down the continents were limited until relatively recently.

When snakes first appeared, over 100 million years ago, the shapes of the landmasses were very different from how they are now. The southern continents, South America, Africa and Australia were joined together and, in addition, the pieces that were later to become Madagascar, India and Southeast Asia, were attached to them. The northern continents, North America, Europe and northern and central Asia, formed the other large landmass. Dispersal of terrestrial animals was therefore much easier than it is now and families that were radiating into different habitats were able to move into many different parts of their respective 'continents'. Because of this, the snake fauna of North America has more in common with that of Europe and central Asia than it does with South America, which shares similarities with the southern continents – Africa, southern Asia and Australia.

Only the more primitive families of snakes, early ancestors of the surviving families, had evolved at the time when some of the large landmasses were joined together. By the time the more familiar families began to appear, the shapes of the landmasses were already beginning to change. Some families evolved after certain pieces broke away and so their opportunities to disperse were more limited than those that evolved when they were together.

Although it is not possible to give a completely accurate account of the sequence of events, the relationships between the snake families, and their distribution, can help to fill in at least some parts of the timetable. For example, the absence of vipers in Australia indicates that this family evolved after Australia broke free from the large landmasses. Conversely, the presence of boas on Madagascar shows us that this family of snakes had already evolved before South America and Africa parted company.

Boas later became extinct on the African mainland (apart from some small burrowing forms) causing the apparent gap in their distribution; exactly the same pattern exists in iguanas, species of which occur in South America and Madagascar but not in Africa.

North America

The North American snake fauna includes five families. Of the primitive snakes, there are a few species of *Leptotyphlops*, and two species of boas, the rubber boa, *Charina bottae*, and the rosy boa, *Charina trivirgata*.

The colubrid fauna of North America is relatively rich in species although only three subfamilies are present. These are the colubrines (typical colubrids such as kingsnakes and rat snakes, *Lampropeltis* and *Pantherophis*), natricines (semi-aquatic snakes such as garter and water snakes, *Thamnophis* and *Nerodia*) and a few species of xenodontines (a poorly understood line of colubrids that includes the hognose snakes, *Heterodon*, among others). Closely related species of rat snakes and natricine snakes occur in Europe and Asia. These links are due to the ancient connection between North America and Eurasia. South America has no natricine snakes, showing that its connection to North America is, by contrast, relatively recent.

In North America, as elsewhere, the colubrids have radiated into many ecological niches. There are burrowing, terrestrial and semi-aquatic species, and a few arboreal ones. The wide variety of habitats and climatic zones has also helped to bring about diversity, with more species being found towards the south of the continent than in the cold northern parts. Especially rich areas include the subtropical swamps of southern Florida and the southwestern deserts.

Elapids are present, but only just, in the form of a small number of coral snakes, *Micrurus* and *Micruroides*: these

◀ Many North American snakes have obvious affinities with their Eurasian counterparts. For example, members of the genus *Nerodia*, such as the green water snake, *N. cyclopion* from Florida (above), are very similar to *Natrix*, species such as the dice snake, *Natrix tessellata* from southern Europe (below).

are predominantly tropical snakes that have larger populations in Central and South America.

Vipers, on the other hand, are well represented in North America but only in the form of pit vipers such as members of the genera *Agkistrodon* and the rattlesnakes, *Crotalus* and *Sistrurus*. Isolated mountain ranges in the southwest help to boost the number of species because they are home to a number of specialised species, especially small rattlesnakes.

Central and South America, including the Caribbean region

All three families of primitive burrowing snakes, the Typhlopidae, Leptotyphlopidae and Anomalepidae, are well represented in South America. Other primitive families that occur here include the pipe snake, *Anilius scytale*, the only member of the Aniliidae, the Boidae and the Tropidophiidae. Of the latter two families, the greater numbers of their species are found on the West Indian islands, although they are represented on the South and Central American mainland by some wide-ranging species, especially *Boa constrictor* and *Epicrates cenchria*. *Loxocemus bicolor*, the only member of the Loxocemidae, is found in the southern parts of Central America.

Although there are many colubrid snakes, most belong either to the Colubrinae or the Xenodontinae. In addition, there are a number of poorly

known species whose relationships have not been assigned yet. Some of these species are wide ranging. but others have very limited distributions. A number of colubrids are highly specialised, including the members of the Dipsadinae, which eat only molluscs.

The South American elapids consist entirely of coral snakes belonging to the genus *Micrurus*, of which there are many species. Vipers of the subfamily Crotalinae include a rattlesnake, large terrestrial pit vipers such as the bushmaster, *Lachesis meta*, and a great many arboreal species.

▲ North America

▲ Central and South America

Europe

This region has a great deal in common with North America, as has already been noted. It also contains small numbers of species from neighbouring regions that, between them, help to increase the number of families represented: these include the Typhlopidae and the Boidae, in the form of a single species of blind snake, *Typhlops vermicularis*, and a single sand boa, *Eryx jaculus*. In addition, a single species of pit viper, *Gloydius halys*, also enters Europe, technically speaking, although its range only includes a very small part of extreme eastern Europe.

The dominant elements of European snake fauna, then, are the colubrids and vipers. The colubrids include the colubrines and the natricines that have close relations in North America, and some rear-fanged species that may have invaded from North Africa and/or the Middle East: the cat snake, *Telescopus fallax*, which is found in southeast Europe, and the Montpellier snake, *Malpolon monspessulanus*, and the hooded snake, *Macroprotodon cucullatus*, which are found in southwest Europe. None of these is dangerous to man. All the European colubrids are terrestrial or semi-aquatic. A few species climb occasionally but there are no specialised arboreal species.

Vipers are well represented in terms of species, and are found in the far north as well as the southern part of the continent, around the Mediterranean region.

North and Central Asia and the Middle East

For the purposes of snake distribution, northern and Central Asia are similar to Europe because there is no barrier to dispersal between them and they all have similar temperate climates, They have many genera in common, therefore, although the pit vipers, *Gloydius*, and the sand boas, *Eryx*, are somewhat better represented in northern and Central Asia than they are in Europe.

The Middle East has a more distinctive snake fauna, largely because of its position, making it accessible to species from Africa as well as southern Asia. The predominant habitat is desert, and so many species are desert specialists.

The snake families Typhlopidae and Leptotyphlopidae are each represented by a single species and there are two boids, the sand boas *Eryx jaculus* and *E. jayakari*. The Colubridae of the region consists mainly of typical terrestrial species such as those belonging to the genus *Coluber*, as well as some smaller, more secretive species and rear-fanged species such as *Telescopus*. A single species of burrowing asp, *Atractaspis engaddensis*, is also found here, as is a single species of the Egyptian cobra, *Walterinnesia aegyptia*.

Vipers are present in the form of three horned vipers, *Cerastes*, up to four saw-scaled or carpet vipers, *Echis*, two false horned vipers, *Pseudocerastes*, and several members of the genus *Vipera*, mainly in the more mountainous parts of the region. The pit viper genera *Gloydius* has its stronghold here.

Southern and Southeast Asia

This region, which includes all of tropical Asia, is very rich herpetologically. Two of the three primitive burrowing blind snake families are present in numbers, only the Anomalepidae being absent. The boas are represented by one or two sand boas that reach these warmer parts and the pythons are well represented by several large species. Two of the three species contained in the Acrochoridae are found here, as are both xenopeltids, *Xenopeltis unicolor* and *X. hainanensis*. The Anomochilidae, Cylindrophiidae and Uropeltidae are also endemic to this region.

The Colubridae family is very well represented, and includes several subfamilies (perhaps families in reality) that are not found elsewhere. These include the

▲ North and Central Asia, and the Middle East

Calamariinae, Homalopsinae, Pareatinae and the Xenoderminae. Other colubrids found in southern and Southeast Asia include very many colubrines and natricines as well as several genera whose relationships with other colubrids are not altogether clear. Colubrids from this region include burrowing, terrestrial, arboreal and aquatic species.

Many species of elapids also occur here, including several cobras, kraits and Asiatic coral snakes but many smaller, less conspicuous species as well. The pit vipers are widely dispersed and include many species in several genera, notably *Trimeresurus* and its close relatives. The true vipers are represented by Russell's viper, *Daboia russelii*, and saw-scaled or carpet vipers, *Echis*. The unusual, and poorly known, Fea's viper, *Azemiops feae*, is found in the mountains of southern China.

▲ Europe

▲ Southern and Southeast Asia

A VERY SUCCESSFUL SNAKE

The adder, or northern viper, *Vipera berus*, is one of the world's most successful snakes. It has the largest geographical range of any terrestrial species (only the yellow-bellied sea snake, *Pelamis platurus*, can theoretically be found over a wider area) and occurs from Britain and Scandinavia, through much of Central Europe, across northern Asia almost as far as the Pacific Ocean. In the southern parts of its range it is restricted mainly to mountain ranges but elsewhere it has an almost continuous distribution, living in a wide variety of habitats, including moors and heaths, meadows, woodlands and marshes. Despite its huge range, there are only two subspecies: the nominate form, *Vipera berus berus*, and a Balkan form, *Vipera berus bosniensis*. (The form from Sakhalin Island, north of Japan, and the mainland opposite, is usually regarded as a separate species, *Vipera sachalinensis* nowadays.)

Not only is the adder the most widespread snake, it also occurs further north than any other, having been recorded to a latitude of 69°N in Scandinavia, well within the Arctic Circle. In northern parts of its range it is the only snake and in many other parts it is the most common species.

Apart from differences between the subspecies, the adder shows little variation throughout its range, although the ground colour, and the contrast between its zigzag markings and the background, may vary slightly. There is a rare form in which the zigzag is replaced by a continual vertebral stripe, and also a totally black form. Black specimens have a velvety appearance and sometimes crop up in otherwise normal colonies. More often, though, they form a substantial

part of a population, often towards the north of the species' range and, more especially, on some of the small islands in the Baltic Sea, where it is common. The dark coloration allows them to warm up quickly and this more than compensates for the costs of reduced camouflage.

That an endothermic animal should be so successful in the cold, northerly regions it inhabits is due to a suite of adaptations: small size, dark coloration and viviparous breeding habits. In parts of its range it may be forced to hibernate for eight months of the year, often emerging in the spring when patches of snow still lie on the ground. Truly a snake for all seasons.

ANIMALS ON ISLANDS

The importance of island size in species diversity has long been recognised. Habitat diversity is obviously relevant but area *per se* may be the overriding factor. The 'Equilibriums Theory' proposed by R. H. MacArthur and E. O. Wilson, in their book *The Theory of Island Biogeography* (Princeton University Press, 1967), attempts to explain this in the form of a mathematical model, as follows.

The number of species living on an island at any given time is thought of as an equilibrium between immigration of new species and extinction of species already there. As the number of species on the island increases, there are fewer new immigrants so the numbers of additional species gets smaller until it reaches zero (when all the mainland forms are present). As the number of species increases, however, the rate of extinction increases, partly because there are more species that can potentially become extinct and partly because, with a greater number of species, competition is likely to increase. Eventually, new immigrants will be arriving at the same rate as old ones are becoming extinct. Now an equilibrium has been reached and the number of species will remain constant.

On large islands, the rate of immigration will be greater than on small islands, all other things being equal, because large islands are bigger targets. The rate of extinction will not be greater, however, and so it will take a longer period of time for the equilibrium to be reached. This will result in a greater number of species.

This model was not concerned specifically with snakes but snakes can be expected to follow the prediction at least as well as other animals.

Africa and Madagascar

There are several members of the Typhlopidae and Leptotyphlopidae in Africa, but neither of these families occur in Madagascar. Boas are represented on the African mainland by the sand boas, *Eryx* and *Gongylophis*, and the Calabar ground boa, *Calabaria reinhardtii*. Three species of large boas, belonging to the endemic genera *Acrantophis* and *Sanzinia*, live on Madagascar, while a number of pythons occur on the African mainland.

Although colubrids are well represented, both on the African mainland and on Madagascar, the relationships of many genera are not clear. In some cases, there appears to be a link with species from South America, as there is with the boas. Most of the Madagascan genera are endemic to the island.

The family Atractaspididae is found almost entirely in Africa, the only exception being the one species that reaches over to the Middle East. African and Madagascan colubrids include burrowing, terrestrial, semi-aquatic and arboreal species, many of which are highly specialised.

There are many elapids, including several *Naja* species, the mambas, *Dendroaspis*, as well as several smaller genera. A similar situation exists within the Viperidae, where a number of typical, terrestrial vipers, including members of the genera *Bitis*, *Caucus* and *Echis*, are found throughout most of the continent in a variety of habitats but have not spread to Madagascar.

Australasia

New Zealand is easily dealt with because it has no snakes. Australia, on the other hand, is well endowed although only a few families are represented. Of the blind snakes, only the worm snakes, Typhlopidae are present. There are many pythons, though, and Australia is one of the centres of evolution for this family; pythons of one sort or another are found throughout the country. Two of the three species of file snakes, *Acrochordus*, also occur here.

The colubrids are thin on the ground, however, with a few species in the north of Australia and in New Guinea. This, and the complete absence of vipers, is due to the separation of the Australasian landmass early on in the continent's history. There are very many elapids, including species that have filled the niche usually occupied elsewhere by colubrids and vipers. Many sea snakes and sea kraits are found around the warmer coastlines and reefs of the continent.

The islands of the Pacific region have a diverse snake fauna and hold many unresolved riddles relating to the dispersal of snakes. Although their snake fauna is predominantly Australasian, the presence of the boid genus *Candoia* is puzzling as there are no other boas in the region. *Candoia* may have spread by rafting from the South American mainland, following the ocean currents in the same way as did the iguanas, also found in the Pacific region. Boas are live-bearing and have long gestation periods, a fact that would act in their favour should a pregnant female become marooned on flotsam.

▲ Africa and Madagascar

▲ Australasia

Snakes on islands

Islands have long held a fascination for biologists and naturalists, due to their often unique and unusual flora and fauna. Darwin's theory of evolution, for instance, germinated after a visit to the Galapagos Islands. Although these particular islands do have a small quota of snakes, other island groups are richer and potentially much more interesting herpetologically.

Islands are also important due to the high proportion of endemic species they support. Isolated populations evolve in ways that may quickly separate them, both in appearance and in behaviour, from the mainland stocks from which they arose. In fragmented island groups, each island may have one or more endemic species. The survival of these populations is vitally important because not only are they unique in their own right, but they are the results of natural experiments, holding the secrets of evolution in their genes.

Unfortunately, island populations are especially vulnerable and the threats to their survival are many. Small areas are very susceptible to rapid environmental changes, especially habitat destruction by human agencies. Introduced grazing animals, especially goats, contribute to and accelerate this process alarmingly and have been implicated in many extinctions, not just of snakes. Introduced vermin, such as rats and cats, find that species which have evolved in the absence of predators are easy targets and they attack eggs, juveniles and adults, quickly wiping out whole populations. Even introduced reptile from other parts of the world can have extremely negative effects, as in the case of the brown tree snake *Boiga irregularis* noted elsewhere (see page 93). Finally, many island forms are of interest to zoos and private collectors, especially when they become rare, and so the dangers of over-collecting are more serious than they would be on mainlands.

Animals that live on islands, then, are especially prone to speciation and to extinction. Other characteristics include greater or smaller size than their close relatives on the mainland. The giant tortoises of the Galapagos Islands and Aldabra are good examples of gigantism among island forms but there are examples among the snakes, too. The Chappell Island tiger snakes, *Notechis ater*

▲ Island species tend to be smaller than their mainland relatives: *Epicrates chrysogaster*, for instance, which comes from the Bahamas and the Turks and Caicos Islands, is among the smallest in its genus.

serventyi, live on two small islands in the Bass Strait between New South Wales and Tasmania, Australia. These tiger snakes are significantly larger than the mainland tiger snakes, with total lengths up to 240 cm (7 ft 10 in) compared to 160 cm (5 ft 3 in) for the Tasmanian form (*N. a. humphrysi*), their nearest relatives. The reason for their large size is almost certainly the unreliability of their food supply. They feed predominantly on sea bird chicks that are only present for a few weeks of the year and they must be capable of storing a large amount of fat to tide them over the remainder of the year: their large body size enables them to do so. Similarly, the speckled rattlesnakes, *Crotalus mitchelli angelensis*, from the island of Angel de la Guarda in the Gulf of California, grow half as big again as the mainland form, whereas those on some of the neighbouring islands are dwarf forms. No ecological studies have been carried out on these populations and the selective pressures that have pushed them in the direction of gigantism and dwarfism, respectively, are not known.

In fact, dwarfism in island snakes is a far more common trait than gigantism and very many small islands have populations of snakes that are significantly smaller than their nearest mainland relatives. For example, the smallest species of *Epicrates* boas on the West Indian islands, such as *E. chrysogaster* and *E. exsul*, are found on the smallest islands whereas the, largest islands (Cuba, Hispaniola and Jamaica) have relatively large species. These are

interspecific differences but there are other examples where the same species differs in its size depending on where it lives.

The European horn-nosed viper, *Vipera ammodytes* normally grows to about 80 cm (2 ft 6 in) on the Greek mainland but on several of the small islands where it occurs it rarely attains 50 cm (1 ft 8 in) and becomes mature at around 30 cm (1 ft). Other dwarf island populations are found among the boas and pythons. In the Pacific region, the subspecies of Macklot's python, *Liasis mackloti savuensis*, that is restricted to the small island of Savu in the Lesser Sunda group, is significantly smaller than the nominate form found on much larger islands, and a form of the common boa, *Boa constrictor*, from a group of small islands off the northern coast of Honduras (possibly extinct now) are considerably smaller than mainland forms.

How do snakes reach islands? There are several answers, and they depend to some extent on the type of island. Some islands are formed when part of the mainland breaks away, through erosion for example, or is separated by rising sea levels. Other islands are formed by volcanic action or by the emergence of coral reefs. Opportunities for the colonisation of each type of island will obviously differ and there are three basic methods by which snakes can reach them.

Firstly, they may already be present when the island is formed, when its connection with the mainland is severed. Secondly, they may reach isolated islands by rafting – precarious voyages made on uprooted trees and rafts of vegetation torn up from the mainland during storms and hurricanes. Thirdly, they may become introduced, either deliberately or accidentally by human agencies. The latter method is, of course, very recent.

Separation of islands through erosion and inundation is a gradual process – the isolation of the British Isles is an example. Many much smaller off-shore islands are also formed this way and they may be formed within lakes as well as in the ocean. Snakes already living on the section of land that becomes separated may continue to thrive there, assuming that conditions such as food supply continue to be suitable. Over long periods of time these populations may change, due either to chance or to selective pressures, and become separate races, subspecies or species. The age of the island will control the amount of speciation that has taken place – snakes living on ancient islands that have been colonised for a long time are likely to have evolved into different species and subspecies, whereas snakes living on more recently formed islands will be similar to their mainland counterparts.

Arriving on islands by rafting is a much more risky business. The chances of trees and other debris reaching an island is very slight indeed. Furthermore, the island on which the creatures land may not be capable of sustaining them, due to an unsuitable climate or lack of food. Even when a suitable habitat is available, a population of snakes will not become established unless at least one male and one female arrive together, or if a gravid or pregnant female is washed ashore. The assumption that island populations may be founded through the arrival of a clutch of eggs is an unlikely one because snake eggs are usually buried and, in addition, they have a low tolerance to salt water. Islands that have been colonised by rafting snakes are likely to lie in one of the main ocean current systems or to be situated opposite a large estuary. The islands of Trinidad and Tobago, for instance, have a rich snake fauna thought to be due, at least in part, to their position directly opposite the mouth of the Orinoco River in South America.

Introduction of snakes by human agency is a recent phenomenon. Snakes may be carried inadvertently in cargoes of wood, food and other produce, or they may be deliberately introduced. There are few cases of deliberate human introduction because snakes are not among the animals with which humans normally like to co-habit. The case of the European Aesculapian snake, *Zamenis longissima*, may be an exception. This species had religious significance in Roman times and its patchy distribution in parts of Central Europe may correspond to the localities of places of worship although some authors have cast doubt on this theory.

The events on Guam (see page 93) are not the only example of introduced snakes posing a threat to local animals. The Indian wolf snake, *Lycodon aulicus*, found its way to several parts of Indonesia and the Philippines and Mauritius in historic times and, most recently, to Christmas Island. This species' potential prey includes birds and lizards and its effects on the fauna of Christmas Island are being studied, while biologists from the Mauritius Wildlife Foundation are considering ways in which they might eliminate it from some of the smaller islands of the Mauritius group. In Europe, the small Mediterranean island of Mallorca is inhabited by two introduced species: the viperine snake, *Natrix maura*, which eats frogs and may have seriously depleted the population of the rare endemic midwife toad, *Alytes muletensis*, and the false smooth snake, *Macroprotodon cucullatus*, which eats geckos and wall lizards. Ironically, it is usually snakes that suffer as a result of introductions to delicate ecosystems whereas these species seem to have turned the tables.

Species introduced accidentally have the same problems to overcome as those that have rafted to islands – a reasonable number, of the right sexes, must be present in order for the population to expand and thrive. A single species of snake, the Braminy blind snake, *Ramphotyphlops braminus*, has overcome this limitation by being parthenogenetic: there are no males, and females begin to lay eggs as soon as they reach reproductive size. This greatly enhances their opportunities for extending their range and, sure enough, this species has a

large and scattered distribution, having established itself far from its natural home. In addition, it is small and lives in soil, therefore escaping detection quite easily. In particular, it has been introduced along with potted plants, especially crops such as rubber and coconut, when these have been exported to other countries. Since the conditions required by the snake are the same as those required by the plants, it is likely to find itself in a suitable environment automatically. Its original home is India but it is now also found on several small islands in the Torres Straits, Christmas Island and Hawaii, as well as parts of South Africa, Australia, Madagascar, Southeast Asia, Mexico and Florida. Its popular name in many of these countries is 'flowerpot snake' (see also page 149).

The snake fauna of any particular island will depend on several factors. The size of the island is obviously important. Large islands may have a range of habitats, making them suitable for a number of different types of snakes. They are also likely to sustain a good supply of other animals that snakes can prey on. Large islands also make easier targets for species that arrive by rafting. Small islands, by contrast, are likely to contain few habitats and are more susceptible to climatic and ecological disasters. They are more difficult targets for drifting debris to hit.

The distance from the mainland is another important factor. Islands closer to the mainland are more likely to be colonised than those at greater distances. Combining this aspect with island size, it is clear that large islands close to the mainland are likely to have a relatively rich snake fauna when compared with small islands that are a long way from shore.

These are not just theoretical assumptions. A number of studies have shown this pattern to apply, although the usual method is to include both lizard and snake species, not just snakes. Studies on West Indian islands of varying sizes and at varying distances from the mainland have shown that the figures are close enough to the predictions to be significant. In another example, of the 12 species of snakes found on at least one island in Lake Erie in North America, there was a strong correlation between island size and numbers of species and between distance from the shore and number of species.

ECOLOGY OF AN INTERLOPER: THE BROWN TREE SNAKE ON GUAM

The brown tree snake, *Boiga irregularis*, is a mildly venomous, back-fanged snake that is native to northeastern Australia, New Guinea and several other islands in the South Pacific region. In the late 1940s it was accidentally introduced to the small island of Guam, which is one of the Mariana group, probably via cargoes delivered to the United States military base towards the south of the island. In the absence of natural predators, it gradually spread throughout the island until, by 1982, it could be found in almost every part except small areas of savannah, where it seems unable to live.

By the 1960s there was concern over the declining populations of several species of forest birds on Guam. This trend continued throughout the 1970s and 1980s until, by 1987, all 10 forest species were in serious trouble: some had not been seen for several years and were presumed extinct on the island and those that remained had retreated to a single small area, in the part of the island that was furthest from the point of the snake's introduction, and their populations were estimated to contain fewer than 100 individuals. Those that were thought to be extinct included two endemic species, the Guam flycatcher, *Myiagra freycineti*, and the Guam rail, *Rallus owstoni*, and a third endemic species, the white tern, *Gygis alba*, was restricted to the northern coastline.

Apart from the birds, brown tree snakes appeared to be feeding on small lizards, including skinks and geckos, were causing power cuts by climbing into overhead cables, eating domestic chickens and causing concern among the human population. Thomas Fritts and colleagues noticed that the snakes

frequently attacked sleeping children, especially those aged between 1 and 3 months. Some of the injuries seemed to result from attempts to eat the children (*Journal of Herpetology*, 28(1):27-33).

Although the disappearance of the birds was closely correlated with the spread of the snakes, experiments carried out by Julie Savidge in 1987 provided additional evidence (*Ecology*, 68:660-668). She placed traps containing quails, *Coturnix coturnix*, in a variety of sites. In order to exclude terrestrial predators, such as rats, the quails were placed in mesh cages that were hung from branches. Three sites were in areas where forest birds had already disappeared and the population of snakes was known to be high; 75 per cent of all the quail had been eaten by snakes within four, seven and nine days. Two other sites were in areas where some birds still remained and which had only recently been colonised by the snakes; the predation rate was

lower in these sites, probably because the snakes were still feeding on wild birds or because there were fewer snakes in areas where they were newly established.

Since the brown tree snake lives in a state of ecological balance in its natural range, why should it have wreaked havoc on Guam? Firstly, it has few predators on Guam and so its population has been able to flourish unchecked. Secondly, the forest on Guam is less complex than forests elsewhere: most importantly, the canopy is lower and the snakes can scale the trees, and so birds are unable to find places to roost and nest where they are immune from attack. Thirdly, the abundant availability of alternative prey, in the form of lizards, provides a reservoir of food that the snake can fall back on when birds are eliminated from an area. Any attempt the birds make to reestablish themselves will be met by a fresh onslaught from the snake.

Island groups and their snake populations

Although it is not possible to catalogue all the small islands worldwide, or to list the snakes that inhabit them, it is interesting to select a few island groups and discuss the snakes that have managed to colonise them.

The West Indies

The West Indies are especially rich in reptile, including snakes, and the origins of these species are hotly debated. The larger islands, Cuba, Hispaniola, Puerto Rico and Jamaica, are thought to have been part of the mainland of Central America at one time. The smaller islands, the Lesser Antilles, are oceanic, however, and rose from the sea bed through volcanic activity and were later capped by the growth of coral reefs. Snakes on the West Indies, therefore, may have arrived by two separate methods – by being present on the various landmasses prior to their separation from Central America, or by rafting. Other authorities maintain that reptiles arrived on all the islands by rafting, the separation from the mainland having occurred too early for reptile to have taken advantage of it.

▼ Cuba is home to over half the known species belonging to the Tropidophiidae (dwarf boas or wood snakes). This is the spotted wood snake, *Tropidophis pardalis*.

Whichever way the snakes arrived on their islands, a great deal of speciation has taken place and very many endemic species are found on various islands. Naturally, the larger islands have the greatest numbers of species, especially Cuba and Hispaniola, with 22 species each. Jamaica, a moderately large island, by comparison has only six species of snakes. This surprisingly small number cannot easily be explained, but extinctions in recent years owing to human disturbance of the habitat and the introduction of domestic livestock and mongooses could be contributory factors. Typhlopids, boas and tropidophiids are the dominant groups in many cases. Cuba, for instance, has 15 tropidophiids. Of the smaller islands, a huge proportion have endemic species or subspecies of snakes, many of which are classed as endangered. A number of these rare snakes are confined to small satellite islands that have remained relatively unaffected by the depredations of the mongooses, rats, cats and goats that have been introduced to the larger islands.

In this context, snakes belonging to the genus *Liophis* have been particularly badly affected. *Liophis cursor*, formerly found on the island of Martinique, now survives only on a small island of 20 hectares (50 acres), while *L. ornatus*, from St Lucia, is now restricted to an island of only 10 hectares (25 acres). According to Henderson and Bourgeois (1993),[2] the main island populations of both these species have been extirpated by mongooses, *Herpestes auropunctatus*. Other species have fared only slightly better.

The Gulf of California

The islands within the Gulf of California form a discrete group and are of interest because they are surrounded by mainland on three sides. Several islands are less than 5 miles (8 km) from either the Sonoran coast or the peninsula of Baja California and were previously joined by land bridges. Other islands, though, are more isolated and are volcanic in origin and colonisation of these can only have taken place by rafting (human introduction of snakes appears not to have occurred). The dominant genus of snakes on these islands is *Crotalus*, the rattlesnakes, and a number of unique forms are found there. Eleven species are each found on at least one island. One of these, *C. catalinensis*, is endemic to one island (and has undergone some interesting ecological changes, see page 130) and seven subspecies of mainland forms are restricted to one or more islands. The larger islands, such as Tiburon, have several species whereas some of the small islands have only one or two (or none).

The Cyclades

The only sizeable groups of small islands in Europe are those of the Aegean Sea.

▲ The Seychelles wolf snake, *Lycognathophis seychellensis*, is one of the two species endemic to the Seychelles Islands.

Of these, the Cyclades has the most diverse snake fauna. At least six taxa are endemic to one or more islands within the group: it is not clear at present which of these are full species and which are subspecies as the taxonomy of the snakes from this region is in the process of revision. Altogether, there are 13 species of snakes and the greatest totals are found on the islands of Tinos (eight), Andros, Milos and Paros (six each) and Kea, Kimilos, Mykonos and Naxos (five each): these are all large islands. Nine islands have only one species each: these are all small islands.

Pacific islands

The Pacific island groups, of which there are many, have not been well colonised by snakes. Many of them are extremely scattered and isolated and they would make difficult targets for floating debris. The boas, *Candoia*, have already been mentioned (see page 90) in connection with the mystery surrounding their presence in what is otherwise python territory. The Solomon Islands, situated to the east of New Guinea, have representatives from six families, including the endemic genus *Salomoneleps*. Many island groups have no native snakes at all and these include Hawaii, although the flowerpot snake, *Ramphotyphlops braminus*, has been introduced here along with several other islands in the region. Perhaps the greatest enigma is the presence of an elapid, *Ogmodon vitianus*, on Fiji. This snake, which lives thousands of miles from its nearest relatives, has only rarely been collected. It grows to 30 cm (12 in) and what little we know of its natural history indicates that it is a burrowing species that eats earthworms and lays eggs.

Indian Ocean islands

The islands of the Indian Ocean, with the exception of Madagascar, tend to be small and isolated. This has meant that snakes have had difficulty in reaching them but there are a few species scattered among them. The Seychelles, for instance, has three species of snakes. One, the flowerpot snake, is an introduction but the other two, the Seychelles house snake, *Lamprophis geometricus*, and the Seychelles wolf snake, *Lycognathus seychellensis*, are endemics. The house snake has close relatives on the African mainland but the wolf snake has no close relatives and is the only member of its genus.

NOTES

1. Stafford, P. J. (1991), 'amphibian and reptile of the joint services scientific expedition to the Upper Raspaculo. Belize, 1991', *British Herpetological Society Bulletin*, (38):10-17.

2. Henderson. R. W. and Bourgeois, R. W. (1993), 'Notes of the diets of West Indian Liophis', *Caribbean Journal of Science*, Vol 29 (3-4): 253-254.

CHAPTER 5
FEEDING

The feeding behaviour of snakes is of great interest because so many unique features are involved. These are partly due to the elongated body shape, which has several implications with regard to capturing, subduing and swallowing prey. This, together with the lack of limbs, has led to the evolution of specialised methods of prey capture and the means of overpowering it before it has a chance to inflict injuries. To this end, the shape and position of their teeth are modified and show great variation, linked to the type of prey and method of hunting employed. Many species have evolved venom and the apparatus with which to deliver it, although, again, there is great variation. In the final stages of feeding, the option of dismembering prey is not available and so it must be swallowed whole. This is made possible by modifications to the skull and skin. Finally, some species have the additional problem of finding enough food in areas that may be of very low food productivity, such as deserts.

A desert horned viper, *Cerastes cerastes*, lies partially buried, in ambush for prey.

TYPES OF FOOD

ALL SNAKES ARE CARNIVOROUS. THE RANGE OF PREY THAT THEY EAT, HOWEVER, IS VERY WIDE AND IT SEEMS HIGHLY LIKELY THAT, COLLECTIVELY SPEAKING, SNAKES WILL EAT JUST ABOUT ANYTHING THAT IS ALIVE (OR HAS BEEN ALIVE) AND THAT WILL FIT INTO THEIR BODIES.

Methods of establishing the diet of snakes include dissection of preserved individuals, analysis of faeces, regurgitation of prey (either voluntary or induced), observations in wild and captive specimens, and implication. Of these, records of snakes in captivity must be used cautiously, while implied diets where, for instance, a snake is seen entering the nest of a bird or mammal, must also be carefully examined and backed up, if possible, by other evidence.

Specialists and generalists

Whatever the methods used, it is well established that some species eat a variety of prey types whereas others are specialists. Some species eat different prey at different stages in their lives. To a large extent, the prey that each species eats depends on availability and, where a species is found over a wide area, its preferred prey may differ if the occurrence of prey species vary within this range. The availability of an animal as prey depends not only on its occurrence in the same area as the snake but also on its habits and the ease with which it can be caught and eaten.

In order to exploit certain types of prey efficiently, morphological and behavioural modifications may be necessary. If this happens, the species concerned is likely to become a specialist and may be ill suited to take an alternative type of prey. The egg-eating snakes belonging to the genera *Dasypeltis* and *Elachistodon* are good examples.

Other types of prey, though, may require similar handling – snakes that eat lizards will usually eat snakes as well and may also eat small mammals if they are available. These snakes are generalists. There are more dietary generalists than specialists among snakes. This is exactly what we would expect: no species wants to exclude a potentially valuable type of prey if it is available, or even if it is available only occasionally. On the other hand, those species that have specialised have staked their existence on the availability of just one type of prey. Although this may make them more vulnerable to an erratic food supply, they are usually better placed and better equipped to deal with that particular type of prey than a generalist would be.

When 'deciding' to become a specialist or a generalist, a species has many factors to weigh up. To become a specialist, it is necessary to 'know' that the chosen food supply is going to be available regularly throughout the year, and there must be plenty of it. It will be easier for a specialist to become successful if its chosen food is one that is not already heavily exploited by generalists. These criteria seem pretty hard to meet, and this is probably why there are so few specialists.

Even so, snakes have tendencies to look for certain types of prey, even though they may not be restricted to them. These could be called 'preferred' prey types. The preferred prey of most species is fairly logical – they prefer the type of prey that is most common, or most easily caught, in the places they frequent. If a particular prey is extremely abundant, a snake may appear to be specialising in it, even though it would take other prey if it were also available. Many West Indian snakes eat *Anolis* lizards, for instance, but also take other lizards and other types of prey – *Anolis* just happen to be incredibly abundant and are often the only item in the stomachs of a series of such snakes. In other places, however, there are no predominant prey types and in these places we would expect most snakes to take a range of prey species.

The following accounts of snakes' diets are broken down into prey types. It is unavoidable that specialists should get most of the attention (they tend to be more interesting when it comes to feeding habits) but it should be obvious from what has already been said that snakes will not always, or often, fit neatly into one or more category of prey types.

▶ (opposite top left) The montane slug-eater, *Asthenodipsas vertebralis*, from Malaysia. This nocturnal snake and several closely related species are the Asian counterparts of the American *Dipsas* and *Sibon* species.

▶ (opposite top right) *Sibon nebulata*, a tropical species that feeds exclusively on slugs and snails.

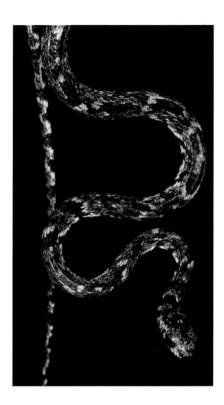

Invertebrates

Starting at the bottom of the scale, the small burrowing snakes belonging to the most primitive families, Typhlopidae, Anomalepididae and Leptotyphlopidae, have small diameters and small mouths. Unlike those of more advanced snakes, the jaws of these species are fairly rigid and so food items must be small in order to be accommodated. Because they eat only small prey, they must eat a great number of them: this further restricts their diet to species that can be found in large numbers. In practice, these are the social insects, especially ants and termites. Many records of the diets of these species are based on casual observations and make certain assumptions. Shine and Webb (1990)[1], however, surveyed the diet of four Australian species of *Ramphotyphlops* by dissecting museum specimens and found that 93-97 per cent of the stomach contents were ant pupae and larvae. Individual snakes contained up to 1,400 prey items. These species rarely ate termites or adult ants. By contrast, White *et al.* (1992)[2] found that the Hispaniolan species *Typhlops syntherus* ate mostly termites but also took adult and larval beetles, and spiders. *Typhlops richardi* and *T. biminiensis* are also thought to eat termites on occasion.

Species of *Leptotyphlops* eat mostly termites and are often found in termite nests. To protect themselves from attack, they smear themselves with a substance they produce in their cloacal glands: this contains pheromones which 'switch off' the aggressive behaviour of the soldier termites, demonstrating a long-term commitment to this particular diet. Research by Nathan J. Kley has thrown light on the methods of feeding in these small and secretive snakes. Leptotyphlopid snakes feed by repeatedly extending and retracting their fused lower jaw – where their teeth are – thereby drawing the prey into their mouth. Typhlopids, on the other hand, have teeth on their upper jaw but not the lower. They have a similar method of pulling the prey into their mouth although the upper jaws are not fused and may be slightly out of synchrony with each other. These two methods of feeding have been described as 'mandibular raking' in leptotyphlopids and 'maxillary raking' in typhlopids and are completely different to the method used by higher snake with flexible jaws, which work each half of the jaw alternately to pull the prey into the mouth and throat, so that jaws almost seem to be walking over the prey.

Many snakes eat insects and other invertebrates. Some specialise in this type of prey whereas others eat them as additional food items. Earthworms are the staple diet of many shield-tailed snakes (uropeltids) such as those belonging to the genera *Rhinophis* and *Uropeltis* of Sri Lanka and southern India. North American colubrids such as the garter snakes, *Thamnophis*, also take earthworms, although some species tend to eat them more than others: Butler's garter snake, *T. butleri*, is thought to specialise in them, at least to some extent. The Mexican garter snake relies heavily on earthworms and leeches when young, moving on to fish and amphibians as it grows. Birth of the young, in July and August, coincides with the greatest availability of these prey species and a similar correlation has been found with two related species, *Thamnophis sirtalis* and *Nerodia sipedon*.

The smaller forms of the ringneck snake, *Diadophis punctatus*, readily eat earthworms in captivity. This species is a generalist and eats pretty much anything it can find. Some of the larger forms live in arid regions where there are few if any earthworms.

Slugs and snails present peculiar problems due to the slime with which they cover themselves and, in the case of snails, a hard, indigestible shell. They are therefore not widely eaten by snakes, except for certain species that have evolved the means of overcoming these problems. Slug- and snail-eating snakes occur in several parts of the world and are found among the members of at least four subfamilies of colubrid snakes. Usually the species involved tend to specialise in these prey and eat little or nothing else, although there are exceptions. The North American red-bellied snake, *Storeria occipitomaculata*, eats mainly slugs and its congener, DeKay's brown snake, *S. dekayi*, eats them sometimes but also eats a wide variety of other soft-bodied invertebrates. Rossman and Myer (1990)[3] describe the methods of feeding of these two species. The snakes grasped the soft bodies of the snails and pushed them along the substrate until the snail became wedged against a piece of rock. The snake then twisted its head through 180° or more and maintained this position until the snail's muscles began to tire. The body of the snail was then pulled from its shell and eaten. The whole process took from 12 to almost 20 minutes. A third North American species, the sharp-tailed snake,

Contia tenuis, also feeds on slugs but it is not known if it also takes snails. *Storeria* and *Contia* both have long teeth on their mandibles, thought to be an adaptation to gripping slugs and snails.

Members of the subfamily Dipsadinae, from Central and South America, are all highly specialised slug and snail eaters. They have characteristically blunt snouts, and long teeth at the front of the lower jaw, which is more rigid than in other snakes. Species in the genus *Dipsas* are further modified by the absence of a groove along the chin (mental groove). These adaptations help the snakes to extract snails from their shells. They brace the shell of the snail against the roof of their mouth and thrust the lower jaw between the shell and the fleshy part of the snail. The long front teeth are used to hook the body out of the shell, with a twisting movement of the jaw. Using this method, *Dipsas* and related species can extract snails' bodies quicker than snakes that have no such modifications: Sanzima (1989)[4] timed the process at one to six minutes (in *Dipsas indica*), and also describes the way in which this species may wedge the snail in its own coils. On the other hand, the same species handled slugs even more quickly (10 to 45 seconds) and ate them by simply lifting them away from the substrate and swallowing them, usually tail first. Other authors have noted that, in related species, slugs seem to be preferred over snails, presumably because of the reduced handling time.

African slug and snail eaters belong to the genus *Duberria*, of which there are two species. They live in damp situations and hunt by following the slime trails of the molluscs. Slugs are merely lifted off the ground and eaten in exactly the same way as they are by the *Dipsas* species. Snails are reputed to be grasped by the body and bashed against a hard surface until the shell breaks, but there appears to be no firsthand confirmation of this.

In Asia, the members of the subfamily Pareatinae are the counterparts to the American dipsadinine snakes; all feed exclusively on slugs and snails and have blunt snouts and lower jaws that can be thrust forward to a greater degree than most other snakes. Their method of snail extraction is unknown and may not have been observed. A specimen of the monotypic *Aplopeltura boa* that ate snails and slugs in captivity always fed at night

▲ The African slug-eater, *Duberria lutrix*, feeds on slugs and snails, which it finds by following their slimy trails. The specimen illustrated is a rare colour mutant, lacking most of its pigment.

and the method of feeding was not observed. It was captured at night, foraging among damp vegetation on the fringes of rainforest.

Soft-bodied insects and their larvae are widely eaten by many small snakes. The North American green snakes feed largely upon them although they also eat other types of insects. The crowned snake, *Tantilla relicta*, eats mainly larval tenebrionid beetles, which may make up as much as 90 per cent of its diet. Many other small, secretive snakes undoubtedly rely heavily on this source of food, although positive information is lacking. A rather surprising case of insect eating is that of the European meadow viper, *Vipera ursinii*. Luisella (1990)[5] found that captive adults ate a significant number of wingless orthopterans while in captivity, especially at certain times of the year. Furthermore, he found that young individuals, less than one year old, would only accept grasshoppers of certain species and usually refused crickets.

Among the more unusual types of invertebrates eaten by snakes are aquatic crustaceans. The sea snake *Aipysurus laevis* will eat prawns and crabs that it finds in crevices in reefs. It also eats fish. The homalopsine colubrid, *Fordonia leucobalia*, lives on mud flats and is highly specialised, feeding exclusively on small crabs that it pins down with its body or constricts. The semi-aquatic Graham's water snake, *Regina grahami* from southeastern North America eats only freshwater crayfish (crawfish) and, according to research carried out by Seigel (1992),[6] takes them only when they have recently moulted and their cuticle is soft, presumably to facilitate

swallowing. Other species in this genus also eat crustaceans. The file snake *Acrochordus granulatus* also eats crabs on occasion as do the *Nerodia* species that are sometimes found in brackish habitats, although fish form the most important part of the diets of all these snakes.

Centipedes are eaten by the specialised *Aparallactus* species, aptly known as centipede eaters, from southern Africa. They are burrowing snakes, sometimes associated with termite nests, which their chosen prey also inhabit. Centipedes may also be eaten by the American hook-nosed snakes, *Ficimia*, which are rear-fanged, although these species apparently prefer spiders. The Central American centipede snake, *Scolecophis atrocinctus*, is also a specialist, as its name suggests, and eats nothing but centipedes.

▲ The Central American centipede snake *Scolecophis atrocinctus* is a centipede-eating specialist.

Fish

Moving on to vertebrate prey, there are no groups that do not form part of the diet of snakes somewhere. Fish are the main prey of most aquatic and semi-aquatic snakes (other than the specialised crustacean eaters mentioned above). With few exceptions, the sea snakes eat fish, often crevice-dwelling reef species which the snakes, with their narrow heads and necks, are well adapted to extricate from their hiding places. For the same reason, fish that live in burrows in mud are often hunted. As a rule, slow-moving fish are the favoured prey but some sea snakes also look for more active fish while they are resting or sleeping at night. Others specialise in particular types of fish; eels are popular, especially among members of the genus *Hydrophis*, and small gobies and blennies form a large part of the diet of other species. An interesting case of resource sharing occurs in the brackish Lake Te-Nngano in the Solomon Islands; two species of sea kraits, *Laticauda colubrina* and *L. crockeri* live here but, whereas the former eats only eels, the latter eats only sleeper gobies.

The two species of sea snakes belonging to the genus *Emydocephalus* and a third species, *Aipysurus eydouxii*, are extreme specialists: they eat only fish eggs, from crevices in coral reefs and sand burrows. As a result, the venom apparatus on all three species has degenerated. There are other sea snakes that eat fish eggs, such as some *Hydrophis* species and *Aipysurus laevis*, but these also eat other prey.

Freshwater fish-eating snakes are numerous and are especially common among the natricines, most of which inhabit marshy areas and the fringes of ponds and lakes. The homalopsine colubrids from Southeast Asia are probably all fish eaters apart from the crab-eating species mentioned above. Together with the sea snakes, these species are among the most aquatic of snakes and some species rarely, if ever, leave the water. Most feed opportunistically, quietly waiting in dense aquatic vegetation and ambushing their prey. The tentacled snake, *Erpeton tentaculatum*, which also belongs to this subfamily, was thought to use the two strange appendages on its snout to lure fish within range. This theory has now been disproved and the structures are thought to break up the outline of the snake, enhancing its camouflage.

All three species of file snakes, *Acrochordus*, are aquatic and feed mostly on fish. They are unusual in that they constrict their prey before swallowing it and the rough, warty skin of these species is an adaptation that enables them to handle slippery prey.

Among the viper group, only the cottonmouth, *Agkistrodon piscivorus*, is an important fish eater, although it also eats an astonishing variety of other prey. A very interesting observation by Wharton (1969)[7] concerns the Florida cottonmouth, *A. p. conanti*, on Sea Horse Key where the snakes feed heavily on marine fish dropped by adult seabirds returning to the nest with food for their chicks. Other readily available items of food, such as rats, squirrels, small birds and lizards, sustain the snakes when the birds are not nesting. A number of island-dwelling lizards also make their living by scavenging around seabird colonies.

Amphibians

Many of the species that eat fish also eat amphibians when they are present. Again, this diet tends to be available mainly to aquatic and semi-aquatic snakes, especially species such as the American and Eurasian water snakes, *Nerodia*, *Natrix* and so on. There are snakes from drier habitats that eat amphibians; these include the American hognose snakes, *Heterodon*, which have modified snouts in the form of an upturned rostral scale that they use to root out toads that have burrowed into the soil, and the African night adders, *Causus* species. Many arboreal snakes, including the young of larger species such as the green tree python, *Morelia viridis*, eat tree frogs. Some of these snakes are generalists, however, eating a wide variety of prey according to availability.

Frogs and toads

Species that eat frogs, either exclusively or casually, tend to swallow them live. Few frogs have defences, although some

▼ The cross-barred tree snake, *Dipsadoboa aulica*, from southern Africa, feeds on geckos and small frogs. Here it is eating a reed frog, *Hyperolius tuberlinguis*.

▲ A green tree snake, *Dendrelaphis punctulatus*, from southeast Australia, eating a reed frog.

species, notably members of the Dendrobatidae (poison dart frogs) from South America, produce highly toxic skin secretions that make them immune to predation. A frog-eating snake, *Liophis epinephelus*, from Central and South America is the only known predator of the world's most toxic animal, the yellow poison-dart frog, *Phyllobates terribilis*. The snake is immune to the toxin of all poison dart frogs, including juvenile *P. terribilis*, but not adults, apparently. Toads belonging to the genera *Bufo* and others also produce toxins and this may deter snakes on occasion although they are most definitely eaten by certain species. The European grass snake, *Natrix natrix*, for instance, will eat them in areas where they are the most abundant prey available although in other areas they may avoid them.

The South and Central American cat-eyed snake *Leptodeira septentrionalis*, and possibly other members of its genus, feed on the eggs of frogs, among other items, a habit that is only made possible by the large number of arboreal frogs that lay their eggs on leaves overhanging pools. Other snakes, for instance *Rhadinea bilineata* and *Liophis atraventer*, both from South America, are also known to eat frogs' eggs, usually those of the terrestrial breeding species belonging to the *Eleutherodactyhus* genera and related kinds.

Salamanders

Salamanders are absent from Australia and from much of Africa, but in areas where they are reasonably common they may be eaten by the same species that eat frogs and toads. Once again, a number of them produce defensive toxins from glands in their skin and they are sometimes brightly marked to give warning of the fact. The European fire salamander, *Salamandra salamandra*, which produces particularly strong toxins, appears not to be eaten by any snakes. Other species, such as the crested newt, *Triturus cristatus*, only gain partial protection by this means as some grass snakes will eat them. In North America, salamanders seem not to have evolved such powerful toxins, and are eaten by a variety of snakes, especially garter snakes and other small species that live in damp environments. Lind and Welsh (1990),[8] for instance, found that *Thamnophis couchii* in northern California ate adults and larvae of the Pacific giant salamander, *Dicampton ensatus*. In one instance a snake weighing 92 g (3.24 oz) ate a salamander weighing an massive 80.9 g (2.85 oz), representing 88 per cent of the weight of the snake. Other snakes in the same study contained the tails of larval salamanders.

At present, South American salamanders belong to the genus *Bolitoglossa*, the tropical lungless salamanders. They are small and arboreal and observations of snakes eating them are necessarily sparse, although there is one record of a *Bolitoglossa altamazonica* that was found in the stomach contents of *Liophis reginae*, a species that also eats fish, frogs and tadpoles.

In a most unusual case, a Rubber Boa, *Charina bottae*, disgorged an adult Ensatina salamander, *Ensatina eschscholtzii*, together with 12 eggs of the same species. The adult had been eaten first, followed by its eggs. This salamander guards its eggs by coiling around them.

Reptiles

Reptiles form the largest part of the diet of a huge number of snakes and at least half the species depend heavily or entirely on them.

Lizards

Small lizards such as geckos, skinks, small iguanids and lacertids can be very abundant in favourable habitats. For this reason they represent an enormous reservoir of food for a wide variety of snakes. Furthermore, lizards are mostly defenceless and are easy prey to snakes, which can catch, overpower and swallow them with little risk of injury.

Although there are lizard-eating snakes from all parts of the world, two areas in particular are worthy of note. In Australia, the number of small mammals is strictly limited due to the mostly dry and arid nature of the country. Reptiles, however, are numerous, especially small species of skinks and geckos. These are the main food for a large variety of snakes, some of which eat nothing else. Even large species such as the whipsnakes, genus *Demansia*, will eat small lizards here because there is a shortage of larger, more substantial prey, and unlike other parts of the world, where larger snakes tend to eat larger prey, there seems to be little such correlation among the Australian snakes that have been studied so far. The sole exceptions are the taipans, which appear to feed exclusively on warm-blooded prey (see below).

A somewhat similar situation exists on the West Indian islands, where the most common vertebrates by far are the slender lizards belonging to the genus *Anolis*. These lizards are eaten by almost all West Indian snakes at some stage in their lives and some species eat almost nothing else. For instance, one study revealed that over 60 per cent of the food

▶ A juvenile diamond python, *Morelia spilota spilota*, eating a small skink. This species switches to a diet of small mammals and birds as it grows larger.

eaten by eight species of colubrids living on the large island of Hispaniola were *Anolis* lizards. In another study, Henderson (1993)[9] found that on a number of West Indian islands, young tree boas, *Corallus cookii*, fed exclusively on *Anolis* lizards. Larger tree boas also ate the lizards but took other types of prey as well. Overall, *Anolis* formed about 66 per cent of the species' diet. By contrast, on the South American mainland, lizards constituted less than 5 per cent of the prey taken by the same species. It is worth remembering that these boas have highly efficient heat sensing facial pits, and may be better equipped to detect and hunt warm-blooded prey than lizards. In the early evening however, the body temperatures of lizards will be above that of their surroundings and can also be detected by the same means. The other group of West Indian boas, those belonging to the genus *Epicrates*, seem not to have adapted to a diet of lizards (with the exception of two

▼ The wolf snakes, *Lycophidion* species, from southern Africa, specialise in eating diurnal lizards, which are captured while asleep.

species, *E. gracilis* and *E. monensis*) and the reason for this is unclear.

A species of spiny-tailed iguana, *Ctenosaura similis*, seems to be a regular if seasonal prey to *Loxocemus bicolor* in Costa Rica, where the snakes have been seen catching hatchling lizards as they emerged from their nests, along with the young of green iguanas, *Iguana iguana*, which share the same nesting sites.

The snakes of the Galapagos islands, of which there are two species and several subspecies, are all lizard eaters and the

largest individuals prey on young Marine Iguanas, *Amblyrhynchus cristatus*. Smaller snakes eat lava lizards, *Microlophus* species.

Although snakes are unable to dismember their prey, lizards sometimes dismember themselves by discarding their tails when they are captured. Lizard tails have been found in the stomachs of a number of species of snakes, and it seems likely that some small snakes exploit the system by catching lizards that would normally be too large to swallow but which can be relied upon to donate their tails!

Amphisbaenians

Amphisbaenians (sometimes known as worm lizards) are closely related to the lizards and the snakes but are more limited in their distribution, being found in the tropical and subtropical parts of the Americas, and in North Africa, southwestern Europe and the Middle East. All are burrowing reptiles, spending the greater part of their time out of sight beneath the surface. This does not eliminate them from the menu of snakes, however, and a number of burrowing snakes actually specialise in eating them. These include members of the coral snake genus *Micrurus*, which follow the amphisbaenians through their tunnels. *M. corallinus* feeds mainly on the amphisbaenian *Leptosternon microcephalum* in southeastern Brazil and *M. laticollaris* eats *Bipes canaliculatus* in Mexico (Papenfuss, 1982).[10] In the latter survey, many *Bipes* were found with damaged tails, possible evidence of predation by snakes. The colubrid burrowing snakes of the genus *Elapomorphus* also seem to specialise in amphisbaenian prey, as does *Pseudoboa neuwiedii*, judging from its behaviour in captivity (Perez-Santos and Moreno, 1987).[11]

In Africa, the atractaspidid snake *Chilorhinophis gerardi*, is a confirmed eater of amphisbaenians although all members of the Atractaspididae are burrowing snakes that feed largely on other burrowing reptiles and there can be no doubt that these include worm lizards whenever they are encountered. The quill-snouted snakes, *Xenocalamus*, however, of which there are five species, are highly specialised and feed only on worm lizards, which they catch and swallow underground.

Turtles

Turtles must rate highly on the list of indigestible food items but are not completely overlooked. Among the species eaten by snakes are musk turtles, a common snapping turtle, box turtle, two species of sliders (and baby American alligators) found in the stomachs of Cottonmouths, *Agkistrodon piscivorus*, and a hatchling hawksbill turtle that was eaten by a Cuban ground snake, *Alsophis cantherigerus*. Less surprisingly, freshwater turtles, and caimans, are eaten by Anacondas, *Eunectes murinus*, in South America.

Snakes

That snakes eat snakes is hardly surprising. After all, they are the ideal shape to accommodate each other. Many lizard-eaters probably eat snakes as well but there are several snake-eating specialists, including some that eat venomous species. The North American common kingsnake, *Lampropeltis getula*, in all its forms, fall into this category as they will tackle rattlesnakes and have some degree of immunity from their venom. Other species of kingsnakes have little immunity, however. None of the kingsnakes appear to be immune to the venom of the Texas coral snake, *Micrurus*

fulvius. On a smaller scale, western populations of the ring-neck snake, *Diadophis punctatus*, eat snakes as well as other prey, while the short-tailed snake, *Stilosoma extenuatum*, preys largely on the crowned snake, *Tantilla relicta*, in peninsular Florida. In Asia, several members of the Elapidae prey mainly on other snakes. These include, most famously, the king cobra, *Ophiophagus hannah*, the kraits, *Bungarus* species, and the Asia coral snakes, *Calliophis*. The members of the Atractaspididae, all but one of which are African, are equipped with specialised fangs that enable them to bite prey while in the confines of a tunnel. Although they eat other prey, burrowing snakes, especially the slender blind snakes, are probably important parts of their diet. The single Middle Eastern species, *Atractaspis engaddensis*, also eats snakes, including the little collared snake, *Eirenis* species. Two Australian pythons, the black-headed python, *Aspidites melanocephalus*, and the woma, *A. ramsayi*, are reptile specialists and will take other snakes, while a Papuan python, *Apodora papuana*, was found with a carpet python, *Morelia spilota*, in its stomach.

Cannibalism

Snakes that eat other *species* of snakes are numerous. Snakes that eat their own species are nowhere near as common, for obvious reasons. Where records exist they often involve captive snakes that may eat cage-mates by accident, often when two snakes start to swallow a single item of food from opposite ends. Polls and Myers (1985)[12] listed 19 species of snakes in which cannibalism had been reported; they consisted of 10 colubrids, three elapids and five vipers. At least seven incidents occurred under captive conditions. Since then, further species have been added to the list of cannibals but, again, they are concerned almost entirely with snakes in captivity.

One episode involved a European ladder snake, *Rhinechis scalaris*, that ate its own eggs and several other cases of oophagy can be added to these: a Mexican hognose snake, *Heterodon nasicus kennerlyi*, ate most of its own clutch on two separate occasions, a northern cat-eyed snake, *Leptodeira annulata*, ate her entire clutch and a striped kukri snake, *Oligodon taeniolatus* ate three of her own eggs. Other cases involve snakes that ate eggs of their own species but not

▼ Many snakes include other snakes as all or part of their diet. This spotted harlequin snake, *Homoroselaps lacteus*, is eating a thread snake, *Leptotyphlops nigrescens*.

necessarily their own. These include a male milk snake, *Lampropeltis triangulum*, that ate its cage-mate's eggs and two instances of scarlet snakes, *Cemophora coccinea*, eating eggs of their own species; in one case the eggs were almost fully developed. Live-bearing snakes may eat dead embryos or infertile egg-masses and this is especially common among boas but was also seen in a pit viper, the cantil, *Agkistrodon bilineatus*.

Autophagy

The most bizarre accounts of snake feeding behaviour have to be those of American rat snakes, *Pantherophis obsoletus*, that have been observed eating themselves! One individual, a captive, did this on two occasions and died at the second attempt. The other individual was wild and was in tight circle, having swallowed about two thirds of its body, when it was found.

Birds

Birds present snakes with two obvious problems; how to catch them and how to hold on to them, so they only figure highly in the diets of certain arboreal snakes have developed special techniques for dealing with them. Green tree pythons, *Morelia viridis*, for instance, have long, curved teeth that penetrate the feathers and retain a firm grip on the bird. Their method of hunting is to hang, head down, from a bough and wait for a bird to pass below. They strike rapidly and accurately, using their ability to sense body heat through their facial pits, as well as their senses of sight and smell. Other species of snakes prey on birds when they are helpless, before they fledge. Black rat snakes, *Pantherophis obsoletus obsoletus*, for instance, feed on nestlings of a number of small birds, some of which nest on the ground and others that nest in trees and bushes. The South American parrot snake, *Leptophis ahaetulla*, has also been observed eating the feathered chicks of a tanager, while the European ladder snake, *Rhinechis scalaris*, and Montpellier snake, *Malpolon monspessulanus*, frequently enter the burrows of European bee-eaters, where they gorge themselves on chicks before coiling up and digesting them, still in the nest chamber. In addition, several European vipers, including the largest species, the Milos viper, *Macrovipera schweizeri*, as well as the smallest, Orsini's viper, *Vipera ursinii*, rely heavily on

nesting birds and at certain times of the year they may eat nothing else.

One of the best examples of extreme feeding specialisation in snakes, concerns the population of tiger snakes, *Notechis ater pserventyi*, on Chappell Island, in the Bass Straits off Australia, a subspecies that is significantly larger than other populations on the mainland or on other islands; these snakes feed almost entirely on the chicks of mutton birds, *Puffinus tenuirostris*, which nest on the island in high densities. The food is highly nourishing but seasonal, and the snakes gorge themselves for a few weeks in order to store enough energy to see them through until the following bird breeding season. The presence of small skinks on the island is important; these are the food of young tiger snakes, until they grow large enough to eat the mutton bird chicks, and so without them the population could not survive.

Generalist feeders will also eat birds but they are restricted largely to ground-nesting species or odd situations where birds come within range by chance. In three studies on the diet of rattlesnakes, for instance, birds made up 2-8 per cent of the total food. On the island of Guam, the brown tree snake, *Boiga irregularis*, which is a generalist, and which was introduced to the island accidentally, has apparently wiped out all the native forest bird species.

Arboreal snakes are not necessarily bird eaters, though. For instance, the Pacific tree boa, *Candoia bibroni*, though thoroughly arboreal, rarely if ever eats birds, and subsists largely on skinks, along with a few frogs and small mammals. Also when Luisella and Rugiero (1993)[13] compared the diets of arboreal Aesculapian snakes, *Zamenis longissima*, with that of the terrestrial asp viper, *Vipera aspis*, from the same region, they found that they were practically identical (both ate lacertid lizards and mice). We have to conclude from these observations that some arboreal snakes take to the trees for reasons other than finding food.

Mammals

Mammals of various types are eaten mainly by medium sized to large snakes. The size of mammals, and the risk of injuries from them, prevents many small snakes from using them as a staple diet, although nestling rodents, for instance, may be taken opportunistically, even by quite small species.

Australia is unusual in having no native rodents, although there are marsupial counterparts. Nevertheless, there are few mammal specialists in Australia, except the two species of taipan, *Oxyuranus microlepidotus* and *O. scutellatus*, which eat small marsupials and introduced rodents. The larger pythons, such as the carpet and diamond pythons, *Morelia spilota*, also eat large numbers of mammals but their diets are not restricted to them. Juveniles, in particular, eat small lizards, especially skinks. This is thought to be a result of their activity patterns; juvenile pythons are diurnal, whereas the adults are more nocturnal in their habits, when there are likely to be more small mammals available.

On other continents, all the larger species of snakes take a large proportion of mammals and many species feed exclusively on them. Common names such as rat snake, applied to numerous snakes in North America, Europe and Asia, highlight the diet of the more common species.

Larger species of mammals, such as ground squirrels and rabbits, form the prey of larger species of snakes. For instance, in an Idaho population studied by Diller and Johnson (1988),[14] these two species made up the majority of prey species eaten by prairie rattlesnakes, *Crotalus viridis*. Furthermore, they estimated that the rattlesnakes accounted for 14 per cent of the population of ground squirrels each year and a further 5-11 per cent of the population of juvenile cottontail rabbits. Gopher snakes, *Pituophis catenifer*, by contrast, ate smaller quantities of ground squirrels (4 per cent of the total population) but more of the cottontails (22-43 per cent of the total population). These figures give a good idea of the efficiency with which snakes control the populations of rodents and related species under natural circumstances and this is well known in some communities where snakes are actively encouraged to take up residence in barns and other areas where grain is stored.

Although rodents are probably the main prey of snakes in the northern hemisphere, in the tropics and elsewhere other groups of mammals are sometimes more common, and therefore more important prey species. Marsupials have already been mentioned in the context of Australian snakes. The New World marsupials, opposums, are known to be eaten by several species including the

▶ Bats are the most common mammals in many parts of the world and are preyed on by several of the more agile species of snakes, such as Children's pythons, *Liasis childreni*.

mussurana, *Clelia clelia*, the neotropical tiger snake, *Spilotes pullatus*, and the rainbow boa, *Epicrates cenchria*.

Bats, though, are the most numerous form of mammal in many tropical regions and are potential prey to many arboreal and semi-arboreal snakes. Species that are known to eat bats in the natural course of events include several boas such as the rainbow boa, *Epicrates cenchria*, and related species such as *E. angulifer* and *Boa constrictor*, and it seems likely that the arboreal boas belonging to the genus *Corallus* also eat them sometimes. The Australian Children's python, *Antaresia childreni*, eats bats on occasion while the cave racer, *Orthriophis taeniura ridleyi*, which is a large Asiatic colubrid, apparently feeds almost exclusively on them. They wait on ledges at the cave entrance and strike at the bats as they fly past on their way in and out of the cave. The American lyre snake, *Trimorphodon biscutatus*, has been seen plucking young bats from the roof of a culvert in Mexico: bats probably do not represent a common prey for this generalist species, however.

Larger prey species probably receive a disproportionately large amount of publicity. Although the giant boas and pythons undoubtedly tackle and eat large animals such as deer, antelope, domestic pigs and goats and even humans, it is likely that they usually subsist on more manageable items of food.

Eggs

Eggs are a useful (and defenceless) source of protein. It is no surprise, then, that snakes exploit this as a food supply. The rare cases of frogs' and amphibians' eggs as food have been listed above, as have the occasions when insects eggs are eaten by thread and worm snakes, but reptile and bird eggs are an important part of the diets of a number of snakes from different families and different parts of the world.

The most famous egg-eating species are, of course, the African egg eaters belonging to the genus *Dasypeltis*, of which there are five species. These snakes are highly specialised and the series of vertebrae running along the top of their throats have modified downward-pointing processes (the hypapophyses), with which

they saw through the shells of birds' eggs, then swallow the contents and regurgitate the shell. Their capacity to swallow eggs that are several times the diameter of their heads is truly amazing. The very rare Indian egg-eating snake, *Elachistodon westermanni*, is said to have similar habits and also has modified vertebrae in the neck region. Unfortunately, it is rare and poorly known.

Other snakes that eat birds' eggs include members of the following genera: *Boiga*, *Conophis*, *Elaphe*, *Lampropeltis*, *Pantherophis*, *Pseustes* and *Spilotes*. All these species are colubrids. A python, *Liasis fuscus*, eats goose eggs when 'in season' and a young yellow anaconda, *Eunectes notaeus*, has been found with eggs of the limpkin, a wading bird, in its stomach. The eggs were swallowed pointed end first. As far as is known, the *Dasypeltis* species are the only ones that reject the eggshell, the others swallow their eggs whole.

Many other snakes eat the eggs of reptiles. Some are specialists while others are opportunists and eat them only if they come across them by chance. As far as is known, all of the snakes belonging to the large Asian genus *Oligodon* are specialists, although they will also eat other kinds of prey. Coleman *et al.* (1993)[15] described the process in *O. formosanus*. The snake used one of its enlarged teeth on the back of its upper jaw to slash the eggshell. It repeatedly drew the tooth along the shell until it had made a slit. The slit was further enlarged by using the cutting edge of the same enlarged tooth until it was large enough for the snake to push its head inside the shell and consume the contents. These snakes are commonly known as kukri snakes, after the ceremonial knives that the enlarged rear teeth are said to resemble.

Oligodon is paralleled in Australia by the small elapids *Simoselaps semifasciatus*,

S. roperi, and possibly other closely related species. These feed entirely on lizard and snake eggs and have a single enlarged tooth on each of the lower jaws, in contrast to *Oligodon*, which have their modified teeth in the upper jaw. It seems that these teeth slit the shells of reptile eggs as they pass through the mouth.

In Africa, the shovel-snouted snakes, *Prosymna*, also feed largely on reptile eggs. They do not appear to have specialised dentition but use the sharp teeth on the maxilla to puncture the shells as they pass into the throat. The shell as well as its contents are swallowed.

A common factor in all the above species (*Oligodon*, *Simoselaps*, *Prosymna*) is an up-turned snout. This is thought to enable the snakes to bring their sharp cutting teeth into play without the need to bite the eggs (which, in many cases, would probably be too large to fit into their gapes). Significantly, the species of *Simoselaps* that do not eat eggs do not have this feature. An upturned snout does not necessarily imply egg-eating tendencies, though, as many burrowing species have also evolved this characteristic (see Chapter 4).

In America, the niche is filled by the two species belonging to the genus *Phyllorhynhus*, known as leaf-nosed snakes. These snakes eat lizards, especially the banded gecko, *Coleonyx variegatus*, but are thought to prey heavily on their eggs as well. (*Coleonyx* are eublepharid geckos

and, as such, they lay soft-shelled eggs, unlike the majority of gecko species, which lay calcareous eggs.)

Species that feed exclusively on reptile eggs must either live in parts of the world where reptiles breed throughout much of the year, that is, the tropical regions, or, if they live in places where reptile breeding is a seasonal event, they must be able to feed heavily when eggs are available and store enough fat to tide them over the rest of the year.

In addition to the specialists, many generalists undoubtedly also eat reptile eggs. The North American kingsnakes, for instance, are known to eat reptile eggs occasionally and there is at least one record of a kingsnake stealing the eggs from the nest of a freshwater turtle. Another opportunist is the Mexican *Loxocemus bicolor*, which eats *Ctenosaura* and *Iguana* eggs in Costa Rica. At certain times of the year, these eggs may make up almost 100 per cent of the food of this species.

Carrion

In the past, there was a widely held view that snakes rarely if ever ate carrion. Problems associated with establishing carrion as a normal food source include the rare and opportunistic nature of happening upon a snake that is feeding on such prey, coupled with the fact that, when stomach contents of snakes are examined, there is no easy way to

distinguish prey items that have been killed by the snake as opposed to those that were already dead when eaten.

Recent observations have changed this view to some extent. There are several reported observations of snakes eating carrion. A large prairie rattlesnake was seen eating a dead cottontail rabbit, for instance. The rabbit had been dead for over one day as maggots and carrion beetles were present on the carcass and the snake took one-and-a-half hours to swallow the rabbit, due to *rigor mortis*. Other instances include a cottonmouth, *Agkistrodon piscivorus*, that ate a dead water snake, *Nerodia erythrogaster*, and another cottonmouth that was seen to scavenge around the nests of sea birds, searching for spilled fish. Venomous snakes may be more disposed to take dead prey than other snakes because their hunting method involves killing and releasing prey, after which they track it down and eat it some time later. The process of finding such prey may take several hours, by which time the body will be well and truly dead.

Non-venomous snakes may also take carrion. A specimen of the West Indian ground snake *Alsophis portoriciensis richardi*, from Congo Cay, Puerto Rico, was watched by Norton (1993)[16] as it found and ate dehydrated fish dropped by brown pelicans while feeding their chicks. The snake appeared to be actively searching in areas where spilled fish may have become lodged. Yet another example concerns a ribbon snake, *Thamnophis sauritus*, which was watched as it tried to peel a squashed toad from a tarmac road, while Bedford (1991)[17] watched an Australian colubrid, the keelback, *Tropidonophis mairii*, taking road-killed frogs from road surfaces on more than one occasion.

These casual observations seem to indicate that snakes are not averse to eating carrion when the opportunity arises. They are, of course, in competition with scavenging birds and mammals and are, by comparison, poorly equipped to find such prey first.

In captivity, most snakes can be encouraged to eat freshly killed prey animals. Many will also eat food that has been frozen and thawed out and a number seem to prefer food that has been left in their cage for several hours and has become 'high'. Observations on captive snakes should be regarded as suspicious but, nevertheless, they do demonstrate the flexibility of feeding behaviour.

Shifts in prey type

Snakes do not necessarily eat the same type of prey throughout their lives, nor do different populations of the same species always eat similar prey. Shifts in prey preference are related to size, the ability of young snakes to overpower and swallow their prey, and the availability of different sorts of prey in different places.

Young snakes are, by definition, smaller than adults of the same species. This places obvious constraints on the type of food they can handle and, whereas the young of some species merely eat smaller versions of the adults' prey, others eat totally different items. Availability plays an important part; fish, for example, are usually available in a range of sizes and fish-eating snakes tend to eat them throughout their lives, tackling progressively larger fish as they grow. At the same time they may drop small fish from their diet altogether, as in most sea snakes, or they may eat all sizes. Foraging behaviour may play a role here because small fish are often found in shallower

water than large fish so, as the snake grows, it may hunt in deeper water and so reduce, or eliminate, the possibility of finding small fish. This behaviour has been found to occur in some garter and ribbon snakes, *Thamnophis*.

Other semi-aquatic species, such as certain water snakes, *Nerodia*, start their lives as fish eaters and graduate to amphibians as they grow. Snakes belonging to the genus *Regina* eat crustaceans as adults but *R. alleni*, and probably the other three species as well, eat smaller species of crustaceans, such as shrimps as well as dragonfly larvae, when they are young.

A common switch is from lizards to mammals. Many mammal-eating snakes are too small at hatching to tackle adult rodents, etc. and, although they may eat nestling mice when the opportunity presents itself, most eat lizards which, due to their shape, are more easily swallowed. The European vipers, for instance, feed almost entirely on small lizards when they are young but gradually work up to small mammals as they grow. Switching does not take place suddenly but their diets change gradually; even the adults of small species continue to take lizards along with small mammals although the larger species may drop lizards from their diets altogether. A similar situation exists with many of the pit vipers in North, Central and South America. Numerous colubrids are known to eat lizards at hatching, then switch to small mammals as they grow: these include several of the kingsnakes, *Lampropeltis* species, especially the smaller montane species that hatch at a time when there is an abundance of small lizards within their habitat. Judging from their behaviour in captivity, many of the young of these species do not eat even newly born mice during the summer and autumn of their first year but will be persuaded to accept them the following spring after a period of hibernation, even though they may not have grown appreciably.

Where populations become isolated, on an island or mountain range for instance, their diets may need to change due to the availability of prey types, which may differ from those of the main population. There has been little research into this area but a couple of examples can be mentioned.

The Santa Catalina rattlesnake, *Crotalus catalinensis*, lives on the island of the same

name in the Gulf of Mexico, and is descended from the red diamond rattlesnake, *C. ruber*. Whereas the mainland form eats small mammals, the island form has undergone a dietary shift, and eats mainly small birds instead, probably because these are more numerous than mammals on the island. To this end, it has become partly arboreal and has evolved a small slender form, for climbing, and longer teeth, for griping prey. More noticeably, its rattle has degenerated (see page 130). On another of the Gulf Islands, Isla Cerralvo, the Baja rattlesnake, *Crotalus enyo cerralvensis*, also climbs into bushes to feed on lizards and birds, although it has not (yet) evolved any noticeable morphological adaptations. And finally, the golden lancehead, *Bothrops insularis*, from the island of Queimada Grande, off the Brazilian coast, has also changed to a diet of birds and has developed powerful, fast-acting venom and longer fangs than its close relatives.

In a study of tree boas, *Corallus*, on the mainland of South America and in the West Indies, Robert Henderson (1993)[18] found that different populations had different diets, with mainland snakes taking mostly mammals with some birds and a few lizards whereas island populations took mostly lizards with a few mammals and hardly any birds. As he points out, this probably reflects prey availability as much as anything else.

Another example involves the North American kingsnake, *Lampropeltis getula*, which ranges over a large geographical area encompassing several different habitat types. Eastern forms, such as the chain kingsnake, *L. g. getula*, are small at hatching and are reluctant to take mice although they will readily accept lizards and smaller snakes. On the other hand, western forms, such as the Mexican black kingsnake, *L. g. nigritus*, are much larger at hatching and are prepared to take mice from the time they hatch. More subtle differences are seen in yet another form, the Californian kingsnake, *L. g. californiae*, in which young from some areas, e.g. the coastal region, take mice readily, whereas young from the desert often prefer lizards. It can only be assumed that prey availability, over a long period of time, has shaped both the ability of the snakes to feed on different types of prey, and their behaviour.

Amount of food

The amount of food eaten by snakes has received little attention. The two

▲ Young Amazon tree boas. *Corallus hortulanus*, living on West Indian islands, undergo a shift in their diets as they grow, from lizards to birds and mammals, whereas those living on the mainland are more likely to feed on birds and mammals from the time they are born.

extremes are represented, on the one hand, by the example of a thread snake that contained 1,400 food items (see page 99) and, on the other hand, by snakes that contained nothing in their stomach. The latter situation appears to be normal: of many surveys carried out by dissecting large numbers of preserved museum specimens, the most common state is for the stomach to be empty. Since snakes take several days to digest their food, an empty stomach indicates that the snake has probably not fed for some time.

The quantity of prey eaten will depend on several factors. Temperature is important, as snakes will not hunt if it is too cold or too hot. The type of prey is also of importance: snakes that eat small items will need to feed more frequently than those that eat larger ones. Superimposed on this are the requirements of the snakes. Active, diurnal species use up energy more quickly than sluggish species that ambush their prey, and so they will need to eat more often, all other things being equal.

Availability is another factor: many snakes probably do not feed as often as they would like. Lack of suitable food can occur for long periods of time. Some prey species are only seasonally available (the mutton bird chicks mentioned on page 105 are an extreme example) and the snakes concerned may need to feed heavily in order to lay down reserves for the rest of the year when there is little or no chance to feed. Female snakes may not feed when they are in advanced stages of pregnancy, presumably because the developing eggs or embryos take up all the available body space leaving insufficient room for a meal: live-bearing species may go without food for several months for this reason. Similarly, snakes fast voluntarily before they shed their skin.

Size of prey

Snakes are capable of eating relatively large prey. Obviously, as they grow the range of prey open to them increases. Small snakes, then, are restricted to small prey, whereas large snakes could eat large *and* small prey. There are costs involved in eating small prey, however, and it may not always be in their interests to do so. For example, snakes that chase their prey are likely to expend as much energy in catching a small lizard as they do in catching a large lizard, although the benefits will be much less. Snakes may also expose themselves to danger each time they hunt and eat their prey and so

one would expect them to forego food items that are of little value. It is important that they optimise their hunting in such a way that the benefits outweigh the costs.

In view of the fact that snakes must swallow their food whole, they must have means of assessing the size of a prey animal before they launch an attack. Smell may play an important role as small species of rodents, for instance, may smell different from large species. Young animals may also smell different from adults. Snakes that kill their prey, either by constriction or by envenomation, often examine their prey closely before beginning to swallow it. This is normally interpreted as a search for the head, but it may also help the snake to decide whether or not the food will fit into its mouth.

The capacity to swallow large prey is not equal throughout the snake kingdom. The limitation of having rigid jaws in the case of many small burrowing snakes has already been mentioned but there are also differences between the more advanced species. On average, vipers are capable of swallowing proportionately larger prey than other types of snakes, over twice as large in some cases. The body shape of vipers obviously helps them to accommodate large prey, as do their lethargic habits. In addition, their sit-and-wait tactics may have forced them into taking larger prey since they must depend, to a large extent, on random meals passing by and cannot afford to reject too many feeding opportunities. Their wide heads may have evolved in response to this necessity. The snakes that eat the largest prey, proportionately, are the vipers. A typical meal would represent about 20 per cent of the snake's body weight but they occasionally eat prey that weighs more than they do.

In absolute terms it is the boas and pythons that eat the largest prey. This is not without its hazards, though, as there are several documented cases of them dying because the horns of their prey have pierced their bodies from inside the gut, and even more cases where bloated pythons and boas have been killed (by humans) because a recently eaten large meal has rendered them unable to escape.

Competition for food and resource partitioning

Within communities of snakes, it often appears that the different species avoid direct competition with each other by concentrating on different types of food. Thus, different species of snakes in a given area may hunt for different types of prey, or they may hunt at different times or in different places.

Although a brief look at the various species of snakes occurring in one area often leads, intuitively, to the conclusion that food partitioning is taking place, there have been very few thorough studies to confirm this. Many snake communities are very complex, especially in the tropics where there may be dozens of species living in the same area, including terrestrial, arboreal and burrowing species, large, medium-sized and small species and nocturnal and diurnal species, in addition to generalists and specialists. Several species may prey on some of the others. For these reasons, it is simpler to look at snake communities that contain only a few species.

In Britain, there are two common species of snakes that may occur together, the adder. *Vipera berus*, which eats lizards and rodents and the grass snake, *Natrix natrix*, which eats fish and amphibians. A third species, the smooth snake, *Coronella austriaca*, also eats lizards and rodents but may avoid competition with the adder by foraging in burrows and crevices. Communities of garter snakes in North America seem to have more subtle differences in their diet. Species occurring together eat worms, slugs, amphibians, fish and mammals, and, although there is some overlap, some species have preferences for

one or more groups of prey. In southwestern Australia, where there are a number of small terrestrial elapids, Shine (1984)[19] found that closely related species sharing the same habitat often specialise in different prey: *Simoselaps bertholdi* and its allies eat only small lizards, *S. semifasciata* eats only reptile eggs, and so on. Several other related species are less specialised and eat lizards and reptile eggs.

Drinking

Most snakes drink. In order to do so, they submerge their snouts and, by pumping with their throats, draw water into their oesophagus. The tongue is not used to lap water.

Some groups of snakes drink rarely or not at all, because they live in habitats where fresh water is not freely available. These include sea snakes and species from deserts. The true sea snakes, belonging to the subfamily Hydropheinae, probably do not drink, but extract water from their food. The sea kraits come ashore occasionally and have been observed drinking from rainwater pools along the sea shore and from overhanging vegetation. Desert snakes drink when they get the opportunity but their main strategy is to extract water from their food and retain it as effectively as possible. Techniques include scale rasping (and possibly rattling) instead of hissing, polishing the scales in order to reduce their permeability, and the production of solid uric acid as their metabolic waste.

It seems likely that some individuals hardly, if ever, drink throughout their lives, and in experimental situations several species, such as the carpet viper, *Echis coloratus*, have been successfully reared without access to water.

▼ Desert snakes, such as the horned adder, *Bitis caudalis*, may drink only rarely, if at all. Some desert species rely entirely on condensed fog for their water.

METHODS OF HUNTING

SNAKES TEND TO BE STEREOTYPED IN THEIR HUNTING METHODS. THAT IS, EACH SPECIES USES A PARTICULAR METHOD AND, BY AND LARGE, STICKS TO IT. THERE MAY, HOWEVER, BE DIFFERENCES IN HUNTING BEHAVIOUR BETWEEN ADULTS AND JUVENILES AND DIFFERENT POPULATIONS OF THE SAME SPECIES MAY ALSO HUNT IN SLIGHTLY DIFFERENT WAYS (OFTEN DEPENDING ON PREY AVAILABILITY). WHEN LOOKING AT HUNTING METHODS, TWO MAIN STRATEGIES CAN BE RECOGNISED: SIT-AND-WAIT PREDATORS THAT AMBUSH THEIR PREY, AND ACTIVE HUNTERS THAT SEEK OUT THEIR PREY, CHASING AND RUNNING IT DOWN IF NECESSARY. THESE ONLY REPRESENT THE TWO EXTREMES OF A CONTINUUM OF STRATEGIES, HOWEVER, AND BETWEEN THEM THERE ARE SEVERAL VARIATIONS AND MODIFICATIONS, EVOLVED TO OPTIMISE THE SNAKE'S SUCCESS RATE.

Hunting strategy obviously depends on the type of prey a snake tends to eat. In an area where small mammals are common, for instance, sitting and waiting may be a very cost effective method, but it is much less likely to succeed where the main prey is birds' eggs or termites!

Active diurnal hunters

Active diurnal hunters are epitomised by the fast-moving and agile diurnal colubrids such as the racers, whipsnakes, coachwhips and sand snakes, *Coluber*, *Masticophis* and *Psammophis*, the Australian elapids *Demansia* (also known as whipsnakes) and others. These species feed by using their sight to locate prey, stalking it carefully in order to get as close as possible, then taking it with a rush. The method is not always successful – lizards, the most common prey of this type of snake, are equally alert and agile and many attacks, possibly most, fail. Characteristics of active hunters are a slender body, long tail, large eyes and a tendency to search by raising the head slightly off the ground as they progress. Many are marked with longitudinal

OPTIMAL FORAGING

Although snakes' food provides the energy they need for other activities, gathering it also incurs a cost. As long as the energy derived from the food is greater than the energy used in gathering it everything will be fine. There comes a point, however, where small items of food do not give a good enough return to make them worth hunting. In order to hunt and feed efficiently, all animals need to take this into account and those that are most efficient are the ones that are most likely to grow and reproduce successfully.

Obviously, larger snakes eat larger prey, because they are able to, but the optimal foraging theory, which predicts the ideal hunting strategy, goes one stage further. It suggests that large snakes should drop small prey items from their diets, because they do not give a good return when compared to the energy used up in capturing them. This ideal system has been confirmed in some populations of rattlesnakes, for instance, in which young snakes of less than one year old eat only shrews but, as they grow, gradually shift their preferences until, by the time they are adult, they feed on larger mammals and birds and rarely take small prey items.

Unfortunately, overall evidence for this type of shift in prey size is not conclusive. There are indications that some species of snakes are more selective when it comes to prey size than others, but there have been too few studies on this aspect of snake biology to draw any general conclusions. Furthermore, many of the feeding records published over the years fail to include the sort of information that is essential for this type of study (they often lump prey items together without giving an indication of size, or they give only the average size of prey).

Even where it has been shown that large snakes do drop small prey items from their diet, optimal foraging may not necessarily be the reason. Small prey sometimes becomes unavailable to large snakes, as in tree boas that hunt for sleeping lizards (because the small lizards sleep on thin branches that will not support large snakes). Fish-eating snakes are in a similar situation because small fish tend to be found in shallow margins of ponds and lakes whereas the larger ones are found in deeper water: once the snake has moved up to larger fish, it will rarely have the opportunity to catch small ones, even if it wanted to. Furthermore, small fish may also be more elusive to large snakes than big ones and therefore the energy spent in catching them may actually be *greater* than that spent in catching large ones. On the other hand, rodent-eating snakes may find nests containing litters of young – it would obviously be worth their while to eat these as, collectively, they constitute a sizeable meal as well as one which represents little risk.

Prey type is another important consideration. Snakes that feed on easily obtained prey, such as invertebrates, can afford to be less fussy about the size of individual items – they expand very little energy in catching and handling their prey anyway and even a small meal will be worthwhile. For this reason, snakes that ambush their prey would also be expected to take any suitable food that passes within range; again, they expend little energy in hunting for their food once they have found a productive place in which to lie in wait. (Most snakes that ambush their prey are large-bodied species, able to accommodate larger prey than active foragers).

Species that have restricted diets are also less likely to be fussy. Australian snakes, for example, have few large prey available to them. They therefore tend to take any prey that comes along, predominantly skinks in many species, and large individuals eat the same sized skinks as small ones do.

stripes along their bodies. Active hunters may be found among terrestrial, arboreal, aquatic and semi-aquatic snakes.

Active foragers

Species that eat sedentary or slow-moving prey, such as molluscs and other invertebrates, or bird and reptiles eggs, are obliged to forage. Finding prey is their main task – once found it is relatively easy to catch and overpower it.

▶ The Namib sand snake, *Psammophis leightoni*, is a typical diurnal hunter with a slender body, large eyes and round pupils.

FORAGING IN BUSHMASTERS: AN OBJECT LESSON IN PATIENCE

Sit-and-wait predators seem to have a fairly simplistic approach to life: they find a productive place to wait and feed whenever they get the chance. Because they do not use much energy by moving around, they do not need to feed very often and, in addition, they reduce the chances of being spotted by a predator.

A radio-tracking experiment carried out on bushmasters by Harry Greene seems to confirm this picture (American Zoologist, 2 3 :89 7).

The bushmaster, *Lachesis muta*, (now reclassified into four species - see page 224) is the largest pit viper. It is quite rare and is found only in the rainforests of Central and South America. It is cryptically coloured and, like most vipers, it ambushes its prey.

Greene tracked three bushmasters for varying periods of time; one of them, a female measuring 90 cm (3 ft) in length, used only three sites over a 45-day period. During the day it rested beneath small plants but it was alert each night and obviously hoping that a meal would materialise. On the 24th night its patience was rewarded: it ate a rodent estimated to weigh at least 40 per cent of its own body weight. After eating, it was inactive for nine more nights before moving to a new site.

The hunting sites chosen by this and two other tracked bushmasters were always near Weltia palms, the seeds of which are eaten by the rodents that the snakes prey on.

▲ The Namib tiger snake, *Telescopus beetzi*, is a nocturnal prowler, with large eyes and vertical pupils. Its flattened head is perhaps an adaptation that allows the snake to thrust it into nooks and crannies where it may find sleeping lizards.

In warm parts of the world, where many snakes are nocturnal, a large proportion are nocturnal foragers. These include species that search for prey such as lizards while they are asleep. To this end they frequent low bushes and shrubs, where species such as the West Indian *Anolis* roost, or poke their heads into crevices in rocks and trees where species such as small skinks, teiid and lacertid lizards sleep. Good examples of these nocturnal foragers are the arboreal neotropical *Imantodes*, the terrestrial *Telescopus* from Europe and Africa, the American lyre snakes, *Trimorphodon*, the Egyptian cobra, *Walterinnesia aegyptia*, and a number of small Australian elapids. As the sleeping lizards are cold and therefore comatose, catching and subduing them is a relatively easy task for these snakes once they have located them, although a short chase may be necessary. Other nocturnal foragers eat frogs which, though active and lively at night, are often preoccupied with calling and mating and are therefore easy prey.

There are also diurnal counterparts of these nocturnal foragers: diurnal snakes that look for resting frogs and other nocturnal creatures that sleep during the day. A position somewhere between hunters and foragers is taken by species such as garter snakes and water snakes, *Thamnophis*, *Nerodia* and *Natrix* species and their relatives. These snakes work their way through marginal vegetation, repeatedly thrusting their heads into it, hoping to flush small amphibians from their hiding places. Once this occurs they give chase, often catching their prey before it has covered more than a few inches. European whipsnakes have also been seen behaving in a similar fashion, poking their heads into the holes in old dry stone walls, where diurnal lizards often hide.

Aquatic species are normally active foragers, although some members of the Homalopsinae, such as the fishing snake, *Erpeton tentaculum*, ambush their prey. The file snakes, *Acrochordus*, forage over the muddy bottoms of estuaries and sea beds, looking for crabs and fish. Other sea snakes investigate nooks and crannies along coral reefs, in search of eels and gobies, or for fish eggs. Snakes such as the American *Nerodia* and the European *Natrix* species often hunt in water and may try to catch fish by swimming in a seemingly random manner with their mouths open. As they swim, they swing their heads to and fro, grasping any fish with which they come into contact.

▲ (top) Terrestrial sit-and-wait predators, like this death adder, *Acanthophis* species, from New Guinea, have large stocky bodies to provide an anchor point and small heads that they can throw forward with great speed. They are invariably well camouflaged and sometimes have brightly coloured tips to their tails, which serve to entice their prey a little closer.

▲ (above) A speckled rattlesnake, *Crotalus mitchelli*, discovered with a flashlight at night and photographed exactly where it lay coiled in ambush among jumbled rocks on Isla Margareta, Baja California, Mexico.

▶ Arboreal sit-and-wait predators, such as the green tree python, *Morelia viridis*, are also well camouflaged but their body size is limited by the size of the branches along which they climb or on which they rest. Their tails are often prehensile, providing an alternative means of anchoring themselves when they strike.

Sit-and-wait predators

Many snakes do not hunt or forage but merely install themselves in a likely spot and wait for their prey to come along. Because their sense of smell is so acute, one would expect snakes to be good at detecting a well-frequented rodent run, for instance, and to optimise their time by waiting in a favourable place. If they were unsuccessful for a long period of time, they could be expected to move to a better location. There appear to have been few studies that have looked at this particular aspect of hunting strategy in snakes.

Snakes that sit and wait for their food are characterised by heavy bodies and large heads. They tend to be well camouflaged, usually having some kind of disruptive coloration. Many boas, pythons and vipers are sit-and-wait predators: the short-tailed pythons, Gaboon viper and the puff adder are three very obvious examples but representatives of several other families also use this strategy. The Australian death adder, *Acanthophis antarcticus*, which, despite its name, is an elapid, is another sit-and-wait predator.

Sit-and-wait arboreal snakes tend not to be as heavy-bodied as their terrestrial

▲ Snakes with contrasting colours on their tails use them as lures. Luring occurs in snakes belonging to several families including several pit vipers, such as the Pope's pit viper, *Trimeresurus popeiorum*, seen here in the highlands of west Malaysia.

counterparts but they are still cryptically marked. They include several arboreal pit vipers such as the Asian *Trimeresurus* species and related genera and the American *Bothrops* and related kinds, as well some boas and pythons, notably the emerald boa, *Corallus caninus*, and the green tree python, *Morelia viridis*. All these species typically grasp a bough with their tail and the back half of their body and hang head-down with a compact S-shaped curve in the front half of their body and their head a few inches from the ground. They will often remain motionless in this position all night if necessary, ready to straighten their body rapidly if prey walks within striking distance underneath them. Mice and other small mammals are the most common prey for these species although they may also take lizards and birds on occasion.

Luring

A number of sit-and-wait species of snakes increase their chances of success by using their tails to lure prey within range. They tend to have cryptically coloured bodies and heads but brightly coloured tails. The technique seems to have evolved separately in several families and has been recorded for numerous unrelated species from various parts of the world.

Luring involves raising the tail above the coils and twitching or waving it in an enticing manner in order to attract the attention of possible prey animals and encourage them to investigate further by approaching the snake. Two types of luring have been noted for several species: slow, speculative luring when no prey has been detected and a more active luring when prey is present. Certain prey types seem to be more susceptible than others and luring tends to be more common among snakes that eat lizards and frogs. In most cases, juvenile snakes have the coloration to lure but lose it as they mature: this usually reflects a change in diet but may also be due to the inability of large snakes to carry out the deception effectively.

Among the pythons, young green tree pythons, *Morelia viridis*, are bright yellow (sometimes brownish orange) but always have yellow coloured tails. Murphy, Carpenter and Gillingham (1976)[20] observed caudal luring in a group of captive-hatched juveniles when rodents were offered to them. Even more remarkably, *Anolis* lizards, which were loose in the laboratory, approached the cages in which the young snakes were housed and tried to attack the tails through the glass.

Among the Tropidophidae, some forms of the Cuban wood snake, *Tropidophis melanurus*, have a black tip to their tail while others have a bright yellow tip. Although luring has not been observed in this secretive species, its coloration suggests that it may occur. Similarly, the closely related *Trachyboa* species have bright orange tips to their tails when young. (Some species may use brightly coloured tails to deflect attack away from their head, however, as discussed in Chapter 6.)

In the Colubridae, luring has not been observed very many times, considering the large number of species in the family. Juveniles of the Brazilian species *Tropidodryas striaticeps* are greenish grey or brown in colour but the tips of their tails are whitish to yellowish. They are also covered with flared scales making them appear broader (juicier?) than they really are. Sazima and Puorto (1993)[21] observed freshly caught captives luring in the presence of potential prey (frogs and lizards) and immediately after feeding.

The African bark snake, *Hemirhagerrhis nototaeniata*, is also cryptically marked but has a bright tip to its tail, pink or orange in this case. It is arboreal and feeds on geckos, small skinks and frogs and may use the tail to lure them, although this has not been observed.

By contrast to the limited number of records of caudal luring in colubrids, many vipers have been observed employing the technique. Greene and Campbell (1972)[22] noted the behaviour in *Bothriopsis bilineata*, while Sazima and Puorto (1993) noted similar behaviour in the Brazilian species *Bothrops jararaca* and *B. jararacussu*. Several other related species, such as the common *B. atrox*, have brightly coloured tips to their tails, at least when young, while the young of *B. asper* seem to be sexually dimorphic, with only the males having bright tail tips: both sexes, however, have been seen using their tail to lure. Luring behaviour is probably quite widespread among the South American pit vipers.

Of the African vipers, *Atheris nitschei* is slate grey with a white tip to its tail when born. Catherine Pook (1990)[23] noticed that they would wriggle their tails in 'a maggot-like motion' when offered food or disturbed. *Atheris chloroechis* also has a light coloured tail tip when young and probably uses this as a lure. Luring seems not to have been recorded in other African vipers. Similarly, caudal luring has not been recorded in any of the European and Middle Eastern vipers belonging to the genus *Vipera*, even though several forms of the horn-nosed viper, *V. ammodytes*, e.g. *V. a. gregortwallneri* and *V. a. ruffoi* have orange tips to their tails when young, while young *V. a. montandoni* have greenish tips to their tails.

Among the Elapidae, only the death adder, *Acanthophis antarcticus*, seems to use its tail as a lure and its behaviour is well documented, by Carpenter *et al.* (1978).[24] This species, which is a particularly bulky sit-and-wait predator, curls its body so that the tail is next to the head. The tail is waved about slowly until prey is detected, when the movements quicken.

An unusual form of luring occur in the African twig snake, *Thelotornis kirtlandii*. This species is very slender and is cryptically marked, resembling a dead branch or vine. It has been observed resting with its bright red tongue extended and is said to entice birds within range by this strategy.

OVERPOWERING PREY

HAVING FOUND THEIR PREY, THE NEXT PROBLEM THAT SNAKES FACE IS THAT OF OVERPOWERING IT. THE DIFFICULTIES INVOLVED WILL DEPEND ON THE TYPE OF PREY, AND FOR SNAKES THAT EAT DEFENCELESS PREY SUCH AS EGGS, SLUGS AND SNAILS THE PROBLEM DOES NOT ARISE. OTHER SPECIES, HOWEVER, MAY NEED TO DEAL WITH PREY THAT IS SLIPPERY AND HARD TO GRIP, PREY THAT MAY DISCARD PART OF ITS ANATOMY IN ORDER TO MAKE AN ESCAPE, OR PREY THAT IS CAPABLE OF INFLICTING SERIOUS DAMAGE.

A number of methods are used by snakes to render their prey helpless. These methods are not always mutually exclusive. The same species, or even the same individual, may use several methods according to the type and size of prey it is tackling and there is strong evidence that snakes can distinguish between potentially harmful and harmless prey. Having said this, feeding behaviour tends to be stereotyped so that, in a given set of conditions, a predictable sequence of events will take place.

In its simplest form, catching, overpowering and swallowing become a more or less continuous process. The European grass snake, *Natrix natrix*, for instance, eats frogs by grasping them in its jaws and beginning to swallow immediately: it sometimes turns the frog around until it can be swallowed head first but often swallows it backwards. The same technique is used by many of the lizard-eating snakes and by snakes that enter rodent nests and take the young. There is plenty of evidence to show that snakes can identify their prey with regard to type and age, and act accordingly. Whereas nestling mice are swallowed alive, sub-adults and adults are invariably rendered helpless before swallowing commences. Identification is not always based on size, though, as the same snake will kill adult mice but swallow nestling rats of the same size and weight without killing them.

Subduing prey completely before swallowing is initiated occurs in snakes from most families, and takes two main forms: constriction and envenomation.

Constriction

There is no clear-cut distinction between swallowing without killing and constriction. A number of snakes grasp their prey and begin to swallow. If the prey struggles, the snake may then throw one or two loose coils around it or use its body to pin the prey down. Species that hunt in the burrows or chambers of rodents, for instance, rarely have enough room in which to constrict their prey effectively but may crush them against the sides of the burrows. Other species are more inclined to constrict their prey as a matter of course. Large boas and pythons, for instance, will often constrict their prey for long periods of time, even when fed with dead food in captivity. This behaviour persists throughout their lives even though they may never be faced with the prospect of killing their own food.

Constriction, in its most extreme form, consists of grasping the body of the prey animal, throwing two or more coils of the body around it in the same instant and then exerting continuous pressure until it expires. Although small bones may be crushed during the process, the prey is killed by asphyxiation – each time it breathes out the coils are tightened until it is unable to breathe at all. The time taken varies with the type and the strength of the prey and can be many minutes in some cases. Constriction tends to be more effective on mammals and birds, which need to breathe frequently, than on lizards or snakes, which can survive long periods without breathing. Species that feed on lizards and snakes, then, may constrict their prey but often begin to swallow it before it is completely dead, so many of the species that feed on these prey types are mildly venomous.

Envenomation

Venomous snakes are found in four families: the Colubridae, Atractaspididae, Elapidae and Viperidae. Their methods of producing the venom are not exactly the same, however.

Rear-fanged colubrids

Many colubrid snakes, including rear-fanged venomous as well as non-venomous species have a Duvernoy's

▲ Constrictors subdue their prey by restraining it in one or more coils, preventing it from drawing breath and restricting the pumping action of the heart. Death ensues from one or other, or both, of these effects. The snake is a small python, *Antaresia maculosus*.

gland. This is a modified salivary gland, and is named after the French anatomist who discovered it in 1832. It is situated towards the back of the mouth, on both sides, and varies greatly in size. A duct carries the toxic saliva, or venom, to the posterior maxillary teeth and discharges it into the furrow between the lips of the snake and the sides of its teeth. A more detailed account of Duvernoy's gland is given in Chapter 2 (see page 49).

Well over 100 genera of colubrids, amounting to about one-third of all species, are known to have a Duvernoy's gland. While some of the species involved have normal dentition, a number have enlarged fangs near the point where the glands discharge. Although the enlarged fangs usually consist of a single pair, some species have two or three adjacent pairs. The enlarged teeth may have grooves running from their bases to their tips in order to allow the venom to travel up them by capillary action once they are embedded in the prey. The venom apparatus is not, therefore, as efficient as

that of the cobras and vipers and the snake has to chew before an appreciable amount finds its way into the prey. Wherever there are enlarged fangs there is a gap, known as the diastema, in front of them, the purpose of which is to allow the fangs to be sunk fully into the prey.

Once the fangs have been thrust into the prey, the chewing action begins. This is thought to fulfil the dual purpose of opening up the wound and improving the flow of the venom along the fangs. The prey is held well back in the mouth and the snake passes through bouts of

chewing alternating with periods of resting. The intermittent chewing bouts, as well as helping to inject the venom, may also serve to stimulate activity from the prey and so tell the snake whether or not the venom has taken effect.

Eventually the prey will die or become unconscious. Once the snake senses this, it moves the prey around in its mouth

▼ The mangrove snake, *Boiga dendrophila*, from Southeast Asia has fangs towards the rear of its mouth and a moderately potent venom with which it immobilises its prey.

and swallows it, usually head first. Should the prey show signs of regaining consciousness, the snake will clamp its jaws on it once more and repeat the process, giving the venom more time to take effect.

The venoms produced by Duvernoy's glands vary slightly between species. Some are more potent than others and certain rear-fanged colubrids have been responsible for human deaths.

Front-fanged snakes

Members of the Elapidae and the Viperidae possess specialised venom fangs at the front of their mouths. They differ in their form, those of the elapids being relatively short and fixed and those of the vipers being relatively long and hinged, so that they can be folded flat when not in use.

Methods of using the venom probably vary little between these two families, although the vipers, especially the American pit vipers, have been studied most. Small and innocuous prey are struck and held while the venom takes effect. Birds, which could fly long distances before succumbing, and which

are unlikely to harm the snake anyway, are always held. Large prey is treated differently. It is struck and then released. The snake then begins to track the dying prey, using it tongue, until it finds the carcass. Swallowing can now take place without danger to the snake. It is interesting to compare the killing methods of different snakes that eat different kinds of prey: the Australian elapids provide a good example. As has already been noted, the taipans are the only species that eat large warm-blooded prey and their technique is to strike and then release their prey, so avoiding possible injury from the struggling victim. All other Australian elapids, which prey predominantly on lizards but some of which also occasionally eat small rodents, bite and hold on to their prey.

The length of time taken for the prey to die will obviously depend on many factors: its size, the potency of the venom and the accuracy of the strike being the most important. Some prey undoubtedly recover, especially if the strike hits an extremity or if venom is absorbed by fur

or feathers. Most snakes, though, strike very accurately: rattlesnakes, for instance, have been shown to hit the chest or lumbar region of rodents and small rabbits in a high proportion of attacks. Death often takes place in less than one minute – sometimes in a few seconds – and the stricken animals may only travel a few feet before dying.

Apart from immobilizing the prey, the venom has a secondary function, that of starting the process of digestion. Snake venoms originate from saliva and contain many of the same components as human saliva, for instance: mucus, fats and different salts of calcium, ammonia and magnesium. The proteins that are responsible for the effects of envenomation are of several different types but basically consist of those which attack the circulatory system and the blood (haemotoxins) and those which attack the nervous system (neurotoxins). Haemotoxins lead to circulatory failure either through anti-coagulation or clotting, whereas neurotoxins affect the nerve centres controlling movement and, more importantly, breathing. Venomous snakes have mixtures, or 'cocktails' of

◀ Large vipers, such as the Gaboon viper, *Bitis gabonica*, envenomate their prey. From this angle, the triangular shape to the head, resulting from the huge venom sacs, is very obvious.

venoms belonging to both groups – death may be caused by one type or the other, or by a combination of both. Generally speaking, neurotoxins produce a more rapid response than haemotoxins but are not necessarily more effective in the long term.

As a very general rule, vipers' venom contains mainly haemotoxins and elapid venom contains mainly neurotoxins. The massive bruising and tissue degeneration associated with bites from dangerous vipers is due to the haemotoxic effects of their venom whereas bites from elapids cause paralysis. There are plenty of exceptions, though. The black-necked cobra, *Naja nigricollis*, produces only haemotoxic venom whereas two vipers, the berg adder, *Bitis atropos*, and the neotropical rattlesnake, *Crotalus durissus terrificus*, produce mainly neurotoxic venom, for example.

The venom of sea snakes acts mainly on the muscles of its prey, and is classed as myotoxic. A few terrestrial elapids from Australia also produce myotoxic venom. Rear-fanged snakes produce mainly haemotoxic venoms.

It should also be noted that the composition of venoms may vary within species. These differences are sometimes due to the age of the snake (i.e. venom composition changes during the life of the snake) or to differences between populations. The latter situation is best documented in the case of the Mojave rattlesnake, *Crotalus scutulatus*, in which two distinct types of venom have been identified, a largely neurotoxic one (Type A) that produces almost no pain or local tissue damage and a haemotoxic one (Type B) that is similar to that of the western diamondback rattlesnake, *C. atrox*, and produces typical viperine venom symptoms consisting of massive local haemorrhaging.

The adder, *Vipera berus*, is also known to produce different types of venom over its wide range as does the asp, *V. aspis*. Richard Clark recently described symptoms of a bite by this species in which there was little local reaction but severe systemic effects, more typical of neurotoxic envenomation.[25]

Differences in the strength of the venom and its resulting effects on the prey may also be correlated with differences between sexes, or different times of the year. This aspect has remained largely unresearched as yet.

SWALLOWING AND DIGESTING

SWALLOWING IS ONE OF THE MORE REMARKABLE FACETS OF SNAKES' FEEDING HABITS, ESPECIALLY TO THE UNINITIATED. ANIMALS SEVERAL TIMES THE DIAMETER OF THE SNAKE'S HEAD AND NECK ARE ENGULFED, SEEMINGLY WITH LITTLE EFFORT AND OFTEN IN A REMARKABLY SHORT TIME.

Swallowing

Relatively small prey is often swallowed without regard to its orientation: large snakes may swallow small rodents head first, tail first or even from the middle, depending on how they are first grasped. Relatively large prey is almost always swallowed head first, however. This aids swallowing because the limbs of lizards and mammals, and the wings of birds and bats, fold more easily in this direction. With birds and mammals, it is likely that

▼ Swallowing large prey is made possible by partial dislocation of the jaws and by a high degree of elasticity in the skin around them.

the snake finds the head by a combination of sensory and olfactory senses. Snakes may take a considerable time in 'deciding' which end to start swallowing, and sometimes make several false starts. The direction of the fur is important while the heads of animals probably have distinctive smells. Nestling rodents, in which there is no fur, are more likely to be swallowed the wrong way round. Similarly, rodents in which an incision is made towards the posterior part of the body also seem to confuse snakes. Captive snakes fed on previously frozen food are more likely to make wrong decisions than those fed on live or freshly killed food, perhaps because it has lost some of its smell, or because it has picked up smells from other food items with which it was stored.

Once the head is found, swallowing begins. The successful consumption of large prey depends on the flexibility of the snake's skull, the shape of its teeth, which are curved backwards, and the elasticity of its skin. The snake first opens its mouth to grip as much of the head as possible. It then hooks the teeth on one side of its jaw into the prey and moves the opposite jaw forwards. This jaw is then hooked into the prey, the teeth on the other jaw are disengaged and that jaw is moved forward. By moving the jaws forward in turn, the food is pulled into the mouth. As the bulk of the prey passes

into the mouth, the two halves of the lower jaw are forced apart and the quadrate bones, which link the posterior ends of the lower jaw with the top of the skull, are spread. In this way, an enormous amount of distension is possible.

At this point, the prey fills the mouth completely and the snake would be in danger of choking were it not for a further modification. The forward portion of the windpipe (the glottis) is strongly muscular and is pushed forward and held open during swallowing, in order to maintain a passage for air.

When eating large prey, or if disturbed, the snake may take a short rest, but the process is usually continuous. Once the food has entered the throat, the snake may, speed up the swallowing process by muscular wave-like contractions. Once the whole of the prey is in the throat, these actions continue to force it down into the stomach. After swallowing, snakes often stretch and manipulate the jaw bones by 'yawning' in order to put them back into their normal positions.

Swallowing large prey is not without its hazards, however. A lyre snake, *Trimorphodon biscutatus* that ate a spiny-tailed iguana, *Ctenosaura pectinata*, took an hour and three quarters to consume its meal and then died twenty minutes later. The lizard was rather large for the snake and its spiny scales had punctured the snake's oesophagus and stomach (Ramirez-Bautista and Uribe, 1992).[26] Similar 'accidents' have been recorded for large pythons that have eaten antelopes whose horns have pierced the stomach.

Digestion

Digestion begins almost as the snake starts the swallowing process, because the saliva, which covers the prey, contains strong enzymes. As it reaches the stomach, further enzymes are secreted and the digestion continues. As this is a biochemical process, the speed with which it takes place is dependent on temperature, as well as the surface area of the prey, and so snakes that have recently fed will normally attempt to raise their body temperatures slightly in order to speed it up. Small snakes may bask by placing their entire bodies on a warm substrate or in the sun, but large snakes sometimes warm only the portion of their body containing the prey, which is easily identified by the bulge it creates about one-third of the way down the body.

The time taken for complete digestion depends on many factors but, in the case of a medium-sized snake that has eaten an average sized meal, such as an adult mouse, it is usually about four days. Should conditions be unfavourable, such as a sudden drop in temperature, digestion may be prolonged and, in exceptional circumstances, stops altogether. When this happens, the snake will usually regurgitate its food. Naulleau (1983),[27] for example, found that all European asps, *Vipera aspis*, would regurgitate their food if maintained at 10°C (50°F) after feeding, about half would regurgitate if they were kept at 15°C (59°F), but less than 10 per cent regurgitated when they were kept above 20°C (68°F).

NOTES

1. Shine, R. and Webb, J. K. (1990), 'Natural history of Australian typhlopid snakes', *Journal of Herpetology*, 24(4):357-363.
2. White, L. R., Powell, R., Parmerlee, J. S., Lathrop, A., and Smith, D. (1992), 'Food habits of three syntopic reptiles from the Barahona Peninsula, Hispaniola', *Journal of Herpetology*, 26(4): 518-520.
3. Rossman, D. A, and Myer, P. A. (1990), 'Behavioural and morphological adaptions for snail extraction in the North American brown snakes (genus *Storeria*)', *Journal of Herpetology*, 24(4):434-438.
4. Sanzima, I. (1989), 'Feeding behaviour of the snail-eating snake, *Dipsas indica*', *Journal of Herpetology*, 23(4):464-468.
5. Luisella, L. M. (1990), 'Captive breeding of *Vipera ursinii ursinii*', *British Herpetological Society Bulletin*, 34:23-30.
6. Seigel, R. A. (1992), 'Ecology of a specialised predator: *Regina grahami* in Missouri', *Journal of Herpetology*, 26(1):32-37.
7. Wharton, C. H. (1969), 'The cottonmouth mocassin on Sea Horse Key, Florida', *Bull.Florida State Mus., Biol. Sci.*, 14:227-272.
8. Lind, A. J. and Welsh, H. H. (1990), 'Predation by *Thamnophis couchii* on *Dicampton ensatus*', *Journal of Herpetology*, 24(1):104-106.
9. Henderson, R. W. (1993), 'Foraging and diet in West Indian *Corallus enhydris*', *Journal of Herpetology*, 27(1):24-28.
10. Papenfuss, T. J. (1982), 'The ecology and systematics of the amphisbaenian genus *Bipes*', *Occ. Pap. California Acad. Sci.*, 136:1-42.
11. Perez-Santos, C. and Moreno, A. G. (1987), 'Feeding behaviour of a false coral snake. *Pseudoboa neuwiedii*', *Herp. Review*, 19(4):69.
12. Polis, G. A. and Myers, C. A. (1985), 'A survey of intraspecific behaviour among reptiles and amphibians', *Journal of Herpetology*, 19(1):99-107.
13. Luisella, L. and Rugiero, L. (1993), 'Food habits of the Aesculapian snake, *Elaphe longissima*, in central Italy: do arboreal snakes eat more birds than terrestrial ones?', *Journal of Herpetology*, 27(1):116-117.
14. Diller, L. V. and Johnson, D. R. (1988), 'Food habits, consumption rates and predation rates of western rattlesnakes and gopher snakes in southwestern Idaho', *Herpetologica*, 26(1):32-37.
15. Coleman, K., Rothfuss, L. A., Ota, H. and Kardong, K. V. (1993) 'Kinematics of egg-eating by the specialised Taiwan snake *Oligodon formosanus*', *Journal of Herpetology*, 27(3):320-327.
16. Norton, R. L. (1993), 'Life History Notes', *Herpetological Review*, 24(1):34.
17. Bedford. G. (1991), 'Record of road kill predation by the fresh water snake (*Tropidonophis mairii*)', *Herpetofauna*, 21(2):35-36.
18. Henderson. R. W. (1993), 'On the diets of some arboreal boids', *Herpetological Natural History*, 1(1):91-96.
19. Shine, R. (1984), 'Ecology of small fossorial Australian snakes of the genera *Neelaps* and *Simoselaps*', *Vertebrate Ecology and Systematics*, Univ. Kans. Mus. Nat. Hist. Spec. Publ. 10:173-184.
20. Murphy, J. B., Carpenter, C. C. and Gillingham, J. C. (1976), 'Caudal luring in the green tree python, *Chondropython viridis*', *Journal of Herpetology*, 12(1):117-119.
21. Sazima, I and Puorto, G. (1993), 'Feeding technique of juvenile *Tropidodryas striaticeps*: probable caudal luring in a colubrid snake', *Copeia*, 1993(1):222-226.
22. Greene, H. W. and Campbell, J. A. (1972), 'Notes on the use of caudal lures by arboreal pit vipers', *Herpetologica*, 28:32-34.
23. Pook, C. (1990), 'Notes on the genus *Atheris*', *British Herpetological Society Bulletin*, (23):31-36.
24. Carpenter, C. C., Murphy, J. B. and Carpenter, G. C. (1976), 'Tail luring in the death adder, *Acanthophis ontarcticus*', *Journal of Herpetology*, -12(4):143-161.
25. Clark, R. (1993), 'Viper bite in France - a cautionary tale', *Herptile*, 18(4):159-164.
26. Ramirez-Bautista, A. and Uribe, Z. (1992), '*Trimorphodon biscutatus* (Lyre snake): predation fatality', *Herpetological Review*, 23(3):82.
27. Naulleau, G. (1983), 'The effects of temperature on digestion in *Vipera aspis*', *Journal of Herpetology*, 17(2):166-170.

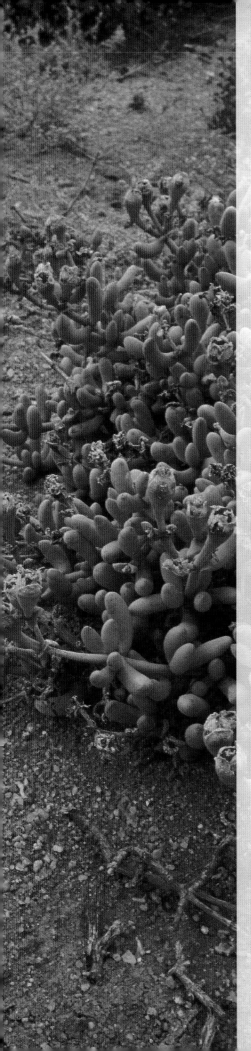

CHAPTER 6
DEFENCE

Despite being predators themselves, snakes have many enemies. These are often other snakes, and Chapter 5 lists a small selection of species that feed on other snakes, or even on their own species. Other types of predators are dealt with here.

A horned adder, *Bitis caudalis*, coiled among succulent plants in Namaqualand, South Africa

PREDATORS OF SNAKES

APART FROM OTHER SNAKES, SIGNIFICANT PREDATORS INCLUDE MANY BIRDS OF PREY, SUCH AS EAGLES, HAWKS, BUZZARDS, STORKS AND HORNBILLS. THE LIST ALSO INCLUDES A FEW SPECIALISTS, SUCH AS THE ROADRUNNER, *GEOCOCCYX CALIFORNIANUS*, THE AFRICAN SECRETARY BIRD, *SAGITTARIUS SERPENTARIUS*, AND THE SERPENT EAGLES BELONGING TO THE GENUS *CIRCAETUS*. OTHER BIRDS THAT HAVE BEEN RECORDED AS HAVING EATEN SNAKES INCLUDE THE RED-TAILED HAWK, *BUTEO JAMAICENSIS*, RED-SHOULDERED HAWKS, *BUTEO LINEATUS*, BALD EAGLES, *HAHAETUS LEUCOCEPHALUS*, CARACARAS, *POLYBORUS PLANCUS*, SEVERAL OWLS – INCLUDING THE MEXICAN SPOTTED OWL *STRIX OCCIDENTALIS* – AND A NUMBER OF CORVIDS, INCLUDING THE RAVEN, *CORVUS CORAX*, AND THE BLUE JAY, *CYANOCITTA CRISTATA*.

Among mammals, their predators range from omnivorous opportunists such as foxes, skunks, the European hedgehog and the North American racoon, to a number of specialists such as the various species of mongooses that are present in several parts of the world. Venomous as well as harmless snakes fall prey to these animals, and a number of predators have devised techniques that help them to avoid being bitten. Snakes in hibernation are particularly vulnerable and surveys have shown that a relatively high proportion are killed at this time, by predators as diverse as foxes, skunks and shrews.

Among the more unusual predators, though probably not significant in terms of the numbers taken, can be included various invertebrates, including spiders such as the large mygalomorphs and the black widow, or red-backed spider, *Lactorodectus mactans*, which was observed by Paul Orange (1990)[1] capturing an Australian elapid, the monk snake, *Rhinoplocephalus monachus*. The same author reported a large centipede that had fatally bitten a worm snake, *Ramphotyphlops australis*.[2] North American scorpions belonging to the genera *Diplocentrus*, *Hadrurus* and *Paruroctonus* also eat thread snakes, *Leptotyphlops humilis*, and also take larger snakes on occasion, including the night snake, *Hypsiglena torquata* (Hibbetts, 1992).[3] Also in North America, the vinegaroon, *Mastigoproctus giganteus*, is known to have eaten small snakes, while aquatic bugs (Belostomatidae) and diving beetle larvae are also recorded predators of semi-aquatic species such as garter and ribbon snakes. Fish may also eat snakes when they get the chance, although the only documented record appears to be that of a brook trout eating a sharp-tailed snake, *Contia tenuis*.

Frogs and toads often eat some of the smaller species of snakes, perhaps mistaking them for worms. Toads are especially voracious, with Asian black-spined toads, *Bufo melanostictus*, having eaten more than one flowerpot snake, *Ramphotyphlops braminus*, and the western toad, *Bufo boreas*, eating a sharp-tailed snake, *Contia tenuis*. A South American bullfrog, *Leptodactylus pentadactylus*, regurgitated a specimen of the terrestrial colubrid snake *Atractus zidoki*, while a more remarkable record involved the investigation of a preserved specimen of the African bullfrog, *Pyxicephalus adspersus*, that had consumed what appeared to have been a newborn litter of 16 rinkhals cobras, *Haemachatus hemachatus*: mysteriously, the front half of an additional young cobra was also present.

▶ (top) Where they occur, crocodiles and alligators are among the predators of snakes, especially aquatic and semi-aquatic species.

▶ (bottom left) Large monitor lizards such as *Varanus albigularis* frequently prey on snakes, including venomous species such as the puff adder, *Bids arietans*.

▶ (bottom right) Although many birds eat snakes, the secretary bird, *Sagittarius serpentarius*, is probably the most famous of them. It is a highly adapted bird of prey that hunts by using its long legs to walk over grasslands in East Africa. When it finds a snake it stamps its feet until the reptile is pounded to death.

DEFENSIVE STRATEGIES

IN ORDER TO AVOID PREDATION, SNAKES, IN THEIR TURN, HAVE EVOLVED DEFENSIVE STRATEGIES. THESE VARY FROM SPECIES TO SPECIES AND A REPERTOIRE OF DEFENSIVE BEHAVIOUR MAY BE USED BY THE SAME SPECIES UNDER DIFFERENT CIRCUMSTANCES. CONVERSELY, SEVERAL DEFENSIVE STRATEGIES MAY BE USED IN CONJUNCTION WITH ONE ANOTHER, OR ONE ATTEMPT TO DETER ENEMIES MAY BE FOLLOWED BY ANOTHER, QUITE DIFFERENT, BEHAVIOURAL SEQUENCE.

Most snakes try to avoid confrontations whenever possible and this they do by concealment, crypsis or by flight. All these techniques are amazingly effective. Just how effective they are, of course, is hard to judge, it being rather difficult to count the number of snakes that are not seen! A good indication of population densities can be sometimes gleaned, however, when a road is cut through a forested habitat or when driving across a desert or swamp on a little-used road. Snakes often turn up in their hundreds in these situations even though many hours of conventional searching will have been completely unproductive.

Concealment

Most snakes conceal themselves when they are not actively trying to raise their body temperature by basking, searching for food or searching for mates. Because of their long, slender shape, they are well suited to entering small crevices in the ground, in tree trunks or between rocks. Many snakes are found when old buildings are pulled down or when rocks are moved during excavations, for instance. Very often, the size of the snake belies the apparent size of the chamber in which it was hiding and snake keepers are often amazed at the small space that even bulky snakes can fit into (and they are equally amazed at the small openings through which they can escape).

In most environments, then, there will almost always be an abundance of places in which snakes may be hidden. Some places are habitually frequented by the same snake, as evidenced by the number of shed skins that may be found in them. Only when the snake outgrows its hideaway will it move to another. Where there are no suitable nooks and crannies for concealment, as in sand deserts, snakes conceal themselves by burrowing, either making permanent tunnels and chambers in which to live or by shuffling or 'swimming' below the surface as the necessity arises.

Crypsis

Snakes are ideally placed to exploit the natural phenomenon of crypsis. In the first place, they can change into an almost infinite number of different shapes – a predator with a search image of an outstretched snake may overlook a tightly coiled one, and vice versa, and there are many intermediate shapes that each snake can assume. Colour and markings are frequently used cryptically. Crypsis relies on the ability to blend into the background, to 'hide in full view'. This is best achieved by a colour scheme that not only matches the surroundings but which also helps to break up the outline of the snake.

Few snakes are uniformly coloured for the simple reason that few substrates are uniformly coloured: a plain brown snake resting on a substrate of dead leaves, for instance, would be easily seen because its outline would separate it visually from the leaves. A mottled brown snake, or a snake with markings comprising irregular blotches of different shades of brown, would blend into the background very well. There are a few black snakes, however, in which the coloration has almost certainly evolved for purposes other than crypsis – there is a trade-off here between the desire to remain concealed and the necessity to absorb heat as efficiently as possible, and the latter has proved to be the most important factor, especially in species from cool environments (see Chapter 3, 'thermoregulation').

Green snakes tend to be arboreal, or they may live in lush understory vegetation such as reeds and grasses. Many green snakes are countershaded – that is, they are lighter in colour underneath so that, when seen from the side, the shaded ventral surface appears roughly the same shade of colour as the dorsal surface. Aquatic snakes may also be marked in this way for the same reason. Other green snakes have some markings, such as the white transverse bands found along the dorsal surface of both the emerald boa *Corallus caninus*, and the green tree python, *Morelia viridis*, in order to break up their outlines. Other arboreal species may be coloured in various shades of green and some from humid rainforest environments are beautifully patterned to match the lichen and moss-covered twigs and branches among which they rest.

Terrestrial snakes occur in a variety of colours, many of which have evolved to match the substrates on which they live. Thus, desert snakes may be grey, yellow, pale brown or even pinkish in colour, often mottled or speckled to simulate light and shadow playing on the sand and gravel on which they rest. Where a species has a wide range over an area with differing soil or rock types, its colour will often vary from place to place. Similarly, snakes that live in rocky places usually closely match the rock colour and they may be additionally

◄ The coloration of the horned adder, *Bitis caudalis*, varies throughout its range according to the colour of the substrate. In Namaqualand, South Africa, this is orange, so the snake also takes on this colour.

▲ A large number of snakes, such as the many-horned viper, *Bitis cornuta*, have patterns or lines that pass through their eyes in order to disrupt the outline of their heads.

▶ Many forest dwelling species, such as *Bothrops atrox*, are well camouflaged.

▼ Arboreal species tend to be well camouflaged, sometimes with lichen-like coloration, as is this form of the eyelash viper, *Bothriechis schlegelii*.

marked to suggest even the texture of the rock or, in the case of the banded rock rattlesnake, *Crotalus lepidus klauberi*, the lichens growing on it.

In other snakes, the principle of breaking up the outline, or disruptive coloration, has become an end in itself. Some of these species have patches of colours that do little to match the snake's usual substrate but which, because of the complexity with which they are arranged, make the overall snake very difficult to discern. The Gaboon viper, *Bitis gabonica*, is the most obvious and famous example but there are several others, especially among the vipers and the pit vipers. Disruptive coloration may be used on the head of an otherwise striped, banded or blotched snake. Dark lines often pass through the eyes and the pigments within the iris itself may form a continuation of the pattern. This disguises the eye, an organ that is easily discernible and which may spoil an otherwise good camouflage.

The outline may also be disguised by using appendages such as those of the fishing snake, *Erpeton tentaculum*, an aquatic species that has two fleshy 'tentacles' arising from its snout. The species is also cryptically marked and hangs motionless among aquatic vegetation waiting for small fishes to swim past. Other species

▲ Despite its seemingly gaudy coloration, the Gaboon viper, *Bitis gabonica*, is well camouflaged when it is resting among leaves and other forest debris.

▼ A large number of snakes, such as the many-horned viper, *Bitis cornuta*, have patterns or lines that pass through their eyes in order to disrupt the outline of their heads.

have single nasal appendages, those of the Madagascan twig snakes, *Langaha*, being the most extreme: males have simple tapered appendages but those of females are lobed.

In order to enhance the effectiveness of their colours and patterns, many cryptic species 'freeze' when disturbed, relying entirely on their camouflage for protection. The twig snakes, *Thelotornis*, from Africa, various vine snakes such as *Ahaetulla* from Asia and *Oxybelis* from North America, as well as the *Langaha* species mentioned above, are well known for this behaviour and some go so far as to protrude their tongues in order to increase the effectiveness of the ruse. Other species, such as the Pacific ground boa, *Candoia carinata*, especially when young, may become quite rigid when handled and, if placed on the ground, sometimes remain motionless for several minutes. More commonly, however, cryptic species will resort to flight once detection seems imminent.

Polymorphism

Another type of defence through coloration is polymorphism. Many species exist in two or more basic colours or patterns. It is important to distinguish between regional species variations, which may be adapted to different situations, and polymorphism.

◀ Many slender snakes, such as the rough green snake, *Liochlorophis aestivus*, lie motionless in order to escape detection.

▼ Polymorphism is relatively common among snakes. In its simplest form, snakes of the same species occur in spotted and striped forms, side by side, as in the European leopard snake, *Zamenis situla*.

may be overlooked. As a rule, predators could be expected to maintain a search image of the most common form and the less common form will benefit. After a while, *it* may find itself to be the most common form, due to the protection it received, and the population of predators may switch their attention accordingly. In the long term, polymorphism will be maintained in the population and both forms can be expected to occur in roughly the same numbers, all other things being equal. Polymorphism is controlled by genes, usually a simple Mendelian system in which one phenotype is dominant over the other.

Colour polymorphism

Colour polymorphism probably has similar benefits. Certain populations of snakes have differently coloured individuals and some species are so diverse that hardly any two are the same – the Amazon tree boa, *Corallus hortulanuis*, is a good example. Furthermore, there are numerous species in which the young and the adults are coloured or marked differently –

Pattern polymorphism

The most common type of pattern polymorphism is the coexistence of banded (or spotted) and striped individuals in the same population. The most often quoted example is that of the Californian kingsnake, *Lampropeltis getulus californiae*, which may have its black and white marking arranged as a series of bands or rings, or as longitudinal stripes.

There are many other examples, however, including the gopher snake, *Pituophis catenifer catenifer*, which is usually blotched but may be striped in parts of its range, the European leopard snake, *Zamenis situla*, and the Caicos boa, *Epicrates chrysogaster chrysogaster*, from the West Indies, which both have a striped and a spotted form.

Other species occur in a bewildering variety of colours and patterns. The sea snake, *Pelamis platurus*, for instance has longitudinal stripes of varying width and which may be black, yellow and brown

(the most common combination), black and yellow or, in a few cases, plain yellow. The small ground snake, *Sonora episcopa*, may be plain coloured, barred with black or it may have longitudinal stripes running along its back. Similarly, *Vipera latifi*, from Iran, is found in four distinct colour morphs. Male boomslangs, *Dispholidus typus*, are not only differently marked from females (see page 165, Chapter 7) but are also highly variable themselves. These are but a few examples of snakes that show polymorphism of one sort or another.

The most feasible explanation for pattern polymorphism relies on the principle of 'search image'. It can be shown that many predators build up a mental picture of their prey. Animals that do not match this picture are often ignored, even though they are equally suitable as food. If a predator builds up a search-image of a striped snake, for instance, spotted or banded individuals

▶ (top) Bold stripes on snakes such as the Mexican rosy boa, *Charina trivirgata trivirgata*, can create an optical illusion as the snake crawls away.

▶ (below) The Californian kingsnake, *Lampropeltis getula californiae*, is usually patterned with bold black and white bands which create an optical illusion when it moves quickly. This species also occurs in a striped form, an example of polymorphism which is thought to be related to another of its defensive strategies.

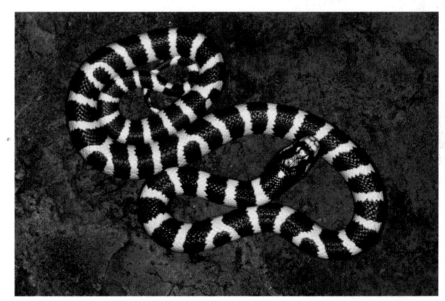

although this is a type of polymorphism, it relies not on the principle of search images but on the differing habitats used by different ages of the snake.

Flight

The overriding impulse for snakes that are caught in the open is to escape. They may do this by fleeing, burrowing or retreating into small crevices. Anyone who has tried to photograph snakes, for instance, will know that the vast majority try repeatedly to escape, even when subjected to excessive handling – only under severe duress do they become aggressive. Even cryptic species will often resort to flight if they feel that their camouflage has failed. Although snakes cannot move very fast, they are able to move unhindered through thick vegetation or over uneven ground. Many do not venture far from crevices whose location they seem to know and to which they return quickly.

A number of species have coloration that makes it difficult for a predator to estimate the speed and even the direction in which they are travelling. Longitudinal stripes, for instance, may appear to remain in the same place even though the snake has started to move away, so fooling a predator into thinking it has more time to spare than it actually does. Transverse bands and saddles can have an even more startling effect. Once the snake is moving quite quickly, the effect of these markings flickering past, possibly glimpsed through a gap in the vegetation, can have an almost hypnotic effect. The speed of travel is hard to estimate and, due to an optical illusion, it can even look as though the snake is travelling in the opposite direction. By the time the brain has processed the information, the snake's tail has disappeared from the spot and it is well on the way to a safe place. Longitudinal stripes and bold transverse bands are commonly seen in the markings of snakes that are relatively fast moving.

Intimidation

When cornered, many snakes put up a great show of aggression. This is often bluff but its effect on predators can be significant. Intimidation usually takes the form of puffing up the body to make it appear larger, facing the enemy and raising or flattening the head, hissing or making other warning sounds and, as a last resort, striking, sometimes with the mouth closed. Temperament varies greatly between the species. Some are invariably docile, even when first captured, whereas others are always aggressive.

Body enlargement

A common strategy among animals that are threatened is to make themselves appear larger than they are. This fulfils a dual function – predators may think twice before tackling them and, in the case of predators that swallow their prey whole, notably other snakes, a large size may cause them to reject an otherwise suitable meal. Enlargement may occur over the whole of the snake's surface or it may be concentrated in a particular area, usually the head and neck.

Puffing snakes

Numerous species inflate their bodies with air, puffing themselves up. Several of these are also 'hissers', exhaling the air forcibly to create a loud warning sound. Examples include the African *Bitis*

CATERPILLARS THAT IMITATE SNAKES

Snakes have numerous ways of intimidating predators, mostly stereotyped behaviour patterns that make them look larger and more fierce than they really are. The signal they send may be real, as in venomous species, or false, as in harmless species that have similar displays to venomous ones. In either case, predators, including humans, frequently back off to avoid further confrontation and possible risk to themselves.

Because the ploy works so well, it is hardly surprising that harmless animals in other groups have evolved displays that make them look superficially like snakes. Legless lizards are well placed to do this and some of the Australian flap-footed lizards belonging to the genus *Delma* appear to be convincing mimics of dangerous snakes whose habitat they share.

Perhaps the most remarkable mimics, though, are found among the insects. Whereas many adult butterflies and moths have large eyespots that are designed to imitate birds of prey, their larvae may imitate snakes. This behaviour is especially common among the caterpillars of the Sphingidae, or hawkmoths. Larvae of the elephant hawkmoth, for instance, have large eyespots on the upper part of their bodies and are frequently mistaken for snakes by human observers.

The larvae belonging to the hawkmoth genus *Leucorampha*, which come from Central America and northern South America, have an even more cunning trick. When disturbed, they detach the front part of their body from the twig on which they were resting and hold it rigid. At the same time it is inflated to form a broad triangular 'head' and turned through 180 degrees to expose the eyespots. Other small markings simulate scales and additional dark areas in front of the eyespots seem to be pits, just like those of the arboreal pit vipers that they mimic. If further disturbed, the caterpillars 'strike' accurately at any object that touches them.

◀ A South American hawkmoth caterpillar mimicking an arboreal pit viper.

▲ The bold marking on the back of the hood of the spectacled cobra is used to warn enemies.

▲ The typical defensive posture of the monocled cobra, *Naja kaouthia*.

species, especially *B. arietans*, which is commonly called the puff adder and the North American *Heterodon* species, which are also known in some areas by the local name of puffing 'adders'.

Spreading hoods

Many cobras raise the front part of their body and spread the ribs of their neck to form a hood. The hood may have bold markings on its back and the cobra may turn in order to display these. Species that use this behaviour as part of their defensive repertoire are those belonging to the genera *Naja*, including both African and Asian species, the King cobra *Ophiophagus hannah* from Asia, both species of *Aspidelaps* and the Rinkhals *Hemachatus haemachatus*, all from southern Africa and some species of black snakes, *Pseudechis*, from Australia. This is purely a defensive action: cobras do not rear or spread their hoods prior to attacking prey.

Apart from the elapids, a number of colubrids also flatten their necks to form hoods. Perhaps some of them are mimicking cobras but others, that occur well outside the range of any cobra, are merely making themselves look larger and more menacing. The Middle Eastern false cobra, *Malpolon monspessulanus*, for example, flattens the front part of its body and raises it off the ground, though not as upright as cobras. The American hognose snakes, *Heterodon*, flatten their heads and necks, hiss angrily and make mock strikes at the same time. Even small species may spread their necks – *Ninia sebae*, from Central America, for instance.

Another strategy is to inflate the throat, often revealing brightly coloured patches of interstitial skin or bold patterns. Snakes that do this include the boomslang, *Dispholidus typus*, the closely related bird

▶ Some species, such as the twig snake, *Thelotornis capensis*, inflate their throat, displaying the bold markings on their interstitial skin, normally hidden by their scales.

▲ The false habu, *Macropisthodon rudis*, a harmless – but aggressive – species from Southeast Asia, has the appearance and demeanour of a terrestrial pit viper.

snakes, *Thelotornis*, and a number of other tree snakes, including some *Boiga* species.

Snakes that flatten their heads, of which their are many, may be displaying brightly coloured lip scales as a warning or they may be attempting to mimic venomous vipers, which characteristically have broad, triangular heads. The African Herald snake, *Crotaphopeltis hotamboeia*, has bright red labial scales, whereas the equivalent scales in the South American *Pseustes sulphureus* and the Asian mangrove snake, *Boiga dendrophila*, are

yellow. Other species with chunky bodies, wide heads and markings similar to vipers, including *Waglerophis* and *Xenodon* species, from Latin America, can easily be mistaken for pit vipers from the region, but perhaps the most convincing viper mimic is the false habu, *Macropisthodon rudis*, which not only looks like terrestrial pit vipers from Asia, but also behaves in a similar manner.

Gaping

Intimidation can also take the form of opening the mouth widely, sometimes exposing brightly coloured interiors. The cottonmouth, *Agkistrodon piscivorus*, has a white mouth that contrasts strongly with its otherwise dark coloration and the parrot snakes, *Leptophis*, of Central and South America have blue areas inside their mouths. These displays are not entirely bluff – they act as preliminary warnings and are followed by striking if the warning is not heeded.

Warning sounds

Although snakes do not hear airborne sounds very well, most of their enemies do. They make use of this fact by producing a variety of sounds in their defence. These take the form of hissing, common to all snakes except the most primitive ones, rattling the tail, an option that is only open to two genera of specialised pit vipers, and rubbing the scales on the body together to produce a buzzing or rasping sound, an even less common strategy only performed by a few species in Africa and the Middle East.

Hissing

With the exception of the primitive burrowing species, most snakes can hiss. Very often hissing accompanies mock strikes or the taking up of a defensive

▲ Snakes other than cobras also spread their necks in an attempt to make themselves look larger and more fierce than they are. The eastern hognose snake, *Heterodon platyrhinos*, and its relatives, are great bluffers.

▶ Where snakes have brightly coloured labial scales, such as this *Pseustes sulphureus*, spreading the head or neck may help to display them more prominently.

THE SNAKE THAT LOST ITS RATTLE

The Santa Catalina rattlesnake, *Crotalus catalinensis*, is unique among members of its genus in lacking a rattle. This island form is most closely related to the red diamond rattlesnake, *C. ruber*, and probably reached Santa Catalina by rafting. During its residence on the island its rattle appears to have become progressively smaller until it disappeared altogether. Why should this species have lost its rattle?

The evolution of a rattle, to be used as a warning device, was probably possible only because most rattlesnakes ambush their prey: it could never have evolved if they actively hunted for their food because the need to drag such an unwieldy and noisy appendage behind them would be a severe handicap, one that would outweigh any advantage that the rattlesnake gained by alerting its enemies.

In the case of the Santa Catalina rattlesnake, two factors may be important. Firstly, because the island has no large predators nor any large hoofed mammals, both of which are threats to rattlesnakes on the mainland, the warning function of the rattle has become largely redundant. Secondly, the snake appears to have undergone a shift in its diet and its feeding habits: it preys largely on spiny lizards and small birds, which it hunts at night while they are roosting in shrubs. The rattle, far from being an asset, would soon become a distinct liability for any snake trying to use stealth to stalk sleeping prey and it may also impede its progress through twigs and branches. There would therefore be a strong selective pressure favouring the individuals that had small or missing rattles.

Along with the loss of its rattle, natural selection seems to have favoured a more elongated body than in related mainland forms, and significantly longer teeth: both of these characteristics are associated with snakes that hunt in trees and shrubs. Furthermore, the Santa Catalina rattlesnake does not bite and release its prey in the usual rattlesnake fashion, but holds it in its jaws until the venom takes effect, thus avoiding the possibility that its prey could drop or fly out of reach before it succumbed.

Two other populations appear to be in the process of losing their rattles and both are confined to islands in the Gulf of California: these are a form of the red diamond rattlesnake, *Crotalus ruber lorenzoensis*, from the island of San Lorenzo Sur, and the San Esteban form of the black-tailed rattlesnake, *Crotalus molossus estebanensis*. The feeding habits of these two rattlesnake subspecies have not yet been studied.

▲ The South American parrot snake, *Leptophis ahaetulla*, has a stereotyped defensive behaviour, in which it gapes widely, displaying the inside of its mouth. If this fails, it bites.

▲ The cottonmouth, *Agklstrodon piscivorus*, is well named: its intimidation display consists of opening its mouth widely to show the white interior.

posture and in some species, notably the American gopher snakes, *Pituophis*, the sound is amplified by the vibration of a flap or membrane of skin in the glottis.

Rattling

Rattles are found only in two genera of snakes, *Crotalus* and *Sistrurus*. By vibrating their tails, which they do when they are alarmed, these snakes cause the segments of their rattles to knock against one another, although the noise produced when rattlers 'sound off' is more of a buzz than a rattle, and often ends with a few tick-like clatters as the vibrations ease off. The structure of the rattle, and how it is formed, are described on page 35.

Contrary to the belief of some nineteenth-century naturalists, the rattlesnake does not use its rattle to serenade lady rattlesnakes, nor does it use it to warn other rattlesnakes of danger! The rattle is only used when the snake finds itself in a potentially dangerous situation. The main function is therefore

▲ Santa Catalina rattlesnake which, through evolution, has lost its rattle.

▲ The tail of a Santa Catalina rattlesnake.

WARNING BEHAVIOUR IN DESERT VIPERS

Because snakes do not hear airborne sounds very well, they do not communicate with each other by sound and have not evolved the same range of vocalizations found in the insects, birds and mammals. They may use sounds as warning, however, since many of their predators hear well: these sounds are mostly limited to hissing, although the rattlesnakes have evolved an alternative method. The saw-scaled vipers, *Echis*, and the closely related horned desert vipers, *Cerastes*, have evolved a third method.

These species produce a loud rasping sound by rubbing together several rows of specialised scales on their flanks. The scales involved are those of the third to the ninth scale rows on each side. Each of these scales is heavily keeled as they are in many other snakes: in *Echis* and *Cerastes*, however, the scales, and the keels, are arranged at an oblique angle instead of being aligned along the body. The keels on these specialised scales are also serrated, like the teeth of a saw.

When the snake is threatened, it forms a characteristic U-shaped defensive coil, in which it folds its body back on itself several times. The snake now moves the coils against one another, so that the saw-toothed ridges on adjacent parts of the body rub together, producing a harsh, rasping sound.

This unique structure and behaviour may have evolved because the snakes live in arid habitats, in parts of North Africa, the Middle East, India and Sri Lanka, where water is precious. If they were to hiss, they would lose water, in the form of vapour, as the air was expelled through their mouth. By rubbing their scales together instead, they may avoid this, and still produce a clear warning.

In Africa, some of the harmless egg-eating snakes, *Dasypeltis* species, which have similar markings to the vipers, also mimic their defensive behaviour where their ranges overlap.

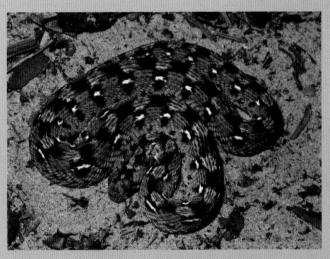

▲ A saw-scaled viper, *Echis ocellatus*, in defensive posture. By coiling in this way the snake brings the serrated scales on its flanks together in a way that produces a sound.

▲ Egg-eating snake, *Dasypeltis fasciata*, mimicking a saw-scaled viper. Notice how it forms a similar horseshoe shaped coil so that it can rub its scales together.

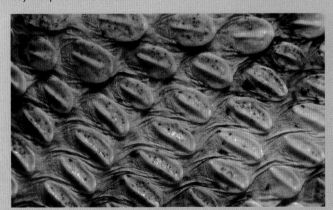

▲ Obliquely arranged, serrated scales on the flanks of the desert horned viper, *Cerastes cerastes*, produce a rasping sound when they are rubbed against similar scales further along the body.

▲ Scales on the flanks of the common egg-eater have oblique keels, just as they do on the venomous species that produce a rasping sound for warning purposes.

▲ A speckled rock rattlesnake, *Crotalus mitchelli pyrrhus*, takes up a defensive posture in the Anza-Borrego Desert, Southern California.

to warn enemies, a theory that is reinforced by the fact that rattlesnakes frequently take up a defensive posture when they are sounding off – the front part of their body is formed into an S-shaped coil and the head is held off the ground, facing the direction of the threat.

In addition, rattlesnakes may benefit by warning larger animals of their presence, so avoiding the risk of being trodden on – a great asset for snakes that are well camouflaged. With the coming of man, it could be that the rattle is now a disadvantage because not only does it draw attention to the snake, which might otherwise be overlooked, but it also identifies it as public enemy number one.

The evolution of the rattle is something of a mystery. There are no snakes with any intermediate stages – they either have a rattle or they don't. Many other snakes, though, do vibrate their tails if they are disturbed and, if they happen to be resting among dead leaves or loose pebbles, a rustling or rattling sound is the result. The first step towards the evolution of a rattle could have been taken by a snake that vibrated its tail which had, by chance, a deformed tip, causing a build-up of shed epidermis.

'Popping'

A few snakes from North and Central America have been observed lifting their tails and emitting a bubbling or popping sound from their vents. Since they do this only when threatened it is assumed to be a defensive mechanism, although why it should be effective is hard to guess.

Warning coloration and mimicry

Animals that are able to inflict injury often perform ritualised behaviour patterns in order to avoid direct confrontation. Others are coloured in such a way that they warn of their ability to cause pain or death.

Venomous snakes are no exception, and behaviour such as spreading of hoods or rattling the tail, while primarily intended to intimidate their enemies, may also serve to identify the snake as a venomous one and issue a warning. Other species use distinctive patterns of colour to identify themselves.

By far the most famous examples of warning coloration among snakes are the coral snakes, *Micrurus* and *Micruroides* of North, Central and South America. The 50 or so species are all coloured with bright bands or rings (annuli) around their bodies. These bands are frequently black, white (or yellow) and red. Some species have black and one other colour but the majority are tri-coloured. All these species are dangerously venomous.

Other members of the Elapidae, in different parts of the world, also have brightly coloured bodies. These include species from Africa, such as *Aspidelaps lubricus*, also known as coral snakes, and garter snakes, *Elapsoidea* species, others from Asia, including the kraits, *Bungarus*, and the coral snakes, *Calliophis*, and yet others from Australia, especially the small species belonging to the genera *Simoselaps* and *Vermicella*.

There has been a great deal of debate as to the way in which warning coloration benefits the snakes. The simplistic theory, that predators learn to avoid such brightly coloured species, is not without its problems, not least of which is the fact that many of these species are deadly and any animal attacking them would be unlikely to live long enough for the lesson to be of benefit, either to itself or to the snakes. In

▲ The Malaysian coral snake is spectacularly coloured. Its underside is red and it will turn itself upside down if threatened.

▲ (left) The brightly coloured Texas coral snake, *Micrurus fulvius*, a small venomous snake related to the cobras and mambas.

▲ (right) Certain kingsnakes and milksnakes, which are harmless, are thought to mimic coral snakes and *Lampropeltis triangulum elapsoides* certainly gives a good imitation of one.

addition, most of the species involved are secretive or burrowing snakes that rarely occur on the surface in daylight. Furthermore, many snake predators, including mammals, are colour-blind.

Several alternative theories have been proposed. One of these is Mertensian mimicry: the deadly coral snakes are mimicking similarly marked snakes that are only mildly venomous. Although these do exist, in the form of the false coral snakes, *Erythrolamprus*, for instance, they are restricted to Central and parts of South America, whereas the American coral snakes have a much wider range. Furthermore, this theory ignores the boldly marked species from other parts of the world. Another theory is that the bright coloration has arisen purely by chance; since the coral snakes are secretive, there is no selective pressure on them to be any particular colour. This theory is equally hard to accept because most other burrowing snakes, such as the worm and thread snakes, tend to be pale in colour, probably because there is a physiological cost involved in producing pigment and this cost can be reduced if pigment is sparse or lacking altogether.

Perhaps the most likely theory is that of 'innate aversion'. In a series of experiments, Susan Smith (1975)[4] showed that young laboratory-reared

▲ (centre) The back-fanged snakes belonging to the genus *Erythrolamprus* are found over much of the range of coral snakes and there are some suggestions of mimicry. Their similarity could equally well be coincidental, however.

▲ (bottom) Many other brightly coloured 'false' coral snakes, such as the Sonoran mountain kingsnake, *Lampropeltis pyromelana*, do not share the same habitat as coral snakes, nor are they very convincing mimics.

▲ The royal python, *Python regius*, is also known as the ball python for a good reason.

birds avoided wooden rods painted with black, yellow and red rings but did not avoid a series of rods painted in other colours and patterns. The implications are that animals have an innate aversion to brightly coloured animals and objects. Humans use such colour patterns to warn of danger on roads, railways, and so on. Many distasteful insects are also brightly coloured. Even colour-blind predators would be able to distinguish the light and dark bands displayed by these snakes.

It has been shown, in other contexts, that predators with plenty of time to examine potential food are far more choosy than those that have to make snap decisions. Because they are so secretive, the colours of the coral snakes need to send a very clear signal so that, if they are suddenly uncovered by the activities of a predator, they can be read instantaneously.

In addition to the true coral snakes (that is, venomous members of the Elapidae), there are any number of 'false' coral snakes among the Colubridae and other families. They are said to be the mimics whereas the true coral snakes are the models. To list just a small number of examples, they include the milksnakes, *Lampropeltis triangulum* (North and Central America); several king snakes including *Lampropeltis pyromelana* and *L. zonata*, and the shovel-nosed snakes, *Chionactis* (North America); the false coral snakes belonging to the genus *Erythrolamprus* and the pipe snake, *Anilius scytale* (Central and South America); the spotted harlequin snake,

Homoroselaps dorsalis (Africa); and two whipsnakes, *Coluber elegantissimus* and *C. sinai* (Middle East).

Supporters of the learned-warning-coloration theory would argue that these species benefit because they look like coral snakes and predators would avoid them just as they have learned to avoid the models. The main flaw in this theory is that many of the mimics inhabit areas where there are no coral snakes. In addition, many of the 'false' coral snakes are not very good mimics – although they have the same basic colours, their arrangements are different, significantly so in several cases. These objections are difficult to refute whereas the 'innate aversion' theory applies equally well to harmless as well as harmful snakes.

Bright, contrasting colours, especially when they are arranged in bands or rings, serve the additional function of disrupting the outline of the snake and, in some cases, of creating an optical illusion when the snake moves quickly. Additional benefits may include startle – the initial reaction of a predator uncovering a brightly coloured snake unexpectedly may be to hesitate, so giving the snake more time to escape.

Balling

A common strategy that can be recognised in a number of snakes from different families has been called 'balling'. The snake forms its body into a tightly coiled mass, with its head towards the centre. The purpose appears to be to present the enemy with a shape that is difficult to deal with, while protecting the vulnerable head.

The royal python, *Python regius*, is also known as the ball python in reference to this behaviour. An African boa, *Calabaria reinhardtii*, also uses the method as do some tropidophiid and colubrid snakes.

Attack deflection (mimetic behaviour)

Although all parts of a snake are important, some are more important than others. Mimetic behaviour may occur when a snake is prepared to sacrifice one part of its anatomy in favour of a less essential part. The least important part of a snake's anatomy is its tail.

Some of the species that hide their head in their coils also offer their tails as false heads in order to deflect attack away from the real head. Rubber boas and Calabar burrowing boas both do this, and many adults have scarred and damaged tails, implying that the technique has served them well. In the latter species, the tail may have a shallow horizontal groove around its tip, simulating a mouth while in other species there may be a pattern of lines and spots to further the deception. The tail of the Asian sand boa, *Eryx tataricus*, consist of a short horizontal line and a black spot, resembling a mouth and an eye. Gerard's black and yellow burrowing snake, *Chilorhinophis gerardii*, has a similar pattern: its head and the tip of its tail are black, while the rest of the tail is blue, with a single black spot. When threatened, all these snakes lift the tip of their tail and wave them around as though they were the head. In extreme cases, the false head may make striking movements. The purpose is clearly to occupy the attacker's attention with the false head while seeking escape, perhaps by burrowing, with the real one.

There are several other examples of snakes that use their tails in defence. Many of these have brightly coloured undersides to their tails: an attack results in the snake raising its tail to expose the bright colours. Examples include the American ringneck snake, *Diadophis punctatus*, which turns its tail over, and forms it into a tight corkscrew shape. The underside of the tail is brilliant red in most forms of this species. The Asian pipe snakes, *Cylindrophis*, are boldly marked in black and white underneath. When they

▲ The 'corkscrew' display of the ringneck snake, *Diadophis punctatus*, exposes the snake's brightly coloured underside. At other times it is well camouflaged.

▲ Rubber boas, *Charina bottae*, may raise their blunt tails above their coils to deflect attack away from their head.

are disturbed, they flatten their body, raise their tail off the ground and curl it over their back, as though they were rearing their head and neck. From the same part of the world, the kukri snakes, *Oligodon*, have tail displays that involve raising and coiling the tail, which is brightly coloured underneath. Further annoyance is registered by using the tail to strike at the aggressor (Mori *et al.*, 1992).[5]

A final example is that of the African shovel-snouted snakes, *Prosymna*, which coil and uncoil their tails rapidly and repeatedly when disturbed. Their tails are not brightly coloured, however, and it is the movement that occupies the attention of the attacker.

Where species have tails that end in a sharp point, they may be pressed against the flesh of a predator, presumably to simulate a bite. This behaviour is common among snakes of the genus *Leptotyphlops* and is also seen in the American mud and rainbow snakes, *Farancia abacura* and *F. erytrogramma*, (sometimes known locally as 'stinging snakes' for this reason) and in the burrowing asp *Atractaspis engaddensis*.

Caudal autotomy

Caudal autotomy, or voluntary tail loss, is common among lizards of many species but is rare in snakes. Even among species that occasionally lose their tails, the mechanism is not as well developed as it is in lizards. In the latter, several vertebrae

towards the base of the tail have fracture planes across them and so, when the tail breaks, it is due to the parting of two halves of a vertebra. With two possible exceptions, snakes do not have this feature, and their tails break off at the point at which two vertebrae join. The two exceptions are the South American colubrids *Urotheca elapoides* and *Scaphiodontophis venustissimus*, neither of which have common names. In these species, examination of the lower part of the tail reveals a slight groove running around the centre of each vertebra; this is circumstantial evidence that they may allow their tails to break off across the vertebrae. Furthermore, the broken tails of snakes do not regenerate, other than forming a small conical scale over the wound, whereas those of lizards do. The

result of this is that an individual lizard may use the technique several times during its lifetime, growing a new tail after each episode, whereas snakes are capable of escaping only once by this means.

In *Enulius*, (four species) and *Enuliophis sclateri*, all from Central and northern South America, the tail is unusually long and thick: from 35 to 47 per cent of the snake's total length. If they are attacked these snakes thrash their tails violently

▼ A Colombian long-tailed snake, *Enuliophis sclateri*, in which a piece of tail has been lost during a previous encounter. Note how long and thick the remaining section of the tail is.

from side to side until a piece breaks off. It continues to twitch, occupying the predator's attention while the snake slips away. Over half the snakes have a portion of the tail missing, a record of past encounters. Unlike lizards, though, these species do not regenerate their tails but, being long, the snake may be able to break off several pieces of its tail in its lifetime. Another colubrid, *Coniophanes fissidens*, from the same region, also shows a high incidence of broken tails - up to 50% of individuals in some areas - and this may be the result of predation by coral snakes, such as *Micrurus nigrocinctus*, which pursue them through their burrows. In Africa, marsh snakes, *Natriciteres*, and sand snakes, *Psammophis*, spin their bodies rapidly if held by their tails, often resulting in a break.

Odour

Most snakes have musk glands situated at the base of their tails, the primary function of which is probably to produce hormone trails used in chemical communication. When attacked, or roughly handled, many of them excrete quantities of these substances, many of which have an unpleasant smell, to say the least. The secretions are milky in appearance and are sometimes produced in copious quantities. Some species are especially adept at wrapping themselves around the hand and liberally smearing their captor. The European grass snake is responsible for a particularly disgusting smell, often enough to persuade human predators to release them. (In my youth I was once evicted from a bus as a result of a particularly pungent grass snake that I had captured and was hoping to take home.) Members of the colubrid genera *Lampropeltis*, *Pantherophis* and *Elaphe* also produce unpleasant substances and the fox snake, *Pantherophis vulpina*, is named for the supposed resemblance of its particular potion to that of foxes.

Autohaemorrhagy

Autohaemorrhagy is the term given to the voluntary rupture of small blood vessels, allowing blood to ooze from various parts of the body. Although certainly a defensive reaction, the way in which it works is uncertain although in lizards which autohaemorrhage (horned lizards, *Phrynosoma*), there is some suggestion that the blood has an unpleasant taste, causing predators to drop them.

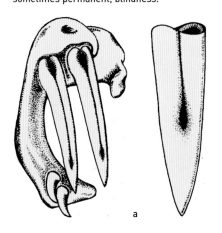

▲ Spitting cobras, such as *Naja mossambica*, have a formidable method of defence. Their venom can cause intense pain and temporary, sometimes permanent, blindness.

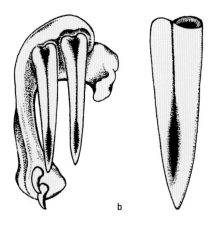

▼ The fangs of spitting cobras (a) have smaller aperatures than non-spitters (b) and they are located in the front rather than towards the tip.

a

b

▲ The Cuban dwarf boa, *Tropidophis melanurus*, is one of just a few snakes that force blood from their eyes and mouth when they are stressed.

▲ Several snakes, including the European grass snake, *Natrix natrix*, feign death if they are threatened.

Autohaemorrhagy has often been observed, in the dwarf boas, *Tropidophis* species, when handled. They first form tight balls then produce relatively large quantities of blood from their eyes and mouth. The species involved are six from the West Indies – *T. greenwayi*, *T. haetianus*, *T. marulatus*, *T. melanurus*, *T pardalis* and *T. semicinctus* – and two mainland species, *T. parkeri* and *T. paucisquamis*: it seems probable that the remaining few species, some of which are poorly known, also use this method of defence.

Other than this genus, autohaemorrhagy has only been noted, occasionally, in three other species, all from North America. These are: the long-nosed snake, *Rhinocheilus lecontei*, which bleeds from its cloaca and, less commonly, nostrils; the eastern hognose snake, *Heterodon platyrhinos*, which bleeds from its cloaca, sometimes prior to feigning death; and the water snake, *Nerodia erythrogaster*, which bleeds from its gums. In these colubrids, bleeding is accompanied by wild thrashing and can be accounted for by increased blood pressure during extreme exertion, possibly incidentally, whereas the dwarf boas appear to have greater control over the bleeding.

Spitting venom

The only snakes that can project their venom are the spitting cobras. Spitting seems to have arisen twice in this family, in the African spitting cobra, or rinkhals, *Hemachatus haemachatus*, and in a group of African and Asian species belonging to the genus *Naja*. The Asian spitting cobras were, until recently, classified as a single species, *Naja naja*, but recent research has shown that there are at least nine species, of which two (*N. naja* and *N. oxiana*) do not spit and the others do (or are thought to do so). Of the African species, *N. mossambica* and *N. nigricollis* are spitters.

Spitting is accomplished by forcing the venom through small apertures in the front of the fangs, causing it to be squirted out at high speed and in a fine spray. This involves a modification of the fangs, in which the aperture, normally fairly large and elongated, is reduced in size and rounded in shape. A strange situation occurs in *N. philippinensis*, where the fangs of males have short openings whereas those of females have long ones. This would suggest that only the males are able to spit.

The venom may be sprayed several metres with a fair degree of accuracy. As the cobras rear their heads prior to spitting, the attacker often receives the venom in its eyes, where it causes instant and intense pain. If not treated, temporary or even permanent blindness may follow in humans.

Feigning death

Pretending to be dead may seem to be a strange form of defensive behaviour as many predators are more than happy to eat carrion. It must be effective, however, for it to have evolved in a number of species of snakes. Foremost among these is the European grass snake, *Natrix natrix*, which may put up a convincing display by turning over and opening its mouth, allowing the tongue to hang out. Not all specimens perform, however, and individuals from some populations never do it. The American hognose snakes, *Heterodon*, and the African spitting cobra, or rinkhals, *Hemachatus haemachatus*, and the Egyptian cobra, *Naja haje*, are also well known for the same technique, but, like the grass snake, their willingness to play dead varies from snake to snake. It is noteworthy that, in all three of these species, death feigning comes at the end of a repertoire of other defensive activities, including intimidation and odour production. Death feigning has also been noted, although rarely, in two of the small North American snakes belonging to the genus *Storeria*, DeKay's brown snake, *S. dekayi* and the red-bellied snake, *S. occipitomaculata*.

NOTES

1. Orange, P. (1990), 'Predation on *Rhinoplocephalus monachus* by the redback spider *Latrodectus matans*', *Herpetofouna*, 20(1):34.
2. Orange, P. (1989), 'Incidents of predation on reptiles by invertebrates', *Herpetofauna*, 19(1):31-32.
3. Hibbetts, T. (1992), in Life history notes, *Herpetological Review*, 23(4):120.
4. Smith, Susan M. (1975), 'Innate recognition of coral snake pattern by a possible avian predator', *Science*, 4178:759-760.
5. Mori, A., Narumi, N. and Kardong, K. V. (1992). 'Unusual putative defensive behavior in *Oligodon formosanus*: head-slashing and tail-striking', *Journal of Herpetology*, 26(2):213-216.

CHAPTER 7
REPRODUCTION

All animals have a basic urge to reproduce in order to pass their genes on to the next generation, and snakes are no exception. The more offspring they can produce, the more their genes will proliferate. All aspects of reproductive behaviour are directed towards this goal.

Two hatchling carpet pythons emerge from the same egg. This is a rare event; perhaps two eggs become surrounded by the same shell in the mother's shell gland or perhaps a single egg splits into two early in its development.

SNAKE REPRODUCTION

THE WAY IN WHICH SNAKES REPRODUCE IS ONE OF THE MOST FASCINATING ASPECTS OF THEIR BIOLOGY AND HAS ATTRACTED A LOT OF INTEREST FROM RESEARCHERS, ESPECIALLY IN RECENT YEARS.

There are several reasons for this.

(1) Snakes may reproduce by laying eggs or giving birth to live young. Strictly speaking, if the snake simply retains the egg in its oviduct until it is on the point of hatching, this is ovoviviparity, whereas viviparity implies some exchange of materials (food and waste products) between mother and embryo.

(2) As well as variation in the reproductive method, snakes also vary in their reproductive output: clutch or litter size may be large or small in relation to the size of the species. The size of each offspring tends to vary in inverse proportion to the number of offspring, i.e. there is a trade-off between number and size of young.

(3) Snakes continue to grow throughout their lives, but reach sexual maturity when they are about half their maximum size. This is known as 'indeterminate growth' and results in an increasing reproductive output, i.e. as females grow larger, they are able to channel more resources into their offspring. This is not seen in other animals, which do not begin to breed until they have finished, or almost finished, growing.

(4) The shape of snakes puts certain constraints on the size of young or eggs they can deliver. This varies with species and their lifestyle. Slow-moving, bulky snakes are less constrained in this respect than active, slender ones.

(5) Female snakes are unusual among animals in that they can separate the time of mating from the time the eggs are fertilised. They do this by storing the sperm in their bodies. Whether or not they delay fertilisation in this way will depend on several factors, foremost of which is the necessity to lay eggs or give birth at a suitable time of the year.

In order to examine these options, it is necessary to understand the reproductive biology of snakes, and their breeding habits.

THE REPRODUCTIVE CYCLE

PHYSIOLOGICAL REPRODUCTIVE CYCLES, i.e. THE VARIATION IN THE STATE OF THE REPRODUCTIVE SYSTEM, ARE DISTINCT FROM BREEDING SEASONS, WHICH REFER TO BEHAVIOURAL ACTIVITIES THAT TAKE PLACE AT VARIOUS TIMES OF THE YEAR. ANNUAL REPRODUCTIVE CYCLES CAN USUALLY BE IDENTIFIED IN MALE AND FEMALE SNAKES, ALTHOUGH THEIR TIMING MAY DIFFER BETWEEN THE SEXES.

The male reproductive cycle

Most of what is known about males' reproductive cycles relates to temperate species, i.e. those species that undergo a period of inactivity in the winter. Males of this type of snake produce sperm in their testes during the part of the year when they are most actively feeding, usually summer and autumn. In tropical species the situation is less clear; it seems likely that males of many such species produce sperm throughout the year, even when there is a distinct breeding season, but males of other species may produce sperm at certain times of the year only, often immediately prior to the breeding season.

Whenever the sperm is produced, it is stored in a bladder-like structure formed from part of the ureter, where it stays until mating takes place. Each male produces and stores enough sperm to mate several times, either with the same female or with a number of different ones. Mating may not occur until the following spring in the case of temperate species. Although mature males are often reproductively active throughout the year, with viable sperm present, mating can only take place when females are receptive, usually at a well-defined time of the year.

The female reproductive cycle

Once again, most of the information relating to female reproductive cycles comes from research into temperate species. The timing of the female reproductive cycle tends to be better defined than that in males and several stages can be recognised.

The ovarian cycle

The first stage is the formation of small, follicular eggs in the ovary. These eggs, or ova, may mature slowly, even taking several years in the case of large, long-lived species, with only a proportion of them maturing each breeding season. Maturation involves surrounding each egg with yolk, a process known as vitellogenesis. Vitellogenesis normally takes place immediately before the breeding season, usually in the spring in temperate species, but it may also occur in the autumn, before hibernation. Snakes appear to produce more yolked follicles than they will ever use to produce fertile eggs. This may be a way of allowing the size of the clutch to be adjusted right up to the last minute: if there is plenty of food immediately before mating they may be able to produce larger clutches than if food is short. Follicular eggs that are not used are reabsorbed by the female.

The fat cycle

The production of yolk is dependent on an adequate store of fat and if the female has not fed well this may be lacking, in which case the follicular eggs do not develop further but are reabsorbed. It has been shown that fat reserves usually accumulate in the female's body until the time of egg maturation. By the time the eggs leave the oviduct, they have grown considerably but the fat store is heavily depleted. The female must feed well before another batch of viable eggs can be produced. Fat cycles are well established in lizards and some large snakes, such as the boas and pythons. There appears to be a fat cycle in most, if not all, temperate colubrids, elapids and vipers. Tropical snakes, especially small species, however, may be in a position to form eggs directly from their food intake, without relying on stored fat.

Ovulation

Once the eggs have been released from the ovary they move into the body cavity and are then 'caught' by a funnel-shaped opening, known as the infundibulum, at the upper end of the oviduct. At the time of ovulation, the infundibulum grows around the ovary in order to reduce the chances of eggs being lost; even so, some eggs do become lost within the body cavity and yet others are caught by the oviduct on the other side of the body, i.e. eggs released by the left ovary end up in the right oviduct and vice versa. This process of transferring the eggs from the ovaries to the oviducts is known as ovulation.

A stimulus may be required before ovulation occurs and this varies from species to species. In temperate snakes, it seems that increasing temperature provides the necessary stimulation whereas in some tropical species it is provided by cooler conditions, such as would occur at the beginning of the wet season. Females of species that have no distinct breeding season may be stimulated by the act of mating or the presence of one or more males in close proximity. Finally, there may be an interplay between environmental conditions, i.e. temperature, and additional stimulation by males.

Fertilisation

Once the eggs have moved into the oviduct they may be fertilised, assuming sperm is present. In the absence of sperm, or if the sperm is not viable, the female will either lay infertile eggs or reabsorb them. Once the eggs have been fertilised, however, they cannot be reabsorbed.

Some snakes are able to store sperm for lengthy periods and so delay fertilisation. This may be useful if males are only present early in the breeding season, before ovulation occurs. Fertile matings can still take place, with the stored sperm fertilising the ova at a later date. Many temperate vipers, for instance, ovulate in early June, irrespective of the time of mating, which may be several months earlier in some species. It is logical to assume that fertilisation and subsequent development will be timed to coincide with warm weather, in order to accelerate the development of the young. Furthermore, the timing of the birth of the young is also important because they must often rely on seasonally available prey, such as young lizards or rodents.

In species that produce more than one clutch in a single breeding season, sperm storage may be used in fertilising the second clutch. In other cases, sperm may be stored from one season to another, so that if the female is unable to find a mate she may still produce fertilised eggs, drawing on the surplus sperm from the previous season. Fertility from clutches produced from stored sperm is, however, usually lower than in clutches fertilised by fresh sperm.

THE SNAKE EGG

The eggs of snakes, like those of all reptiles, and birds, have large amounts of yolk. The yolk contains the fats and carbohydrates necessary for development of the embryo. The embryo starts its development as a flat disc lying on the surface of the yolk and, as it develops, it lifts away from the yolk and begins to form itself into a young snake. The yolk nourishes it throughout development and, towards the final stages, is drawn into the snake through a slit in its underside, visible as a small scar at the time of hatching.

The embryo is surrounded by two sets of membranes. One set is formed in the oviduct of the mother, and includes an outer layer, the shell, containing calcium salts. The other, much thinner set of membranes, is produced by the embryo, and comprises the amnion, the chorion and the allantois. These membranes usually develop after the egg has been laid. All the membranes help to conserve water and are one of the fundamental differences between amphibians' and reptiles' eggs.

In addition to the shell, embryo and yolk, snake eggs contain a small amount of albumin and an air bubble. The albumin is composed of a solution of proteins which, through osmosis, attracts water into the egg while the air bubble controls the exchange of oxygen and carbon dioxide and also acts as a pressure regulator.

Towards the end of incubation, some of the calcium is extracted from the shell by the embryo and is used to form its skeleton: the shell becomes thinner and more flexible around this time. Oxygen passes through the shell more readily and, for a while, this compensates for the embryo's increased oxygen requirement. Eventually, though, it will need to leave its shell to breathe.

▶ An Australian diamond python, *Morelia spilota spilota*, with her eggs.

▼ The internal structure of the snake egg.

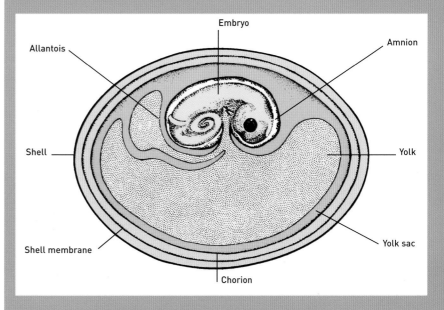

▲ African egg-eating snakes frequently store sperm, laying several clutches of fertile eggs following a single mating. This hatchling may be the result of a mating many months previously.

Finally, sperm storage may be used by species that are widely scattered and have difficulty finding one another at a specific time of the year. These species may mate whenever the opportunity arises, with the females storing the sperm until they ovulate, maybe as a result of environmental stimuli. The sperm is stored at the lower end of the oviduct in special chambers known as seminal receptacles.

Developing eggs are retained in the oviduct and, if the species is oviparous, each is provided with a parchment-like shell which is produced in a specialised area in the lower portion of the oviduct. Very occasionally, two developing ova are encased in a single shell, so that when the egg hatches two young emerge instead or one. (Although these are commonly known as twins, all the offspring from a single clutch of eggs are twins, or triplets, or whatever, and the emergence of two young from one egg is probably the result of a malfunction in the shell-producing process.) Live-bearing species do not produce a shell but each developing embryo is enclosed in a separate membrane.

BREEDING SEASONS

MOST SNAKES HAVE BREEDING SEASONS THAT ARE UNDER THE CONTROL OF EXTERNAL FACTORS SUCH AS TEMPERATURE. UNLIKE LIZARDS, THERE IS NO EVIDENCE AT PRESENT THAT SNAKES' BREEDING CYCLES ARE AFFECTED BY DAYLENGTH. THIS WOULD SEEM TO BE A LOGICAL RESULT OF THEIR ORIGINS AS BURROWING ANIMALS, AND THEIR SECRETIVE HABITS, WHERE ANY DIFFERENCES IN DAYLENGTH WOULD GO LARGELY UNNOTICED.

It seems that the reproductive behaviour of very many snakes follows a fairly standard sequence and other systems can be considered as variations. Most of our knowledge comes from studies on temperate snakes, especially North American and European species such as the kingsnakes, rat snakes, water snakes, garter snakes, rattlesnakes and vipers, and so these can be used as a starting point.

A typical cycle for these snakes would be for mating to take place in the spring, shortly after they emerge from hibernation, for fertilisation to occur shortly afterwards and for the young to be born, or to hatch, before the end of the summer. Species that come from places where there is no well-defined winter, such as the tropics, may have similar cycles but they may be timed to synchronise with wet and dry seasons. Other species appear not to cycle at all and may be thought of as opportunists, breeding whenever they are in a reproductively active state, regardless of season.

Temperate species

Snakes from temperate regions usually hibernate or go through a period of reduced activity during the time of year when average temperatures are insufficient to allow them to maintain a suitable body temperature. Depending on their whereabouts, they may pass through a period of deep hibernation lasting many months, during which time they are more or less comatose, or they may merely hide away for short cold

periods. Either way, they seem to have little interest in reproduction until the weather warms up permanently in the spring. At this time males usually actively seek females.

Courtship and mating may take place immediately after hibernation or a few weeks later; each species has its own system, with some species differing from population to population. For example, chequered garter snakes, *Thamnophis marcianus*, in Arizona mate as soon as they have emerged from hibernation, but in Texas mating takes place about twenty days after they have emerged.

Spring matings allow females to lay their eggs at a time when the weather is still warm enough to incubate them (or to allow their young to develop in the oviduct if they are of a live-bearing species) and to ensure that when the young hatch or are born conditions are suitable for them to disperse and find food. In addition, hatching or birth often coincides with a time when there is an abundance of young lizards, amphibians and rodents, so that the young can feed and grow quickly before the coming winter.

The timing of mating and egg laying may be shifted slightly, according to species. The American Trans-Pecos rat snake, *Bogertophis subocularis*, for example, mates in the summer, several months after other snakes from the same region, and its eggs are not laid until the end of summer or the beginning of autumn. Hatching takes place in the winter. This species is found in southern Texas and northern Mexico, where summers are hot and dry and winters are mild.

Other species mate during one period of activity and give birth, or lay eggs, during the next. There are actually two systems operating here. In its most simple form, autumn mating seems to be an insurance against not finding a mate in the spring and therefore wasting a breeding season. Females of these species enter hibernation with a store of sperm in their reproductive system. This sperm is still active in the following spring and may be used to fertilise the eggs that ovulate at this time. If she gets the opportunity, however, the female will mate again in the spring and so the autumn mating is not always essential in order to produce fertile eggs.

One such species is the crowned snake, *Tantilla coronata*, from North America, whose reproductive cycle was investigated

▲ The breeding cycle of the chequered garter snake, *Thamnophis marcianus*, varies according to where it lives.

by Aldridge (1992).[1] Apparently mating can take place in late summer and the sperm is stored in receptacles in the lower part of the oviduct. During the following spring, mating may take place again but, whether or not this is the case, females have viable sperm in their oviduct, at the same time as the eggs are maturing. The eggs are laid at the beginning of summer and, by the end of summer, the females have little or no sperm in their oviducts or their storage receptacles, perhaps because the eggs carry unused sperm out of the body when they are laid. The female must mate again to replenish her store of sperm. Autumn mating, in which the female stores sperm over the winter, has also been recorded in hognose snakes, *Heterodon*, another egg-laying species. Again, this species also mates in the spring.

Autumn matings also take place in the pygmy rattlesnake, *Sistrurus miliarius* (Montgomery and Schuett, 1989),[2] and the massasauga, *S. catenatus*. The latter species has also being observed to mate in the spring. It seems most likely that these two viviparous species store sperm over the winter and ovulate in the following spring, using either the stored

sperm or sperm from more recent matings to fertilise their ova, just as the crowned snake does.

Other viviparous vipers, including some populations of the prairie rattlesnake, *Crotalus viridis*, and the ridge-nosed rattlesnake, *C. willardi*, have been known to mate in late summer and store their sperm over the winter. Ovulation and fertilisation take place the following

spring and the young are born in the following summer (Graves and Duvall, 1993[3] and Martin, 1976[4]). Spring matings have not (as yet) been recorded for these species, however.

Biennial breeding cycles

Species or populations that live in cold places may not breed every year. Most of these species are live-bearers, for reasons that are discussed later. Females that are carrying young or eggs are often unable to feed, either because the burden of the young, and the amount of time they spend basking, prevents them from hunting, or because the developing young or eggs take up so much space in their bodies that they are unable to accommodate food. If the summer is short, as it is at higher latitudes, the females may be gravid for almost all of the active season. This being the case, they will not be in a position to regain their condition before hibernation and will emerge the following year with very little fat reserves. A 'fallow' year will then be necessary in order for them to build up enough reserves to produce eggs or young. There is even a possibility that snakes at very high latitudes, such as the adders in northern Scandinavia, breed only every third year, requiring two

▼ Western hognose snakes may mate in the autumn as well as the spring but they lay their eggs in spring or early summer.

SPERM STORAGE IN A SMALL RATTLESNAKE

The ridge-nosed, or Willard's, rattlesnake, *Crotalus willardi*, is a small species found only in a few isolated mountain ranges in southern Arizona, southern New Mexico and northern Mexico. It is specialised in its habitat preference and is only found at high altitudes, where it is subjected to extended periods of inactivity during the long, cold winters.

Mating takes place in the summer in July and August. Development begins the following spring, after a long hibernation, and the females give birth to small broods of offspring the following August or September. The period of time that elapses between mating and birth therefore totals about 14 months. This precludes the possibility of females breeding in successive years.

This, coupled with the small litters and their exacting habitat requirements, has led to great concern over their future survival, especially of the subspecies *C. w. obscurus*, the New Mexican ridge-nosed rattlesnake.

▲ Snake breeders have found that many species, such as the Pueblan milksnake, *Lampropeltis triangulum campbelli*, will lay more than one clutch in a single breeding season.

feeding seasons in order to become fit enough for one breeding season.

These biennial breeding cycles may or may not be fixed genetically in the snakes. Prevailing conditions, particularly the amount of food available during a particular year (itself sometimes dependent on rainfall), will control the frequency of breeding in populations that are borderline. Some species that normally breed every other year, such as European adders, will breed every year in captivity if they are provided with plenty of food and a longer active season.

Conversely, a poor year, in terms of food availability, can lead to small numbers of females breeding during the following year, regardless of when they last bred. Where the food supply is

unreliable, then, breeding is not regular but opportunistic and in any given year the proportion of females breeding can vary from a quarter to three-quarters or more. Other species seem more or less locked in to biennial breeding, regardless of food supply and conditions, the Tasmanian tiger snake, *Notechis scutatus*, being an example of the latter type of species.

There are also viviparous species that have annual as well as biennial populations. The northern Pacific rattlesnake, *Crotalus viridis oreganus*, may breed every year even though related subspecies are biennial breeders (Wallace and Diller, 1990[5]). Bearing in mind that this species mates in the summer (see above), females feed throughout the spring and again in the autumn, after they have given birth, and may be fit enough to breed again the following year.

Multiple clutches

Cases of snakes that breed every other year are well documented, but examples of species that breed more than once each year are not as well known. Some species certainly have the potential to do so, because in captivity they will often produce a second or even third clutch in the same breeding season provided they are well fed and in good condition. These

may result from separate matings or, in some cases, females that have only been mated once, in the spring, will go on to lay another clutch later in the year, even though the male has not been present after the first clutch. In order to do this, she must store sperm from the initial mating and use it to fertilise the subsequent clutch of eggs.

Because of the difficulty of monitoring individual snakes throughout the season, it is hard to say how often multiple clutches occur in wild snakes. It does seem likely that it occurs at least occasionally, if for no other reason than that it is physiologically possible. If multiple clutching does occur, it will be found in species that have long active seasons.

These variations in breeding seasons, all concerning temperate species, serve as a reminder that each species of snake has adapted its reproductive timetable to its requirements and to the prevailing conditions. Although many species have similar systems, others will have evolved unusual or unique systems if they happen to suit them better.

Tropical species

Even though most snakes are tropical in origin, there has been less research into the controlling factors of breeding seasons in these species. Like temperate species, they may also respond to temperature but seasonal differences are likely to be more subtle. The beginning of the wet season is normally accompanied by lower temperatures, at least during some part of the day. This may stimulate the snakes to breed. On the other hand, they may mate at the end of the wet season, when temperatures rise slightly, so that the birth or hatching of their young is timed to coincide with the next wet season and therefore provide more food and cover. The olive sand snake, *Psammophis phillipsi*, from northern Africa, seems to fit into the latter category. Egg formation in this species begins around the end of the rainy season and the eggs are fertilised and laid by the middle of the dry season. Hatching occurs at the onset of the next rainy season (Butler, 1993).[6]

Overall, the timing will depend on the length of the gestation coupled with the length of the wet and dry seasons. Both these factors are variable. In parts of the tropics where wet and dry seasons are not predictable, female as well as male snakes may be in more or less permanent readiness to breed, perhaps as a response to increased food supply or a sudden lowering of temperature during occasional downpours.

One of the problems with unravelling the seasonal breeding rhythms of tropical snakes is that, unlike temperate species, few tropical species are kept and bred in captivity. Of those that are, most are large boas and pythons but, as these species have long gestation times, they may breed at different times of the year from small species. If preserved specimens are dissected it is sometimes possible, by examining their reproductive tracts, to establish some seasonal patterns, and this has been carried out with some species. Results seem to vary across the species though, with some snakes showing distinct breeding seasons, others with less distinct, or extended, seasons, and yet others in which no obvious pattern can be discerned. It seems likely that regional differences occur – even within the same species – especially with those that range widely and over areas that have different climatic conditions.

The Hispaniolan snake *Antillophis parvifrons protenus* is a case in point. Where it occurs on the main island there is a fairly consistent rainfall throughout the year and plenty of moist habitat; in these regions the reproductive season is extended and may even continue throughout the year. Where it occurs on two small satellite islands, however, there is seasonal variation in rainfall and on these islands the snakes' breeding seasons are timed to coincide with the rainy season (Powell *et al.*, 1991).[7]

Other examples are not so straightforward. Solorzano and Cerdas (1989)[8] studied the terciopelo *Bothrops asper*, which has a fairly extensive range in South America. The seasons vary throughout this species' range: in Costa Rica, for instance, it occurs on both sides of the Central mountain range, which divides the country into two different climatic zones. On the Pacific side, females mate from September to November and give birth from April to June, at the beginning of the rainy season. The newborn snakes eat frogs, which are plentiful at this time of the year. On the Atlantic side of the country, the seasons are almost reversed, and mating takes place in March, at the end of the rainy season, when the temperature rises. The young are born from September to November, which is the beginning of the rainy season in *this* part of the country.

Females of both populations, then, give birth at the beginning of the rainy season. But, because the duration of the rainy seasons vary from one side of the country to the other, one group of snakes can time its mating to coincide with rising temperatures at the end of the previous rainy season whereas members of the other population have no such environmental trigger. They mate at a time when conditions are more or less constant, and there is no way of knowing what stimulates them. Another interesting difference between the populations, for which there is no explanation as yet, is that of litter size: females from the Pacific population have litters of five to 40 young (average 18.6) whereas females from the Atlantic population have larger litters, of 14 to 86 (average 41.1).

Biennial cycling in boas and pythons

Biennial cycling occurs in some of the larger boas and pythons, none of which comes from especially cool climates. These species carry their young for long periods of time, up to ten months in some cases, and often fast for most of this time. There simply would not be enough time to feed sufficiently during the remainder of the year. Under captive conditions, many of these species can be induced to breed every year by intensive feeding immediately after the birth and during the early part of pregnancy. On other occasions, however, they may mate every year but produce young only every second year.

▼ The timing of the reproductive cycle and the litter size of the pit viper, *Bothrops asper*, vary according to location: in some parts of Costa Rica, for instance, it is more prolific than in others.

MATING SYSTEMS

THE ANIMAL MATING SYSTEMS THAT ARE APPLICABLE TO SNAKES CAN BE BROADLY DIVIDED INTO THREE TYPES. ONE IS WHERE A MALE AND A FEMALE STAY TOGETHER, EITHER FOR LIFE OR FOR THE DURATION OF THE BREEDING SEASON, AND ALL THE OFFSPRING HAVE THE SAME MOTHER AND THE SAME FATHER (MONOGAMY). A SECOND IS WHERE MALES MATE WITH SEVERAL FEMALES (POLYGAMY) AND THE THIRD IS WHERE FEMALES MATE WITH SEVERAL MALES (POLYANDRY).

All three systems can be found among snake populations. Lifelong monogamy has not been proved, because it is difficult to observe pairs of snakes from one year to the next, but there are several examples of species in which males and females stay together throughout the breeding season.

Polygamy and polyandry often go together. Whereas in monogamy, the presence of a male will limit the female's opportunity to mate with other males, with polygamous systems, once the male goes in search of additional mates, the female may be found and mated by a second, third or subsequent males and it has been shown that females may produce a batch of eggs or young that have been fertilised by more than one male. One way around this problem, from the male's point of view, is described below.

Mate finding

As with seasonality, the systems by which snakes find and court members of the opposite sex vary with species and the particular lifestyles they lead. Where snakes congregate in large numbers to hibernate, such as in rattlesnake dens, mating usually takes place before the animals have dispersed, often within a few weeks of their emergence. Finding a mate in these situations is not a problem, although increased competition may mean that only a small proportion of males is fortunate enough to father a batch of young. Other species, including those that pass the winter in small groups or as individuals, must search for mates over a larger area. This is made easier by the production of pheromone trails, invisible chemical tracks that are left by snakes as they move around. Males are adept at locating and homing in on females, especially when they are in a state of reproductive receptivity.

From a collector's standpoint, it will often happen that some species are most easily found at the time of year in which matings take place, but invariably the samples contain more males than females, indicating that males go in search of females rather than the other way round. Females are able to remain

ENFORCED CHASTITY IN GARTER SNAKES

Males of some species use a 'trick' in order to get the best of both worlds. This involves the use of copulatory plugs. Plugs are formed from fluid secretions, made in a specialised part of the male's kidney, and deposited into the lower part of the female's oviduct immediately after sperm is ejected. The fluid hardens after a few minutes, forming an effective barrier to further impregnation of the female by other males. The male is then free to search for more mates, secure in the knowledge that another male cannot replace or dilute his sperm. The plug, which was first discovered in a few species of garter snakes, *Thamnophis*, remains in place for two to four days, after which time it begins to break down and is ejected by the female. It is doubtful if the period of time during which the plug is in place is sufficient to prevent further fertile mating altogether, as female snakes may remain receptive for several weeks but, when mating aggregations take place, as they do among garter snakes, the most vulnerable time for additional matings probably occurs in the first few days of sexual activity, after which the adults begin to disperse.

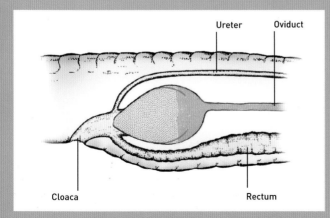

▲ Male garter snakes secrete a fluid that hardens after a few minutes to form a plug in the entrance to the female's oviduct. This is thought to prevent subsequent males from impregnating the female in mating balls.

▲ Black-necked garter snake, *Thamnophis cyrtopsis ocellatus*.

near familiar territory and are less likely
to be caught.

Courtship and mating

When males and females meet, mating
does not necessarily take place
immediately. Although the ritual of
courtship in snakes is not in the same
league as that of birds, for example, males
do need to stimulate females before they
will mate with them. Stimulation is
usually tactile, although odour probably
plays an additional role. During courtship,
it is usual for the male to crawl along the
back of the female, often making regular
jerking movements. In pythons and boas,
the rudimentary spurs are used to scratch
or tickle the back of the female. When the
female is ready to mate, she allows the
male to lift her tail with his and coil his
tail around hers. As their cloacae come
into contact, the male inserts one of his
hemipenes into the female's cloaca and
copulation takes place. Copulation can
last from a few minutes to several hours,
depending on species.

Once the snakes are joined, they are
not easily separated. If one of the pair
decides to move off, the other will be
dragged along too. Large females are
often seen dragging smaller males behind
them, but sometimes it is the male that
takes the lead: Lillywhite (1985),[9]
reported on a male black racer, *Coluber
constrictor*, that he watched as it climbed
into a tree, dragging the female behind
him to a height of 5 m (16 ft).

During the breeding season, males of
some species may remain with females
for several days or even weeks. The
purpose of this may be to ensure that
they are able to mate as soon as the
female is receptive and to copulate
several times. Multiple copulations
ensure that the male's sperm outnumber
those of any other male that may have
mated with the female previously. Once
the female ceases to become receptive,
the male's attachment to her ceases and
they usually go their separate ways.

Male to male combat

During the time that a male is attending a
receptive female, rival males may
approach. The resident male will attempt
to drive them away by ritualised combat
dances in which each male raises its head,
neck and the fore part of its body off the
ground, entwines the other's body and
tries to press him to the ground. These

bouts last varying amounts of time,
depending on how well matched the
adversaries are, and the combatants may
take rests between bouts. Eventually, one
of the males, usually the smaller
individual, concedes defeat and crawls
away. The victorious male then returns to
the female, who normally remains nearby
during these proceedings, and mating may
take place. The male snakes rarely, if ever,
do serious damage to one another,
although under the artificial circumstances
of captivity, where the submissive male is
unable to leave the scene, the dominant
animal may bite him savagely, sometimes
inflicting deep wounds. In boids, males
sometimes use their spurs to scratch at
their rivals.

▲ Copulation in some of the more arboreal
snakes takes place while they are coiled around
branches. Green tree pythons, *Morelia viridis*,
seen here, and emerald boas, *Corallus caninus*,
intertwine their tails to keep their cloacae
adjacent to each other. Other snakes usually
intertwine their tails while lying on the ground
but the methods of courtship and mating in
aquatic and burrowing species is unknown.
Most observations on courtship and mating
in snakes have involved captive individuals.

Combat of one form or another has
been noted in a wide array of species,
including boids, numerous colubrids,
many vipers and pit vipers, including
rattlesnakes, and many elapids, particularly
Australian species, such as blacksnakes,
Pseudechis, whipsnakes, *Demansia*, white-

THREE BREEDING SYSTEMS COMPARED:
MALE-MALE COMPETITION, SCRAMBLE COMPETITION AND EXTENDED MATE SEARCHING

Different breeding systems evolve in response to different circumstances: the best strategy for one species may not be equally good for another. Studies have also shown that, in addition to variations between species, different populations of the same species can also vary. Although it can sometimes be hard to see exactly which system is at work, a few detailed studies have identified at least three distinct patterns of reproductive behaviour.

Male-male competition in the adder
One of the first species to be thoroughly studied was the European adder, *Vipera berus*, in southern England, by Ian Prestt (*J. Zool. London*, 164:373-418). He found that adders spend the winter in communal dens, containing large numbers of males and females. They emerge in the spring, with males emerging before females. The males move away from the den to nearby favoured basking sites, which they may use year after year. They remain at these sites for several weeks during which time they shed their skin but do not feed. When the females emerge from the den, they tend to congregate at nearby 'mating sites', and the males gravitate towards these sites.

In many years, only a small proportion of females breed, with the result that there are often many more males than breeding females. The males then have to compete for mates, sometimes clashing with each other to establish dominance in the spectacular and well-known 'combat dances'. The victorious males, which are usually the largest, drive the losers away from the vicinity of the females, and may immediately mate with the females.

In other years, the number of receptive females may be almost as high as that of males: in these years competition between males is less intense and most of them may find mates regardless of size.

The mating season lasts about four weeks, after which the males and females disperse to find food. The females give birth towards the end of the summer and males, females and juveniles congregate around hibernation sites again in the autumn.

Scramble competition in wandering garter snakes
Brent Graves and David Duvall studied two species, the wandering garter snake, *Thamnophis elegans vagrans*, and the prairie rattlesnake, *Cratalus viridis*, in Wyoming (*Journal of Herpetology*, 24(4):351-356). They found interesting differences; both differed from that of the adder.

Wandering garter snakes spend the winter in communal hibernation dens. Males always emerge before females but remain in the vicinity.

When the females emerge, the males do not engage in combat with one another but scramble to mate with them; each male tries forcibly to dislodge other males in order to effect copulation, resulting in large 'mating balls'. Once all the females have been mated, both sexes disperse to begin feeding and the females give birth later in the summer.

▲ Adders, *Vipera berus*, typically congregate during the breeding season, with several males competing for the opportunity to mate with females. Here one male is mating with the larger female while another stays nearby in the hope of sneaking a mating.

Mate searching in prairie rattlesnakes
Prairie rattlesnakes also overwinter in communal dens but their subsequent behaviour is somewhat different from that of the garter snake. They emerge from their hibernation dens later, and males and females emerge at the same time. There is no mating activity at this time and both sexes make their way immediately to feeding areas: this may take them several kilometres (miles), away from the den site. Not until later, in early summer, do the males begin to look for mates, probably using pheromone trails to locate them. Because females are so widely dispersed, males find them singly, and combat is not thought to take place (although it does in many other species of rattlesnakes). They mate after a few days of courtship and the mating season is over by the end of August. Shortly afterwards, both sexes make their way back to the den in readiness for hibernation. The young are born the following spring or early summer.

lipped snakes, *Drysdalia*, brown snakes, *Pseudonaja*, taipans, *Oxyuranus*, swamp snakes, *Hemiaspis*, small-eyed snakes, *Cryptophis*, tiger snakes, *Notechis*, and copperheads, *Austrelaps*.

Because larger males nearly always win these bouts of combat, there will be strong evolutionary pressure for males to become bigger: large males mate more often than small ones and so the genes for being large will be passed on. The males of species that engage in combats tend to be relatively larger than males of the species that do not.

The significance of male to male combat is that the female mates with the strongest male and, thanks to his 'good' genes, their offspring will have a better chance of survival. On the other hand, small males may never win a combat and therefore would never get to mate. Sometimes, small males can be seen in the vicinity of mated pairs of snakes and there is a strong possibility that these are 'satellite' males that, given the fact that they can never win a female through fair means, try to steal matings while the dominant male is otherwise occupied, such as when he is defending his female from other rivals.

The activities described probably apply to many temperate snakes, although only a small proportion of species have been studied. In other species, matings are more casual, with males tracking down and mating with females, then departing immediately, presumably to look for other females. This leads to the possibility that several males may find and mate with a single female and that her eggs may be fertilised with sperm from a number of them. Males of species that employ this mating system do not engage in combat as they rarely meet with rivals. Competition between sperm, i.e. which sperm reach the unfertilised ova first, then becomes the significant factor in controlling which male fathers the most young, instead of competition between individuals. Nearly everything we know about mating and mating systems in snakes is based on observations made of the most common and most conspicuous species. There is still an enormous amount not known and, in particular, the methods of mate finding, courtship and mating in snakes belonging to some of the more primitive snake families, particularly the worm and thread snakes, is virtually unknown.

SNAKES WITHOUT FATHERS

Parthenogenesis is the term given to a method of reproducing without the help of a member of the opposite sex; that is, without males. A number of invertebrates have evolved methods of reproducing parthenogenetically, as have some fish and a few lizard species but, as far as is known, only one species of snake is parthenogenetic.

This is the small worm snake *Ramphotyphlops braminus*, sometimes called the flowerpot snake. Although nobody has yet succeeded in rearing and breeding this species in captivity, and thereby proving beyond doubt that it is parthenogenetic, there is strong circumstantial evidence. Firstly, all the specimens that have ever been found have turned out to be females: since it is not a rare snake, one would expect to find at least some males if they existed. In addition, colonies of the species have become established in many parts of the tropical and subtropical world through accidental human introduction: parthenogenetic species are far more likely to establish themselves in new places because only a single individual is needed to found each new colony.

Being parthenogenetic has costs as well as benefits. Looking at the benefits first, not having to find a mate is an obvious advantage when it comes to establishing new colonies—one solitary individual, even an immature one, is enough to get things started. Also, populations of parthenogenetic species tend to grow very quickly, because each individual is female and therefore able to produce young (i.e., the number of individuals that can lay eggs is doubled).

There is a drawback, however. In normal (sexual) reproduction, genes from both parents mingle and express themselves in various combinations in their offspring. This causes an almost infinite amount of variation within the population. Variation is important if conditions change because, in all likelihood, some individuals will be better able to adapt to the change than others. (This is the basis of natural selection and speciation.)

With parthenogenesis, however, all individuals are identical (they are clones of the female that bore them) except in the rare cases of spontaneous mutation. Being identical is fine for as long as conditions remain unchanged but, sooner or later, for the survival of the species, a need to adapt to new conditions is likely to arise. Without variation, the species cannot respond to changing conditions and is likely to die out.

Parthenogenesis, then, gives short-term advantages and long-term disadvantages.

▲ Flowerpot snake, *Ramphotyphlops braminus*.

MATTING SYSTEMS

THE FACT THAT SNAKES CAN STORE SPERM CREATES PROBLEMS WHEN TRYING TO ESTIMATE THE LENGTH OF GESTATION PERIOD – OBVIOUSLY, UNLESS THE EXACT TIME OF FERTILISATION IS KNOWN, IT IS NOT POSSIBLE TO CALCULATE THE TIME FROM FERTILISATION TO EGG LAYING OR BIRTH, AND INSTANCES IN WHICH WIDELY VARYING GESTATION PERIODS HAVE BEEN RECORDED MAY WELL RESULT FROM CASES OF SPERM STORAGE. FURTHERMORE, MANY SNAKES MATE SEVERAL TIMES OVER A LONG PERIOD OF TIME – SEVERAL WEEKS OR EVEN MONTHS IN PYTHONS AND BOAS, FOR INSTANCE. CALCULATIONS ARE NORMALLY MADE USING THE LATEST DATE OF OBSERVED MATING BUT THIS METHOD IS PRONE TO ERRORS SINCE EGGS MAY HAVE ALREADY BEEN FERTILISED BY THIS TIME, BY SPERM INTRODUCED AT A PREVIOUS MATING.

The period of time from mating to egg laying or birth is also subject to variation for other reasons. Egg-laying species naturally have a shorter gestation than viviparous species but even egg layers may retain their eggs until they are partially developed. It is dangerous, therefore to generalise. Temperature also plays a role and cool weather may prolong the gestation period, despite attempts by the female to absorb as much heat as possible.

Having said this, there is plenty of reasonably sound information, based on snakes that have been allowed to mate only once. Gestation periods for many medium-sized colubrid snakes seems fairly constant at about 40 to 50 days. Elapids seem to have a similar gestation period. Pythons generally take longer, however, sometimes twice this length of time. This may be partly due to their larger size, although even the smaller species, such as the Australian Children's and spotted pythons, *Antaresia childreni* and *A. maculosus*, take longer than colubrids of equivalent size.

Pregnancy in viviparous species also varies greatly. Indeed, it is subject to even

greater variation because of the greater likelihood of vagaries in the weather over this longer period. As we have already seen, some species, such as the prairie rattlesnake, *Crotalus viridis*, and the ridge-nosed rattlesnake, *C. willardi*, mate one year and give birth the next, at least in some parts of their range. If the months when the snakes are hibernating is included in the calculations of gestation period, it will appear to be unusually long. Most temperate viviparous species, though, mate early in the spring and give birth to their young towards the end of the summer, with a gestation period of four to six months. Tropical viviparous species have similar gestation periods.

Females with developing eggs may need to maintain a high body temperature in order to speed up the development of their eggs. For tropical species this is not usually a problem but snakes from cool climates tend to bask for long periods when they are gravid. This increases the risk of predation, but is preferable to delaying development until the weather becomes even cooler. Females of a few species are darker in colour than males, and, in one or two species, such as the Madagascan tree boa, *Sanzinia madagascariensis*, there may be a colour change during pregnancy, so increasing heat absorption and speeding up development.

Many female pythons assume a peculiar posture when they are carrying eggs, coiling upside down to expose most or all of their ventral surface. Perhaps they are attempting to raise the temperature of their developing eggs, by moving them away from a cold substrate.

EGG LAYING AND BIRTH

AS WE HAVE SEEN, EGG LAYING AND BIRTH MUST BE TIMED IN SUCH A WAY THAT THE YOUNG SNAKES HATCH, OR ARE BORN, AT A TIME WHEN THERE IS SUITABLE FOOD AVAILABLE. THEY MUST ALSO FIND THEMSELVES IN AN ENVIRONMENT WHERE THEY CAN GET OFF TO A GOOD START. THIS WILL NORMALLY BE THE SAME ENVIRONMENT IN WHICH THE ADULTS LIVE BUT, WHERE THE HOME RANGE DOES NOT CONTAIN ANY SUITABLE SITES, FEMALES MAY MOVE SOME DISTANCE IN ORDER TO FIND PLACES IN WHICH TO LAY THE EGGS.

Live-bearing species

The young of live-bearing species are born in the thin membrane that was surrounding them in the oviduct during their development. They have to break free from this before they disperse and this is achieved simply by wriggling, usually within seconds of birth.

The birth itself usually takes place in a secluded place, perhaps a retreat that the female has used for the late stages of her pregnancy. It may consist of an underground tunnel, a space beneath a rock or log, or a cavity among the roots of a tree. Sometimes, however, the young snakes are born in the open, and live-bearing arboreal species may give birth among the branches where they live. The membrane surrounding their young may help to prevent them from falling by sticking to foliage. Birth in completely aquatic species, such as the sea snakes, is rarely observed but always takes place in the water. Semi-aquatic snakes, such as the garter and ribbon snakes, *Thamnophis*, however, give birth away from the water.

Females may eat any infertile egg-masses that accompany the birth of the young, and they have also been known to eat dead young. This may merely be a way of recycling waste material. It is widely assumed that parental care in snakes is rare or non-existent but little research has been carried out. Females are often found with newly born young

although there is no knowing whether these are chance observations or not.

Egg-laying species

Oviparous snakes must also find a suitable place in which to deposit their eggs, and this is more demanding because certain basic requirements must be met if the eggs are to develop to hatching. Snakes' eggs absorb water throughout their development, but especially during the early part of incubation. The substrate in which they are laid must therefore be moist. The eggs also require oxygen, however, and a substrate that is too wet will impede the oxygen exchange across the egg shell and the development of the young will be adversely affected. Since the incubation can last for up to three months, the properties of site chosen for laying the clutch must be very constant. Finally, snakes' eggs are not pigmented to any great degree and therefore make an easy target for predators, so they must be hidden or buried.

Egg-laying sites

As it happens, snakes are so good at hiding their eggs that nests are rarely found by human observers, even in areas where they are numerous. Much of what we know about egg laying, clutch sizes and incubation periods comes either from dissection of preserved specimens, from the behaviour of captive snakes or, more rarely, from lucky observations.

Clutches are probably secreted in safe, secluded places where they will be able to develop and hatch without interference. These sites are likely to be within the area that the female uses for her other activities although females of some species need to travel to separate areas in order to find sites with the correct conditions. Rough green snakes, *Opheodrys aestivus*, for instance, have been observed leaving their usual habitat,

▲ Viviparous snakes, such as the Argentine rainbow boa, *Epicrates cenchria alvarezi*, are born inside a thin membrane, supplied with blood vessels. The young snake usually frees itself as soon as it is born, but it may remain inside the membrane for up to 24 hours, while it absorbs its yolk sac.

▼ A horned adder, *Bitis caudalis*, with part of her brood of young.

▲ A female Baird's rat snake, *Pantherophis bairdi*, in the process of laying her eggs.

alongside a small lake, and moving away from the shore in order to lay their eggs in cavities in trees (Plummer, 1989).[10] They probably use the same holes year after year because the remains of previous clutches were found in them. One individual tried repeatedly to gain access to a hole that was too small, presumably because the growth of the tree had reduced the size of the opening or

▼ A clutch of eggs, belonging to the golden-crowned snake, *Cacophis squamulosus*, discovered beneath a stone. Snakes hide their eggs so well that finding a clutch in nature is a rare event.

because the female had grown slightly since her last visit.

The sea kraits, which are the only marine species to lay eggs, come ashore to lay them. Tu *et al.* (1990)[11] found that on Orchid Island, off Taiwan, eggs of *Laticauda semifasciata* and *L. laticauda* were laid above sea level in tidal caves, where they would not be inundated with sea water. The correct moisture level to allow the hatchlings to properly develop was maintained by fresh water dripping from the roof of the caves, and this also served to dilute any sea water that entered during storms. The humidity within the caves was 100 per cent and the temperature was fairly constant at 23-26.8°C (73.4-80.2°F). The eggs took from four to five months to hatch. Several females of both species had used the same cave and broken egg shells, from previous clutches, were also present.

Communal egg laying

On the basis of other studies on egg laying, and on a number of chance observations as well, it is clear that when egg-laying sites are in short supply several females may all lay their eggs in especially suitable places, sometimes using them year after year.

In addition to the sea kraits mentioned above, communal nesting is also known in several other species, including the European grass snake, *Natrix natrix*. Females of this species choose piles of decaying vegetation in which to lay, in order to make use of the additional heat produced by the process of decomposition to accelerate development. Farmyard manure heaps, compost heaps and piles of sawdust have been used in addition to natural sites, especially in agricultural areas. They often become the focal point for several females in the same area, which each lay their moderately large clutches in them. The total number of eggs may even exceed 1,000. As breeding is fairly well synchronised in this species, the eggs all tend to hatch over a short period of time, causing a local population explosion of young snakes.

Communal egg laying also occurs in both species of the American green snakes, large batches of eggs of the smooth green snake, *Liochlorophis vernalis*, have been found together, despite an average clutch size of about five to six, while Palmer and Braswell (1976)[12] reported on a group of 74 eggs of the rough green snake, *Opheodrys aestivus*, in a panel from an abandoned refrigerator, packed with insulating material. Since the species also lays small clutches of five or six eggs, this batch must have been produced by at least ten females, probably more.

Communal nesting has also been recorded in several other North American snakes and in the Australian whipsnake, *Demansia psammophis*. It may be more widespread than these isolated cases indicate but, until more naturally occurring nest sites are found, this cannot be confirmed.

Burger and Zappalorti (1991)[13] studied nesting behaviour in the northern pine snake *Pituophis melanoleucus melanoleucus*. They found that the female digs burrows in sandy soil, bending its neck to scoop the soil out of the burrow. It digs down until it finds a layer of soil in which the moisture content is suitable, taking two to three days to excavate the tunnel. The tunnels measure about 1.5 m (5 ft) and slope downwards at first but then rise slightly before ending in a chamber. The eggs are laid in this chamber. It appears that females use the same egg-laying site every year, but dig new tunnels. Not every female digs her own tunnel, however, and several females may use the same one. This cannot be accounted for by a shortage of nest sites, so some females appear to specialise in using the tunnels dug by others in order to save time and energy.

Alligator nests as egg-laying sites
In Florida, eggs of the mud snake, *Farancia abacura*, have been found inside the nests of alligators, *Alligator mississippiensis*. Alligator nests consist of large piles of dead and rotting vegetation, situated in or near swamps. The female attends the nest, guarding the eggs until they hatch. Both active and abandoned nests have been used by the mud snakes (and also by turtles).

The pile of damp and rotting vegetation must create a good environment for the snake eggs and, when the alligator is in residence, they would also gain a highly effective 'babysitter'.

Ant and termite nests as egg-laying sites
Mention should be made of another specialised type of egg-laying site, used by a variety of mainly tropical snakes. These species lay their eggs in ant and termite nests, making use of the constant temperature and humidity inside them. The temperatures of the inner chambers

of these structures have been found to be stable at 27-29°C (80.6-84.2°F) in relevant ant nests despite fluctuations in the outside air temperature. Termite nests can average 5-11°C (9-20°F) higher than outside temperature because they are usually oriented in such a way as to catch the rays of the sun in the early morning and late evening, when air temperatures are low. Other advantages of such sites may include a degree of protection from predators and also from bacterial and fungal attack of the eggs, as ants and termites are meticulous in their attention to hygiene in their nests.

Eggs of at least 18 species of snakes have been found in this type of site, and were listed by Riley *et al.* (1985).[14] They include two species of blind snakes, both of which use termite nests, and one elapid, the coral snake *Micrurus frontalis*, which uses ant nests. All the other species are colubrids, including two species, *Liophis obtusus* and *Philodryas patagoniensis*, that between them accounted for 146 clutches of eggs found in 83 nests in Uruguay. Most colubrids use ant nests rather than those of termites, probably because hatchling snakes would have problems in finding their way out of the nests of termites, which construct nests of hard-baked clay and quickly repair any damage that occurs to its outer surface. Having said this, eggs of the colubrid, *Adelphicos quadrivirgatus*, have been found in a termite nest that was situated 1-1.5 m (3-5 ft) from the ground in a tree (Pedrez–Hidareda and Smith, 1989).[15]

This is a small species with a pointed snout and slender body, better adapted to finding its way in and out of termite nests than many other colubrids. Eggs of two species of *Boiga*, *B. drapiezii* and *B. jaspidea*, have also been found in termite nests in Java.

Although the eggs of at least one species (the African house snake, *Lamprophis fuliginosus*) have been found in a variety of sites, apart from termite nests, it seems that many species *only* lay in them. Most are West Indian or South American, where large nests of species such as leafcutter ants, genera *Acromyrmex* and *Atta*, are a prominent feature of the rainforest floor, and most eggs have been found in the central fungus chamber, where the ants cultivate the fungus on which they feed.

One other snake that has a strong association with termite nests is the anthill python, *Antaresia perthensis*, which preys heavily on a gecko, *Gehyra pilbara*, that also uses the nests as egg-laying sites. The eggs of *A. perthensis*, however, are unknown in the field.

Clutch size
Taking snakes as a whole, their clutch size (including litters of live young) ranges from one to over 100 but only a few species have ever been recorded with clutches or broods of more than 100. These include three pythons, the Indian,

▼ The mud snake, *Farancia abacura*, has truly enormous clutches of eggs, with over 100 having been recorded.

African and reticulated pythons, *Python molurus*, *P. sebae*, and *P. reticulatus*, and two vipers, the puff adder and the common lancehead, *Bitis arietans* and *Bothrops atrox*. The remaining four species are all colubrids: the mud snake, *Farancia abacura*, the green water snake, *Nerodia cyclopion*, the African mole snake, *Pseudaspis cana* and the common garter snake, *Thamnophis sirtalis*. The largest single brood appears to be that of a puff adder reported from the Dvur Kralove Zoo, in Czechoslovakia, which produced 157 living young. The snake measured 1.1 m (3 ft 7 in) in length.

All of these records are exceptional, and clutches or broods of more than 50 are unusual for any snake but it is worth noting that, of the nine species listed above, three are very large pythons, two are large-bodied vipers and three are large-bodied colubrids. Only the garter snake could be considered of average, or below average build.

Very small snakes tend to lay very small clutches. Thus species in the families Typhlopidae and Leptotyphlopidae, as well as a number of small colubrids, lay

▼ Part of a clutch of eggs from a heavily built snake (a well grown Baird's rat snake, *Pantherophis bairdi*), and a clutch from a more slender snake (a young milk snake, *Lampropeltis triangulum*). Because of its body size, the milk snake can only lay eggs with a small diameter: this means that they must be relatively elongated in order to be large enough to produce a viable hatchling. The rat snake, being thicker, can lay eggs with a greater diameter and therefore they are more rounded.

clutches as small as one and may only average two to three eggs per clutch (although clutches of up to 34 eggs have been recorded for an Australian worm snake). These examples are extremes, however, and the vast majority of clutches number between three and 16. The average clutch size, taking all snakes into account, works out at about seven.

As females grow, so they can produce larger numbers of eggs or young. An average colubrid, such as a corn snake, *Elaphe guttata*, may produce about six eggs in her first season but steadily increases her productivity until, when she is fully grown, her clutches will consist of about 20 eggs. Animals that produce exceptionally large numbers of offspring, like those listed above, were probably very old, large individuals.

Egg size and shape

Being cylindrical and slender is not the ideal shape for carrying large eggs around. Snakes therefore tend to lay relatively smaller eggs than their closest relatives, the lizards. Because each egg is smaller, they can afford to produce more of them, and this is probably why snakes lay, on average, a greater number of small eggs than lizards, which tend to lay a small number of relatively large eggs.

The size of snakes' eggs is obviously closely connected to the size of the species. As a very rough figure, the total reproductive output of a female (the weight of her whole clutch or brood), accounts for about 20 per cent of her own body weight. This figure is sometimes known as the relative clutch mass, or simply the RCM. So, if the snake produces an average-size clutch of, say, seven eggs, each egg will weigh about 3 per cent of the weight of the female.

Snakes of similar size, therefore, tend to produce eggs of similar size. There is some variability, though. Within closely related species of snakes, different strategies can sometimes be recognised. Females of two different species may 'decide' (in an evolutionary sense) to share out their reproductive output in different ways, one laying a few large eggs and the other a lot of small eggs. Even within the same species, members of some populations or subspecies may lay larger or smaller eggs than others.

Leaving aside variations such as this and looking at snakes as a whole, small snakes, and very slender snakes, always seem to lay clutches consisting of a few large eggs: the clutches are smaller, and each egg is larger, relative to the size of the female, than in other snakes. The European leopard snake, *Zamenis situla*, for instance, which is one of the smallest species in its genus, lays clutches of between three and six large, elongated eggs, whereas other members of the genus lay much larger clutches, over 20 eggs in some cases.

Why do small snakes have relatively large young when compared with large snakes? Perhaps there is a lower size limit below which young snakes cannot survive. They may have trouble finding food, avoiding predators or just maintaining a suitable body temperature if they fall below this lower limit.

This means that small species of snakes need to produce relatively large young, even at the cost of producing fewer of them. Since, as we have already seen, slender animals and large eggs do not go together very well, they must find a way around the problem. The solution is to lay eggs that are long and slender, sausage-shaped, and which therefore fit into the body of the snake more easily; small snakes, and slender tree snakes, then, lay elongated eggs, larger snakes lay more rounded eggs. Somewhere around the borderline are those species that begin breeding when they are small and carry on growing until they are large. Very often, the eggs of these species are elongated when they begin to breed and become more rounded in later years, as they grow.

INCUBATION

SNAKE EGGS DEVELOP ONLY IF THEY HAVE THE RIGHT CONDITIONS. THESE INCLUDE SOME DEGREE OF MOISTURE IN THE SUBSTRATE AND A SUITABLE TEMPERATURE. THE IDEAL TEMPERATURE SEEMS TO BE ABOUT 28°C (82°F) FOR TEMPERATE SPECIES, A FEW DEGREES HIGHER FOR TROPICAL SPECIES, INCLUDING PYTHONS. TEMPERATE SPECIES WILL CONTINUE TO DEVELOP AT MUCH LOWER TEMPERATURES, ALTHOUGH DEVELOPMENT SLOWS DOWN AND HATCHING IS DELAYED. ALSO, EGGS INCUBATED AT SIGNIFICANTLY HIGHER OR LOWER TEMPERATURES THAN THE IDEAL, PRODUCE YOUNG THAT ARE SMALLER AND WEAKER THAN AVERAGE. AS EXPECTED, TROPICAL SNAKES HAVE LESS TOLERANCE IN THIS RESPECT THAN TEMPERATE SPECIES DO.

During incubation, snake eggs swell, especially in the days immediately following laying. The biggest increase is in their width rather than their length and, by the time they hatch, their weight will have increased by about 50 per cent. This is largely due to the influx of water, which passes through the semi-permeable eggshell and is used by the developing embryo. If the moisture content of the substrate is too low, water will flow in the other direction, i.e. from the inside to the outside of the shell, and the embryo will dehydrate.

Parental care
Parental care is, apparently, very rare in snakes. When it does occur it invariably involves only the female. In addition, it is confined to egg-laying species: as far as we know, live-bearing species show no interest in their offspring after they are born.

Brooding in pythons
Although parental care of eggs is found in snakes from several families, nowhere is it as strongly developed as in pythons. Female pythons gather their eggs together as they are laid, manipulating them into a pyramid-shaped pile and surrounding them with their coils. Brooding may have evolved originally as a means of protecting the eggs against predation – pythons tend to be large, powerful species that are well able to drive away most of the small predatory animals that may attempt to steal their eggs. At some point in the evolution of brooding behaviour, however, temperature control became an important factor.

Females of at least one python species are able to produce a small amount of metabolic heat from their own bodies: this is the only occasion on which any snake becomes endothermic. External signs of the process are spasmodic contractions of the muscles along the body. Brooding pythons appear to shiver at regular intervals: the time between bouts of shivering varies with the temperature – the lower the temperature, the more often they shiver. Female Indian pythons, *Python molurus*, maintain a temperature of 32-33°C (90-91°F) within their pile of eggs, as much as 7°C (13°F) above that of the surrounding air. Although all species of pythons brood their eggs, and shivering has been observed in several of them, it is debatable whether or not they raise their temperature. In most cases, it has not been possible to show temperature rises within the pile of eggs, although the brooding behaviour may help to prevent heat loss. In addition, the dark colour of the female may allow her to absorb radiant heat and transfer it to the pale-coloured eggs by conduction. It is significant that the temperature at which python eggs develop is much more critical than it is in other snakes and relatively slight drops in temperature can result in poorly developed, abnormally pigmented or deformed young. At 23°C (73°F) they fail to develop altogether.

Egg guarding in other snakes
Other snakes coil around their eggs purely in order to guard them; there is no evidence that temperature control is within their capabilities. Species in which this type of behaviour has been seen include the king cobra, *Ophiophagus hannah*, which is also unusual in constructing its own nest by using its coils to pull together a pile of dead vegetation. It then coils around the eggs until they hatch. Other Asian species of cobras, *Naja*, may also remain with their

▲ Even small species of python, such as this Children's python, *Antaresia children*, brood their eggs, coiling around them during incubation to protect them from predators and, in some cases at least, helping to regulate their temperature.

eggs throughout at least part of their incubation. Egg guarding is also found in the spotted skaapsteker, *Psammophylax rhombeatus*, from southern Africa, which lays its eggs in a hole in the ground then coils around them. Similar behaviour has been observed in the related *P. variabilis* in areas where it is oviparous: this species can also be viviparous (see page 159). The Chinese colubrid snake *Sinonatrix percarinata* also guards its eggs: like *Psammophylax rhombeatus*, this species is part of a genus in which viviparity has evolved in other species.

Other species in which some degree of guarding has been seen include some members of the genus *Elaphe*, the North American mud snake, *Farancia abacura*, the same species that sometimes uses alligator nests in which to lay its eggs, and the Texas thread snake, *Leptotyphlops dulcis*. A final example is found among the Viperidae, where one of the few oviparous species, the Malaysian pit viper, *Calloselasma rhodostoma*, lays clutches of about 20 eggs and coils around them for the duration of their incubation, which normally takes about 40 days.

Though egg guarding is a rarity among snakes, it is found in at least five families: the Leptotyphlopidae, Boidae, Colubridae, Elapidae and Viperidae. Considering the huge proportion of species about which little is known, especially the colubrids, it may be more widespread than we realise.

HATCHING

HATCHING TAKES PLACE WHEN THE YOUNG SNAKE IS FULLY DEVELOPED AND WHEN THE YOLK HAS BEEN ABSORBED. BECAUSE THE SHELL CONSISTS OF A PARCHMENT-LIKE MATERIAL, AND IS NOT HEAVILY CALCIFIED, IT MUST BE SLIT RATHER THAN BROKEN. ESCAPE FROM THE EGG IS HELPED BY A SMALL THORN-LIKE GROWTH ON THE SNOUT OF THE YOUNG SNAKE, POPULARLY KNOWN AS THE EGG-TOOTH. THE EVENTS THAT STIMULATE THE YOUNG SNAKE TO BEGIN SLASHING AT THE INSIDE OF ITS SHELL HAVE NOT BEEN STUDIED IN SNAKES BUT ARE LIKELY TO BE SIMILAR TO THOSE THAT TAKE PLACE INSIDE THE SHELL OF TURTLES AND BIRDS.

As the embryo develops inside the egg its requirement for oxygen goes up. At first, this requirement is met by oxygen passing through the permeable shell but, eventually, the young animal requires more oxygen than can be supplied in this way. It begins to become restless, twisting and turning inside its shell and pushing at the inner surface with its snout. There is a tiny egg-tooth on the end of the snout and this cuts through the material. Several long slits are usually made. It seems that snakes may slit their eggshell at any time of the night or day – since the eggs are normally buried or hidden in cavities, the time would be immaterial in any case.

After their initial breakthrough, the hatchlings usually rest. They will often poke their head through one of the slits they have made, but seem reluctant to leave their shell. If they are disturbed they will draw back their heads and disappear again, sometimes for several hours. It may be two or more days after first slitting the shell that they finally leave it altogether. They disperse within a few days of hatching but they may stay in their nest until they have shed their skins, usually within the first week. There is no information about subsequent contact with their siblings and it is not known whether or not they are able to discriminate between related and unrelated snakes at a later date.

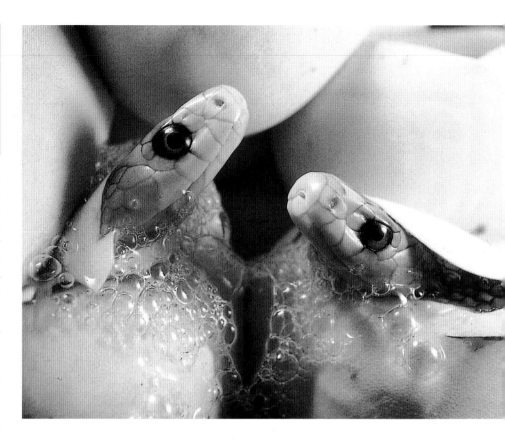

▲ Taipans, *Oxyuranus scutellatus*, hatching.

◄ A hognose snake, *Heterodon nasicus*, emerges from the egg in which it has been developing for several weeks.

◄ Bibron's blind snake, *Typhlops bibronii*, lays thin-walled eggs that hatch in a matter of days.

GROWTH AND DEVELOPMENT

THE RATE AT WHICH SNAKES GROW IS LARGELY UNDER THE CONTROL OF GENETIC PROGRAMMING AND SEVERAL FACTORS ARE INVOLVED – HOW LARGE THEY ARE AT HATCHING, HOW EFFICIENTLY THEY ASSIMILATE THEIR FOOD AND THEIR EVENTUAL ADULT SIZE. ENVIRONMENTAL FACTORS, INCLUDING THE AMOUNT OF FOOD THEY FIND, THE CLIMATIC CONDITIONS UNDER WHICH THEY LIVE (ESPECIALLY THE LENGTH OF THEIR ACTIVE SEASON) AND THEIR SUSCEPTIBILITY TO PARASITES AND DISEASES, ALSO PLAY THEIR PART. BECAUSE OF THE AMOUNT OF VARIATION WITHIN ALL THESE CATEGORIES OVER ALL THE SPECIES, GENERALISATIONS ABOUT THE GROWTH RATE OF SNAKES ARE NOT VERY USEFUL.

Sexual maturity is always a good landmark in the life of animals, and is especially useful for snakes because they continue growing after they have reached sexual maturity. Therefore, 'adult' snakes are considered to be those that have reached breeding size, regardless of their eventual maximum size. As a very rough guide, snakes begin to breed when they are about half their potential maximum size. Some individuals, of course, never reach their adult size, owing to predation and disease, whereas others may live a long time but still not reach the same size as other members of the same species. This may be due simply to different amounts of food eaten by different individuals, or different kinds of food, or differences between the sexes. Sexual dimorphism in size is dealt with below.

The age at which snakes mature seems to range from less than one year to four or five years. In most of the species that have been studied, males mature earlier, and at a smaller size than females, even though they may eventually become the larger of the two sexes. Sometimes, both sexes mature at about the same age but there are no species in which females mature earlier than males. The reason for this is that larger females can produce more young, whereas the number of

▲ Two corn snakes, *Pantherophis guttata*, emerge from their eggs. Hatching is surprisingly synchronous in most clutches.

young a male can produce is not linked to his size. It is therefore in the interests of females to wait until they have reached a reasonable size before they start to breed: males have no need to wait. Reproduction also involves a greater cost to the female in terms of energy lost, mainly through the amount of energy she puts into the developing young, but also because she often will not feed during the times she is gravid. If she breeds too soon, she may not be able to recover and her future chances of breeding may be less.

Other patterns that emerge are that small species tend to mature earlier than large ones living under similar climatic conditions, and that live-bearing species mature later than egg-laying species, all other things being equal.

Combining all these factors, the longest period for maturation should be found in females of large, live-bearing species from cool regions. This appears to be so. Females of several species of bulky vipers from high latitudes, for instance, mature at four years or more of age, males slightly earlier. Conversely, the species that reach maturity quickest should be small, egg-laying tropical species. Again, this appears to be so and, although there is not much information to go on, some species in this category mature at less than one year of age.

In captivity, abundant food, reduced disease and parasites and a long active season can combine to accelerate maturity. Most frequently kept colubrids, such as kingsnakes, *Lampropeltis*, and American rat snakes, *Pantherophis*, for instance, can be made to mature at less than two years of age, i.e. they breed in their second summer, even though the same species may require three, four, or perhaps even more years to reach maturity in the wild. Even large species, such as common boas, *Boa constrictor*, and Indian pythons, *Python molurus*, are known to have reached breeding size in less than two years, yet other species in this family are less flexible: they seem reluctant to breed until they are at least three or four years of age, regardless of how well they are fed or how quickly they grow.

REPRODUCTIVE STRATEGIES

WE HAVE LOOKED AT THE WAYS MALE AND FEMALE SNAKES GET TOGETHER AND WHAT HAPPENS WHEN THEY DO. THIS SECTION IS DIRECTED MORE TOWARDS THE EVOLUTIONARY ASPECTS OF REPRODUCTION, AND, IN PARTICULAR, ATTEMPTS TO EXPLAIN SOME OF THE VARIATIONS.

There are many facets to the problem of how best to optimise reproductive effort. Each individual tries to produce as many viable young as possible and any advantage that it gains, through a change in its physiology or behaviour, is likely to spread through the population as its genes become more numerous through its comparative success. The best reproductive strategy, then, is the one that will enable the snake to produce the maximum number of offspring, but a strategy that works well for one species may not do so for another because its circumstances may be different.

It should be made clear that terms like 'decisions', 'choices' and 'trade-offs' are used for convenience, not because they are made by individual snakes. A female viper does not 'decide' whether to lay eggs or give birth to live young. That decision has already been made for her, in

other words, by natural selection. If her ancestors had made the 'wrong' decision they would have left no offspring. Because they did leave offspring, we can assume that they made the 'right' decision.

Egg laying versus live bearing

Of the four orders of reptiles (the crocodilians, chelonians, tuataras and squamates), only the latter have evolved viviparity. Even so, the more primitive snakes lay eggs and so the ability to give birth to live young can be regarded as a system that evolved through selective pressures. The evolution towards viviparity begins with egg retention. Females of some species retain eggs inside their bodies until the embryos are well developed and the incubation period is very short. The smooth green snake, *Liochlorophis vernalis*, for example, lays eggs that are partially developed; in the southern part of its range, in the Chicago region, they need about 30 days to hatch but further north, in northern Michigan, they sometimes hatch after just four days. Indeed, it is possible that, under certain conditions, they hatch before they are laid. Although they are normally regarded as oviparous, species of this kind can be thought of as intermediate in their reproductive method: they are some way along the evolutionary route to viviparity.

▼ The European smooth snake, *Coronella austriaca*, is live-bearing, whereas the other European members of its genus lay eggs. This is an adaptation to the cooler regions where this species lives.

The line between oviparity and viviparity is not clearly defined, therefore, and closely related species may differ in their reproductive modes. A good example of this reproductive flexibility can be seen in the African genus *Psammophylax*. Two of the three species, *P. tritaeniatus* and *P. rhombeatus*, lay eggs, while the third, *P. variabilis*, lives up to its name: the subspecies *P. v. multisquamis* lays eggs but the other subspecies, *P. v. variabilis*, gives birth to live young. One of the egg-laying species, *P. rhombeatus*, guards its eggs. A second example concerns the two species of smooth snakes *Coronella*, from Europe: *C. girondica* lays eggs whereas *C. austriaca* is viviparous. The third species in the genus, *C. brachyura*, comes from Asia and is oviparous. Finally, the South American colubrid *Helicops angulatus* may be oviparous or viviparous, depending on where it lives. Other members of its genus are oviparous.

Whether a snake should give birth or lay eggs is an ecological 'decision', with advantages and disadvantages that must be carefully weighed up. The reasons for the evolution of viviparity, and therefore the way in which this system is advantageous in certain cases, has several explanations, some of which may be superimposed on the others. In other words, there is a 'trade-off' between the costs and benefits. The reasons for the evolution of viviparity can be divided into several categories. These categories – climate, lifestyle, habitat and ancestry – are often interrelated and may act together. Because of this, it can sometimes be difficult to see exactly which is the deciding factor or factors.

Climate
The most important factor is probably temperature. Snakes that live in cold climates, either because of high latitudes or high altitudes, tend to be viviparous. The reasons for this are not difficult to understand. The development of reptile eggs is entirely dependent on outside sources of heat, and development rates vary, with eggs at cool temperatures developing much more slowly than those at warm temperatures. At very cold temperatures (the exact level may depend on the species) development stops altogether and the embryo dies.

Females that lay eggs, then, must rely on the weather. Where this is constantly warm, the eggs will develop normally, hatch in a reasonable time and the young will emerge to a suitable environment to feed and grow. Where the weather is cold, or where unpredictable cold periods are possible, the eggs may fail to develop, or they may develop so slowly that the young hatch at a time when temperatures are not suitable for their continued activity. Under these circumstances, it is advantageous for the female to retain her eggs inside her body so that she can optimise temperatures by alternately basking and seeking refuge from the cold. She may then lay the eggs when they are part of the way through their development or, more commonly, wait until they have hatched and give birth to live young.

Of the examples listed above, where some members within a genus lay eggs while others give birth to live young (*Psammophylax*, *Coronella* and *Helicops*), in every case the live-bearing species live in cooler regions than the egg-laying species, and there are several other examples that bear out this theory.

Frequency of reproduction may also play a part but is firmly linked with climatic effects. If a species has the potential to breed more than once each year, because of a suitable climate, we would expect it to lay eggs because the female would be able to breed again sooner than if she were to carry her young for the whole of their development. Species that could only breed once every year (because the active season was short, for instance) would not benefit to the same degree. Since multiple breeding is probably restricted to tropical and subtropical species anyway, it is difficult to assess the importance of this particular factor.

▲ Active, slender snakes, such as coachwhips, *Masticophis flagellum*, tend to lay eggs because they rely heavily on speed and must eat regularly: they cannot afford to carry developing embryos around with them. Heavy-bodied snakes, most of which are sedentary, sit-and-wait predators, are more likely to be live-bearers: the extra burden of developing young has little effect on their activities.

Lifestyle
Other factors involved in the evolution of viviparity include methods of defence and hunting. When female snakes retain their eggs, they place an extra burden on their ability to move rapidly. This is more of a limitation in some species than in others. For example, large, inactive snakes, such as several of the vipers, rely heavily on camouflage, both for defence and for catching their prey, which they ambush. The extra burden of a clutch of developing young would not be such a strong disadvantage in this type of species as it would in slimmer, more agile species that rely more heavily on speed and agility to escape from predators and to catch their prey. All of the fast-moving diurnal hunters listed in Chapter 5, page 110, for instance, (*Coluber*, *Demansia*, *Masticophis* and *Psammophis*) are oviparous.

Using the same argument, we would also expect burrowing snakes, which are out of sight most of the time and do not need to worry quite so much about predation, to be viviparous. Unfortunately, the picture is not clear here because many of them belong to primitive families such as the Typhlopidae and the Leptotyphlopidae in which viviparity seems not to have evolved: they don't have the option of giving birth to live young. In addition, most burrowing snakes are tropical in origin, and so the benefits of egg laying may outweigh the benefits of live bearing. Some families of burrowing snakes, however, such as the shield-tails and their relatives, Uropeltidae, *are* viviparous.

Habitat

Certain groups of snakes may evolve viviparity because of the habitat they live in: this consideration may be more important than other factors, such as climate. They are the species that have thoroughly adapted to environments that have no suitable sites for laying their eggs, and include totally aquatic snakes. Laying eggs would involve, for these species, leaving the environment to which they are best adapted and becoming vulnerable to predation. Most aquatic species are therefore viviparous, regardless of their distribution, the only notable exception being that of the sea kraits, belonging to the subfamily Laticaudinae, which must leave the sea to lay their eggs ashore.

Some tree snakes find themselves in a similar situation. If they are only semi-arboreal, egg laying may be most advantageous to them, remembering that most tree snakes are long and slender and would therefore want to unload their eggs at the earliest possible opportunity. If they are so highly adapted that they never come down to the ground, however, live bearing is the best option. Species in this category include the long-nosed tree snakes, *Ahaetulla*, of Asia.

Ancestry

Finally, viviparity may be a legacy of snakes' ancestry. The strength of the selective pressure will determine the degree to which a particular species deviates from its close relatives, but some lineages of snakes seem to be more flexible than others when it comes to taking up the viviparous option.

The three families of burrowing snakes, Anomalepididae, Typhlopidae and Leptotyphlopidae, are all oviparous.

The Boidae are all viviparous save the Calabar ground boa, *Calabaria reinhardtii*, and possibly two species of sand boa, whereas the pythons are all egg layers, regardless of size or habitat. All these species therefore appear to have little flexibility in their breeding methods and it is especially interesting to note that ecological counterparts still maintain the ancestral trend; the emerald boa from

▲ Most boas are viviparous. Live-bearing in this family is well established as a breeding strategy because even relatively slender species such as the Madagascan tree boa, *Sanzinia madagascariensis*, give birth to live young.

South America is viviparous whereas the green tree python, from southeast Asia, is oviparous, despite their similarity in every other aspect of their appearance and lifestyles.

The python family is an especially interesting case because they appear to go against the argument that large, heavy-bodied snakes tend to be viviparous; many pythons fall into this category but viviparity has not evolved. What seems to have happened is that pythons use their size in another way. Female pythons brood their eggs for the duration of their incubation. Brooding is, in a way, similar to viviparity, in that the developing embryos remain with the female, who protects them and has some control over their environment. Brooding may have evolved as an alternative to viviparity.

The colubrids consist of such an assorted assemblage of species, some of which are known from only a few specimens and many whose relationships are not clear, that reproductive patterns are difficult to pick out. Some subfamilies are reasonably consistent: the Homalopsinae, for example, are all aquatic and all give birth to live young, as expected. The Natricinae also tend to be aquatic or

semi-aquatic and viviparity is common in this subfamily, although some species lay eggs. Other sub-families are more variable and, as has already been mentioned, species in the same genus, or even individuals within a species, may differ in their reproductive mode. Where variations occur, the viviparous species, subspecies or populations tend to be found in cooler regions than their oviparous counterparts.

Among the elapids, oviparity seems to be the rule, particularly among African and Asian species; most are slender snakes that actively hunt for their prey and rely on flight rather than camouflage for defence, and they are mainly tropical in their distribution. Exceptions include the African spitting cobra (or rinkhals), *Hemachatus haemachatus*, which is oviparous, perhaps because it inhabits cooler regions than most cobras, and several of the Australian elapids, notably those occurring towards the south of the continent. The death adder is an interesting case because, although it is an elapid, it has moved into the niche that vipers would normally occupy if they were present. It has become short, stocky and well camouflaged, and it ambushes its prey. Viviparity is a natural extension of this parallelism.

Vipers have a tendency to be viviparous, perhaps because they are heavy-bodied species that ambush their prey. In addition, many species come from cold places. For example, all the *Vipera* species breed this way as do the

African *Bitis* species. Even so, there are plenty of exceptions. All the night adders, *Causus* are egg layers and the large Eurasian species *Macrovipera lebetina, M. schweizeri* are both egg layers, as is Russell's viper. Similarly, the North African desert horned adder, *Cerastes cerastes*, is oviparous, perhaps because its specialised form of locomotion – sidewinding – may have influenced its breeding system, even though the North American sidewinder, which leads a similar life, has retained the viviparous mode of reproduction (like all the other rattlesnakes). The African and Asian genus

▷ A few vipers, such as the West African night adder, *Causus maculatus*, lay eggs.

▽ Like most of the more advanced vipers, the green bush viper, *Atheris chloroechis*, from tropical Africa is a livebearing species.

▲ Like most vipers, the American copperhead, *Agkistrodon contortrix*, gives birth to live young.

▶ Members of the genus *Trimeresurus*, such as the Sri Lanka green pit viper, *T. trigonocephalus*, are live-bearers whereas related kinds, especially if they are terrestrial, lay eggs.

Echis, known variously as saw-scaled vipers and carpet vipers, includes oviparous as well as viviparous species.

Pit vipers occur in North and South America, where they are all viviparous with the sole exception of the bushmasters, *Lachesis*, and in Asia, where their reproductive mode is more varied. Most Asian pit vipers, such as *Trimeresurus* and *Protobothrops* are live-bearers but several closely related, but terrestrial, species, lay eggs. They include the members of the genera *Ovophis* (literally "egg snake"), the Malaysian pit viper, *Calloselasma rhodostoma* and the Chinese moccasin, *Deinagkistrodon acutus*.

Parental effort

Parental effort is the term given to the amount of effort that parents put into producing young. It covers every stage of reproduction, including the amount of food that is diverted into the production of sperm or ova, the amount of energy spent searching for a mate and in courtship, and the amount of time devoted to producing and rearing young.

Parental effort in female snakes is easier to measure than in many other groups of animals because parental care of the young is almost non-existent: the few exceptions are dealt with later in this section. Males put less effort into the production of the sex cells (sperm) than females, which produce relatively large eggs. The major contribution to the next generation, therefore, in terms of energy, comes from females. This can be considered a disadvantage to females, but being a male snake also has drawbacks.

Whereas every female in a population of snakes is almost bound to reproduce, at least at some stage of its life, it seems likely that some males never breed. Other males, though, may father many offspring by mating with many females each breeding season. This is due to sexual selection, in which dominant males, or males that are especially good at finding mates, get to mate with more females than subordinate ones. Dominance, where it exists, is achieved through male to male combat, and appears to be present in some boids, colubrids, elapids and vipers, though not in all species belonging to these families. Sexual selection within the other families of snakes has not been established one way or the other.

Parental effort in males is difficult to measure. It would be necessary to look at the amount of energy each male spends in finding and defending a mate, and in the amount of food it gives up during these activities. Searching for a mate may also make it more vulnerable to predation and, as has already been mentioned, males that have to range over a large area in order to find females are more likely to come to the attention of predators than are females of the same species.

Female reproductive effort can be measured in part by measuring the proportion of her body weight that each female contributes towards her batch of eggs or young. This is usually referred to as her 'relative clutch mass'. As female snakes grow, they have more resources to divert towards reproductive effort. They can use these extra resources in two ways: they can either produce more offspring, or each offspring can be larger. This is another example of a trade off, where the factors that need to be balanced are: is it better to produce a lot of small babies, or a few large ones?

Relative clutch mass among most snakes is somewhere around 20 per cent — a female snake that weighs 1 kg (2 lb) will produce a clutch of eggs or a litter of young weighing, on average, a total of 200 g (7 oz), for example. Females of some species, however, put more or less effort into their reproduction. Why should this be so?

Mode of reproduction plays a part: viviparous snakes have, on average, a lower relative clutch mass than oviparous species. This suggests that the other costs of reproduction (leaving aside weight) are higher in viviparous species, perhaps because they carry their young for a longer period of time and would therefore be more prone to predation.

Sea snakes, which are viviparous, have even lower relative clutch masses than other viviparous snakes, probably because their body is partially filled with an organ that regulates their buoyancy, and so they have less room for developing embryos.

In general, small snakes have higher relative clutch masses than large ones. This is difficult to explain but may be related to life expectancy. Large snakes tend to live longer. Their reproductive effort in any one year must be weighed against their chances of surviving until the next year. If they put too much effort into reproducing, they may not survive. Small snakes, on the other hand, are more likely to die or to be killed before they get another chance to breed and so it may be in their interests to produce more young while they have the chance.

More young or bigger young?

This is another 'decision' that must be made. Given that a female has only a limited amount of energy to devote to reproduction, how should it be shared out? As she grows, she may produce more young, or the same number of bigger young, or a compromise – slightly more young, each of which is slightly bigger. In most species that have been studied, it seems that females tend to compromise for the best chance of survival.

Differences between species are much more complicated. Closely related species of about the same size may use different strategies: one will lay a large number of small eggs and the other a few large eggs. Differences may arise because of the feeding habits of the young. Where a species eats prey that is available in a range of sizes, such as frogs, it may be able to produce small young that have a good chance of surviving. It may pay the female to lay a lot of small eggs. If the available prey comes in large 'packages', such as mammals, young that are too small will not be able to find enough food and will all die. In this case the best strategy is to lay a few large eggs.

Sexual dimorphism

Just as male and female snakes behave differently, or rather, *because* they behave differently, these differences may be reflected in their appearances. Where males and females differ in design, they are said to be sexually dimorphic.

Internal differences, which are not visible in the living animal, usually involve the reproductive organs (see below) and are referred to as primary sex characteristics. Secondary sex characteristics are those not directly concerned with the reproductive system, although some of them may also play a part in reproductive behaviour.

Snakes do not usually show the same degree of sexual dimorphism found in many other animals, such as lizards and birds, for instance. This is largely due to the lack of visual displays in snakes' interactions with one another. There are, however, various more subtle differences between the sexes, although these are not found generally across all species or families.

Differences in size

There are two factors that significantly affect the size of snakes. Females can produce more offspring if they are larger, whereas this is not an important factor in males, which do not carry eggs or young. But in species in which males fight one another, large males tend to be more successful than small ones. Males may still be smaller than females even in this scenario, however, because the benefits of being larger may be more important to females than males. Bearing these two points in mind, we would expect males to be relatively larger (compared to females) in those species that fight than in those species that do not fight.

By looking at comparative sizes of males and females within a species, it should be possible to pick out those species in which fighting takes place. This does seem to be generally true, despite some problems associated with how sizes are compared (because snakes grow throughout their lives). In some species that fight, males ultimately reach larger sizes than females – in rattlesnakes, Australian whipsnakes, *Demansia*, and in some populations of Australian tiger snakes, *Notechis scutatus*, for instance, even though they may start breeding when they are smaller. In species in which combat almost definitely does not take place, blind snakes, for instance, females are larger than males.

Differences in shape
Female snakes are often more heavy-bodied than males of the same species and similar size. This is apparent in many vipers, including pit vipers, and also in some boids, such as *Boa constrictor*. Greater girth is beneficial to females in allowing more room for developing eggs and young. The relative length of the tails usually differs significantly between male and female snakes, with those of males being longer. This is due to the presence of the hemipenes in males, which must be accommodated in the base of the tail when retracted.

Less easily explained is the fact that females often have relatively larger heads than males, or the shape of their heads may differ. The differences have been noted especially in semi-aquatic natricine snakes, including *Nerodia* and *Thamnophis* from North America and *Natrix tessellata* from Turkey, but also occur in other species. This difference may be apparent right from the moment of hatching or birth and in some cases it

▲ The green water snake, *Nerodia cyclopion*, a species in which males do not combat and in which they are often noticeably smaller than females.

▼ The differences between male (below) and female (above) *Langaha nasuta* are plain to see, but the reason for their strange appendages is unknown.

may be associated with differences in prey between the sexes of young snakes.

Other differences in head shape involve the various ornamentations that some snakes carry, as in the strange protuberances on the snouts of the Madagascan snakes belonging to the genus *Langaha*, which are more elaborate in females. Some male tree snakes, including *Ahaetulla pieta* and *Bothrops moojeni*, have larger eyes than females, and, in at least two species belonging to the South American genus *Imantodes*, males have longer tongues!

In cobras belonging to the genus *Naja*, the males of *Naja naja*, *N. samarensis* and *N. oxiana* have longer fangs than females. Two of these species spit venom, but *N. naja* does not. In another species, *N. philippinensis*, the males have short orifices in their fangs, in keeping with species that spit, whereas the females have long ones; although the species is known to spit, it is not known if both sexes do so.

Minor differences are found in the body scales of some species, and these differences concern two groups of scales. In some species, including several North American water snakes, *Nerodia* and garter snakes, *Thamnophis*, males have small warty tubercles on the chin. This may serve to stimulate the female during courtship, when the male rubs his chin along the length of the female. In these same species, but also in several others that are not closely related, males have a group of heavily keeled scales in the region of their vent. These may assist in helping the male to locate the vent of the female during mating or they may help him to retain a better grip during copulation. Similar scales, but not so localised, have been found in some species of sea snakes, where their function is also uncertain.

In boas and pythons, males have vestigial limbs in the form of spurs on either side of the vent. These are used to stimulate the female during courtship and, sometimes, to damage other males during combat. Females may also have spurs, although these are often smaller. In some species, or in certain populations, spurs are lacking altogether in females. In the tropidophids, males have spurs but they are completely lacking in females. Indeed, female *Ungaliophis continentalis* and *U. panamensis* have lost all traces of their hind limb girdles.

Coloration

Differences between the coloration of males and females are not widespread among snakes and, when they do occur, they tend to be rather subtle. In several European vipers, *Vipera*, males are more brightly marked than females, usually as a result of a lighter background colour. Shine and Madsen, 1994[16] have suggested that the reason for this difference lies in the fact that males move more rapidly than females, especially in the spring when they are defending females, and that under these circumstances their markings may help to fool predators by 'flickering' as the snakes move. Females are more sedentary and rely heavily on camouflage and so their markings will have evolved in a different way.

In some populations of the boomslang, *Dispholidus typhus*, males are also more brightly coloured than females, and show great variation, being bright green, red or pinkish, yellow, or even blue, sometimes with black-edged scales or speckles, while others are uniformly coloured. Females, on the other hand, are usually plain brown or olive. The banded rock rattlesnake, *Crotalus lepidus klauberi*, shows dimorphism in some areas, where males may have a greenish hue but the females are grey. In other populations, both sexes are identically coloured. In *Bothrops asper*, juvenile males have brightly coloured tips to the tail whereas females do not. Both sexes apparently use their tails to lure prey.

NOTES

1. Aldridge, R. D. (1992), 'Oviductal anatomy and seasonal sperm storage in the southeastern crowned snake (*Tantilla coronatum*)', *Copeia*, 1992(4):1103-1106.
2. Monugomery, W.B. and Schuett, G. W. (1989), 'Autumnal mating with subsequent production of offspring in the rattlesnake *Sistrurus miliarius streckeri*', *Bull. Chi, Herp. Soc.*, 24(11):205-207.
3. Graves, B. M. and Duvall, D. (1993), 'Reproduction, rookery use and thermoregulation in free-ranging, pregnant prairie rattlesnakes, *Crotalus viridis*', *Journal of Herpetology*, 27(433-41.
4. Maruin, B. E. (1976), 'A reproductive record for the New Mexican ridge-nosed rattlesnake (*Crotalus willardii obscurus*)', *Bulletin Maryland Herpetological Society*, 12(4):126-128.
5. Wallace. R. L. and Diller, L. V. (1990), 'Feeding ecology of the rattlesnake. *Crotalus viridis oreganus*, in northern Idaho', *Journal of Herpetology*, 24(3):246-253.
6. Butler, J. A. (1993), 'Seasonal reproduction in the African olive grass snake, *Psammophis phillipsi*', *Journal of Herpctology*, 27(2):144-148.
7. Powell, R., Maxey, S. A., Parmerlee, J. S. and Smith, D. D. (1991), 'Notes on the reproductive biology of a montane population of *Antillophis parvifrons protenus* from the Dominican Republic', *Journal of Herpetology*, 25(1): 121-122.
8. Solorzano, A. and Cerdas, L. (1989), 'Reproductive biology and distribution of the terciopelo, *Bothrops asper* in Costa Rica', *Herpetologica*, 45(4):444-450.
9. Lillywhite. FL B. (1985). 'Trailing movements and sexual behaviour in *Coluber constrictor*', *Journal of Herpetology*. 19(2):306-308.
10. Plummer, M. V. (1989), 'Observations on the nesting ecology of green snakes (*Opheodryas aestivus*)'. *Herp. Review*, 20(4): 87-89.
11. Tu, M. C., Fong, S. C. and Lue, K. Y. (1990), 'Reproductive biology of the sea snake, *Laticauda semifasciata* in Taiwan'. *Journal of Herpetology*, 24(2):119-126.
12. Palmer, W. M. and Braswell, A. L. (1976), 'Communal egg-laying and hatchlings of the rough green snake, *Opheodrys aestivus*', *Journal of Herpetology*, 10(3): 257-259.
13. Burger, J. and Zappalorti, R. T. (1991), 'Nesting behaviour of pine snakes (*Pituophis m. melanoleucus*) in the New Jersey Pine Barrens', *Journal of Herpetology*, 25(2):152-160.
14. Riley, J., Stimson, A. F. and Winch, J. M. (1985), 'A review of squamata ovipositing in ant and termite nests', *Herp. Review*, 16(2):38-43.
15. Pedrez-Hidareda, G. and Smith, II. M. (1989), 'Termite nest incubation of the Mexican colubrid snake *Adelphicos quadrivirgatus*', *Herp. Review*, 20(1):5-6.
16. Shine. R and Madsen, T. (1994), 'Sexual dichromatism in snakes of the genus *Vipera*: a review and a new evolutionary hypothesis', *Journal of Herpetology*, 28(1):114-117.

CHAPTER 8
SNAKES AND HUMANS

People's interactions with snakes down through the ages form an interesting study. Much of it is within the realms of anthropology, however, and has only a limited place in a book about snakes. For this reason, only a very brief overview is given here.

The African house snake often lives in and around farm buildings, where it does a useful job of keeping down rodents.

SNAKE MYTHS AND SNAKE WORSHIP

SNAKES HAVE BEEN OBJECTS OF FASCINATION, FEAR AND WORSHIP IN MANY CULTURES THROUGHOUT THE WORLD, ALMOST WHEREVER THEY ARE FOUND, IN FACT.

Snakes in ancient cultures

The earliest evidence of man's interest in snakes comes from cave paintings in southern Europe, some of which date from at least twenty to thirty thousand years ago. Additional scratchings and engravings have been found on fragments of bone and wood from the same era.

From more recent times, rock and cave paintings depicting snakes can be found in regions inhabited by tribal peoples whose lifestyles have changed little until recently. These include bushman paintings in part of southern Africa and aboriginal paintings in many parts of Australia. Aborigines also decorated their own bodies in the form of stylised snakes in certain of their ceremonies.

Although little can be deduced about the motivation of prehistoric snake images, the stories behind the aboriginal paintings are well known because many of the painters still practise their art. Snakes play a number of different roles in the mythology of these people. Their importance as food is obviously relevant as is the regularity with which they appear from seemingly sterile habitats during rainy periods. The various rites and ceremonies associated with them may therefore serve to increase the fertility of snakes, thereby ensuring a good supply of food, or to ensure that the rains come. The rainbow serpents are among the most dramatic manifestations of snakes in their mythology. They live deep in permanent waterholes during the dry season but leave them and take to the skies, where they appear as rainbows, during the rainy season. The importance of such a custodian of natural water supplies is obvious when one considers the arid nature of the Australian interior, and the paintings of them are carefully restored at the approach of each rainy season.

▲ The Aesculapian snake, *Zamenis longissimus*, named for the Roman god Aesculapius.

▶ The staff of Aesculapius, incorporating an entwined snake, is commonly used throughout the world as a symbol of the medical profession.

The worship of snakes, as part of religious activities, is also widespread. It was common in Africa, where the python was singled out for special attention, and African slaves later carried snake worship to Haiti where it took the form of the voodoo cult, still apparently practised to the present day.

In India the cobra has been widely worshipped since ancient times. Snake gods, in the form of Nagas and their wives, Naginis, are associated with everyday village life and may be good or bad depending on their mood; in former times, human sacrifices were made to them as a form of appeasement.

In China, the dragon takes the place of the Indian Nagas. Although it has legs, it owes it origin to snake worship and was also thought to have control of several natural phenomena such as rain making.

The ancient Egyptians are thought to have kept 'asps' in their homes and temples. Judging from their painting and inscriptions, these were probably cobras, even though the modern day asp is a

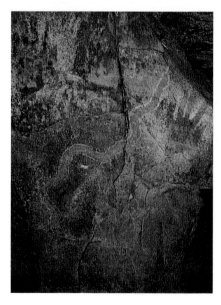

▶ An Australian aboriginal painting, depicting a snake along with other animals and symbols.

viper (*Vipera aspis*), which is not found in North Africa. As in many other cultures, the Egyptians associated snakes with rain, and therefore fertility. Also with the river Nile, which brought fertility, and therefore wealth, to their land. A rearing cobra, with hood extended, was the symbol of one of their goddesses, Ejo, and a similar symbol was incorporated into the headdress of the Pharaoh.

Snakes were also sacred to the Greeks, the Romans and the Minoans. Many of their gods appeared as snakes or with them, although Hercules, the Greek hero, was famed as a slayer of serpents. The oracle serpent, Gaea, was defeated in a fight by Apollo but its wisdom continued to be of use through the oracle at Delphi, the 'navel of the earth', while the generic name of the sand boas, *Eryx*, commemorates a magic spear, thrown on to the flanks of Mount Olympus, whereupon it promptly turned into a snake.

There are many other legends and myths concerning snakes, and their associations with the gods, one of which has persisted into the present time. It concerns the widespread belief that snakes are immortal, usually attributed to their habit of shedding their skin periodically, looked upon in ancient times as a type of rebirth. For this reason, the Greek god Asklepios (later incorporated into Roman mythology as Aesculapius) is portrayed as a man with a snake as a staff. The emblem of two entwined snakes is still widely used as the emblem of the medical profession. The species most often identified with Aesculapius is the European colubrid *Zamenis longissimus*, which is commonly known as the Aesculapian snake. It has a disjunct population throughout parts of Europe and this is thought to be due to its having been introduced to sites of Roman baths and spas in various parts of the Roman empire.

In the New World, as in the Old, snakes were associated with rain. North American Indians held snakes in high esteem for this reason and in some of the more arid parts of North America rain dances involved the use of living snakes, those of the Hopi Indians being the best documented because they were continued until very recently. After parading with the snakes, they were released into crevices in the ground in the hope that they would carry the Indians' prayers to the rain gods. The snakes, then, were not worshipped as

THE SNAKE FESTIVAL OF COCULLO

Dominic de Guzman, a Spaniard and founder of the Dominican Order, lived from about CE 1170 to 1221. In 1215 he travelled throughout the Abruzzese Mountains in central Italy, preaching to the heretical Albigenses, who deviated from the Roman Catholic faith. The Albigenses were represented by snakes, to whose venom he was supposedly immune; thus his snake association.

In the village of Cocullo he is still honoured with an annual procession, in which his effigy, draped with snakes, is paraded through the streets. The festival of San Domenico, 'Il rito die serpari', takes place early in May. During the morning a mass is held in his honour then, at midday, the church doors are swung open and the statue is carried out into the village square. It is placed in front of the church and local people approach the statue and place live snakes around the head and body, where they stay for the duration of the ceremony. The species used is the four-lined snake, *Elaphe quatuorlineata*, a large and impressive colubrid that is found in the region. Each snake is marked with a spot of paint on the top of its head.

The litter containing the statue is then lifted and the procession begins. The priest and the mayor of the village walk ahead, followed by young girls dressed in local costume. The litter is carried by local men and is flanked by policemen dressed in their ceremonial finery and wearing cocked hats topped with black and red feathers. The procession wends its way round the village, accompanied by local people and tourists. Afterwards, the snakes are released or sold to tourists.

gods but acted as messengers. It is not hard to see how snakes that live in underground chambers, and emerge only when conditions are favourable, can be linked with the underworld and the forces of nature.

In Central America the Aztecs and Mayans decorated their temples and monuments with gigantic carvings of stylised snakes, often in gruesome attitudes. Although it is not known what part they played in their culture or religion it is most obvious that it was an important one. Furthermore, many of their important deities were depicted with serpents entwined around them in the form of cloaks, skirts or belts and some of them carry staffs in the shape of snakes.

The Christian religion may have done more harm to the way in which we view snakes than any other. The snake, being symbolic of so many heathen cults and cultures, was an obvious scapegoat. It became synonymous with evil, an attitude typified by the episode in the Garden of Eden, and even today some communities, especially in the Mediterranean region still regard snakes as fundamentally evil and persecute them mercilessly, whether venomous or harmless.

Legends and superstitions

Several of the ancient beliefs and prejudices surrounding snakes live on into the twentieth century, often modified as 'old wives' tales'. There are hundreds, if not thousands, of these stories throughout the world, most of them without any scientific basis whatsoever but they are none the less important to the people whose daily lives often bring them into contact with wild snakes.

Throughout the ages, humans have assumed that other animals were placed on earth because they were of some potential use to them. The trick was to find out what that use was. Snakes, with their potent symbolic and actual properties, have been thoroughly investigated by medicine men, herbalists, quack doctors and bona fide medical practitioners in almost every part of the world.

Some traditional remedies call for various parts of snakes' anatomy, including their shed skins. Ailments that they are said to cure include rheumatism, sore throats, headaches and backaches. Snake skins were sometimes used to ease childbirth and snakes' gall bladders have also been used for the same purpose. The flesh of snakes has been used to improve the complexion, while snake fat was thought to be a cure for premature baldness. The Chinese ate snake flesh for the prevention of tuberculosis and sea snakes were thought to be effective against malaria and epilepsy.

Rattlesnake oil, of course, was widely sold in travelling medicine shows in North America, mainly as a cure for backache and stiffness but also for use in cases of toothache, deafness, sties, ringworm and mosquito bite. Medicines made from various snake preparations have also been claimed effective against the black death, measles, smallpox and leprosy, among other diseases. The list is almost endless!

Snake venom has always been held in high regard by the medical profession and is credited with many special properties and its use in medicine is under current investigation in a number of fields. Some of the claims are obviously fanciful but dried Russell's viper venom acts as a blood coagulant and was used in cases of haemorrhage and haemophilia until recently. Cobra venom may act as a pain reliever under certain circumstances and its use also continued until recently.

Snake bite has always been a hazard to people living in areas where venomous species are common. Although their fears were mostly justified, there were, and still are, superstitions surrounding the power of poisonous snakes. According to some cultures, snakes are able to spit their venom for great distances and one mythological serpent, the basilisk, could apparently kill with a single glance from its fiery red eyes. Snakes were also thought to sting with their tails, a myth that may have arisen

because a number of species have sharp pointed tails that they press into the skin if they are restrained. Several species, especially burrowing snakes, have blunt tails that could be mistaken for their heads, although none of them are venomous.

To protect against snake bite, spells and charms were widely used, many of them using parts of snakes, such as teeth and skin. Quite recently, ropes of hair were used in North America to encircle camps in the belief that snakes would not cross them. Plants such as the ash tree were also thought to repel snakes, as were the ashes and extracts of numerous plants. Even human saliva was thought to be effective.

Immunity to snake bite was claimed by a number of clans of native peoples and many acted as Shamans, to cure snake bite in others. Cleopatra was apparently attended by Shamans from two tribes in an attempt to save her life after her self-imposed asp bite. Many cures involve the use of parts of the culprit, such as wine in which the head of an asp has been pickled or a broth made from the snake. These cures were held in high regard in Europe until the eighteenth century. The most universally used cure was suction, no doubt as a result of the natural reaction of humans to suck any small injury. Suction can be beneficial, as snake venoms are relatively harmless when swallowed. Various devices were used to draw out the venom, including porous stones, pieces of burnt bone and poultices made from a variety of natural products.

Cauterisation has been widely used to prevent snake venom spreading, as have the applications of ligatures and, more drastic, summary amputation. As only a small proportion of snake bites are potentially lethal, one is left to ponder to what degree these mutilations were actually necessary.

More recently, alcohol was thought to counteract the effects of the venom and this proved to be a most popular cure, for obvious reasons. The patient was given enough to make him or her well and truly drunk and there are many stories of fictitious bites and prophylactic treatments. Some years ago, an Australian character, interviewed on television, maintained that a shot of whisky was the best cure for snake bite, adding that it was most effective taken before the bite! In fact, alcohol may increase the effects of a bite by speeding up the circulation, and the enormous doses recommended may kill the patient before the venom has had time to work.

CURRENT ATTITUDES

CURRENT PUBLIC ATTITUDES TOWARDS SNAKES VARY GREATLY. WHILE THERE IS GREATER AWARENESS IN THE WESTERN WORLD OF THE VALUE OF WILDLIFE AS A WHOLE, THERE IS STILL AN UNDERLYING DISTRUST OF SNAKES. THIS OBVIOUSLY STEMS IN PART FROM THE FACT THAT MANY SPECIES ARE CAPABLE OF CAUSING RAPID AND SPECTACULAR DEATH, BUT IS ALSO FUELLED BY AN IRRATIONAL REVULSION.

Prejudices

Snakes rank higher than spiders, cockroaches or rats as the most disliked animal. The majority of people who fear them will never have seen a wild snake. Even fewer will have been bitten by one. Events in the Garden of Eden have undoubtedly done a great deal to engender this attitude. Many popular sayings, such as 'snake in the grass' and 'speaking with a forked tongue', perpetuate the negative view of snakes.

A healthy respect for snakes is no bad thing, especially where venomous species are concerned, but there is little reason to loathe them nor is there any excuse to persecute them. Interestingly, young children are rarely afraid of snakes and are perfectly happy to handle them; as they grow, their dislike and mistrust of them is encouraged, mostly by their parents.

Snake bite

Snake bite is a serious problem in only a few parts of the world, mainly rural tropical areas. Several factors contribute to this. Firstly, venomous snakes are more common in tropical areas. In addition, many rural workers in tropical countries make themselves more vulnerable by wearing inadequate or no protection on their feet or lower legs. Finally, many of these countries have poor medical facilities and people may, in any case, be reluctant to use them, preferring instead to rely on traditional 'cures'.

The carpet, or saw-scaled, viper, *Echis carinata*, is usually regarded as the world's most dangerous species. This is due to its wide distribution over much of Africa and

Asia, where it is often extremely common. It relies heavily on camouflage, making it all too easy to be trodden on, and has an aggressive nature, never hesitating to bite if it feels it is in danger. Other dangerous species include Russell's viper, *Daboia russeli*, in Asia, the puff adder, *Bitis arietans*, in Africa, the Malayan pit viper, *Callosclasma rhodostoma*, in Asia and the terciopelo, *Bothrops atrox*, in Central and South America. It is notable that many of the more notorious venomous snakes – the mambas, cobras, taipans, rattlesnakes and the bushmaster – are absent from this list; although these species may cause a substantial number of fatalities, they are not regarded as significant as is popularly believed. This may be because they are relatively rare (the bushmaster and the taipans, for example) or because they live in regions where people are well protected (the rattlesnakes and, again, the taipans). Other venomous species are shy and reluctant to bite except under extreme provocation and this applies to many of the less dangerous species as well, including the European vipers, many small rattlesnakes, coral snakes and cobras.

The effects of snake bite on man vary according to the species. Many bites are mild and their effects are insignificant, any symptoms being slight and clearing up without treatment after a few days or hours. On the other hand, serious bites often produce the most alarming symptoms. These may be localised, as in bites from species that produce haemotoxic venom (mainly vipers and back-fanged colubrids), or systemic, as in bites from species that produce neurotoxic venom (mainly cobras).

Bites from haemotoxic species produce local pain that may be immediate and severe. Swelling and discoloration often follows within a few minutes and may spread up the limbs and on to the trunk. Internal haemorrhage is caused through the breakdown of blood vessels and may be exacerbated by damage to the clotting agents in the blood. In other cases, clotting is caused, leading to thrombosis. In extreme cases, irreversible tissue damage may occur, leading to gangrene or even death. Death usually results from damage to internal organs or low blood pressure.

Bites from neurotoxic species produce little or no local effects. Muscles become weak, leading to drooping eyelids in the early stages. Paralysis follows and breathing may become difficult. In

SNAKE BITE

Snake bite statistics are notoriously difficult to obtain. In many countries, where medical facilities in rural areas are non-existent, many cases must go unrecorded. Confusion may also exist over the species that was responsible.

A fairly recent estimate gives a figure of about 25,000 deaths per year from snake bite. More than half of these are thought to occur in India and Burma, where rural populations are dense, medical facilities are often less than ideal and several potentially lethal species are fairly common. It is thought that Russell's viper is responsible for at least 10,000 bites and 1,000 deaths in Burma alone. Other significant species in the region include the carpet viper and several species of pit vipers, cobras and kraits.

Figures for South America are extremely difficult to estimate. Among the Waorani tribe of Ecuador, it has been estimated that almost 5 per cent of deaths are caused by snake bite, and that nearly 80 per cent of the population is bitten at least once during their lifetime. In other parts of South America about 0.5 per cent of the population is bitten per year, but only a fraction of these are fatal. Figures for parts of tropical Africa point to a similar incidence.

Snake bite fatalities in westernised societies are far less frequent. Snakes have all but disappeared from many urban and agricultural areas, the population is usually better informed and protected, and medical facilities are of a high standard. In Australia, which has the distinction of having more venomous than non-venomous species, deaths number less than 10 per year on average while in North America, with a fair sprinkling of potentially lethal rattlesnakes, about 15 people become victims each year. A similar figure is often quoted for Europe, where most of the more dangerous species of vipers live in the south and east. Of these deaths, a number can be put down to casual handling by snake keepers and unnecessary heroics.

▲ Russell's viper, *Daboia russelii*, a species responsible for many serious snake bites in southern Asia.

extreme cases, death can result from asphyxiation. In serious cases, where the bite penetrates a major blood vessel, death can occur in a matter of minutes.

Sea snakes rarely bite people, and their venom apparatus is not adapted for giving a deep bite. Fishermen may be vulnerable in some parts of the world as the snakes often become entangled in nets. They are usually reluctant to bite, however, and are often handled casually. Their venom affects the muscles and symptoms include swelling, muscular pain and stiffness. The muscle cells are destroyed, releasing potassium ions into the system. This may lead to death through cardiac arrest. On other occasions, death is caused by respiratory

failure due to paralysis of the muscles responsible for breathing.

The rear-fanged colubrids are not normally regarded as especially dangerous. At least three species have caused fatalities, however: these are the boomslang, *Dispholidus typus*, the twig snake, *Thelotornis capensis*, and the Asian tiger snake or yamakagashi, *Rhabdophis tigrinus*. These species produce symptoms similar to those of vipers, with local tissue damage, bleeding, bruising and reduced blood clotting. Death from boomslang bite usually occurs within 24 hours due to respiratory failure but in the case of the other two species it may occur several days, or even weeks, after the bite, due to kidney failure.

TREATING SNAKE BITE

The most effective treatment for serious snake bite involves the use of antivenom. The first stage in manufacturing antivenom is obtaining pure venom by 'milking' the snake: its fangs are hooked over the lip of a glass vessel and its venom gland massaged until the venom is ejected through the apertures in the fangs. After processing, small quantities of the venom are injected into animals, usually horses but sometimes cattle, sheep or goats, at regular intervals until they have built up an immunity. Blood taken from the animal is then separated so that the serum containing the antibodies can be isolated and used in the treatment of snake bite.

Antivenom is made in laboratories throughout the world, some of which produce antivenom against common local species and some of which produce a range of antivenoms for sale and distribution in other countries or for use in zoos, etc. Most antivenoms are expensive, due to the difficulty involved in producing them, ranging in price from U.S.$25 to U.S.$1,000 per ampoule, depending on species. In severe bites, the use of several ampoules may be necessary. They also have limited shelf lives, often only two or three years: in countries where snake bite is frequent, such as Papua New Guinea, the purchase of antivenom can absorb a significant proportion of the annual health budget.

Antivenoms may be polyvalent (i.e. effective against a range of species) or specific (i.e. effective against a single species or a group of closely related species). Polyvalent antivenoms are useful in regions where there is a number of venomous snakes, and where the species involved cannot always be positively identified. The range of species against which they are effective may be limited to snakes that produce broadly similar venoms, such as polyvalent *Crotalus* (which is effective against bites of a number of dangerous rattlesnake species), polyvalent coral snake (effective against bites from a number of *Micrurus* species) and so on. Others contain antivenom of two or more species; they are mixtures that are designed to target the most dangerous species from the same region, regardless of which type of venom they produce, e.g. Indian cobra and Russell's viper (produced by Central Hills Research, Kasauli, India), or Indian cobra, Indian krait, Russell's viper and carpet viper (produced by the Serum Institute of India).

Specific antivenoms, e.g. anti-bushmaster, black snake antivenom, mamushi antivenom (against *Agkistrodon halys*), etc., are intended to be used where the species has been positively identified, although they may also be effective against bites from similar snakes.

Because they can have harmful side effects, antivenoms should only be used by qualified medical staff. In particular, some people are allergic to horse serum, and the anaphylactic shock it produces can be even more dangerous than the bite. Since the venom must be given intravenously, there are the additional dangers of infection and injury associated with inexpert administration.

In practice, antivenom is not normally necessary except in cases of a serious bite. In an information sheet produced by the Liverpool School of Tropical Medicine, 30 per cent of viper bites, 50 per cent of elapid bites and 80 per cent of sea snake bites are reckoned to produce no clinical symptoms whatsoever: the snakes often produce 'dry' bites. Local symptoms are produced as a result of 80 per cent of effective viper bites and 50 per cent of bites from spitting cobras; systemic symptoms, including bleeding gums, shock, respiratory and cardiac problems, occur in 40 per cent of viper bites, 20 per cent of elapid bites and 20 per cent of sea snake bites. Not all the bites that produce symptoms are lethal, of course, and natural recovery is likely in the majority of cases. The death rate, in the absence of treatment, is thought to be somewhere in the region of 1 per cent for viper bites, 5 per cent for elapid bites and 10 per cent for sea snake bites. These are generalised estimates and in certain parts of the world, where some of the more dangerous species are found, the death rate is likely to be higher than average.

In the event of snake bite, medical help should always be sought. First-aid treatment should be confined to reassuring the patient and keeping him or her calm. Avoid movement, especially of the bitten limb, so that the venom is not carried around the body any faster than is necessary. Tourniquets are no longer recommended, nor is opening the wound or sucking out the venom. The most effective interim measure is to apply a firm crepe or elasticated bandage to the entire limb. This will slow down the circulation of lymph and delay symptoms for several hours, by which time expert medical attention should be possible. Given proper care, full recovery is highly likely.

EXPLOITATION OF SNAKES

SNAKES AS A WHOLE HAVE VERY LITTLE COMMERCIAL VALUE COMPARED WITH OTHER GROUPS OF ANIMALS. THE VARIOUS WAYS IN WHICH THEY ARE EXPLOITED TEND TO BE LIMITED TO SPECIFIC REGIONS OR TO A FEW SPECIES.

Food

Snakes are eaten, though not as much as in former times, by a number of native peoples. They are easily caught and killed and, although they often yield only a small amount of flesh, their occurrence in areas where other animals are scarce or hard to catch must have made them an important addition to the diet in times of need. Australian aborigines, for instance, eat all varieties of snakes and relish pythons in particular. In parts of tropical Africa the rock python is held in high esteem and anacondas and common boas are eaten in South America.

In Asia, snakes are widely eaten, even by the urban population. Sea snakes are especially prized and huge numbers are consumed. A wide range of other species is eaten, however, including cobras and kraits. In Hong Kong, snakes' gall bladders are thought to be a tonic and are often removed from the living snake and swallowed whole. Other parts of snakes are sold and eaten as aphrodisiacs and cures for various ailments. Snake-eating in China is commonplace in the Canton region where certain species, especially the python, fetch very high prices in markets.

In North America rattlesnakes were eaten by early settlers but only in times of hardship — prejudice came to the snake's aid in this instance. On the other hand, tinned rattlesnake is still available, often originating from animals killed during rattlesnake round-ups.

Snakes in entertainment

The entertainment value of snakes has not been overlooked. Revulsion often goes hand in hand with fascination and snake charmers, snake dancers and side-shows play on this quirk of human nature.

RATTLESNAKE ROUND-UPS

Rattlesnake round-ups, or rattlesnake 'bees' as they used to be known, have a history dating back to at least 1680, when men were employed at two shillings a day to kill rattlesnakes in Massachusetts. This programme of extermination developed until, by 1740, a day was set aside each year for a general snake hunt, during which men would gather to kill as many snakes as possible. These early rattlesnake hunts were carried out with the purpose of eliminating rattlesnakes in areas where settlers were attempting to make their land safe for themselves, their children and their livestock.

As communities grew, the rattlesnake hunts became progressively more competitive, with prizes awarded to the participants who killed the greatest number of snakes; one account, of a hunt in Iowa which took place in 1849, describes how two men killed 90 rattlesnakes each in one hour and a half, and the total killed in the year was 3,750.

Rattlesnake round-ups became popular 'sport' in many areas, including those where rattlesnakes presented little or no threat to human life or livestock. The hunt developed into a carnival, where local spectators would take picnics along to watch the proceedings. Civic authorities and charities often sponsored the events to raise money and to provide entertainment; they included exhibitions of rattlesnake handling, after which the snakes were killed and the skins and flesh sold.

Incredibly rattlesnake round-ups are still carried out in several states, the most notorious being that of Sweetwater, Texas, where 70,773 snakes were reported to have been killed over a 16-year period. Other figures include 751 timber rattlesnakes, *Crotalus h. horridus*, killed over a nine-year period at the Morris snake hunt, Pennsylvania and 3,205 in 17 years at the Keystone Reptile Club, also in Pennsylvania. Other States where rattlesnake round-ups still take place are Alabama, Florida, Georgia and Oklahoma.

In the early years, rattlesnakes were caught in the open and round-ups were timed to coincide with the most productive time, just after they had emerged from the hibernation dens but before they had dispersed. Later developments included dynamiting the dens. At present, a common method is to pour gasoline into the dens and into gopher tortoise burrows, with the aim of driving out the snakes; this method is particularly insidious because the rattlesnakes often remain in the burrows and die, along with harmless snakes and other wildlife that may be sheltering there.

Snake charmers are found in North Africa, the Middle East and India. Their origins are thought to go back to ancient Egyptian times, where power over snakes was regarded as a divine gift. The mystique surrounding snake charming can be put down to an intimate knowledge of snake behaviour. Accomplished charmers use 'intact' highly venomous species and fatal accidents are not unheard of. Less principled performers remove the fangs of venomous species, sew up their mouths, milk the venom regularly or use non-venomous species. The snakes most used by snake charmers are, of course, the cobras, whose hooded stance makes them instantly recognisable for what they are. Where it occurs, the king cobra is the most favoured species. Other species are often used, however, including pythons and vipers.

Other snake shows include exotic dancers and various types of cabaret act in which snakes figure. Large pythons are the obvious choice for these performers as they are spectacular and quite easily handled. The American snake side-shows, previously to be seen at roadside petrol stations and restaurants, are less of an attraction than they used to be.

A more specific case is that of the snake temple in Penang, Malaysia, where

WHERE DO ALL THE SNAKES GO?

Exploitation and persecution of snakes takes many forms. Often, it is difficult or impossible to quantify the effects on their populations — for instance, the numbers of snakes killed through habitat destruction, consumed as food or medicine, out of prejudice and on the roads are incalculable. When snakes enter commercial trade, however, we have some measure of numbers involved, through the licensing system operated by CITES. Even these figures need to be viewed with caution, however, because certain species are exempt from CITES control and some countries are not party to CITES. Furthermore, the movement of snakes and snake products around the world are difficult to keep track of and, whereas some items may not be counted at all, others are counted more than once. Then again, a number of snakeskin products may be made from a single skin.

In Britain, trade in snakes is controlled by the Department of the Environment. Since the relaxation of licensing regulations in 1993 (due to the free trade agreement within the European Community) these figures are less complete. The figures for previous years, however, may be considered useful indicators of the extent of trade, and the uses to which snakes and snake products are put.

They show that in 1992 the total imports of snakes, snake skin and snake products totalled almost 350,000 items. Of these, about 230,000 were imported as skins, 112,000 were imported as products (mostly shoes, boots and handbags) and the remaining 3,500 or so were imported live, presumably for the pet trade and for exhibit in zoos, and use in laboratories.

Of this total, the greatest numbers consisted of Asian species, including *Ptyas mucosus*, which accounted for roughly 133,500, of which most (125,000) were imported as skins, *Python reticulatus* (about 64,500 of which over 58,000 were skins), *Elaphe carinata* (53,500 of which over 48,000 were snakeskin products) and *Zaochys dhumades* (nearly 42,000 of which over 27,500 were snakeskin products). In addition, almost 16,500 skins of the Java file snake, *Acrochordus javanicus* were imported and there were nearly 38,000 importations of other species, as snakeskin products (22,000), skins (12,000) or alive (3,500). The 'other species' comprised a wide range of snakes, some of which were imported in small numbers (often one or two) and some of which were bred in captivity.

During the same period, nearly 40,000 skins or snakeskin products were re-exported to other parts of the world.

As may be expected from the species concerned, the main exporting countries were Asian, especially Indonesia, Hong Kong and Singapore. Many of the skins and products exported from the latter two countries originated in China.

Bearing in mind that these figures represent trade passing through only one country, it is difficult to see how snake populations can continue to sustain trade of this magnitude.

▲ An Asian rat snake, *Ptyas mucosus*, a species that is heavily exploited in the skin trade.

pit vipers, *Tropidolaemus wagleri*, are draped around ornaments throughout the temple and are used as 'props' with which tourists may be photographed for a fee. The snakes are normally sluggish during the day and may also be stupefied by the atmosphere inside the temple. These snakes are not maintained in a healthy state and casualties must be continually replaced with fresh stock taken from the wild.

Snakes as pets

The trade in living snakes destined for the pet trade is growing. Tens, if not hundreds, of thousands of snakes change hands every year for the enjoyment of amateur enthusiasts. Smaller, but significant, numbers are collected for display in zoos and snake parks. Fortunately, the trend is moving away from trade in wild-caught specimens towards captive-bred ones. Several commercial breeding operations have been set up in North America and Europe to supply the demand, producing many thousands of young snakes each year. Countless more part-time breeders produce varying quantities to supplement these. There is still a trade in wild snakes, however, either because certain species are not easily bred in sufficient quantities or because the cost of producing them often exceeds the paltry amounts for which they can be purchased from native collectors.

Regulation of the trade in wild animals is controlled by the Convention on International Trade in Endangered Species of Wild Fauna and Flora (CITES), which came into force on 1 July 1975. Member countries issue permits for the import and export of snakes, among other animals, only where they feel that trade is not likely to endanger the survival of that species. Several rare snakes are subject to severe restrictions by CITES and the numbers of many others are carefully monitored.

Overall, collecting for the pet trade probably has little serious effect on the populations of most species, although there has been little or no research into wild populations that are regularly 'harvested' in this way. Desirable species are obviously at more risk than others although, again, many of these are widely bred in captivity. Accurate numbers reflecting the trade in wild snakes are very difficult to obtain. Since the setting up of CITES, data have become more easily obtainable.

Snake skins

The colours and patterns of snake skins, as well as their curiosity value, have created a demand for them in the fashion industry. Figures are even harder to estimate than those pertaining to the trade in live snakes. Certain species are more useful than others. The main markets for these products are North America, Europe and Japan and the species mostly exploited are two of the large pythons, *Python reticulatus* and *P. molurus*, two species of anacondas and the common boa. These species alone represent an industry generating several million dollars annually in the United States. Other species, such as the file snakes, *Acrochordus*, and the Indian rat snake, *Ptyas mucosus*, have been equally heavily exploited. The latter species has shown a marked decline in several areas where the snakes were formerly common. Trade figures measure exports of species such as this in pounds (kilograms), rather than individual numbers. Recently, some countries, including India and Sri Lanka, have become concerned about the effects of the skin trade on snake populations and have banned exportations.

Snakes in research

The scientific community must take responsibility for the exploitation of snakes in the past. Museums and universities throughout the Western world are often crammed with preserved specimens, including many that have never been properly studied or even classified. Nineteenth-century zoologists collected huge numbers of animals for shipment back to their sponsors in Europe and North America, often without regard to the effects on local populations and sometimes without the collection data that would have made them more useful to future workers. Taxonomists and anatomists failed to cooperate with one another and so many collections were duplicated unnecessarily. Even quite recently, published papers have reported the killing of large numbers of individuals for the sake of research, sometimes to confirm facts that were already well known, such as the diets of various species. More responsible researchers, however, have used the store of preserved material already in collections or have developed methods of research that do not involve killing the subjects.

CONSERVATION

SNAKES MAY BECOME RARE OR ENDANGERED AS A RESULT OF SEVERAL FACTORS, SEVERAL OF THESE ARE LISTED ABOVE UNDER THE HEADING OF EXPLOITATION. OTHER THREATS INCLUDE HABITAT DESTRUCTION, WHICH IS FAR AND AWAY THE MOST SERIOUS, AND POLLUTION, EITHER KILLING THE SNAKES DIRECTLY OR INDIRECTLY, BY AFFECTING THEIR FOOD SUPPLY.

Most biologists would agree that many species of snakes are in need of protection but, where the general public is concerned, snake conservation has a low priority. This is largely due to prejudice and a 'what use are they' factor. Where species are afforded some degree of protection, it is usually through chance – they happen to live in a region where other, more appealing species are found and become protected incidentally, along with their habitat. In National Parks and National Monuments, for instance, all species of plants and animals are protected and there are many such areas, especially in North America and Europe, and also, increasingly, in other parts of the world.

Local protection

Laws and regulations designed to protect snakes are rarely specific, although many U. S. states list snakes that are protected within that state. In Massachusetts, for example, it is illegal to kill or otherwise interfere with four species: the worm snake; black rat snake, timber rattlesnake and copperhead. Other states have similar laws designed to protect species that are rare or declining. Unfortunately, they often do little to prevent habitat destruction, although developments have been prevented in a few places because they would be detrimental to an endangered snake. Road casualties are hard to legislate for, however, and some laws pay lip service to protection. Token protection is given to all Australian species, which may not legally be exported from the country and similar restrictions apply in other part of the world.

Specific protection *per se* is afforded to a few species, as opposed to protection acquired through blanket restrictions on all wildlife in a country or region. The albino rat snakes, *Elaphe climacophora*, living in the city of Iwakumi, Yamaguchi Prefecture, Japan, are protected as a national monument. In China, Pallas' pit vipers are protected on Snake Island, 40 km (25 miles) south of Lushun on the Liaoning peninsula. These snakes occur in high densities, with a total population of about 13,000 on the small island. The island has been declared a nature protection zone and measures have been taken to safeguard the snakes.

A notable U-turn was taken by the Greek government who, in 1977, protected the endemic viper *Macrovipera schweizeri* (formerly regarded as *Vipera lebetina schweizeri*) on Milos and a few neighbouring islands in the Cyclades group, having previously placed a bounty of 10 drachma on each snake.

Snakes that are federally protected in the United States include the indigo snake, San Francisco garter snake, Lake Erie water snake and the New Mexico ridge-nosed rattlesnake. Many other species are

▲ Much natural habitat has been displaced by farming, reducing the original flora and fauna.

▲ Logging of tropical rainforests continues to be a major source of habitat destruction.

DEATH ON THE ROADS

In many parts of the world snakes suffer greatly at the hands of motorists: their elongated bodies make them easy targets, whether intentional or accidental, and they are relatively slow moving. In addition, many linger on the warm tarmac surfaces during their nocturnal wanderings. The corpses of dead snakes often litter roads passing through good habitat. Drivers frequently go out of their way to hit snakes, sometimes swerving on to the shoulder or even across to the wrong side of the road; several accidents have been caused in the process. Other studies have shown that drivers will often stop and reverse over snakes, sometimes several times, in order to make sure they are dead.

▲ A harmless mole snake, *Pseudaspis cana*, killed by traffic in South Africa.

Two recent studies have highlighted the problem. Bush, Browne-Cooper and Maryan counted dead snakes along sections of the Great Northern Highway and the North West Coastal Highway, Western Australia (*Herpetofauna* 21 (2):23-24). In several places, the road passes through small reserves, intended to provide a haven for flora and fauna that would otherwise be eliminated due to increased agricultural activities in the region. In under 9,000 km (5,600 miles) of driving they found a total of 396 dead reptiles, of which 109 were snakes, belonging to 12 species (four species of pythons and eight species of elapids).

In a separate study, Philip Rosen and Charles Lowe surveyed U.S. Highways 85 and 86, which pass through the Organ Pipe Cactus National Monument, in southern Arizona (*Biological Conservation* 68:143-148). This area is well known for its rich herpetofauna, including one species and one subspecies of snake that are not found elsewhere in the United States (*Chionactis palarostris* and *Charina trivirguta trivirgata*). Several other rare species, such as the saddled leaf-nosed snake, *Phyllorhynchus browni*, also have their strongholds in the region. In 15,585 km (9,740 miles) of driving they recorded 368 snakes belonging to 20 species on the road: over two-thirds were dead.

Allowing for the number of snakes that were overlooked, especially small species, and those taken away by scavenging animals before they could be recorded, it is not difficult to see that, over an extended period of time, heavily used roads throughout the world must account for many hundreds of thousands of snakes annually. Furthermore, roads often cross reserves and other protected areas, as in the two studies above, creating a conflict of interests between road users and wildlife.

protected in parts of their range. Similarly, in Europe, species that are common in places may still be protected where they are rare, perhaps because they are living at the edges of their range: the smooth snake, *Coronella austriaca*, is an example. Restrictions do not always give complete protection but legislate against trade, or may limit the number that can be kept.

International protection

The International Union for Conservation of Nature and Natural Resources (IUCN) lists 10 species of snakes as 'critically endangered', 20 species or subspecies as 'endangered' and many more are listed as 'vulnerable'. This list has grown considerably in the last ten years and will no doubt continue to grow as common species become rare and rare species become endangered.

The other important organisation that concerns itself with reptile conservation is the 'Washington' Convention on International Trade in Endangered Species of Wild Fauna and Flora, known as CITES. The convention is administered by the United Nations and protects plants and animals by regulating international trade in them to ensure that they do not become depleted. It came into force in 1975 and to date about 170 countries have joined up. Of the 33,000 species on the CITES list, 223 are snakes. They include all the boas, pythons and dwarf boas (Tropidophiidae). Trade is not necessarily prohibited in CITES species but depends on their rating – each species is placed in an "Appendix" depending on its perceived vulnerability. Thus, all three Madagascan boas are considered vulnerable to trade and are placed on Appendix I, the highest degree of protection. Most other snakes are on Appendix II, in which some trade is allowed but figures are monitored to see if further action is required. Appendix III lists species that are protected in parts of their range where they are considered to be most at risk. Anyone intending to import CITES species needs to obtain a license from the relevant authorities.

Dodd (1987)[1] identifies a total of 186 species as in need of conservation, Some of these may not be rare, but are rarely collected owing either to their secretive natures or a remote and little-studied distribution. Others may always have been naturally scarce and are destined to remain so. There are undoubtedly many other endangered species that are not listed, however, which would more than compensate for these.

Conservation of snakes could take place through several pathways. Prohibiting commercial collecting is an obvious method and may help to stem the flood of certain species that reach the pet trade in huge numbers. Collection for the skin trade is another area that could be similarly controlled. Regulations such as these are in force already, although they probably do not go far enough. Even with tighter restrictions, however, they can only protect individual snakes from individual collectors. Habitat protection is far more effective and logical. This, in effect, means the setting up of reserves where rare species are known to live. The reserves must be large enough to be effective although, in the short term, even small reserves may sustain some populations.

Captive breeding

Many species of snakes are bred in large numbers in captivity. The purpose of this is often to make the species available to other snake keepers and, while it may reduce the drain on natural populations, it does little to conserve species in the true sense of the word. Captive breeding programmes may be useful where certain species' habitats are seriously degraded or have disappeared entirely. There should, however, be an ultimate goal of restoring the species to its natural habitat at some time in the future and, if this is to be achieved, its genetic integrity should be carefully managed, i.e. crosses between subspecies, or even between animals from different populations, should be avoided.

There is little evidence so far that reintroductions have been a significant success. The African rock python, *Python sebae*, has apparently been successfully reintroduced to the East Cape region of South Africa, where it had been extinct since 1927. This impressive snake is considered useful by farmers because it feeds largely on cane rats. The eastern indigo snake, *Drymarchon corais couperi*, has been reintroduced into parts of the southeastern United States by 'head starting' juveniles, that is by raising them in captivity until they are of a less vulnerable size, a technique pioneered by sea turtle conservationists. At the present time it is still too early to say whether this has been successful.

Some success has been achieved with the critically endangered Aruba Island rattlesnake, *Crotalus unicolor*. This species is the subject of a species survival plan operated by the American Zoo and Aquarium Association (AZA – formerly the AAZPA) in which several institutions cooperate in planning effective breeding programmes to increase numbers of threatened species. Captive populations of many other snakes are recorded through a series of studbooks maintained by zoos in North America, Europe, Australia and elsewhere. Many snakes breed readily in captivity and numbers can quickly build up over just a few years. The San Francisco garter snake, *Thamnophis sirtalis tetrataenia*, for example, a stunningly colourful garter snake whose habitat has largely disappeared, is bred by zoos and enthusiasts in America and Europe and the captive population of the very attractive and adaptable Dumeril's boa, *Acrantophis dumerili*, possibly exceeds that in its native Madagascar so successful has captive breeding been.

Long term plans to improve these species' chances of survival through captive breeding depend on breeding programmes that avoid inbreeding and a realistic chance of re-introduction in the future. A number of such species come from habitats that are so severely damaged that reintroduction is unlikely to be possible without considerable work on the ground. A rare success story is that of the Round Island boa where the species being bred with some success at Jersey Zoo, the habitat has been improved by weeding out alien plants and replacing them with native ones, and a permanent field station has been established on the island.

▲ The Aruba Island rattlesnake, *Crotalus unicolor*, is the subject of a captive breeding programme with the eventual aim of repopulating the island where it has been almost exterminated.

Education

Perhaps the best means of conservation is education. An urban population is unlikely to seriously consider setting aside areas of land for snakes while current prejudices prevail. Zoos and snake parks have an important role to play and there has been a noticeable change in attitudes towards this in recent years. Amateur herpetological societies also have a part to play, through putting on responsible demonstrations and displays to the public and, in particular, by encouraging young members.

▼ Dumeril's boa, *Acrantophis dumerili*, an endangered species from Madagascar, which is widely bred in zoological institutes and private collections.

STUDYING SNAKES

THE STUDY OF SNAKES IS A BRANCH OF THE SCIENCE OF HERPETOLOGY. THE TERM COMES FROM TWO GREEK WORDS, *HERPETON*, WHICH MEANS 'CRAWLING THING' AND *LOGOS*, MEANING 'KNOWLEDGE' OR 'REASON'. HERPETOLOGY, THEN, IS THE STUDY OF CRAWLING THINGS, ALTHOUGH ITS CURRENT MEANING HAS BECOME NARROWER, THE STUDY OF REPTILES AND AMPHIBIANS.

The history of herpetology

In 1989 the Society for the Study of Amphibians and Reptiles published *Contributions to the History of Herpetology*, edited by Kraig Adler.[2] This book is essential reading for anyone interested in a detailed account of the main players in herpetological research or in classic herpetological literature. Much of the following information has been summarised from this publication.

Snakes have been seriously studied for several centuries. The earliest studies, such as those by Aristotle, were more concerned with classifying animals, and snakes were placed within the reptiles by him. In 1587 Gessner's *Serpentium Natura*, an account of snakes and scorpions, was published posthumously. The Italian Francesco Redi was the first to establish the nature of viper venom through experiments performed in the 1660s. Several other books included snakes in the late seventeenth and early eighteenth centuries, many of them crossing the boundaries between fact and fiction and written from a herbalist's point of view.

Carl Linnaeus, one of the most famous names in the study of biology, published various editions of his *Systema Natura* from 1735 to 1766, in which the reptiles are classified within the order 'Amphibia', along with the cartilaginous fish. Linnaeus's most important contribution, however, was in his development of the binomial system by which all plants and animals are now named, often referred to as the Linnaean system. Linnaeus described many species of snakes, including the common boa, anaconda

and several other large South American snakes, and established the genus *Coluber*. His name for the common boa, *Boa constrictor*, still stands, although many of his other species have since been reclassified.

With the discovery of new worlds and the travels of explorer-naturalists over the next century, numerous new species were discovered and described and Linnaeus's original classification began to become chaotic. This was corrected by the Frenchman Constant Dumeril when he published his *Erpétologie Générale ou Histoire Naturelle Complète des Reptiles* between 1834 and 1854. In this work he organised the genera of reptiles into natural groups and described 1,393 species, of which many are illustrated. His work was continued after his death by his son, who succeeded him at the Natural History Museum of Paris.

There was now an explosion of literature on reptiles, including snakes, with new species being added at an ever increasing rate. Great herpetologists of the time included John Edwards Holbrook, Louis Agassiz, Spenser Fullerton Baird and Edward Drinker Cope in North America, and John Edward Gray, Thomas Bell and George A. Boulenger in England. Some of these men were amazingly prolific writers. Cope, for instance, published almost 1,400 titles, most of them on fossil reptiles and amphibians, but many on new species from North America and Mexico. As well as naming and describing new species, he also studied the anatomy of reptiles, establishing some of the principles that are used in snake classification today, such as the lungs and the anatomy of snake hemipenes. In Europe, Boulenger published a series of catalogues of reptiles and amphibians, a monumental task in which 8,469 species are covered. The snakes were dealt with in three volumes published between 1893 and 1896.

Alexander Strauch was the first serious Russian herpetologist and the rich herpetofauna of Australia was first thoroughly studied by Gerard Krefft, who was born in Germany and later emigrated, first to the United States, and then to Australia. His *Snakes of Australia* was first published in 1869 and reprinted as recently as 1984. Snakes from other countries were often studied by ex-patriots stationed abroad. Foremost among these was Frank Wall, an English medical officer who lived in various parts of India, Burma and Sri Lanka. He

published several important articles in the *Journal of the Bombay Natural History Society* and wrote a number of books, including *The Poisonous Snakes of our British Indian Dominions* in 1907 and *Ophidia Tapronica or the Snakes of Ceylon* in 1921. This work is characterised by accurate and astute observations of the natural history of the species he describes, making it as useful today as it was when first written.

Most of the early books on snakes are scientific treatises, intended for serious students of the subject and often written in styles that the layperson would have difficulty in understanding. From the turn of the nineteenth century, however, more popular books on snakes began to appear, of interest to the amateur naturalist and the general public. This tradition began in North America, with books such as *The Reptile Book* in 1907 (later revised and reissued in 1936 as *The Reptiles of North America*) and *Snakes of the World* in 1931, both by Raymond L. Ditmars, Assistant Curator of reptiles at the Bronx Zoo. In Europe, George Boulenger found time to write *The Snakes of Europe*, a popular account of European snakes, in 1913.

Books such as these popularised herpetology as a science and spawned a new generation of keen amateur and professional herpetologists. By the latter half of the twentieth century herpetology had come of age, with a large number of students working in the many areas of research, including the taxonomy, anatomy, physiology and ecology of reptiles.

Research areas

Although early herpetologists concentrated largely on the taxonomy and classification of snakes, so laying the foundations for their further investigation, more recent trends have seen the diversification of herpetology into specialised disciplines. Taxonomy is still continuing, of course, and serves the very important dual purpose of firstly labelling species so that other workers can communicate their findings accurately and, secondly, of organising the various species, genera and families into natural groupings and assemblages in an attempt to establish their inter-relationships.

Although taxonomy takes place mainly in museums, many taxonomists are also field workers, searching for new species and subspecies in areas that have not

▲ The Oenpelli python, *Morella oenpelliensis*, a large snake overlooked in a remote part of northern Australia until 1977.

been explored thoroughly. Regrettably, there are few such areas left nowadays but many regions of the world have only been superficially sampled and new species are still turning up, sometimes unexpectedly, even in countries that are usually regarded as well known from a herpetological standpoint. The discovery of a huge python, *Morelia oenpelliensis*, in northern Australia as recently as 1977 is a good example.

Other parts of the world are virtually 'no go' areas for various reasons and there are almost certainly interesting discoveries waiting to be witnessed and recorded by scientists. These areas include much of tropical Africa, parts of the Middle East and remote regions in South America.

Other new species are established by looking more closely at series of specimens formerly classified as one but which transpire to have minor but significant differences between them and this is the way in which most new species have been 'discovered' in recent years. Countering this, species that were formerly thought to be distinct are sometimes shown to be identical to others and they are suppressed. Taxonomy often consists, therefore, of 'lumping' and 'splitting' species, genera and families, much to the dismay of amateur herpetologists who have neither

the time nor the inclination to keep abreast of recent developments.

The anatomy of snakes has been fairly thoroughly established on a general scale, with unique organs such as Jacobson's organ, the heat-sensitive pits of some boas and pythons and the pit vipers, and the hemipenes of male snakes having been intensively studied. Minor anatomical differences, especially in the structure of the skull and the arrangement and structure of the scales are other useful tools in classifying snakes.

Biochemists have long been fascinated by the composition and effects of snake venom due to its medical importance but, again, biochemical differences in venom and blood have become useful tools that can be used in classification. The physiology of snakes has been studied mostly from the standpoint of thermoregulation, but reproductive biology is also an important field.

Studies on the behaviour and ecology of snakes has historically been the most neglected aspect of their biology. This stems from the difficulty with which they can be observed, because they remain hidden for a large amount of the time and are easily disturbed by the observers, leading to the cessation of natural behaviour. Much of what we know about snake behaviour relies on

anecdotal evidence – chance encounters with snakes doing something interesting such as eating or mating. Using this erratic method, it would take an infinite amount of time to compile a reasonably comprehensive picture of wild snake behaviour. Similarly, studies on captive snakes, though useful, are difficult to back up with parallel studies on free-ranging, wild snakes.

One method is to catch and mark snakes, usually by clipping a number of ventral scales in a unique pattern so that the snake can be identified if it is caught again, even if several years have elapsed. By this means, growth rates, movement and breeding behaviour can be established. A lot is left to chance, though, as it must be possible to find the same animals again at a later date, and so it is only really effective for species that occur in fairly high densities in a specific place.

The availability of sophisticated electronic equipment for monitoring the movement of snakes that are out of sight has revolutionised this type of research. Snakes are first caught and then implanted with a small electronic transmitter. This generates a signal that is

RADIO-TRACKING SNAKES

In the past, one of the biggest obstacles to snake research has been the difficulty of observing them going about their activities in a natural and undisturbed situation: much of the information that is available has had to come from anecdotal evidence or from observations made in captivity.

The development of miniaturised electronic systems has had a great impact in this area. Small transmitters can be located on the snake and its subsequent movements can then be tracked over the following months or even years. The transmitter contains a battery which provides enough power for a regular signal to be transmitted every few seconds. Additional information, such as the temperature of the transmitter (and therefore the snake) can also be relayed if necessary although this depletes the battery more quickly. Similarly, the range of the equipment can be altered but long-range transmitters are also heavy on battery power. Larger batteries can be incorporated but this may only be possible in large snakes.

A typical system consists of a battery and transmitter capsule about 3-4 cm (1-1.5 in) long with a diameter of 1 cm (0.4 in) or less. For a medium-sized snake this represents a 'payload' of less than an average meal. The capsule can be force-fed to the snake, then it will only be operational for the length of time that food normally stays in the system, 4 to 12 days on average.

Alternatively, it can be inserted surgically, by making a short incision and positioning the capsule between the skin and the body wall. The antenna is then threaded along the body, also between the skin and the body wall. After the incision has been sealed and the snake has recovered from the anaesthetic, it is released at the site of capture.

Subsequently, the snake can be located. An antenna is held aloft and will pick up a signal from the transmitter, in the form of a series of 'bleeps', which become louder if the antenna is orientated towards the snake. Different designs of antenna may be used, one to locate the snake's whereabouts at long distance, and another to pinpoint its position with more accuracy.

Results obtained from these studies can provide much information which would otherwise not be available. Daily and annual activity patterns can be established, for instance. Preferred habitats can be identified at different times of the year and snakes can even be located during hibernation. Activity patterns of males can be compared to those of females and juveniles. In the long term, growth rates and reproductive rates can be investigated.

This information is used to find out more about the private lives of snakes. It can also be a powerful tool in snake conservation.

▲ Tracking a radio-tagged snake.

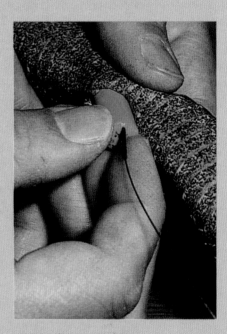

▲ Implanting a transmitter.

used to locate the snake again at a later date and it may be possible to obtain additional information such as the snake's body temperature. A number of snake species have been studied in this way, especially in Australia and North America, where snakes are reasonably numerous, and some interesting results have been obtained.

Although much of the research is directed towards finding out more about snakes *per se*, sometimes more far-reaching biological principles can be investigated. Evolutionary ecology is the term that describes the study of various aspects of animal behaviour in which predictions of how animals should react to various situations can be tested. Birds and insects are widely used in this field because they are relatively easily studied but snakes have certain qualities that make them equally useful in some cases.

By using them as biological models, aspects of thermoregulation, feeding strategies and reproductive strategies can help us to understand how the behaviour of animals has evolved.

The role of the amateur

Traditionally, the study of animals, especially those which had little or no commercial value, was almost exclusively the bailiwick of the amateur. Early naturalists were frequently well-heeled persons who financed their own travels and studies and often paid for the publication of their own observations. Charles Darwin epitomises the 'gentleman naturalist' of the time and, although he did not work specifically in the field of herpetology, his voyage on the Beagle produced many new species of reptiles and amphibians, including snakes.

More recently, the great American amateur herpetologist, Laurence M. Klauber, an electrical engineer by training, not only discovered about 50 new species and sub-species of reptiles but published extensively on the natural history of many of the snakes found in the southwestern United States. He developed several statistical methods of analysing large quantities of data, accumulated a collection of over 35,000 preserved specimens and was the first to see the potential of driving a car along desert roads in order to find and capture snakes, a technique that is still regarded as the best method of sampling large areas. His speciality was rattlesnakes and he published many papers on their natural history and distribution, culminating in his two-volume *Rattlesnakes*, published in 1956, possibly one of the finest monographs ever produced on a single group of animals, and including many facts about the folklore, superstitions and bite of rattlesnake.

Since Klauber's day no amateur has matched his dedication in pursuit of knowledge about snakes, nor his output of literature, but a vast army of amateur snake fanciers continues to make useful and original observations about the natural history, distribution, reproduction and feeding habits of snakes, either by keeping them in captivity or by making regular field trips, often squeezed in between professional and personal commitments and invariably self-financed.

Although their resources are usually somewhat limited compared to those of professional herpetologists, there are plenty of areas where even basic information is lacking about snakes. Observations by amateur herpetologists are regularly published in society newsletters and bulletins, and even the more scientific journals are pleased to accept and publish papers by amateurs provided they are well written, original and thoroughly researched.

BRUSHER MILLS

Henry 'Brusher' Mills was born in 1838 in the New Forest in Hampshire, England. He became a well-known character in the area, where for most of his life he pursued the occupation of snake catcher. He reputedly caught between five and six thousand snakes, supplying most of them to zoos, where they were used to feed other, exotic, species of snakes. Other specimens went to collectors or scientific laboratories where their venom was extracted, or were used in the preparation of snake fat, which was supposed to possess medicinal properties.

Although no records were kept, most of the snakes he caught would certainly have been adders, *Vipera berus*, which is the most common species in the area. These he caught using the traditional forked 'snake-stick' although he was also known to handle them freely without getting bitten. Along with the stick, he carried with him a sailcloth sack and a tin, in which to carry his catch.

Brusher Mills became a famous attraction with the visitors that began to visit the New Forest around the turn of the century; he was then able to supplement his income by exhibiting his snakes and his snake catching techniques to day trippers. He was also known to surreptitiously release a snake in a crowded street and then catch it again after it had caused widespread panic, so earning gratitude, and a handsome tip.

For 20 years Brusher Mills lived in a small hut, similar to those used by the charcoal burners of the day. When he was not catching snakes, he followed the game of cricket, making it his responsibility to sweep the pitch at Lyndhurst between innings, and it was this occupation that led to his nickname of Brusher.

He died in 1905, shortly after he had been evicted from his squatter's hut by the local authorities, and is buried in the village churchyard at Brockenhurst. His local public house, the Railway Inn, was renamed The Snakecatcher in 1993.

▲ An old postcard showing Brusher Mills in the New Forest.

SNAKES IN CAPTIVITY

PEOPLE KEEP SNAKES IN CAPTIVITY FOR A VARIETY OF REASONS: FOR PUBLIC EXHIBITION IN ZOOS, ETC., FOR RESEARCH PURPOSES, FOR COMMERCIAL BREEDING PURPOSES OR JUST BECAUSE THEY LIKE THEM. TECHNIQUES FOR KEEPING SNAKES HEALTHY HAVE IMPROVED GREATLY OVER THE LAST 20 OR SO YEARS AND MANY NOW BREED REGULARLY UNDER CONTROLLED CONDITIONS.

There are several excellent books that deal in detail with keeping and breeding snakes in captivity and so this section is intended to give an overview, without specific reference to any single species. Additional brief notes are given in the final chapter where applicable.

An understanding of the biology of snakes is important. As they are not domesticated animals, their habits and behaviour are still under the control of natural instincts. Placing them in a totally artificial situation, where they cannot behave normally, will lead to stress, resulting in poor health and, in extreme cases, death. This does not mean that their cages should represent exact replicas of the habitats from which they come, but that certain physical features, namely heat, light, security as well as a natural diet, should be carefully considered. Furthermore, snakes are not 'pets' in the true sense of the word. Some of them may give the appearance of enjoying being handled but it is likely that this is due to the warmth of the human hand rather than the warmth of the human spirit.

Although snakes do not respond to affection they do respond to other stimuli, and amateur snake keepers may be in a better position to make original observations than full-time professional herpetologists who have restricted time. For this reason, accurate records should be kept, especially of unusual behaviour and, even more especially, if rare species are being kept. Interesting observations should be written up and submitted to one of the herpetological journals or newsletters.

Obtaining snakes

Snakes can be obtained from a variety of sources. Foremost among them, and the starting point for most snake keepers, are other hobbyists who have surplus animals to sell or exchange due to a successful breeding programme. Obtaining snakes in this way has several advantages, including the greater likelihood that the snake will be free from diseases or parasites, and will adapt to captivity better than a similar individual plucked from the wild. Advice on its care and breeding will be freely available from the breeder at the time of purchase.

Alternatively, snakes can be obtained from the wild, either by personal collecting or by purchase through an animal importer or dealer. The pitfalls of this method can be inferred from the above comments. On the other hand, if your interest is in species that are not widely bred in captivity, then there is little alternative. Collecting your own snakes is usually preferable to obtaining them through the animal trade, where they may have been kept under poor conditions for several weeks or even months before purchase and where they may have been mixed with species from other parts of the world and picked up diseases and parasites to which they have little or no resistance.

▼ There are many colour variants of the corn snake. This one, which lacks red pigment and has reduced black pigment as well, is sometimes known as a 'ghost' corn snake.

Be aware, however, that there are often restrictions on the capture of wild snakes, especially of rare species or in National Parks, and that there may also be restrictions on importing animals collected abroad. Each country has its own set of rules and regulations; the onus is on the collector to ensure that he or she keeps within the law and that any necessary paperwork is in order.

Choice of species

Of the 2,500 or so species of snakes described, only a very small proportion of these is suitable for captivity. Many are too small, too large, too dangerous or too rare to be considered. Some have specialised diets that cannot be satisfied in captivity and others are so secretive, or dull in colour, or both, that keeping them in captivity is boring, to say the least, unless they are the subjects of a particular study.

The most popular snakes are found among the boas, pythons and colubrids. Some boas and pythons suffer from the problem of size: when buying a young snake make sure that you will still be able to accommodate it when it reaches its full size a few years later. Other species in this family are rare or endangered and should only be considered by responsible and experienced specialists who stand a good chance of breeding from them. A few are aggressive, and would not normally be considered by amateurs wanting a snake that can be handled without fear of injury.

Of the colubrids, by far the best choices of snake belong to genera such as the rat snakes, *Elaphe and Pantherophis*, the kingsnakes, *Lampropeltis*, and the gopher snakes, *Pituophis*. All the species in these genera eat rodents and adapt well to captivity. They occur in a variety of colours, and often there are a number of distinct forms even within the same species so an interesting and varied collection can be built up. All species are widely bred in captivity and there should be no need to encourage the trade in wild snakes by buying imported animals. There are plenty of other colubrids that are worth considering, the main requirements being that they eat food that is readily available (mice and rats being the obvious choice for most people), that they adapt well to captivity and are not endangered or otherwise restricted species.

It is possible to keep snakes from other families but many have their drawbacks. The primitive snakes are not freely available and, being mainly burrowing kinds, they have specialised requirements (and are rarely seen). Their dietary habits are also somewhat inconvenient unless an inexhaustible supply of termites and similar small invertebrates is to hand. Members of the small families – Acrochordidae, Loxocemidae, Xenopeltidae, Aniliidae, Uropeltidae – are not easily obtained. *Loxocemus* and *Xenopeltis*, though, often do quite well in captivity. Potentially dangerous rear-fanged colubrids, elapids and vipers should not even be considered by amateur hobbyists that have had limited experience of keeping snakes. In addition, there are often legal restrictions on keeping dangerous snakes and licences are only granted to persons who can demonstrate that they have adequate facilities and knowledge to keep them in such a way that they will not become a danger to themselves and to members of the public.

Housing

Snakes do not necessarily require large cages. Many species normally spend the greater part of their lives coiled in a cavity beneath a rock or within a log and venture out only when the pangs of hunger or the mating instinct is upon them. If these species are provided with all their needs, they will normally be content to live in a cage that measures less than their body length. More active species, especially if they are nervous or aggressive, will be stressed if they hit the sides of the cage each time they try to move quickly, and they require much larger accommodation. In practice, many of the diurnal hunting species do not make good captives for this very reason.

The possible designs for snake cages are numerous and varied. A simple cage is often based on a glass aquarium, with a modified lid to make it escape-proof and to provide adequate ventilation. These cages can be bought ready-made, together with a vivarium-type lid, in a variety of sizes, or they can be made. If they are homemade, the shape and size can, to a certain extent, be tailored to accommodate the animals or to fit a specific space in the home. Security is especially important when venomous or aggressive snakes are concerned and a design that can be locked should be seriously considered.

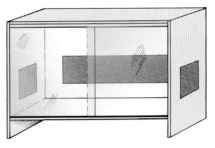

▲ A simple but effective snake cage, with ventilation panels in the back and sides, and a sliding glass front.

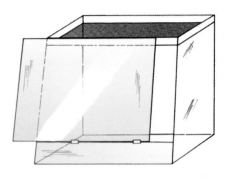

▲ A snake cage made entirely of glass, with a removable front.

A rather better design consists of a glass or wooden cage with sliding glass doors. As well as being easier to service, cages of this type have the distinct advantage that ventilation can be incorporated at a lower level, and therefore a better rate of air exchange can be expected. In addition, they can be stacked on top of one another if necessary. Again, the dimensions of this type of cage can be tailored to suit its use, within reason, and it is often easier to fix heating and lighting equipment, etc. to a cage that has at least part of its structure made from wood or plastic. The glass doors can be wedged, or even locked, in order to prevent the escape of the snakes and care should be taken to see that the doors are fully closed after the cage has been serviced – failure to do this often results in the snake working away at the opening until it either damages its snout or enlarges the opening and escapes.

If tall cages are required for arboreal snakes, sliding glass fronts do not work too well and some other arrangement will be necessary. Sometimes a removable front is most convenient and the cage can be designed so that it slopes backwards slightly, helping to hold it in place (although clips should also be used). In large cages, the front can be plastic, rather than glass, for safety reasons.

▲ The twin-spotted rat snake, *Elaphe bimaculata*, used to be imported in vast numbers for sale through the pet trade. Most died at the hands of inexperienced keepers and dealers.

For large snake collections, or where the snakes are required solely for experimental purposes or for commercial breeding, large plastic containers may be used. These are easily cleaned and a large number can be stacked in a system of racking with heating built into it. Such cages are also useful for housing young snakes temporarily, and for newly acquired snakes that are in quarantine.

Heating and lighting

Because snakes are not able to generate their own body heat, they are entirely dependent on heat sources outside their bodies. In captivity, this means an electrical heater of some description. Temperature control is one of the most important aspects of snake keeping.

Different species of snakes may have different temperature requirements, and even the same individual may prefer to be at different temperatures at certain times of the day or season. As there is no way of knowing exactly what temperature to keep every snake every minute of every day, the answer is to give them a choice. This is very easily arranged by installing all heating equipment towards one end of the cage. This provides a temperature gradient and the snake can move about until it finds the temperature that best suits it. Upper temperatures, i.e. in the warmest part of the cage, should be about 30°C (86°F) and temperatures in the coolest part of the cage should be about 20°C (68°F). This range will suit most tropical and temperate species under normal conditions. It will not matter if the overall temperature falls slightly at night – indeed, it may be beneficial.

The preferred means of providing heat for most types of snake is the undercage heat mat or heat pad. These low-power units can be placed under the cage, obviating the need for electrical supply to enter the cage itself. They give out a continuous, gentle heat and, if only part of the cage is placed over them, they will warm one end while allowing the other end to remain cool. Often there is no need for a thermostat, although the manufacturer's instructions should be carefully studied. Alternative methods include the installation of radiant light sources in the lid of the cage, either in the form of an incandescent light bulb or an infra-red heater. Both methods are more suitable for larger snakes in larger cages. Light bulbs have an obvious drawback – they are only effective when they are switched on, and the snakes must either be cooled at night or they must be subject to perpetual light. If light bulbs are used with a thermostat, the situation is worsened – the light will flash on and off throughout the day and night. Dull infra-red emitters come in several forms, including powerful ceramic heaters designed mainly for the agricultural industry, as well as less powerful units designed specifically for reptile keeping. Before buying and installing equipment, it is as well to investigate all the possibilities and to use the equipment that seems best suited to each particular situation.

Lighting is probably not strictly necessary for snakes unless they are kept in a room with no daylight. There is no evidence to suggest that day length has any great influence on snakes' feeding or breeding regimes, and temperature, coupled to their inbuilt biological rhythm, is by far the most important factor. Lighting may be applied to snakes that are on public display in order to enhance the appearance of the cages, but it must be said that most of the species that are normally kept shun intense lighting and will usually hide themselves away if their cage is too bright. A few diurnal snakes, however, may display themselves well by basking in the heat of a spotlight in much the same way that diurnal lizards do.

Feeding

If the species are chosen wisely, feeding should not present a problem. Most of the more popular snakes eat rodents at all stages of their lives, although the size of the food items will obviously vary according to their age. Rodents such as mice and rats can be bred for the purpose of providing snake food. This is not usually a favourite task with most snake keepers due to the time and space required but has the advantage of ensuring a reliable and cheap food supply and, perhaps more importantly, offering a range of sizes so that a mixed collection of snakes can be fed with suitable prey. Small collections of snakes, however, are more easily maintained on a diet of frozen rodents, which can be purchased in bulk, stored in the freezer and thawed as required.

Species that require prey other than rodents are not so easily kept. The American garter, ribbon and water snakes, *Thamnophis* and *Nerodia*, and European water snakes, *Natrix*, can sometimes be persuaded to accept strips of raw fish, whole, small frozen fish or alternative foods such as earthworms (for garter snakes) or rodents. Some of these diets are more satisfactory than others, and some experimentation with vitamin and mineral supplements, with

special regard to Vitamin D and calcium, may be necessary.

It may be possible to obtain a regular supply of small lizards, amphibians or fish for other species, depending on your locality. Catching large numbers of these items from the wild may be frowned on however, and may also introduce parasites into the snake collection. Frozen lizards and frogs are sometimes available through reptile importers, who often suffer large losses when trading in these animals. Each individual must examine his or her own conscience when deciding whether or not to use this food source.

Snakes that eat invertebrates have attracted little attention from amateur or professional herpetologists and there is some scope here to make interesting contributions to the natural history of

some of these little-known species. In general, a fair amount of success has been had with keeping snake species such as the American shovel-nosed snakes *Chionactis* ground snakes *Sonora* ring-necked snakes *Diadophis* and green snakes *Opheodrys*, but none of these are widely kept or bred and captive-bred specimens are rarely available.

Apart from the fish-eating species mentioned above, vitamin and mineral supplements are not normally required for any of the rodent or lizard-eating species that are fed on natural diets.

▼ Few insectivorous snakes enter the pet trade. An exception is the rough green snake, *Opheodrys aestivus*, which, unfortunately, is not widely bred in captivity.

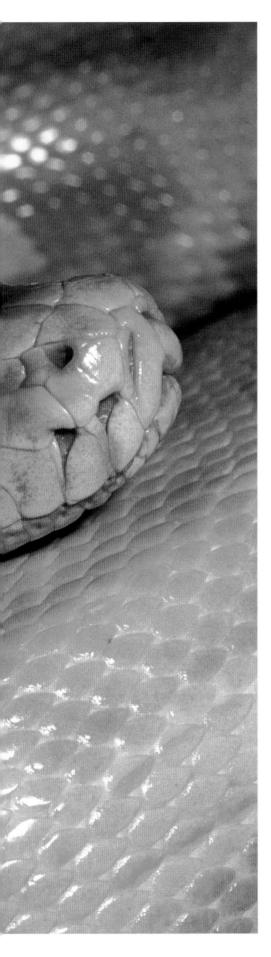

Breeding

Encouraging captive snakes to breed is a worthy aim for a number of reasons. Most obviously, by breeding desirable species in captivity, the strain on natural populations is relieved. Some species are protected and would not otherwise be available to others. Captive breeding can provide useful information of a type that is often difficult to obtain from free-living snakes and, although such data must be used cautiously, information on clutch size, incubation periods, frequency of breeding and so on, has traditionally been provided by amateur or professional snake keepers. Captive breeding also indicates that the conditions under which the snakes are kept are suitable for the species concerned. Snakes will not breed if they are in poor health or if their environment is less than satisfactory.

Captive breeding also provides an opportunity for selective breeding experiments. These may involve naturally occurring variations in colour or pattern and are often the only way in which the genetic mechanisms controlling these variations can be thoroughly investigated. Alternatively, selective breeding may serve to increase the numbers of a particular colour form originating from a chance mutation and some of the more popular species of snakes, notably the corn snake,

◀ Of the larger snakes, the Burmese python, *Python molurus bivittatus*, is the most commonly available species, and may be obtained in several colour variations, all of which have been produced by selectively breeding from mutants. The most common form is the albino or 'golden' python.

Pantherophis guttatus, and the Burmese python, *Python molurus bivittatus*, occur in a plethora of colour and pattern forms, some of which are more attractive than others.

The practical aspects of breeding snakes are not difficult to master, being a natural progression from keeping them properly. If they are in good condition, and a male and female are available, they should breed. Whereas some species require some environmental manipulation, others will breed under almost any conditions.

It is important to know the natural breeding season, if there is one, for the species you intend to breed. As described in Chapter 7, snakes may be seasonal or aseasonal in their reproductive habits. Seasonal species may breed in the spring or summer (most colubrids from temperate and subtropical regions breed at this time, for example) or in winter (most tropical boas and pythons).

Sex determination

Although some species show a certain degree of sexual dimorphism in the form of different colours or markings, this is not the most reliable way in which to determine the sexes for the majority of species. Usually, adult males can be recognised by their longer tails and greater number of sub-caudal scales. In addition, the base of the tail of male snakes is often noticeably swollen when compared with that of a female of a similar species and size. This swelling is due to the presence of the hemipenes, which lie inverted in a pair of pockets opening into the cloaca. For a more reliable diagnosis, the hemipenes can be probed internally with an appropriately

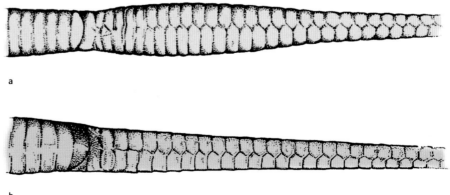

a

b

▲ The retracted hemipenes of male snakes may create a bulge at the base of their tail (a), which may also be longer than that of females (b).

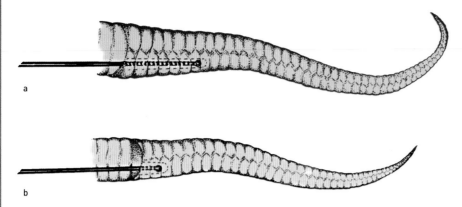

▲ The retracted hemipenes of male snakes can be located by careful probing with a smooth instrument of appropriate size. The probe will typically enter to a depth of more than five subcaudal scales in males (a) but only two or three scales in females (b).

sized rod of metal or plastic, when it will be found that the probe will pass into the base of the tail for a considerable distance in the case of males but hardly at all in females. The probe should be lubricated with water, liquid paraffin or petroleum jelly, and eased very gently back into one of the openings. It sometimes helps if the probe is slowly twirled between the thumb and forefinger as it is inserted, and only minimal pressure should be used. If the probe can only be inserted to the depth of two or three subcaudal scales, the snake is probably a female. The other side should now be probed in confirmation. Should the probe pass into the tail for a depth of six or more subcaudals, the snake is almost certainly a male. There is no need to continue probing to the bottom of the pocket as damage can be inflicted if the snake suddenly twists or twitches. This method is very reliable once it has been mastered, although a few species are difficult if the male has short hemipenes; females have musk glands at the base of the tail into which the probe can also pass and there may be little difference in the depth to which the probe can be inserted.

Probing small hatchling snakes is not recommended, except as a last resort, as the size of the probe must be such that it would be all too easy to injure the snake. A better, and equally reliable, method is to evert the male's hemipenes by applying pressure at the base of the tail (often known as 'popping'). The base of the tail is grasped and the thumb is used to push the hemipenes gently out of the cloaca. Males are very obvious once their hemipenes have been everted, females often evert their musk glands, which are shorter than the male's hemipenes, and at the bottom

there is a very small red spot. This method requires practice and some operators are better than others. Once mastered, though, it can be used with a high degree of accuracy and probing need only be used where results are inconclusive.

Once snakes have been sexed with a fair degree of confidence they should be identified in some way so that probing or popping does not need to be done any more than is necessary, normally only once in the snake's lifetime. Identification can take the form of noting or sketching some unique marking or scale pattern on the snake's record.

Conditioning
Snakes will not breed unless they are in good condition. They should be well fed, though not overfed, and free of diseases or parasites. Seasonal breeders should be introduced at the correct time of the year. Note that snakes from the opposite hemisphere will have their biological rhythms reversed. Winter in the south is summer in the north and vice versa. Winter breeders from South Africa, for instance, will be programmed to breed in the northern summer. It may be necessary to reverse the local temperate regime by cooling them in the summer and warming them in the winter. Captive-bred snakes seem to adapt to local conditions at the first generation and such inconvenient manipulations are then rarely necessary.

Species that breed in the spring may require a period of cooling. How essential this is will depend on their origin: snakes from Canada or northern Europe are likely to need a longer and more severe cooling period than those from Florida or the Mediterranean

region. Heat can be removed from hardy species as long as they are in good condition but feeding should cease at least 10 days beforehand so that the digestive system is empty. Some individuals stop feeding in the late summer or early autumn anyway, and these should be cooled once this has occurred, otherwise they will lose body weight during the resting period. During the cooling-off period, snakes should have access to drinking water; some species remain quite active at this time and even go through the skin shedding process, probably because they are not cooled to the same degree that they would experience in the wild. No harm will come to them, however.

Mating
Serious snake breeders usually keep the sexes in separate cages when they are not expected to breed, introducing them to one another when they are considered 'ripe'. Other people prefer to leave the snakes permanently together as pairs or breeding groups and allow the courtship and mating process to occur spontaneously and naturally.

Snakes that have been cooled off should be warmed up for a few days before they are introduced. Some breeders like to give both sexes two or three meals before mating them, and others wait until they have undergone their spring shed. All sorts of variations have been tried and they all seem to be equally successful as long as the snakes are in good condition and are of the opposite sex. Where males and females are paired just for breeding purposes, they often mate immediately. It is still advisable to leave them together for a while, or to separate them and reintroduce them a few days later in order that mating can take place several times. Fertility is likely to be higher if this is done and it is especially important with boas and pythons. Once the female begins to swell with eggs the pair can be separated until the next mating is required. The male may be used to mate with another female if necessary.

Egg laying or birth
There is now some deviation in the procedure, depending on the reproductive habits of the species concerned. Viviparous species can be left to their own devices and birth will take place without

any assistance. The only precaution to take is to ensure that the cage is escape-proof as the young will obviously be much smaller than their mother. Some species also seem to benefit if they are given a hide box with a layer of damp moss in which to give birth, although this is by no means essential in every case.

Egg-laying species will require a suitable egg-laying site, otherwise they may retain their eggs or lay them in an unsuitable place, such as the water bowl, where they will perish. Colubrid snakes give some warning that egg laying is imminent by shedding their skin six to 12 days before laying. A suitable container should be partially filled with a damp substrate, such as moss or peat, and placed inside the cage at this time. The female will begin to frequent this and, if all goes well, will lay her clutch in it.

Incubation and hatching

Females often remain with their clutches, at least for a few days. Pythons coil around their eggs and may remain with them for the duration of incubation if given the opportunity, and you may decide to allow the female to incubate her own eggs. Otherwise, they should be removed at the earliest opportunity and placed in a clean substrate in an incubator set at the correct temperature. Vermiculite is the most commonly used medium as it will hold a considerable amount of water over a long period of time and, being non-organic, will not encourage bacteria or moulds. A fairly coarse grade of vermiculite works best and it should first be thoroughly soaked with clean water and then gently squeezed until all the surplus has drained off. A layer of 5-10 cm (2-4 in) of moistened vermiculite should be placed in a clean plastic container. The depth is important as it will ensure that any remaining water does not come into contact with the eggs, which must have an adequate flow of oxygen around them. Python eggs require a somewhat drier mix than colubrids. Three parts water in four parts vermiculite, by weight, usually works well, although some experimentation may be necessary because vermiculite from different sources can vary in its moisture content.

The eggs are placed in shallow depressions in the vermiculite, but not buried. If the eggs have adhered to one another, no attempt should be made to

separate them and the clump should be arranged in such a way that the greatest number of eggs is in contact with the medium: it may be necessary to draw it up around the clump slightly. The container in which the eggs are placed should be ventilated with a few small holes. Too much ventilation will allow the incubating medium to dry out too quickly, and too little will lead to oxygen starvation resulting in dead or poorly developed hatchlings.

An incubation temperature of 28°C (82°F) is recommended for colubrid eggs. Python eggs require a rather higher temperature and 30-32°C (86-89.6°F) usually gives good results. The incubation period varies with species. Most of the commonly bred colubrids hatch after 60-90 days but some take less time. Pythons usually hatch in about 60 days or slightly less. Hatching is usually synchronous among a clutch of eggs, provided they have all been kept at the same temperature. If part of the clutch hatches but some eggs are still not slit, it may be advantageous to cut into them carefully in order to help the young snakes to emerge. Often these stragglers are dead or weak but occasionally they can be saved in this way.

The hatchlings should then be removed from the container and housed individually. Most breeders use small plastic boxes for initial housing, and a clean substrate of paper towels. A water bowl is essential and some species benefit from a small box into which they can crawl and hide. Most young snakes shed their skins about one week after hatching, and begin to feed afterwards. Hatchling pythons and new-born boas, on the other hand, may go several weeks before this initial shed and may begin to feed before it takes place.

NOTES

1. Dodd, C. K. (1987), 'Status, conservation and management', in *Snakes: Ecology and Evolutionary Ecology* (edited by R. A. Seigel, J. T. Collins and S. S. Novak), Macmillan Publishing Company, New York.
2. Adler, K., *Contributions to the History of Herpetology*, Society for the Study of Amphibians and Reptiles, Oxford, Ohio, 1989.

▼ Snake eggs are usually incubated artificially in an absorbent and inert material such as vermiculite.

CHAPTER 9
TAXONOMY

There is probably no area of biology that causes as much frustration, especially among amateur naturalists, as taxonomy. And yet, taxonomy is of great value, not only in allowing the communication of information between interested parties, but also in helping us to understand the relationships between different animals: once a group of animals begins to be studied, some method of arranging them into groups, and naming them, becomes essential.

The red diamond rattlesnake from Mexico has recently been subject to a name change, from *Crotalus exsul*, to *Crotalus ruber*.

Taxonomy, or systematics, consists of two disciplines: *classification* and *nomenclature*. Classification is the process of establishing relationships between and arranging animals into taxonomic groups. The groups that are produced are known as taxa (singular *taxon*). Nomenclature is the allocation of names to these groups.

Classification must be carried out first, so that the groups can be identified. Only when the taxonomist is sure that he has achieved the best possible arrangement, based on the evidence at his disposal, can the groups be named: classification precedes nomenclature.

Chapter 1 dealt with the way in which snakes evolved from their early ancestors. At points during their evolutionary history, groups of species broke away from the main stock and began to evolve and radiate into the side branches that we call families. Families are one level within the system of classification. The other important levels are: order, class and phylum, all higher than the family level, and genus and species, both at a lower level. Between these levels, others are sometimes inserted: suborder, subfamily, subspecies, etc.

The level with which most people are familiar is that of the species. The concept of species is not easily understood as there is no universally accepted definition of it (which is why taxonomists spend much of their time arguing over whether a certain animal belongs to this species or that). A common way of regarding species is to think of them as populations that can interbreed to produce fertile offspring. Animals of different species do not, as a rule, interbreed. If they do, their offspring are known as hybrids and may be infertile. Although there are numerous exceptions to this definition, including some snakes, it is probably the best we have at present.

Animals of the same species tend to look alike, although there may be differences between the sexes and between adults and juveniles. When a species is distributed over a large area, local differences in colour and pattern may arise and these can be regarded as subspecies. Different subspecies may interbreed but would not naturally be able to because they live in different places. In areas where the range of one subspecies merges into another, the animals may show characteristics intermediate between both subspecies, and are known as intergrades. Other subspecies, though, are physically separated (by a mountain range for instance) and so they have no opportunity to intergrade. If they are isolated for long enough they may evolve in different ways from one another and eventually become full species. But at what point does a subspecies become a full species? There are no hard and fast rules, so this can be another cause of dispute. If two species are only slightly different from one another, perhaps because they have not been isolated for long, they may be placed in the same genus (plural genera). Genera that are not too different may be placed in the same family, and so on.

This produces a logical hierarchy of groupings which serves two purposes. Most importantly, the various levels within the hierarchy reflect different degrees of evolutionary divergence. It also serves as an aid to memory. Taxonomic hierarchy can be thought of as a series of boxes that fit inside one another. The biggest box, the one that contains all the others is, in our case, the suborder of snakes. Inside this box are the 18 smaller boxes representing the 18 families of snakes. Within each of these boxes are more boxes, representing the genera that are assigned to each family, and down through species, then subspecies and, finally, individual snakes. Taxonomists, then, decide which boxes to put inside which. So far, so good. The problems arise when individual snakes do not fit readily into any of the boxes.

Since the 1990s there has been a revolution, as better techniques for investigating organisms' relationships with each other develop. These include DNA mapping, computerised programmes for handling large amount of data and a better understanding of which characteristics can be used to determine lineages, and they have created a far better picture of who is related to whom, and how closely. That is not to say that there are still areas where snake taxonomy is woefully inadequate.

CLASSIFICATION

THE PROBLEM WITH HIGHER CLASSIFICATION IS THAT THE CHARACTERS USED MUST NOT BE SUBJECT TO THE LOSSES AND GAINS THAT GO WITH ADAPTATION. SPECIES FROM MANY DIFFERENT ANCESTRAL LINES MAY EVOLVE TO LOOK SIMILAR TO ONE ANOTHER IF THEY LEAD SIMILAR LIFESTYLES. SEVERAL EXAMPLES OF THIS CONVERGENCE HAVE BEEN GIVEN. ON THE OTHER HAND, SPECIES THAT ARE FROM THE SAME LINE MAY GROW TO BE VERY DIFFERENT FROM EACH OTHER IF THEY RADIATE INTO DIFFERENT ECOLOGICAL NICHES.

Thus, boas may be long and slender if they are arboreal or short and stout if they are burrowers. How then can we tell that the different species are both boas? Or vipers, or whatever? Herpetologists hoping to classify snakes at levels higher than species must find characters that are less subject to evolutionary pressures than shape, size, colour and so on. Furthermore, the characters they use should not be immediately connected to a particular lifestyle. This invariably involves delving beneath the surface to look for features such as pelvic girdles, coronoid bones, hypapophyses, various muscles, various internal organs and, more recently, proteins and chromosomes.

None of these are much use in identifying a live snake in the hand, even less useful if it is seen rapidly gliding away through the vegetation. Identification normally takes place at the species level. Most parts of the world have some type of field guide or key to species that can be used to name the snakes found there, or at least the common ones. Problematical species may require close examination, even dissection in the case of blind snakes, *Typhlops*, and thread snakes, *Leptotyphlops*, for instance. Usually, though, identifying snakes is fairly straightforward. Having identified our snake, how do we know which family or subfamily it belongs to? And does it matter anyway? To the general field naturalist it probably doesn't matter too much. To the amateur or professional herpetologist, however, higher classification

is important because it attempts to link species in a way that reflects their relationships with one another. Thus, if two species are very closely related they will be placed in the same genus.

So far, the criteria for placing snakes in the same genera or families have been rather vaguely presented. This is because evolution does not proceed in jumps but as a continuum. Variation within a population may be so great that specimens taken from either extreme look very different but all the intermediate stages between them are present. In this case they do not represent separate species but merely a single, highly variable species. But if populations at either end of the continuum become physically separated from the rest, they can evolve in different directions and become distinct.

Often, when specimens of snakes are first collected, preserved and deposited in museums, it is not always possible to know if there are intermediate forms. At a later date, intermediates may be collected and early opinions may have to be revised. Then again, the degree of difference required to constitute a species varies according to the researcher: some would like to see more species with less variability whereas others prefer fewer species, taking in a much wider range of variation.

The same argument exists at higher levels, for example, as to whether pythons and boas differ enough to constitute separate families. In other words, are the differences between the *genera* greater than the differences between the *families*?

Every time new evidence arises, the classification system may need to be brought up to date. This may involve name changes. If all this seems confusing, it is worth remembering that humans have assigned the names to genera, species, subspecies etc. Nature does not adhere to rules made by people and any difficulties we experience in this field are due to the inherent drawbacks in the system we use.

There is probably no field of biology in which the higher classification presents greater problems than in that of snakes. Problems that seem to be solved by one generation of classifiers rear their heads again when a later generation starts to use a more sophisticated technique. At the end of the day, academic arguments that centre on the relative importance of an obscure characteristic are of little concern to the average herpetologist. All that is required is a fairly stable system that is understood, if not totally accepted, by everyone.

NOMENCLATURE
HOW SNAKES ARE NAMED

THE CLASSIFICATION OF SNAKES INTO A LOGICAL SYSTEM WOULD BE OF LITTLE USE IF THEY WERE NAMED IN A HAPHAZARD WAY. NOMENCLATURE IS THE DISCIPLINE OF DECIDING HOW THEY ARE NAMED.

Names given to snakes are of two types: common names and scientific names. Common names are useful for everyday use but have drawbacks. They may vary from one part of the species' range to another and some species have several common names. Red rat snake, corn snake, Great Plains rat snake and rosy rat snake all refer to the same species – the red rat snake is another name for the corn snake but the other two names refer to subspecies, one of which is no longer accepted as valid! Scientific names are less variable. *Pantherophis guttatus* and *Lachesis muta* are understood by herpetologists throughout the world.

This system of nomenclature, in which each species is given a latinised name, was first used by Carl Linnaeus in 1753 when he published his *Species Plantarum*. The system he proposed gained wide acceptance and is the one in use today.

Basically, each species is given two names, or a 'binomial' comprising the genus followed by the species. Sometimes a third name is added, in the case of subspecies (in which case the name is a 'trinomial') but the species is the basic unit of classification. The first, or generic, name is always written with a capital letter but the second, or specific, name is not (even if it commemorates someone's name or the name of a place). Occasionally, specific names repeat generic names, as in the European grass snake, *Natrix natrix*, and the desert horned adder, *Cerastes cerastes*, in which case they are known as 'tautonyms'. Furthermore, where there are subspecies, one of them must be the *nominate* subspecies (i.e. the one on which the species was based) and its subspecific name repeats the specific name. Thus the nominate subspecies of the grass snake becomes *Natrix natrix natrix*, and the nominate subspecies of the American rat snake is *Pantherophis obsoletus obsoletus*. If there are no subspecies, it is incorrect to use the trinomial form of the name.

The whole name is normally written in italics. Finally, the full name is often written with the name of its 'author' (the person who first described the species) after the latinised name, written in normal type. This is often abbreviated and may be in brackets. The brackets indicate that, although the species was first described by the stated author, the species has since been removed from the genus he or she originally placed it in and put in another. For example, the common boa was named *Boa constrictor* by Linnaeus in 1758. The name remains valid today and may be written in full: *Boa constrictor* Linnaeus. The Indian python was also named originally by Linnaeus but he placed it in the genus *Coluber*. Once it had been reclassified into another genus its full name became *Python molurus* (Linnaeus). Some species are renamed many times, but the name of the original author is still placed in the brackets. Obsolete names are known as synonyms.

Describing new species

When new species are discovered they must be formally described in the scientific literature and at this time they are given a name by the person describing them. There are numerous rules governing the naming of new species in order to avoid confusion and duplication. The new names must also be grammatically correct. Different authors favour different ways of describing new species. The names may be descriptive of the animal, e.g. *scalaris*, meaning ladder, and referring to a ladder-like marking along the back of *Rhinophis scalaris*, or descriptive of its lifestyle, e.g. *Natrix*, meaning 'the swimmer'. They may be named after the place where the original specimen was found (*Arizona elegans*) or in recognition of the collector, as in Fea's viper, *Azemiops feae*, after the European explorer M. L. Fea, who first collected the snake in China.

Several snake names may contain the same stem, especially if they are derived from classical languages. Many contain the word *ophis*, for example, which is derived from the ancient Greek word for snake. We have *Cylindrophis* meaning 'cylindrical snake' and *Tropidophis*, meaning 'keeled snake'. Other snakes are named after mythical creatures, such as *Python*, the fabled monster of Greek mythology, killed by Apollo in the Pythian Vale near Mount Parnassus.

Each species has to be assigned to a family. If a new species does not fit into any of the existing families, a new one must be formed, although this occurs very rarely. Family names begin with capital letters and have the suffix -idae. Some families are divided into subfamilies. The names of these also begin with a capital, but they are suffixed -inae.

'Types'

Another aspect of nomenclature that sometimes causes problems is that of 'type' and it is worth noting some of the different ways in which type can be used.

Type specimen
The type specimen refers to the original specimen from which a species or subspecies is described. If the specimen was collected by the author of the description it is known as the holotype. Types and holotypes are deposited in major museum collections where they can be referred to by future researchers.

Type locality
The type locality is the place where the type specimen was collected.

Type species
The type species is used in conjunction with genera and is the species that was first placed in that genus. *Boa constrictor* is the type species of the genus *Boa*, for instance (in fact, it is the only member).

Type genus
The type genus is the genus chosen as the standard reference for a family. For instance, the type genus of the Colubridae is *Coluber*. Problems sometimes arise when the type genus is moved to another family. This occurred in the case of the genus *Elaps*, which was the type genus for the cobras and their allies, the Elapidae. When the genus was moved into the Atractaspididae its name was changed to *Homoroselaps* in order to avoid having to change the name of the family, which would have caused no end of confusion (although the genus has since been moved back into the Elapidae).

The general rule is that, once a species has been named, its specific name cannot be changed. (The only exception to this rule is where the name given has already been used for another animal.) This sometimes causes confusion if the given name is inappropriate or incorrectly spelled. Russell's viper, for example, is named in honour of Dr. Patrick Russell, who pioneered work on snakes and their venom in India in the eighteenth century. Through a clerical error, however, it was given the scientific name *Coluber* (later changed to *Daboia*) *russelii*, with a single 'l' and, although incorrect, this cannot be changed. Similarly, the large shield-tailed snake, *Pseudotyphlops philippinus*, occurs in Sri Lanka, but not in the Philippines, as its original describer (Cuvier) believed.

◀ A scientific name in which a species' specific name repeats its generic name, is known as a tautonym. This is the European grass snake, *Natrix natrix*, originally named by Linnaeus in 1758 as *Coluber natrix*. Later research showed that it did not belong in the same genus as other species of *Coluber* so it was removed in 1768 and called *Natrix vulgaris*. After a brief spell in the genus *Tropidonotus*, it was eventually named *Natrix natrix* by Stejneger in 1907.

CHAPTER 10
THE CLASSIFICATION OF SNAKES

THE FAMILIES OF SNAKES – A QUICK REFERENCE

Family	Number of genera	Approx. number of species	Page
Scolecophidia			
Anomalepididae	4	16	196
Leptotyphlopidae	2	95	197
Typhlopidae	5	235	197
Alethinophidia			
Anomochilidae	1	2	198
Aniliidae	1	1	199
Cylindrophiidae	1	10	199
Uropeltidae	8	47	200
Loxocemidae	1	1	201
Xenopeltidae	1	2	202
Boidae	11	43	202
Pythonidae	7	35	208
Bolyeriidae	2	2	212
Tropidophiidae	4	28	214
Xenophidiidae★	1	2	215
Caenophidia			
Acrochordidae	1	3	216
Viperidae	36	263	217
Atractaspididae	11	69	226
Colubridae	310	1881	228
Elapidae	59	140	255

★ The Xenophiidae is a new family described on the basis of few specimens and this has led some authorities to reserve judgement until more material is available.

Wagler's pit viper, *Tropidolaemus wagleri*, the only member of its genus

HOW BIG AND HOW SMALL?

Sizes of snakes, though interesting to most people, are difficult to state. Maximum sizes, often quoted in field guides, may refer to extra large 'freak' individuals and bear no relation to the size of the average specimens that the reader is likely to come across. Then again, some snakes are poorly known and it is difficult to know if larger or smaller individuals are waiting to be found. In extreme cases, where only one specimen is recorded, the maximum size will also be the minimum size!

Because of this, I have decided to give approximations. In the following descriptions of genera, the terms 'very small', 'small', 'medium-sized', 'large' and 'very large' are used to describe the sizes of the members of each genus.

These sizes are equivalent, roughly, to the following measurements:

Very small	less than 30 cm (12 in)
Small	30-75 cm (12-30 in)
Medium-sized	76-150 cm (30-60 in)
Large	150-300 cm (60-120 in)
Very large	Over 300 cm (over 120 in)

In large genera, there may be species of different lengths, and here it has been necessary to give a range of sizes, e.g. small to medium sized, etc.

Length is not the only measure of size, of course, and some attempt has also been made to give an impression of the relative bulk of the various snakes by describing the overall body form, e.g. heavily built, slender, etc., giving a reasonably good impression of the snakes in question.

ANOMALEPIDIDAE

MEMBERS OF THE ANOMALEPIDIDAE (SOMETIMES CALLED ANOMALEPIDAE) ARE AMONG THE MOST PRIMITIVE SNAKES. ALTHOUGH THEY LACK PELVIC GIRDLES, THEY ARE CLEARLY CLOSELY RELATED TO THE BLIND SNAKES AND THREAD SNAKES. ALL ARE VERY SMALL SNAKES WITH CYLINDRICAL BODIES, SMOOTH, GLOSSY SCALES AND A SHORT TAIL. THEY HAVE LONG, NARROW LOWER JAWBONES, WHICH ARE HINGED AND TYPICALLY BEAR A SINGLE SMALL TOOTH EACH, OR NONE AT ALL. THEY ARE MOSTLY BROWN OR BLACK AND SOME SPECIES HAVE WHITE OR YELLOW HEADS AND TAILS.

They are all burrowing species that are rarely seen on the surface and which feed on termites and, possibly, other soft-bodied invertebrates. Almost nothing is known about their natural history although they are presumed to lay eggs. Four genera are recognised and the family's range is restricted to Central and South America.

Anomalepis Four species found in Central America and northern South America. They have a single tooth in each side of their lower jaw.

Helminthophis Three species from Central America and northern South America. There are no teeth in their lower jaw.

Liotyphlophis Seven species found in Central America and northern and eastern South America. There is a single tooth in the lower jaw.

Typhlophis Two species from northeastern South America. There are no teeth in the lower jaw.

◄ Distribution of Anomalepidiae.

LEPTOTYPHLOPIDAE
THREAD SNAKES

THE THREAD SNAKES COMPRISE ABOUT 95 SPECIES FOUND IN THE SOUTHERN PARTS OF NORTH AMERICA (TEXAS AND CALIFORNIA) CENTRAL AND SOUTH AMERICA, THE WHOLE OF AFRICA EXCEPT THE SAHARA DESERT, THE ARABIAN PENINSULA AND PARTS OF THE MIDDLE EAST. THEY ARE SMALL, SLENDER SNAKES WITH SMOOTH, SHINY SCALES. THEY HAVE A WELL-DEVELOPED PELVIC GIRDLE AND SOME SPECIES HAVE VESTIGIAL HIND LIMBS IN THE FORM OF SPURS. THERE ARE NO TEETH IN THEIR UPPER JAW, WHICH IS RIGID, AND THE LOWER JAW IS SHORT AND HINGED ABOUT HALF WAY ALONG THE SKULL. THERE IS NO LEFT LUNG AND NO LEFT OVIDUCT. THEIR EYES ARE SMALL AND ARE COVERED BY A SCALE RATHER THAN A BRILLE. MOST ARE SILVERY PINK IN COLOUR, BUT THERE ARE A FEW MORE HEAVILY PIGMENTED SPECIES.

All species are burrowing snakes, seen on the surface only occasionally at night or when washed from their burrows by heavy rain. They eat only termites and their larvae and produce pheromones that prevent the soldier termites from attacking them. Because of their small mouths, the soft abdomens of large insects are grasped and the contents squeezed out. Two genera are recognised.

Leptotyphlops This is the largest genus, containing all the species in the family except one. The range of the genus is as for the family. Found in a variety of habitats including semi-arid regions. They are usually found in the nests of the termites on which they feed. They lay small clutches of tiny eggs, as small as grains of rice in some species, and one species at least, the Texas thread snake, *L. dulcis*, coils around its eggs.

Rhinoleptus A monotypic genus, containing only *R. koniagui*, from West Africa. It is distinguished by a hook-like rostral scale and its large size (for a thread snake) of 50 cm (1 ft 8 in). Its biology is poorly known.

▼ Distribution of Leptotyphlopidae.

TYPHLOPIDAE
BLIND SNAKES

A RELATIVELY LARGE FAMILY WITH ALMOST 200 SPECIES FOUND OVER MOST OF THE TROPICAL AND SUBTROPICAL WORLD, ALSO FOUND THROUGHOUT AUSTRALIA AND ON SEVERAL GROUPS OF ISLANDS. THEY ARE VERY SMALL TO SMALL SNAKES WITH SMOOTH SHINY SCALES AND RUDIMENTARY EYES THAT ARE COVERED OVER BY SCALES. THEY HAVE CYLINDRICAL BODIES AND SHORT TAILS. MOST SPECIES ARE VERY SLENDER, BUT THERE ARE A FEW LARGER, MORE ROBUST SPECIES. THEY HAVE A PELVIC GIRDLE AND A SINGLE OVIDUCT. THE LEFT LUNG IS VESTIGIAL OR ABSENT ALTOGETHER BUT THERE IS A TRACHEAL LUNG. THEY HAVE TEETH ON THE UPPER JAW, ATTACHED TO THE MAXILLA, BUT NO TEETH ON THE PREMAXILLA. THE LOWER JAW HAS NO TEETH AND IS RIGID. MOST SPECIES ARE PALE IN COLOUR, OFTEN PINKISH, BUT OTHERS ARE BROWN, BLACK OR GREY.

They are exclusively burrowing snakes, which eat ants and termites and their larvae and, possibly, other soft-bodied invertebrates. Despite the large geographical range of the family, only three genera are recognised at present, although more are due to be described shortly, including one from Madagascar.

Acutotyphlops Four species from the Solomon Islands and the Bismarck Archipelago, previously placed in *Typhlops*.

Cyclotyphlops A monotypic genus containing only *C. deharvengi*, described in 1994 from Sulawesi. The single specimen is unique among snakes in having a large circular scale in the centre of its head, perhaps covering a parietal eye, surrounded by smaller scales.

Ramphotyphlops About 60 species, formerly placed in the genus *Typhlina*, which is now suppressed. This genus is naturally confined to the Old World and is found from India, through Southeast Asia, on many South Pacific Islands, New

Guinea and into Australia. One species, the Brahminy blind snake, *R. braminus*, is parthenogenetic and has been introduced to many parts of the world outside its natural range. These include Australia, South Africa, Central America and Florida. It is commonly known as the flowerpot snake because of the frequency with which it has been accidentally transported around the world along with potted plants. Several other species are known from only one or two specimens.

Description of the *Ramphotyphlops* species is as in the family description. Males of this genus are unique in having a solid portion to their protrusible copulatory organ, as opposed to the soft tube-like structure found in other snakes. Some species are quite colourful, especially where they occur in areas where the soil is red or yellow. A number are associated with termite mounds, where they move about through a network of burrows and probably feed on the insects and their larvae. As far as is known, all species lay small clutches of elongated eggs.

Rhinotyphlops About 30 species, under revision at present. The genus is not recognised by some authorities, who consider that its members should be placed in the genus *Typhlops*. Otherwise,

they are separated from them by having a horizontal edge to their rostral shield. Most species are found in Africa south of the Sahara, but one comes from the Middle East (*R. simoni*) and there are two species in Asia. Their habits are similar to other typhlopids: they feed on termites and other soft-bodied invertebrates and lay clutches of tiny eggs.

Typhlops About 140 species found in Central and South America, the whole of Africa south of the Sahara Desert, the Middle East, and south Asia. A single species, *T. vermicularis*, reaches Europe in the Balkan region. They are very small or small (exceptionally, medium-sized) burrowing snakes, usually grey, brownish or pinkish in colour, often resembling earthworms, Some species have black markings on pale grey or pink backgrounds. They probably feed largely on termites, ants and their larvae. As far as is known, all species lay eggs, with clutches of up to 60 in exceptional cases (e.g. *T. schlegelii*) but more usually less than 10. The eggs may be retained by the female until they are well developed, however, as in Bibron's blind snake, *T. bibronii*, and they hatch after five or six days. *T. diardi*, from India and Southeast Asia, is said to retain the eggs until they are fully developed.

ANOMOCHILIDAE
DWARF PIPE SNAKES

FORMERLY INCLUDED WITH THE PIPE SNAKES, AND CLASSIFIED WITH THE UROPELTIDAE, BUT NOW ELEVATED TO A FAMILY OF THEIR OWN. APPARENTLY INTERMEDIATE BETWEEN THE SCOLECOPHIDIANS AND THE MORE ADVANCED SNAKES..

Anomochilus Two species, Leonard's pipe snake, *A. leonardi*, with five specimens from peninsular Malaysia and one from Sabah, Borneo, and Weber's pipe snake, *A. weberi*, with one specimen from Sumatra and another from Kalimantan, Borneo. They are small snakes with cylindrical bodies and small heads. They live in rain forests habitats and appear to burrow in mud but with so few known specimens any information is speculative. Possibly oviparous.

▼ Distribution of Typhlopidae.

▶ Schinz's blind snake, *Rhinotypholops schinzi*, a member of the Typhlopidae from the drier parts of Africa.

ANILIIDAE
SOUTH AMERICAN PIPE SNAKE

THE ANILIIDAE CONTAINS ONLY A SINGLE SPECIES. IT HAS A PELVIC GIRDLE AND VESTIGIAL HIND LIMBS. THE EYES OF THIS SPECIES ARE SMALL AND ARE NOT COVERED BY A BRILLE, BUT BY A LARGE TRANSPARENT SCALE. THE VENTRAL SCALES ARE HARDLY LARGER THAN THE DORSAL ONES AND THE BODY IS CYLINDRICAL IN SHAPE. THE SKULL IS NOT VERY FLEXIBLE, WITH ONLY A LIMITED AMOUNT OF ARTICULATION IN THE LOWER JAW AND NONE AT ALL IN THE UPPER JAW. THE LEFT LUNG IS VESTIGIAL, AS IN MORE ADVANCED SNAKES. THIS SNAKE THEREFORE COMBINES FEATURES OF THE PRIMITIVE SNAKES (TYPHLOPIDAE, ETC.) WITH SOME OF THOSE OF THE MORE ADVANCED FAMILIES (COLUBRIDAE, ETC.).

▶ Distribution of Anilidae.

▼ The South American pipe snake, *Anilius scytale*, is the sole member of the family Anilidae.

Anilius A monotypic genus containing only the South American pipe snake, *A. scytale*, found in the Amazon Basin. It is a medium-sized snake with a bold coloration of black and red rings and is sometimes regarded as a 'false' coral snake. It is a burrowing species, usually found in moist habitats including rainforests and more lightly forested areas. It is most active at night and is thought to feed on small vertebrates, including smaller snakes. It is thought to be viviparous but details are lacking.

CYLINDROPHIIDAE
PIPE SNAKES

THE CYLINDROPHIIDAE CONSIST OF TEN SPECIES FOUND FROM SRI LANKA, INDIA, BURMA, INTO INDO-CHINA AND TO PARTS OF INDONESIA. SMALL TO MEDIUM-SIZED SNAKES WITH CYLINDRICAL BODIES BUT CONSPICUOUSLY FLATTENED TAILS.

Cylindrophis Mostly burrowing snakes from moist or damp habitats. Their heads are small and flattened and their eyes are also small. When threatened they may raise their tails, exposing bright coloration beneath. At the same time, they hide their heads among their coils. Little is known about their natural history or diet although some species at least feed mainly on other burrowing snakes. Viviparous, giving birth to up to 15 young.

UROPELTIDAE
SHIELD-TAILED SNAKES

THE SHIELD-TAILED SNAKES ARE DISTINGUISHED FROM THE PIPE SNAKES IN NOT HAVING PELVIC GIRDLES. THE 47 SPECIES ARE ALL SPECIALISED BURROWING SNAKES WITH RIGID SKULLS AND JAWS.

The head is narrow and pointed and is used to drive a burrow through the soil. Through modifications to the first few vertebrae the neck can be twisted to a very sharp angle and this presumably allows the snake to use its head to enlarge the burrow by ramming the soil to one side and the other. The specialised locomotion of these snakes is described elsewhere. Their eyes are covered by a large polygonal scale rather than a brille and teeth are absent from their maxillae. The left lung is very small. The most notable feature of members of this family concerns their tails. This may end in a scale bearing a single pointed spine or a pair of spines, it may be oblique and covered with keeled scales and tubercles, or it may be conical and roughened with small tubercles. There is a bony plate immediately below this area. The eight genera are restricted to southern India and Sri Lanka.

Brachyophidium A monotypic genus containing only *B. rhodogaster*, from southern India. A very small snake in which the tail ends in a spine rather than a shield. Presumed to be viviparous, otherwise very poorly known.

Melanophidium Three species from southern India. Rare, medium-sized snakes found in forested montane regions about which little is known. Viviparous.

Platyplectrurus Two species, *P. trilineatus*, which is endemic to southern India and *P. madurensis*, from southern India and Sri Lanka. Small snakes in which the tails end in a spine. Viviparous.

Plecturus Four species from the south of India. Small snakes in which the tail ends in a pair of spines. Poorly known. Viviparous.

Pseudotyphlops A monotypic genus containing only *P. philippinus*, from Sri Lanka (the specific name was given in error). A small species in which the tail ends in a circular, roughened plate, armed with a ring of spines around its rim. Found in wet or damp soil, especially in agricultural areas. It apparently feeds on earthworms. Viviparous.

Rhinophis Twelve species found in southern India and Sri Lanka. Small snakes with large tail shields covered with tubercles. They live in a variety of habitats, including under decaying vegetation and logs and in silted up drainage ditches. They are often found in small colonies and appear to feed mainly on earthworms. Viviparous.

Teretrurus A monotypic genus containing only *T. sanguineus* from southern India. A very small snake about which almost nothing is known. Presumed to be viviparous.

Uropeltis Twenty-three species, three of which are found in Sri Lanka, the remainder in southern India. Very small to small snakes with small tail shields ending in a pair of spines. Thought to feed on earthworms. Viviparous.

▶ Black shield-tailed snake, *Uropeltis melanogaster*, from the Central Hill Country, Sri Lanka.

▼ Distribution of Uropeltidae

LOXOCEMIDAE
CENTRAL AMERICAN BURROWING SNAKE

THE CENTRAL AMERICAN BURROWING SNAKE COMPRISES A FAMILY OF ONE. IT WAS FORMERLY PLACED WITHIN THE BOIDAE, AND IS SOMETIMES CALLED THE MEXICAN BURROWING PYTHON. A PELVIC GIRDLE IS PRESENT, AND CONSISTS OF TWO BONES. THE LEFT LUNG IS ABOUT HALF THE SIZE OF THE RIGHT ONE.

Loxocemus A monotypic genus containing *L. bicolor*. The species is found in Mexico and adjacent parts of Central America. It is a medium-sized snake with a stout, muscular body and large scales on the top of its head. The scales on its body are smooth and slightly iridescent and there are often irregular patches of white scales: these occasionally cover extensive areas. Otherwise, the upper side of the body is brown, the lower parts white. A semi-burrowing species that is active mainly at night. Its behaviour in the wild is poorly known. It is known to eat the eggs and young of turtles and iguanid lizards, but, judging from its behaviour in captivity, it probably takes a variety of vertebrate prey. It is oviparous.

■ *Captivity* Easily cared for in a vivarium containing a deep layer of peat or moss into which it can burrow. Alternatively, it should be given a hide-box containing similar material. It feeds readily on small rodents and is docile and easily handled. Captive breeding is, mysteriously, hardly ever achieved. It seems that a period of substantial cooling may be required.

▲ Distribution of Loxocemiadae.

▼ An unusual example of the Central American burrowing snake, *Loxocemus bicolor*, in which most of the dark pigment is missing.

XENOPELTIDAE
SUNBEAM SNAKES

THE FAMILY XENOPELTIDAE CONTAINS BUT TWO SPECIES, THE SUNBEAM SNAKE, *XENOPELTIS UNICOLOR* AND *X. HAINANENSIS*. THESE SPECIES, AND THEREFORE THE FAMILY, ARE RESTRICTED TO SOUTHEAST ASIA AND SOUTHERN CHINA. THEY HAVE NO PELVIC GIRDLE OR SPURS, AND THEIR LEFT LUNG IS WELL DEVELOPED, BEING ABOUT HALF THE SIZE OF THE RIGHT ONE.

Xenopeltis Natural history information relating to the Chinese species, *X. hainanensis*, described in 1972, is largely lacking but its habits are thought to resemble those of the sunbeam snake. *X. unicolor*, which is better known. This is a burrowing species that is rarely seen on the surface. It is found in a range of habitats including lightly forested areas but also among the suburbs of cities on waste ground. It is a medium-sized snake with a cylindrical body, dark above and white or creamish below. Its scales are smooth and highly polished, and are more iridescent that those of any other snake. The head and snout are flattened and shovel-shaped and the eyes are small. It is mainly nocturnal, and feeds on small mammals, amphibians and reptiles, including other snakes. It is oviparous.

■ *Captivity* The Chinese species, *Xenopeltis hainanensis*, is unknown in captivity. *Xenopeltis unicolor* is a rather specialised snake, not commonly offered for sale. Wild individuals may be in poor condition but, once acclimatised, they fare well and are easily accommodated. They should be given a slightly humid vivarium with a deep layer of peat or moss covering the base. They will spend most of their time below the surface, coming out at night to take small rodents. Captive breeding has taken place on a few occasions. Clutches of up to 10 eggs are laid. The young are small and may require force feeding at first, although some will take newborn mice. Once they begin to feed they grow quickly and are trouble-free.

▼ **Distribution of Xenopeltidae.**

BOIDAE
BOAS

THIS IS A DIFFICULT GROUP OF SNAKES BUT ONE THAT IS OF GREAT INTEREST TO HERPETOCULTURALISTS AND NATURALISTS. SOME AUTHORITIES CONSIDER THE BOAS AND PYTHONS TO BE PART OF A SINGLE FAMILY, THE BOIDAE, WHEREAS OTHERS PREFER TO SEE THE PYTHONS IN A SEPARATE FAMILY, THE PYTHONIDAE. I HAVE TAKEN THE LATTER PATHWAY AND DEALT WITH THEM AS SEPARATE FAMILIES, WHILST RECOGNISING THAT THIS IS NOT UNIVERSALLY ACCEPTED.

The various arguments for different systems of classification are put forward in the following important articles:

Kluge, A. (1991), *Boine snake phylogeny and research cycles*, Misc. Publ. Mus. Zool. Univ. Michigan, 178:iv+ 58 pages.
Kluge, A. (1993), *'Calabaria and the phylogeny of erycine snakes'*, Zool. Journal of the Linnean Society, 107:293-357.
McDowell, S. M. (1987), *'Systematics', in Snakes, Ecology and Evolutionary Biology*, pp. 3-50, edited by R. A. Seigel, J. T. Collins and S. S. Novak, Macmillan Publishing Company, New York.
Underwood, G. (1976). *'A systematic analysis of boid snakes'*, in Morphology and Biology of Reptiles, pp. 151-175, edited by A. d'A. Bellairs and C. B. Cox, Linnean Society Symp. Series 3, Academic Press, London.

THE BOAS, BOIDAE
In addition to the boas, the Boidae formerly included the pythons, now placed in their own family, the Pythonidae, the dwarf boas or wood snakes, and the Round Island boas, which now form the Tropidophiidae and the Bolyeriidae. As now understood, the Boidae contains 43 species in 12 genera and two subfamilies. They occur in North, Central and South America, Africa, Madagascar and Asia but not Australia. One species is found, on the edge of its range, in southeastern Europe. All members of the family, apart from one or two, give birth to live young.

The family is divided into two well-defined subfamilies, the Boinae and the Erycinae, the latter being small burrowing forms. The Boinae is dealt with first.

Boinae

Seven genera are included in the Boinae. Heat-sensitive pits are present in some members of this subfamily and, when present, they are situated between the labial scales, not within the scales as in the pythons.

Acrantophis The two species forming this genus are restricted to Madagascar. They have no heat-sensitive pits. *A. madagascariensis* is the Madagascan ground boa and *A. dumerilii* is Dumeril's ground boa. They are heavy-bodied species, superficially similar to the common boa, but more intricately marked. Dumeril's boa grows to moderate sizes, 2 m (65 ft) at most, whereas the Madagascan boa is larger, to almost 3 m (10 ft). Both species feed on birds and small mammals and both favour humid habitats and are therefore most commonly found near rivers and streams. Dumeril's boa is restricted to the south and south-west of the island whereas *A. madagascariensis* is found in the north

and east. Both species have been placed on Appendix I by CITES.

■ *Captivity* Both species fare very well in captivity under a typical tropical regime and with a diet of rodents. *A. madagascariensis*, however, is not seen as often as its congener. This may be because it has proved to be the more difficult of the two to breed under artificial conditions and because it has smaller broods: a maximum of 8 as opposed to a maximum of 20.

Boa This is a monotypic genus containing only the common boa, *Boa constrictor*. There are no heat-sensitive pits and the species seems to be more closely related to the Madagascan *Acrantophis*, despite their geographical separation, than any other genus of boas. This species is so well known that a description appears superfluous, although there is much confusion over geographical forms and subspecies. No fewer than nine forms have been given subspecific recognition at various times but the differences between them are difficult, or impossible, to quantify. The Argentinian form, *B. c. occidentalis*, is the most distinct of the mainland forms. The proliferation of names such as 'Colombian red-tailed boa', used by snake-keeping hobbyists to

describe particular colour forms and slight variations only add to the confusion as individuals from many parts of the range can have red or reddish coloured tails and this character is of no value in ascribing a particular snake to a subspecies.

This snake has a truly enormous range, from Argentina in the south to as far north as Guaymas on the northwest coast of Mexico (*Boa constrictor 'imperator'*). It is primarily a rainforest species, inhabiting clearings and forest fringes, although it can be found in semi-arid thorn scrub in parts of Sonora and in dry tropical forests in parts of Central America. It is also found on several islands including those of Trinidad, Tobago, Dominica (subspecies *nebulosa*) and St Lucia (subspecies *orophias*) in the West Indies as well as a number of smaller off-shore islands along the coast of Honduras. *B. c. sabogae* comes from Saboga Island and a dwarf, nameless form, possibly extinct in the wild, from Cayos Cochinos off the Caribbean coast of Honduras (commonly known as Hog Island boas).

The common boa may grow to a maximum length of about 4 m (13 ft): most specimens are appreciably less than this. It is a generalist, feeding on mammals and birds, and may be arboreal in areas where large trees grow. It is equally at home on the ground, however, and is often encountered along rivers, either in the water or lying out on the banks. It is also commonly found in the vicinity of human settlements.

■ *Captivity* Common boas are among the most popular and undemanding of all large snakes. They require accommodation in keeping with their size but, this apart, they rarely present any serious problems. Captive-bred animals are less inclined to be aggressive and adapt better than wild ones. Common boas nearly always feed well on dead rodents, although a few seem to favour birds. This applies especially to some of the small island races although captive-bred offspring from the original collected animals are usually as easy to feed and raise as any of the other forms. Where the temperature is kept constant throughout the year, they may mate at any time. Otherwise mating usually takes place in the winter months in response to cooler conditions. Up to 50 live young are born after a gestation

◀ **Distribution of Boidae.**

period that varies from five to eight months, depending on temperature.

Candoia This genus contains three well-defined species from New Guinea and neighbouring islands. The scales on the body of these species are heavily keeled and the head is covered with numerous small scales. None of the species has heat-sensitive pits. Characteristic of the genus is a flat, angled rostral scale that gives the snout an oblique profile. There is great variation in size and coloration within the species. Some of this is due to their distribution, scattered as they are among many oceanic islands, but even within groups from the same locality many different colours and patterns can be recognised. In *C. carinata*, 'long-tailed' and 'short-tailed' populations can also be recognised and there is some correlation between tail length and distribution. The three species clearly come from a common ancestor and demonstrate adaptive radiation: *C. aspera*, the smallest species, is short and stocky with a prehensile but very short tail. It is a

▼ Young Amazon tree boa, *Corallus hortulanus*.

terrestrial or semi-fossorial species. *C. bibroni* is long and slender with a highly prehensile tail and is totally arboreal in its habits. *C. carinata* is intermediate in form and may be found in either habitat although it climbs less than *C. bibroni*.

■ *Captivity* All species are quite easily cared for but require a dark, secluded cage with hiding places. Adults usually feed readily but young specimens sometimes refuse to eat rodents. *C. carinata* gives birth to very large litters of live young: almost 100 in some cases. The other two species also have relatively large litters and the newborn young are very small in every case.

Corallus At least six and probably eight species, although the rare Cropan's boa, *C. cropanii*, is often placed in a separate genus, *Xenoboa*. All are South and Central American and slender, arboreal snakes. They have large, vertically aligned heat pits in their labial and rostral scales. *C. caninus*, the emerald tree boa, is the most familiar species. It is highly arboreal and closely parallels the green tree python, *Morelia viridis*, from Asia, both in appearance and behaviour. It grows to

2 m (6 ft 6 in). It is bright green when adult but juveniles are brick red or dull orange at birth and begin to turn green after a few months. The species is flattened laterally and feeds mainly on rodents, occasionally lizards and rarely, if ever, on birds. It has long curved teeth to prevent its prey from escaping once it has grasped them.

The annulated boa, *C. annulatus*, occurs in Central and northern South America where it is uncommon and a similar species (or possibly subspecies) *C. blombergi*, replaces it in Ecuador. Cropan's boa, *C. cropanii*, is the rarest and least known of all, though, and perhaps the world's rarest large snake, known from only three examples from the shrinking coastal rain forest around São Paulo, Brazil.

The other tree boas are more problematic. *Corallus hortulanus*, the Amazon tree boa, may grow to the same length as the emerald boa but is a smaller species, being more slender in build. Its markings are highly variable. It is found throughout the Amazon Basin and in northern South America, while further west, from Venezuela to Costa Rica, and

on Trinidad and Tobago, it is replaced with a similar species, *C. ruschenbergerii*, although this is not always recognised. Cooke's tree boa, *C. cookii* and a possible additional species, *C. grenadensis*, occur in the West Indies. All these species were often lumped together under the catch-all name of *Corallus enhydris*, which is no longer recognised. Problems in assigning species stem from the great variability of colours and markings within some populations, and the lack of reference material from some places.

■ *Captivity* The emerald boa is far and away the most widely kept of the three species, followed by the Amazon tree boa and then the annulated boa, which is hardly ever available. All species are tropical and require constant high temperatures or around 25-30°C (77-86°F). Because they are arboreal, they require tall cages so that they can coil on a branch well above ground level. This is especially important in the case of the emerald tree boa because it has great difficulty in feeding unless it can hang downwards while it swallows its prey. Breeding may take place at any time of the year, although it is most commonly recorded in the winter. The gestation period lasts approximately six months and litters of up to 20 have been recorded. Care of the other species is similar, and *C. hortulanus* has been bred in captivity on numerous occasions with litters of up to 15 young. Some difficulty may be experienced in getting the young to accept small rodents, although they will often take lizards.

Epicrates Ten species, distributed throughout the West Indies (nine species) and the South American mainland, this one is the rainbow boa, *E. cenchria*, which is divided into nine subspecies, one of which, the Colombian rainbow boa, is sometimes treated as a full species, *E. maurus*. Some species, e.g. *E. cenchria*, have heat-sensitive pits in the lower labial scales and also in the upper labials towards the snout. In others, e.g. *E. angulifer*, they are very shallow while *E. gracilis* and *E. exsul*, for instance, lack pits altogether. There is probably a correlation with prey types, those species with pits being the larger ones, which eat endothermic animals (birds, bats and other mammals) whereas the smaller species, which have no pits, eat mainly lizards and, possibly, frogs. Two forms, *E. m. monensis* and *E. gracilis*, appear to eat only reptiles, especially lizards.

Epicrates is the largest genus of boas, mainly because it is distributed throughout the West Indian islands, where a high degree of speciation has taken place. Many species are endemic to small islands, where their future is bleak. Of the 10 species, several have been divided into two or more sub-species. *E. cenchria*, the only species found on the mainland of South America (and on the offshore islands of Trinidad and Tobago), has a very large range, from Columbia (subspecies *maurus*) in the north to Argentina (subspecies *alvarezi*) in the south, and from the Pacific to the Atlantic coasts. Up to nine subspecies are recognised. This species reaches 2 m (6½ ft) in parts of its range and, like the other five larger species, has a rather generalised life-style. Four of the West Indian species, *E. angulifer*, *E. inornatus*, *E. striatus* and *E. subflavus*, are also quite large, exceptionally growing to 4 m (13 ft) in the case of *E. angulifer*, and about 2 m (6½ ft) in the others. They are also generalists. The five small species, *E. chrysogaster*, *E. exsul*, *E. fordi*, *E. gracilis* and *E. monensis*, are smaller, growing to about 1 m (3 ft 4 in). These tend to be more arboreal and are rather slender in build, although none of them shows the same degree of adaptation as *Corallus* species, for instance. The Puerto Rican boa, *E. inornatus*, is listed as endangered by the IUCN and the Jamaican species, *E. subflavus*, as vulnerable. Both are included on Appendix I by CITES, as is the Mona Island boa, *E. m. monensis*. The Bimini boa, *E. striatus fosteri*, is also in grave danger of extinction, while the Virgin Islands boa, *E. m. granti*, is known from several small islands but is nowhere common.

■ *Captivity* The rainbow boa, *Epicrates cenchria*, is by far the most commonly kept species, especially the Brazilian, Colombian and Argentinian subspecies (*E. c. cenchria*, *E. c. maurus* and *E. c. alvarezi* respectively). All these species are easily cared for and will breed under fairly simple conditions and will eat rodents readily. The Argentinian subspecies probably requires cooler conditions than the others, which are more or less tropical in origin, and it may require a significant period of lower temperatures to induce it to breed. In all these subspecies, mating usually takes place during the cooler months of winter and the young are born about six months later, the exact period depending on temperature. Litters may number up to 30 in exceptional cases, although the Argentinian subspecies has significantly smaller broods of relatively large young. The young of most forms are noticeably brighter than the adults – this is especially so in the case of *E. c. maurus*, the young of which are often indistinguishable from those of *E. c. cenchria*, even though, as adults, they will fade to a fairly uniform brown coloration. *E. c. alvarezi* are again an exception, as the juveniles and adults are identically marked.

Of the other species, *Epicrates striatus*, are occasionally kept, and pose no special problems, while the rare Jamaican boa, *E. subflavus*, and the Mona Island boa, *E. monensis*, are subjects of captive breeding programmes in an attempt to increase stocks. The small species are difficult, however, as they feed primarily on lizards, at least when they are young.

Eunectes This South American genus consists of four species, two of which, the green anaconda (usually referred to simply as the anaconda), *E. murinus*, and the yellow anaconda, *E. notaeus*, are fairly well known. The others are the dark-spotted anaconda, *E. deschauenseei*, from Marajo Island, Brazil and adjacent parts of the mainland, and the recently described Beni River anaconda, *E. beniensis*, from Bolivia. There are no heat-sensitive pits on the labial scales of any members of the genus.

Eunectes murinus is the world's largest snake, growing to at least 9 m (29.5 ft) in length. Its length may just be exceeded by that of the reticulated python but that species is far more slender in build. It has a large range over much of tropical South America, including the island of Trinidad. It is a semi-aquatic species that is strongly associated with swamps and slow moving rivers and is rarely found far from water. This species has even been known to give birth under water in captivity. Its prey includes freshwater turtles and even small South American alligators (caiman), as well as mammals and birds. Anacondas are aggressive and dangerous snakes and undoubtedly overpower and eat humans occasionally.

The yellow anaconda, *Eunectes notaeus*, is a much smaller animal, growing to less

▲ Yellow anaconda, *Eunectes notaeus*, from South America.

than half the length of it congener (and therefore only a small proportion of its weight). It, too, is highly aquatic but it has a more restricted range, occurring in the southern parts of the Amazon basin.

■ *Captivity* The larger of the two species is rarely kept, owing to its enormous size and potentially vicious disposition. The yellow anaconda is kept and bred on a limited scale. It only rarely becomes tame but will usually eat rodents readily. Mating takes place during the cooler months and the gestation period is six months or more, depending on temperature. Litters of up to 20 young are born.

Sanzinia A monotypic genus containing only the Madagascan tree boa, *S. madagascariensis*. This arboreal species has conspicuous heat-sensitive pits in its upper and lower labial scales. Its coloration is variable but most are some shade of green or greyish green. A larger, brown and yellow form also occurs in parts of the island. Tree boas are amongst the most common snakes on Madagascar but deforestation has severely reduced suitable habitat. The species is placed on Appendix I of CITES.

■ *Captivity* Although rare, the species is

highly prized for its attractive coloration and usually calm temperament. It feeds readily on rodents and has been bred on numerous occasions. Four to 16 young are born after a gestation period lasting six to eight months. The young are red and change to the adult greenish coloration within their first year.

Erycinae

The Erycinae consists of four genera, and 15 species. All erycine boas are small fossorial or semi-fossorial snakes, with many of the adaptations typical of burrowing snakes, such as a cylindrical body, smooth scales, broad head (with the eyes directed upwards in some species) and short tail. The tail may be used to deflect attention away from the head when the snake is under threat.

Calabaria This is a monotypic genus containing only the Calabar ground boa, *C. reinhardtii*, from West Africa. This species, under the same name, was previously included with the pythons, partly because it lays eggs. It is a small, cylindrical burrowing snake, with a short tail, smooth scales and small eyes. It is variable in colour, usually being brown or reddish with a suffusion of irregular black mottling. The tail is especially blunt and rounded and is used as a false head if

the snake is threatened. Otherwise, little is known about its natural history.

■ *Captivity* Difficult. Imported animals often fail to adapt well and there is little or no supply of captive-bred young. The best results have been obtained by housing the animals in cages with a deep layer of moss into which they can burrow, or by providing a dark retreat, such as an upturned clay plant pot. They feed on rodents and lay small clutches of one to three large, elongated eggs.

Charina Two species, the rubber boa, *C. bottae*, and the rosy boa, *C. trivirgata*, formerly placed in a separate genus, *Lichanura*. Both are from western North America. The rubber boa, *C. bottae*, only grows to about 75 cm (30 in). It occurs from British Columbia, Canada, in the north to southern California in the south, In places it may be found at altitudes of more than 3000 metres (about 10,000 feet) and prefers cool, humid conditions. Three subspecies are recognised. Although primarily a burrowing snake, the rubber boa has been found in low vegetation and on top of stumps. It feeds mainly on small nestling mammals but also takes amphibians and smaller snakes. Litters of three to eight young are born after a gestation period of three to four months. There is some evidence that females only reproduce every two or three years.

The rosy boa occurs in the more arid areas of southwestern United States and northwestern Mexico. Four or five subspecies have been named. Although a desert species, it is associated with rocks and is rarely found more than a few metres from the rocky outcrops characteristic of the region. In all its forms, this is a longitudinally striped snake, although the clarity and colour of the stripes vary with locality and subspecies. The rosy boa grows to just over one metre (3 ft 4 in) and feeds largely on rodents. It gives birth to three to five young, although much larger litters, up to 12, are on record.

■ *Captivity* The rubber boa is not often seen in captivity because of its rarity and the fact that it is protected over much of its natural range. It requires conditions that are not too hot and a substrate into which it can burrow. Occasional light spraying of the substrate appears to be beneficial. The species rarely feeds in the winter irrespective of the temperature at which it is maintained. The rosy boa, on the other hand, is a popular species that usually fares well in captivity. Captive-bred specimens feed well and grow quickly. As this is a temperate species it should not be subjected to constant heat – a thermal gradient, with heat applied to one end of the cage only is recommended and heat can be withdrawn altogether in the winter provided the temperature does not fall below about 10°C (50°F). Breeding takes place in the spring and the young are born after a gestation of about five months. Newborn rosy boas sometimes refuse to feed. If this behaviour persists it is best to remove the heat and allow them to remain cool until the following spring, when they will usually begin to feed voluntarily.

Eryx (sand boas) Nine species, from northern Africa, the Middle East, Central Asia and India. The Javelin sand boa, *E. jaculus*, is the only boa occurring in Europe, where it is restricted to the south-east. Members of the genus are small, burrowing snakes that live in arid places. They have stout, cylindrical bodies and short, blunt tails. Their heads are the same width as their bodies and there is no discernable neck. Their eyes are positioned towards the top of their heads, especially in the Arabian sand boa, *E. jayakari*. The largest species, *E. johnii*, grows to about 1 m (3 ft 4 in) but several species, such as *E. miliaris* and *E. tataricus*, are less than half this size. Most are cryptically coloured in shades of brown, yellow, orange or reddish, depending on the soil where they live but the black sand boa, *E. miliaris nogaiorum*, which lives to the north and northwest of the Caspian Sea, is heavily suffused with black. All sand boas eat small mammals, which they ambush from a half-buried position, and probably take other prey such as lizards and birds if they get the chance. *E. elegans*, from Central Asia and *E. somalicus*, from North Africa, are known from very few specimens.

■ *Captivity* All available species fare well in captivity under a variety of conditions. They should be given a suitable substrate for burrowing in, although this need not be sand. All species take rodents of appropriate size although a dwarf form of *E. jaculus turcicus* from several Greek islands appears to eat only small lizards. Breeding takes place in the spring and the young are born about four to six months later. Litters may number up to 30 or more young (in *E. tataricus*) but more commonly consist of around 10.

Gongylophis (sand boas) Three species, formerly placed in *Eryx*. They are the East African sand boa, *G. colubrinus*, the rough-scaled (or tough-tailed) sand boa, *G. conicus*, and the Sahara sand boa, *G. muelleri*. Their collective distribution extends from East Africa to India and Sri Lanka, with rather a large break in the Middle East.

■ *Captivity* As for *Eryx* species. *Gongylophis colubrinus* and *G. conicus* are among the most attractive and popular sand boas.

◀ (top) The West African ground boa, *Calabaria reinhardtii*, previously regarded as a python.

◀ Rosy boa, *Charina trivirgata*, an example from Baja California, Mexico.

PYTHONIDAE
PYTHONS

As previously noted, the pythons used to be included in the Boidae. They differ from boas mainly in the arrangement of bones in their skulls and also in their distribution and breeding habits.

Pythons are restricted to the Old World, but are not found on Madagascar. Their centres of evolution appear to be Africa and Australasia. All species lay eggs and a number are known to brood them throughout the incubation period. Many species are well known and they include four of the six so-called 'giant' snakes. Other species, however, are more moderate in size. Pythons feed on a variety of warm-blooded prey, amphibians or other reptiles. Some species have heat-sensitive pits situated within the scales bordering their mouth. The presence or absence of these pits, the size and arrangement of the scales covering the top of their heads and the presence or absence of teeth on the premaxilla are the characters that have been most used in their classification.

Taxonomically, the family is in a state of complete chaos where the Australasian species are concerned. A minimum of five genera are recognised but some authorities consider that this should be expanded to at least seven. A conservative approach has been adopted here, using the six most widely accepted genera, with short notes outlining some of the other proposals.

Antaresia Four small brown pythons from Australia. They lead much the same lifestyle as medium-sized colubrids (which are absent from much of Australia) and are mostly nocturnal. The anthill python, *A. perthensis*, is the smallest python in the world. and is often found in termite nests. The other three, Children's python, *A. childreni*, the spotted python, *A. maculosa*, and Stimson's python, *A. stimsoni*, are only slightly larger and are more variable in their habits.

■ *Captivity* Easily kept and bred, apart from the anthill python, which is, in any case, hardly ever available. Stimson's python is also rare in captivity. The other two can be treated as mouse-eating colubrids but they should only be cooled slightly in the winter. Mating normally takes place during, or at the end of, winter, and the females coil around their eggs in typical python fashion. They may be removed for artificial incubation if desired.

Bothrochilus A monotypic genus containing only the Bismarck ringed python, *B. boa*. Juveniles are stunningly beautiful, being marked in alternating rings of black and salmon-pink, or orange. As the grow they become darker and some adults show hardly any trace of their juvenile markings, however. They grow to about 1–1.4m (3ft 4in–4ft 7in). Previously part of Liasis.
■ *Captivity* They can be treated like most other pythons. They are terrestrial and so tall cages are not required, and do better with high humidity. A hide box should be provided as they are secretive, and this can be part-filled with moist sphagnum.

Aspidites A clearly defined genus consisting of two medium sized pythons, endemic to Australia and characterised by the absence of heat-sensitive pits, large symmetrical scales on the top of the head and lack of teeth on the premaxilla. The species are the black-headed python, *A. melanocephalus* and the woma, *A ramsayi*. Both are restricted to Australia and grow to approximately the same size, 2.5 m (8.5 ft), although they average rather less than this, about 1.5 m (5 ft). The species are rather similar in appearance, and their most obvious difference is the black head and neck of *A. melanocephalus*. The latter is more northerly in its distribution and is found along the north coast of Australia and ranges south into the more arid regions of the interior. The woma, on the other hand, is confined to the desert regions of central Australia. Both species eat reptiles, including other snakes, in addition to a wide range of bird and mammal prey.
■ *Captivity* These pythons are rarely seen outside Australia. There are no obvious problems, however, and both species have been bred under captive conditions. They mate mainly in the winter, December to May inclusive in the Northern

hemisphere. Although they will accept rodents in captivity, *Aspidites* also feed on snakes and there is a tendency towards cannibalism. This would indicate that they are best housed separately except for breeding.

Leiopython A monotypic genus containing D'Albertis' python, *L. albertisii*, also known as the white-lipped python, from New Guinea, parts of Indonesia and islands in the Torres Straits. A long and slender species with a narrow head. There are several colour forms, one of which is black with white scales bordering its mouth and another that has a black head and neck and a golden brown body and tail. All are attractive, but aggressive. It is nocturnal and lives in humid forest habitats, often near streams or swamps. It grows to almost 3m (9ft). This species was previously included in *Liasis*.
■ *Captivity* Popular on account of its attractive appearance, but the snake can be difficult to control due to its uncertain temperament. This genus is only suitable for experienced breeders but it can be rewarding in the right hands.

Liasis This genus contained 11 species until recently but has been reduced to three due to the shuffling of species and creation of new genera. The survivors are the water python, *L. fuscus*, Macklot's python, *L. mackloti*, and the olive python, *L. olivaceus*. They live in Australia, Papua New Guinea and parts of Indonesia. These are medium-sized snakes, up to 3m (10ft) of slightly more in the case of the olive python, and mostly drab brown or olive in colour. They live in moist or locally humid microclimates.
■ *Captivity* Only for the dedicated snake-breeder, as these are not the most attractive snakes, although they are interesting. They usually resent handling and may bite, struggle or spray the handler with the contents of their lower intestine. Unpleasant, to say the least. Most will eat rodents or fowl.

Morelia An Australasian genus and one that has been the subject of much revision over the years. At one time it contained only the carpet python, *M. spilota*, and its variants but at present it includes at least eight species with, one suspects, more to come. Apart from the carpet and diamond python (both belonging to the species *M. spilota*) the

▲ D'Alberti's python, *Liasis albertisii*, a slender, elegant species from Papau New Guinea.

established members of the genus are the amethystine python, *M. amethistinus*, from Indonesia, Boelen's python, M. boeleni, from New Guinea, Bredl's python, *M. bredli*, from Central Australia, the rough-scaled python, *M. carinata*, from the Kimberley region of Australia, Kinghorn's python or the Australian scrub python, *Morelia kinghorni*, the Oenpelli rock python, *M. oenpelliensis*, from northern Australia and the green tree python, *M. viridis*, from extreme northern Australia (Cape York), Papua New Guinea and several other Indonesian islands. Three other species have been described from Indonesian localities (*M. clastolepis, nauta* and *tracyae*) but there is still much to do as there is variation among the small Indonesian islands over which it is spread.

Species in this genus have heat-sensitive pits in their labial and rostral scales. Their heads may be covered with small irregular scales (*M. carinata, M. spilota* and *M. viridis*, for example) or

with larger, regularly arranged scales (*M. amethistinus* and *M. oenpelliensis*). The scales on the body are smooth or slightly keeled, with the notable exception of *M. carinata*, in which they are heavily keeled. These pythons are medium-sized to large, the largest species averaging about 3.5m (11ft 6in) but sometimes exceeding 4m (13ft).

The green tree python, *Morelia viridis* has only recently been added to the genus, having previously been placed in its own genus, *Chondropython*, which no longer exists. It is an arboreal rain forest species, rarely leaving the canopy except to lay its eggs. The young are bright yellow, or sometimes orange, but gradually change to the typical green coloration of the adults in the first year of their lives. Some individuals are uniform in colour whereas others have a series of white marking along their dorsal midline. Others have scattered groups of yellow scales and populations seem to vary slightly between the different islands

on which they occur. It is remarkable for its similarity to the South American emerald boa, *Corallus caninus*.

■ *Captivity* The carpet python and the green tree python are by far the most interesting to breeders. The Carpet python occurs in numerous region colour patterns, some of which have been recognised as subspecies. The forms from Queensland and from Irian Jaya are particularly distinctive and sought-after. Care of this species is quite straightforward. It can be aggressive but usually settles down quickly in captivity and is undemanding with regard to temperature, etc. It eats small rodents and some individuals may develop preferences for a particular species of prey, e.g. rats or mice. It is widely bred in Australia and elsewhere and fully-grown

◀ A particularly colourful form of the carpet python, *Morelia spilota cheynei*, from Queensland, Australia.

▼ Boelen's python, *Morelia boeleni*, from highland regions of New Guinea

females lay clutches of about 20 eggs. The care and breeding of Bredl's Python, which is perhaps even more attractive, is the same. Other than these, the Amethystine Python has a small following, stimulated mainly by the arrival of various interesting and attractive forms from Indonesia, some of which are referred to above as new species. Some are small forms and therefore very suitable for captivity and many are more gentle than the rather unpredictable *M. amethistinus*.

The green tree python is widely kept and bred and its popularity is fully justified. It requires a tall cage with a perch near the top so that it can coil comfortably and hang down to ambush its prey. It eats rodents and birds although hatchlings sometimes require manipulation before they start to feed. Most specimens are moderately aggressive and cannot be handled easily but this is probably just as well as they are easily stressed. Breeding is achieved regularly, with most matings occurring during the cooler months, mainly from

September to December inclusive. The eggs number from four to 20. They sometimes fail to hatch unless they are incubated in such a way as to allow plenty of air to circulate around them. Few breeders leave the eggs for the females to brood, although this can bring good results.

Python A well-known (and relatively stable) genus with up to 10 members in Africa, southern and Southeast Asia. The reticulated python and the Indian python, *P. reticulatus* and *P. molurus*, are the two largest snakes in Asia, while the African python, *P. sebae*, is the largest snake in Africa. There are also a number of small, stout-bodied species such as the royal python or ball python, *P. regius*, and the Angolan python, *P. anchietae*, from Africa, and the short-tailed python, *P. curtus*, from Southeast Asia. This species is commonly divided into three: the Borneo short-tailed python, *P. breitensteini*, the Malaysian short-tailed python, or blood python, *P. brongersmai*, and the Sumatran short-tailed python, *P. curtus*, although some experts consider that these are simply regional forms (subspecies) of a single species. Another 'new' species is *P. natalensis* from East and southern Africa, previously incorporated into the African rock python, *P. sebae*. All

▲ The Malaysian short-tailed python, *Python brongersmai.*

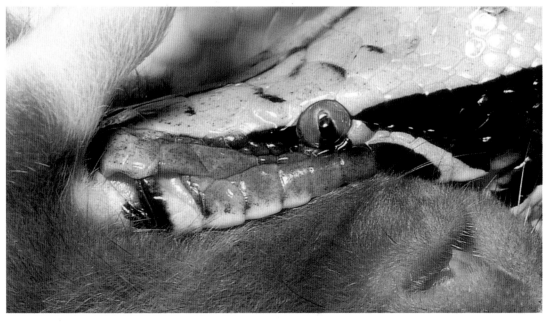

◀ Borneo short-tailed python, *Python breitensteini.*

members of the genus have heat-sensitive pits in the labial and rostral scales. The Timor python, *P. timoriensis*, is intermediate in size and is the least known species. It is restricted to the island of Timor and appears to form a link, both geographically and morphologically, between the pythons from northern Australia, such as *Morelia kinghorni*, and those from Southeast Asia, such as *Python reticulatus*.

■ *Captivity* Pythons of this genus are among the most popular captives. The royal, or ball, python, *P. regius*, is, for the time being, one of the most popular of all snakes and is bred in a wide variety of colour forms, mostly from chance mutations. This is probably a fad, similar to the tulip craze of Victorian times, when rare varieties sold for huge sums of money only for the bubble to burst leaving many people with stock they could not sell. Only time will tell. Normal royal pythons, however, are good choices as long as they are captive-bred as they are small, have good temperaments and adapt well to captivity. The very large species have special requirements and are recommended only for those keepers with the facilities to accommodate them, although I would question the motives of many of the people who keep snakes that are large enough to eat the family. Other than the size problem, members of the genus are hardy and trouble-free. The Burmese python is widely bred in captivity and several mutant forms are available. This species lays clutches of 30–50 eggs and captive females often make good mothers, coiling around the eggs and brooding them throughout their development. The African rock python and the reticulated python tend to have less attractive temperaments, although there are certainly exceptions, and are not as widely kept or bred. The various forms, or species, of the short-tailed python, often do very well but need large cages. Wild-caught animals are invariably infested with parasites and are aggressive but captive-bred animals are completely different and are infinitely easier to cater for. The Timor python is only rarely seen in captivity and the Angolan python almost never.

BOLYERIIDAE
ROUND ISLAND BOAS

THIS SMALL FAMILY CONTAINS ONLY TWO SPECIES, CONFINED TO THE DIMINUTIVE ROUND ISLAND, IN THE INDIAN OCEAN. THEY ARE OFTEN GROUPED WITH THE BOIDAE, BUT SOMETIMES WITH THE TROPIDOPHIIDAE, WITH WHICH THEY HAVE MANY SIMILARITIES. THEY SHOULD PROBABLY BE PLACED IN A FAMILY OF THEIR OWN, HOWEVER, MAINLY BECAUSE OF THE FORM OF THE MAXILLA, WHICH IS JOINTED, AND THE ABSENCE OF PELVIC GIRDLES, PRESENT IN ALL OTHER BOLD GROUPS. IN ADDITION, THE LEFT LUNG IS GREATLY REDUCED ALTHOUGH THERE IS NO TRACHEAL LUNG.

Bolyeria A monotypic genus containing *B. multicarinata*, the Round Island burrowing boa. Probably extinct; the last individual was recorded in 1975, Apparently, this is a fossorial species, despite its long tapering tail. Little more is known of it. It is not even known if it is live-bearing or whether it lays eggs, like its partner.

Casarea A monotypic genus containing *C. dussumieri*, the Round Island keel-scaled boa. This species has strongly keeled scales and a narrow head. It appears to feed exclusively on the two lizard species that share its island. Although commonly known as a 'boa' it lays eggs, clutches of three to ten having been noted in captivity.

▶ (opposite above) Aerial view of Round Island.

▶ (opposite below) The Round Island boa, *Casarea dussumieri*.

◀ ▲ (above) Distribution of Bolyeriidae and detail (left).

THE BOAS OF ROUND ISLAND

Round Island is a small volcanic island off the north coast of Mauritius, in the Indian Ocean. Although its area is only 151 hectares (less than one square mile) it forms the total range of two boa-like snakes that are the only members of the family Bolyeriidae. (The Bolyeriidae is sometimes included in the Boidae or the Tropidopheidae.) The two species are *Bolyeria multicarinata*, the Round Island burrowing boa, and *Casarea dussumieri*, the Round Island keel-scaled boa.

Owing to habitat destruction, by goats and rabbits introduced during the nineteenth century, all the Round Island flora and fauna were brought to the brink of extinction. Apart from the boas, there are two other endemic reptiles on the island, a gecko, *Phelsuma guentheri* and a skink, *Leiolopisma telfairi*, and several endemic plant species.

Remedial action was instigated in 1976, with a programme to eradicate the goats. Extermination of the rabbits followed during the next decade. Regeneration of the endemic trees and understorey plants was encouraged by the absence of these two browsers and most of the reptile fauna began to recover slowly. Unfortunately, the action may have been too late for *Bolyeria*. The last live specimen was caught on the island in 1975 and no signs of it have been seen since. This species is especially vulnerable because it is (or was) a burrowing snake. The loss of the trees on the island led to rapid erosion of what little soil had collected over the island's rocky core. If *Bolyeria* has indeed survived it will be in one of the small fissures where a small amount of leaf-litter and soil may have been retained.

Casarea dussumieri, however, has responded favourably to the help it has been given by conservationists. Its numbers have increased significantly due, on the one hand, to the regeneration of the vegetation among which it lives and forages and, on the other, to a knock-on increase in the numbers of the small geckos and skinks which form its main prey. In addition, this species is being bred successfully at Jersey Zoo.

Since 2000 a major restoration programme has been funded by the World Bank, Global Environmental Agency and operated by the Mauritian Wildlife Fund. This includes a self-sustaining field station so that weeding of alien species and planting of native ones can continue year-round. Routine reptile censuses also take place and these include a mark and recapture project to estimate the numbers of boas. The rediscovery of the Round Island burrowing boa is now a fading hope, however.

TROPIDOPHIIDAE
WOOD SNAKES OR WEST INDIAN BOAS

MEMBERS OF THIS FAMILY WERE FORMERLY PLACED IN THE BOIDAE, HENCE ONE OF THEIR COMMON NAMES. AT OTHER TIMES THEY HAVE BEEN ALLIED WITH THE ROUND ISLAND BOAS. THEY ARE DISTINGUISHED MAINLY BY THE PRESENCE OF A WELL-DEVELOPED TRACHEAL LUNG, A CONDITION THAT IS ABSENT IN THE TRUE BOAS AND THE ROUND ISLAND BOAS. THE LEFT LUNG IS GREATLY REDUCED AND FEMALES OF SOME SPECIES LACK A PELVIC GIRDLE. THEIR EYES HAVE VERTICALLY ELLIPTICAL PUPILS. THEY ARE SECRETIVE, NOCTURNAL SNAKES THAT ARE USUALLY FOUND AMONG FOREST DEBRIS, UNDER ROTTING LOGS, ETC. ALL SPECIES ARE VIVIPAROUS. THE FAMILY COMPRISES 21 SPECIES IN FOUR GENERA AND HAS A RESTRICTED RANGE IN CENTRAL AND SOUTH AMERICA AND THE WEST INDIES. THEY ARE DIVIDED INTO TWO SUBFAMILIES, ON THE BASIS OF THEIR HEMIPENAL MORPHOLOGY. EACH SUBFAMILY HAS TWO GENERA.

TROPIDOPHEINAE

Species in this subfamily have prehensile, though short, tails. The body is thickset and roughly cylindrical and the scales may be smooth or keeled.

Trachyboa Two species are known, *T. boulengeri* and *T. gularis.* They are known as eyelash boas because of small protruding scales above their eyes. They are found only in lowland rainforests of southern Central America and northern South America, as far south as Ecuador. They have rough scales and dull coloration and appear to be terrestrial in habits. Rarely seen snakes about which little is known, but captives have produced litters of six and seven young.

Tropidophis Twenty-one species, 18 of which are found on various West Indian islands, including 15 on Cuba. The other three occur on the South American mainland, ranging as far south as Peru (*T. taczanowskyi*), Ecuador (*T. battersbyi*) and Sao Paulo Province, Brazil (*T. paucisquamis*). Small to medium-sized snakes, ranging in size from about 30 cm-1 m (1-3 ft). All species are opportunistic nocturnal hunters, taking frogs, lizards and small rodents. Some species force blood from their eyes and mouth when under stress: this unusual defensive behaviour may be unique among snakes. Some have brightly coloured tips to their tails: they may use these as lures. Many species and subspecies have very restricted ranges,

▼ Haitian wood snake, *Tropidophis haetianus*.

▲ **Distribution of *Tropidophiidae*.**

often only one small island, and several are rare, having only been collected on a few occasions.

■ *Captivity* They are rarely kept in captivity, although *T. melanurus* is kept and bred on a limited scale. They prefer a cage with a substrate into which they can burrow or plenty of small holes into which they can crawl. Moderate humidity should be provided. Mating takes place in the early spring and the young are born about six to nine months later. They require small lizards or frogs at first but are also said to accept small fish. Later on they will take nestling mice, which they constrict

UNGALIOPHEINAE

Only three species, in two genera, are placed in this subfamily. They are sometimes considered to constitute a separate family, the Ungaliophiidae.

Exiliboa A monotypic genus that contains only the Oaxaca boa, *E. placata*, from southern Mexico. It is a rare and little-known snake found only in cool montane cloud forests. It is uniform glossy black in colour with only a small, light facial marking. Nothing is known of its diet, behaviour or reproduction.

Ungaliophis The genus contains two species, *U. continentalis* and *U. panamensis*, from Central America. They are sometimes called banana boas because they have been accidentally transported in shipments of bananas. They differ from the other members of the family by having a large, conspicuous, internasal scale. Small to medium-sized snakes, rarely reaching 1 m (3 ft) in length, which appear to be largely arboreal and nocturnal. Their natural prey is probably small lizards and frogs. *U. continentalis* has given birth to small numbers of live young under captive conditions.

■ *Captivity* One species, *Ungaliophis continentalis*, is occasionally kept. Its requirements are straightforward, although it is secretive and must be given somewhere to hide. Adults will accept small mice but feeding the small young is sometimes problematical.

XENOPHIDIIDAE

IN 1988 AN AMATEUR HERPETOLOGIST FOUND AN UNUSUAL SMALL SNAKE IN A PATCH OF LOWLAND RAIN FOREST A FEW MILES NORTH OF KUALA LUMPUR, MALAYSIA. IT WAS NOT STUDIED FOR SEVERAL YEARS BUT IN 1993 CLOSE EXAMINATION OF THIS SNAKE LED TO THE CONCLUSION THAT IT WAS A NEW SPECIES. DURING THIS STUDY, HOWEVER, IT WAS LINKED TO ANOTHER UNIDENTIFIED SNAKE COLLECTED IN SABAH, BORNEO, IN 1987.

The two snakes were described as new species and placed in the new genus *Xenophidion* and given the English name of 'spine-jawed snakes'. The Kuala Lumpur snake was named *X. schaeferi* and the Borneo snake was named *X. acanthognathus*. They were provisionally placed in the Colubridae. Subsequent studies of the new snakes concluded that they were probably not colubrids but were more closely related to more primitive snakes, particularly the dwarf boas, Tropidophiidae, from the Caribbean region, and the Round Island boas, Bolyeridae, from the Indian Ocean region. At this point the spine-jawed snakes were placed in a new family, the Xenophidiidae. Further studies indicate a closer relationship with the Round Island boas (one of which is extinct) while yet others have proved inconclusive. Neither species has been collected again since their discovery and are represented by a single preserved specimen each, so the puzzle may not be solved until more material is collected.

ACROCHORDIDAE
WART OR FILE SNAKES

THE WART SNAKES ARE SET APART FROM OTHER FAMILIES OF SNAKES BY A COMBINATION OF UNIQUE FEATURES. THEY ARE HIGHLY SPECIALIZED FOR AQUATIC LIFE AND OCCUR ONLY IN TROPICAL FRESHWATER, ESTUARINE AND SEAWATER ENVIRONMENTS. THEY ARE PRACTICALLY HELPLESS ON LAND AND APPEAR NEVER TO LEAVE THE WATER VOLUNTARILY. THEY HAVE A SINGLE LUNG BUT THE TRACHEAL LUNG IS LARGE AND WELL DEVELOPED. THERE ARE NO TRACES OF A PELVIC GIRDLE AND THE LOWER JAW IS FLEXIBLE, AS IN THE COLUBRIDS.

When the snakes submerge themselves, the nostrils can be closed by means of a flap in the roof of the mouth, while the lingual fossa (the notch in the upper jaw through which the tongue is protruded) can also be closed, by a pad on the lower jaw. The skin is loose and hangs in folds, especially when the snakes are removed from the water. The scales are unlike those of any other snakes and are small, granular and do not overlap one another – their common names are derived from the superficial appearance of the scales. Furthermore, the skin has microscopic hair-like bristles, the function of which is uncertain. The family contains a single genus.

Acrochordus (file snakes) Three species with a large distribution, from India through Indo-China and Southeast Asia to the South Pacific region and northern Australia. The Javan file snake, *A. javanicus*, is found in fresh waters of Asia and is replaced in New Guinea and Australia by the Arafura file snake, *A. arafurae*. The little file snake, *A. granulatus*, may be found in fresh water but also occurs in mangrove forests, estuaries and coastal marine waters throughout the area. The file snake are medium-sized to large snakes, with the largest species, *A. javanicus*, sometimes reaching 2.5m (8ft). This large species is sometimes known as the elephant trunk snake. Two of the species are brown or grey above and dirty white below but *A. granulatus* is boldly banded in black and white. All species feed on fish and give birth to live young.

■ *Captivity* File snakes are rarely kept in captivity because of their specialist requirements, and their collection should be discouraged. They would require very large heated aquaria and a steady supply of live fish. Captive breeding has not been achieved.

▲ Distribution of Acrochordidae.

▼ Small file snake, *Acrochordus javanicus*.

VIPERIDAE
VIPERS

THE VIPERS FORM A WELL-DEFINED AND ADVANCED FAMILY OF SNAKES FOUND THROUGHOUT MUCH OF THE WORLD BUT ABSENT FROM MADAGASCAR AND AUSTRALIA. THEIR MOST DISTINCTIVE CHARACTERISTIC IS A PAIR OF SHORTENED MAXILLAE TO EACH OF WHICH IS ATTACHED A SINGLE LONG FANG. EACH MAXILLA IS HINGED SO THAT THE FANGS CAN BE FOLDED BACK WHEN NOT IN USE. THE FANGS HAVE AN ENCLOSED CANAL THROUGH WHICH VENOM IS FORCED.

Vipers are typically short and stocky with broad heads. The scales are usually heavily keeled (except night adders, in which they are smooth) and the head is covered with small irregular scales: the night adder is, again, an exception and there are a few others. They are mainly terrestrial or arboreal but there are a few burrowing species and some are semi-aquatic. They may be diurnal or nocturnal, depending largely on their distribution: several species come from cold environments and are then mainly diurnal. Many are well camouflaged snakes that ambush their prey, which consists mostly of warm-blooded vertebrates, although some also eat reptiles and a few are partly insectivorous. Most species are viviparous but a few lay eggs.

The family is divided into four subfamilies: the Viperinae and the Crotalinae each have many species whereas the Azemiopinae and Causinae have few. The Crotalinae are unique among snakes in possessing a pair of large heat-sensitive pits between the eye and the nostril.

▲ Distribution of Viperidae.

AZEMIOPINAE

This subfamily contains a single species. There are no heat-sensitive pits, while peculiarities of the skull separate it from the true vipers.

Azemiops A monotypic genus containing only *A. feae*. This rare and poorly-known snake comes from the Himalayan foothills of Burma, Tibet, central and southern China, where it lives in cloud forests. It is a medium-sized snake with smooth dorsal scales, large scales on the top of its head and short fangs. Its coloration is particularly striking, consisting of narrow orange rings on a dark grey or black background. The head is also orange. It is a terrestrial montane species, found up to 2,000 m (6,500 ft), and hibernates during the winter. Its eats small mammals and possibly other types of prey. Otherwise, little is known of its biology.

CAUSINAE Night adders

This subfamily contains a single genus, from Africa. Primitive vipers, with large scales on their heads.

Causus (night adders) Six species, found in Africa south of the Sahara. Small to medium-sized snakes with moderately stout bodies. They have smooth or weakly keeled scales and short tails. The snouted night adder, *C. defilippi*, has an upturned snout but the head is blunt in the other species. Nocturnal snakes that live in

◀ Fea's viper, *Azemiops feae*, a primitive and unique member of the viper family, from China.

forests or grasslands and feed on amphibians, especially toads. Although their venom glands are large, the venom is not very powerful and their bites are not normally considered dangerous to humans, although there have been occasional fatalities. Oviparous, with clutches of over 20 eggs in some species.

VIPERINAE 'True' vipers

Members of the Viperinae are found in Europe, Asia and Africa, but not Madagascar. They lack facial heat-sensitive pits. They tend to be heavily built though not especially long. Their heads are broad and covered with small scales and their tails are short. A variety of habitats are used and they may be diurnal or nocturnal. Using a conservative arrangement, there are 12 genera and about 74 species.

Adenorhinos A monotypic genus containing only *A. harbouri* from Africa. This species was previously placed in the genus *Atheris*. Poorly known but assumed to be viviparous.

Atheris (bush vipers) Twelve species from central and West Africa. Small to medium-sized snakes with strongly keeled scales. The heads are covered with many small scales. Found in tropical forests and mainly arboreal, although the two species mentioned above are terrestrial. They apparently feed on frogs, lizards, small birds and mammals. The effects of the venom on man are not known. Viviparous, giving birth to up to 10 young.
■ *Captivity* Rarely available and rather delicate for reasons not yet fully understood. They require a tall cage with branches for climbing and a humid environment. Feeding can be a problem as not all specimens will accept rodents and alternatives, in the form of lizards and frogs, have to be found. Captive breeding has occurred but is a rare event.

Bitis Sixteen species found throughout Africa south of the Sahara. Small to large species (mostly medium sized) but often massively built with broad, triangular heads. All species are terrestrial, and those from desert regions, of which Peringuey's viper, *B. peringueyi* is the best known, are efficient sidewinders. Other habitats include mountains, rocky hillsides, forests and river courses. The small species prey

▲ (top) *Causus maculatus*, a night adder from Central Africa.

▲ (above) A common night adder, *Causus rhombeatus*, found over much of Africa south of the Sahara, eating a toad, its preferred prey.

▶ (opposite top) A young puff adder, *Bitis arietans*.

▶ (opposite below) Desert horned viper, *Cerastes cerastes*.

mostly on lizards but the larger ones eat birds and mammals. The large species are cryptically coloured and epitomise 'sit-and-wait' predators, while small species may bury themselves beneath sand and loose soil in order to ambush their prey. All species are dangerous, especially the larger ones such as the puff adder, *B. arietans*, and the Gaboon viper, *B. gabonica*. Viviparous, producing from four to almost 100 young. A litter of 154 young *B. arietans* has been recorded.

■ *Captivity* Not often kept because of the danger to human life. Most species fare well in captivity, however, with the possible exception of the rhinoceros viper, *B. nasicornis*, which has proved rather delicate. The small species may require a diet of lizards. Captive breeding of *B. arietans* and, to a lesser extent, *B. gabonica*, takes place fairly regularly and the young are easily reared.

Cerastes Three species from North Africa and the Middle East. Small vipers with moderately slender bodies, broad heads and rounded snouts. *C. cerastes*, the desert horned viper, and *C. gasparettii* may have prominent horns or spines over their eyes but they are sometimes small or lacking in some populations. The other species, *C. vipera*, lacks horns. Confined to desert areas with loose sandy substrates, which they move across by sidewinding. They feed by ambushing their prey from a buried position with just their eyes showing. Lizards probably form the bulk of their prey although small mammals may also be taken. They have serrated lateral scales with which they produce a rasping sound when disturbed. Bad-tempered and dangerous to man, although their bites are rarely fatal. Oviparous, laying up to 25 eggs.

■ *Captivity* The horned viper, *Cerastes cerastes*, fares quite well in captivity provided it can be persuaded to accept rodents. It requires a cage with a substrate of sand, which should be deep enough for the snake to shuffle down into.

Daboia A single species, Russell's viper, *D. russelii*, a wide ranging species from Sri Lanka and India, through Southeast Asia and into southern China. The form *D.r. formosensis* lives on Taiwan and the species also occurs throughout the Indonesian archipelago, with *D.r. siamensis on Java and Sumatra* and *D.r. limitis* on Flores and Timor.

▲ Lataste's viper, *Vipera latastei*, a small species from Spain, Portugal and North Africa.

A dangerously venomous species possibly responsible for more deaths in Asia than any other species. Attractively marked, though well camouflaged when resting among dead leaves and forest debris. The venom of this species varies from place to place and produces a range of symptoms, often fatal unless treated properly and promptly.

Echis (carpet or saw-scaled vipers) Six to eight species from North and West Africa, the Middle East, India and Sri Lanka. Small to medium-sized snakes with heavily keeled scales. When threatened, they will coil up and rub their scales together to produce a rasping sound. Mostly found in arid habitats, including sandy deserts, where they may move by sidewinding. They feed on lizards and small mammals. Dangerous to man because of their abundance in populated areas and their aggressive temperaments. They are the main cause of death by snake bite in some areas. Viviparous, producing small litters of young.

Eristicophis A monotypic genus containing only McMahon's viper, *E. mcmahoni* from Afghanistan and northern Pakistan. Found in high deserts among sand dunes. It buries itself rapidly by shuffling down into the sand. It is probably nocturnal or crepuscular and feeds on lizards and small mammals. Although it is docile and not inclined to bite, it is potentially dangerous to man. Rarely collected and poorly known.

Macrovipera A recently resurrected genus containing four species previously regarded as belonging to *Vipera*. They are found in North Africa, southeastern Europe and western Asia: *M. schweizeri* is confined to a few small islands in the Cyclades group. The other species are *M. deserti, M. lebetina* and *M. mauritanica*. Medium-sized snakes with thick bodies and broad heads covered with small scales. Terrestrial species that feed mainly on small mammals. Their venom is more toxic than that of the *Vipera* species and they are potentially dangerous to man. Unlike the *Vipera* species, they are oviparous.

Montatheris A monotypic genus containing only the Kenyan montane viper, *M. hindii*. An unusual terrestrial viper from the highlands of Kenya between 2700 and 3800 metres in montane moorland. It has been placed in *Vipera, Bitis,* and *Atheris* in the past. A diurnal species (because nights are too cold for it to be active) that eats lizards, small frogs and, possibly, small rodents. It is quite common in places but active only on sunny days. Viviparous, with small litters of young.

Montaspis A monotypic genus containing only the cream-spotted mountain snake, *M. gilvomaculata*, from South Africa. This snake is not very viper-like, and may, indeed, not be a viper; its relationships with other snakes are not understood. It was discovered in 1990 high in the Drakensberg Mountains. It is secretive and hunts for frogs in reed beds and other emergent vegetation at the edges of mountain streams. Not thought to be dangerous to humans.

Pseudocerastes A monotypic genus containing only *P. persicus* from the

Middle East; there are several geographical races that are sometimes regarded as full species. Medium-sized snakes with moderately heavy bodies and keeled scales. There is a group of raised scales over each eye, forming a horn, but not spine-like as in Cerastes. They move by sidewinding in suitable areas, and feed largely upon lizards. Viviparous.

Vipera Currently about 27 recognised species ranging from northern Scandinavia, where the adder, *Vipera berus*, extends into the Arctic circle, east to Japan. One or two species are found in North Africa. Many species are found in Turkey and the Middle East, where the most recent discoveries have been made (*V. wagneri* was described as recently as 1984, *V. pontica* and *V. albizona* in 1990). These tend to live in montane habitats, as do several of the European species:

▼ Wagner's viper, *Vipera wagneri*, from Turkey.

V. aspis in the Alps and other mountain ranges of central Europe, *V. ursinii* in scattered colonies in mountain ranges throughout southern and eastern Europe and western Asia, etc. Other species are found in a variety of habitats, including arid regions around the Mediterranean, heathlands, moors and lightly wooded regions. The adder, *V. berus*, is the most widely-distributed snake whereas some other species have very small ranges and are vunerable to habitat disturbances. Small to medium-sized snakes with moderately thick bodies. The top of the head may be covered in many small scales, e.g. *V. ammodytes*, or with several large plates, e.g. *V. berus*. Some species have upturned or horned snouts – these are formed by groups of small scales rather than a single spine. Predominantly terrestrial, although some species may climb occasionally. They feed on lizards and small mammals and, apparently, invertebrates. The venom of the European species is not particularly toxic

and, although they are slightly dangerous to man, few fatalities have been recorded. ■ *Captivity* A number of species are regularly kept and bred in captivity, especially in Europe. They adapt well and are usually trouble-free, although feeding juveniles, and the adults of smaller species, can sometimes present something of a problem as their natural prey is lizards. European and Middle Eastern species breed regularly, mating in the spring and giving birth in late summer. The young are easily reared once they begin to feed.

CROTALINAE Pit vipers

Species in this subfamily include the rattlesnakes and other pit vipers of North and South America, and a group of genera from Southeast Asia. A prominent, heat-sensitive pit is situated on each side of the head, just below a line drawn between the nostril and the eye. It is larger than the nostril and the membrane lining it can clearly be seen at the base.

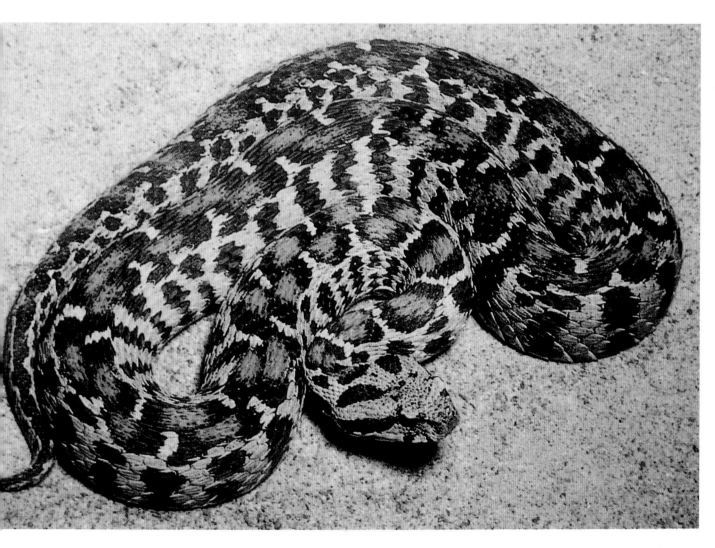

All pit vipers are potentially dangerous to man. Predominantly viviparous but members of a few genera lay eggs.

Agkistrodon Four species from North and Central America. Medium-sized snakes with keeled scales, broad, triangular heads and pointed snouts. They use a range of habitats, from swamps to deserts. The cottonmouth, *A. piscivorus*, is found at sea-level in the Florida Keys and sometimes hunts around seabird colonies, whereas the copperhead, *A. contortrix*, is a snake of woodlands, rocky hillsides and shady canyons. The other two species are the cantil, *A. bilineatus*, and the Mexican moccasin, *A. taylori*, both from Mexico.

Atropoides (jumping vipers) Three species of short, chunky vipers known as jumping vipers because they sometimes strike so forcefully that their whole bodies move forwards. They occur in humid forests of Central America, from southern Mexico to Panama. All three species were formerly placed in *Bothrops*. Live-bearers.

Bothriechis (palm vipers) Eight species, six of which occur in Central America and the seventh extends into northern South America. This is *B. schlegelii* the eyelash pit viper, a polymorphic species with distinctive horn-like scales over each eye. Medium-sized, slender, arboreal snakes with keeled scales and prehensile tails. Mostly coloured green, with the exception of *B. schlegelii* which may also be yellow or orange. Found in tropical montane forests, they feed on lizards, frogs, small birds and mammals. The bites of these species produces localized pain and swelling but are not normally fatal to man. Viviparous.

Bothriopsis Eight species from South and Central America. Small to large, slender species, most of which are arboreal. They are found in a variety of forest habitats but several are very rare and are poorly known. Presumed to be viviparous.

Bothrops Formerly including practically all the Central and South American arboreal or semi-arboreal pit vipers, this genus is now reduced to 31 species, commonly known as lance-headed snakes, owing to the shape of their heads. Three species are found only on Caribbean islands. *B. atrox*, the common lancehead, is a dangerous species with a wide range over much of northern South America. *B. ammodytoides*, from Argentina, is the most southerly

▼ Black-speckled palm viper, *Bothriechis nigroviridis*, from Central America.

▲ Emerald pit viper, *Bothriopsis bilineata*, from the Amazon Basin.

occurring snake. Small to large species with moderately stout bodies and keeled scales. All apparently terrestrial but occasionally climbing, and feeding on a

▼ Baja rattlesnake, *Crotalus enyo*.

variety of vertebrate prey. Dangerous snakes owing to their abundance and their aggressive natures. *Bothrops* species account for most of the snake bite deaths in South America. Viviparous.

Calloselasma A monotypic genus containing only *C. rhodostoma*, the Malayan pit viper. Found in Indo-China,

the Malaysian peninsular and on Java. Apparently common where it occurs. Highly aggressive. Mainly nocturnal but sometimes diurnal, feeding on a variety of small vertebrates. This species is unusual among Asian pit vipers in laying eggs, with clutches of 20 to 40 eggs having been noted. The females coil around their eggs during incubation, apparently in order to protect them from predators.

Cerrophidion Four species of small vipers, three of which are restricted to Mexico and a fourth (*C. godmani*) that also occurs further south, as far as Panama. Upland species that are mostly diurnal, previously included in *Porthidium* and other genera. Live-bearers.

Crotalus (rattlesnakes) The best-known genus of pit vipers. Twenty-nine species are recognised, ranging from Canada in the north to Argentina in the south, and they include all of the rattlesnakes except the three species of *Sistrurus*. Adaptations to many environments have taken place but there are no arboreal species. Typically desert species although some are found in more humid environments, even rainforests. Others occur in scrub, grasslands and prairies. Nocturnal or diurnal, according to distribution and season – even primarily nocturnal species will become diurnal during cool weather. They feed on a variety of vertebrate prey, small species mainly on lizards and the larger species on ground-nesting birds and mammals up to the size of rabbits. All species are viviparous, giving birth to a variable number of young, depending on species and size.
■ *Captivity* Several of the more common species are kept by specialists. They present no obvious problems but should be kept dry at all times. Some species need a period of cool conditions in the winter.

Deinagkistrodon A monotypic genus containing only *D. acutus*, from southeastern China and Taiwan. A large, heavy-bodied species with a characteristic upturned snout. Found in wooded mountains and hills. A variety of prey is taken, including amphibians, lizards, snakes and mammals. A highly venomous species whose bite often proves fatal to man – the local common name of 'hundred-pace snake' refers to the distance covered by victims before

▲ Hump-nosed viper, *Hypnale hypnale*, a small but fiery pit viper from India and Sri Lanka.

they succumb. Oviparous, like *Calloselasma*, laying around 20 eggs which the female guards.

Gloydius Ten species of Asiatic pit vipers previously referred to *Agkistrodon*, which is now restricted to the New World species. Terrestrial and diurnal vipers, including a single species, *G. halys*, that, theoretically at least, reaches eastern Europe. Also included are several species from high mountains, notably, *G. himalayanus*, and *G. monticola*. Viviparous.

Hypnale (hump-nosed vipers) Three species, found in Sri Lanka and southwestern India. One of these, *H. wali* may be a subspecies of *H. nepa*. Small snakes with short tails and keeled scales. Found in dry and moist habitats, often wooded and sometimes in association with human settlements. They feed on frogs, lizards, snakes, reptile eggs and small mammals. Although venomous and therefore dangerous to man, they are generally inoffensive. Viviparous, bearing four to 17 young.

Lachesis Four species from Central and South America. Until recently there was a single species of bushmaster, *L. muta*, with several geographical races, but these have now been accorded specific status, as follows: *L. stenophrys* from the Atlantic lowlands of Costa Rica and Panama, reaching the Pacific coast in southern Panama and Colombia, *L. melanocephala*, from an isolated region of the Pacific lowlands of Costa Rica, *L. muta*, with by far the largest range in the Amazon Basin and the Guyana shield, and *L. rhombeata* from the Atlantic forests of southeast Brazil. Bushmasters are the largest pit vipers, growing to 3m (10ft) or more. They live only in undisturbed forests which can bring them into contact with humans when the forests are cleared for logging or agriculture. Despite their size and potent venom, deaths are relatively rare as this is usually a placid species which shuns confrontation with humans. Unique among the American pit vipers in being oviparous.

Ophryacus Two species, *O. melanurus* and *O. undulatus*, from Mexico. Small, rather stout vipers from Mexico, with very limited ranges in the cool uplands of the Central Mexican mountain ranges. Both species are 'horned' with raised scales above their eyes. Diurnal and viviparous.

Ovophis Four species from Asia previously placed in *Trimeresurus*. Collectively, they range widely from Bangladesh, Indonesia, Vietnam, China and Japan. Dull coloured, terrestrial species that lay eggs, unlike the remaining *Trimeresurus* species.

Popeia A single species, *P. inornata*, described in 2004 from the Malaysian Peninsula, and Borneo, from specimens previously assigned to *Trimeresurus popeiorum*.

Porthidium Eight species found in Central and northern South America. One species, *P. hyoprora*, is found in the Amazon Basin. Small to medium-sized, terrestrial pit vipers, including several chunky 'jumping' vipers such as *P. nummifer*. Mostly stout-bodied but some species are quite slender. Mainly nocturnal in habits but several species are poorly known. Dangerous to man though not usually fatal. Viviparous.

Protobothrops (Asian lanceheads) Eight species previously placed in *Trimeresurus*. Some are poorly known whereas others are common. *P. flavoviridis* is the notorious 'habu' from the Japanese Ryukyu Islands, which, until recently, held the dubious honour of experiencing the highest incidence of snake-bite anywhere in the world. Some species are oviparous while others are viviparous.

Sistrurus The three species in this genus are known as the massasauga (*S. catenatas*) and the pygmy rattlesnakes (*S. miliaris* and *S. ravus*). They are found in North America and Mexico. Although they have rattles, they differ from members of the genus *Crotalus* in having several large scales on the tops of their heads. A variety of habitats are used, from wetlands and coniferous forests to deserts to cloud forest, depending on species and location. They are all terrestrial, feeding on small vertebrates such as lizards and rodents. Although bites are painful, they are not normally considered a danger to life. Viviparous.

Triceratolepidophis A monotypic genus containing only *T. sieversorum*, the three-horned pit viper, from Vietnam. This species was only described in 2000, from a single specimen caught in the Annam Mountains of Vietnam. It had three thorn-like projections over its eyes and on its snout, and no others have been found at the time of writing. Feeding, breeding, venom, etc. are unknown.

Trimeresurus A confusing genus of 30-40 species as currently understood, although many species have been split off into new genera. *Popeia* is one such (see above) but there are five others (*Cryptelytrops*, *Himalayophis*, *Pareas*, *Peltopelor* and *Viridovipera*) for which I prefer to reserve judgement. They are distributed across southern and Southeast Asia. Small to medium-sized vipers, with broad heads and moderately stout bodies. Most are arboreal although there are some terrestrial species. They live in a variety of habitats, including rainforest, cloud forest, mangrove swamps and mountains. Some are commonly found around human settlements. The arboreal species are often green in colour whereas the terrestrial ones are usually brown, with a variety of markings. They feed on lizards, frogs and small mammals, and possibly birds. Bites from these species are painful and can be potentially dangerous, causing local tissue damage at the least. All species are viviparous as far as is known.

■ *Captivity* Several of the arboreal species in this genus are kept in captivity. They usually adapt well and are easily cared for in tall cages with branches for them to rest. Tropical temperatures of about 25-30°C (77-86°F) should be provided and the cages should be sprayed occasionally. Adults will usually eat rodents but the young, which are small, require small frogs or lizards.

Tropidolaemus Two species, Wagler's pit viper, *T. wagleri*, which is widespread in Southeast Asia and well-known as the species kept at the Snake Temple in Penang, Malaysia, and Hutton's pit viper, *T. huttoni*, known from just two

▼ McGregor's pit viper, *Trimeresurus mcgregori*.

specimens collected in southern India in the 1940s. Wagler's pit vipers vary in coloration depending on whether they are male, female or juveniles. Viviparous.

Zhaoermia A single species, the Mangshan pit viper, *z. mangshanensis* described in 1990 and originally placed in the genus *Trimeresurus*. A rare, green, terrestrial species from a small area of forest in the Nan Ling Mountains, China. It reportedly spits venom, which, if correct, is unique among the viper family. Oviparous.

▶ (opposite) Duerden's burrowing asp, *Atractaspis duerdeni*, from southern Africa, a member of the small and poorly understood family Atractaspididae.

▼ Wagler's pit viper, *Tropidolaemus wagleri*, from Southeast Asia.

ATRACTASPIDIDAE
BURROWING ASPS

THE ATRACTASPIDIDAE IS A PROBLEMATICAL GROUP OF COLUBRID-LIKE SNAKES FROM AFRICA AND THE MIDDLE EAST. IT CONTAINS A SMALL ASSEMBLAGE OF SNAKES THAT SEEM TO HAVE AFFINITIES WITH ONE ANOTHER BUT WHICH CANNOT BE EASILY LINKED BY ANY SINGLE CHARACTERISTIC. IT MAY BE THAT THERE IS MORE THAN ONE LINEAGE INVOLVED. FOR THIS REASON, PREVIOUS AUTHORITIES HAVE BEEN IN CONSIDERABLE DISAGREEMENT OVER WHERE THE VARIOUS GENERA FIT INTO THE SCHEME OF SNAKE EVOLUTION AND RELATIONSHIPS. THEY HAVE BEEN VARIOUSLY TREATED AS COLUBRIDS, VIPERS OR ELAPIDS IN THE PAST. THE CURRENT FEELING IS THAT THEY CONSTITUTE EITHER A SUB-FAMILY OF THE COLUBRIDAE OR A FAMILY IN THEIR OWN RIGHT. IF THEY CONSTITUTE A SEPARATE FAMILY, WHICH SEEMS LIKELY, THERE WILL STILL BE DISAGREEMENT OVER WHICH GENERA SHOULD BE PLACED IN IT AND WHICH SHOULD REMAIN WITHIN THE COLUBRIDAE.

The Atractaspididae, as regarded here, contains ten genera. Members of the genus *Atractaspis* are venomous and the others have Duvernoy's glands, extending a long way back into the front half of the snake's body. The venom-delivering apparatus varies from genus to genus, however. *Atractaspis* has large erectile fangs on the front of its maxilla and no other teeth. *Amblyodipsas*, *Chilorhinophis*, *Macrelaps*, and *Xenocalamus* all have a short maxilla bearing three to five normal teeth and a pair of grooved fangs under the eye. Most members of the specialized genus *Aparallactus* also have enlarged fangs below the eye: in some species the fangs have no grooves and in *A. modestus* they are lacking altogether.

Amblyodipsas Nine species from Africa south of the Sahara. Small to medium-sized snakes with cylindrical bodies, small eyes and smooth, shiny scales. They burrow in loose soil and feed on other burrowing reptiles, amphibians and small mammals. Nocturnal. Mostly oviparous, but it is thought that *A. concolor* may give birth to live young.

Aparallactus (centipede eaters) Eleven species found throughout Africa south of the Sahara, sometimes included in the Colubridae. Small snakes with cylindrical bodies and smooth scales. Their venom apparatus is variable: back fangs may be present or absent. They are burrowers often associated with termite nests, rotting logs, etc., and feed exclusively on centipedes. Mostly oviparous, but *A. jacksoni* gives birth to live young.

Atractaspis (stiletto snakes) About 18 species found throughout much of Africa and with one species, *A. engaddensis*, in the Middle East. Small snakes with small heads, cylindrical bodies and smooth scales. Their hollow fangs may be erected while the mouth is closed, an adaptation to feeding in confined spaces. They are all burrowing snakes that may be seen on the surface at night. They feed on other burrowing reptiles and small rodents. Difficult to handle safely, and capable of giving potentially dangerous bites. Oviparous.

Brachyophis A single species, *B. revoili*, from Somalia and Kenya. Its biology is unknown.

Chilorhinophis Three species from East and central Africa. Medium-sized snakes with small heads, small eyes and slender bodies. The tail is rounded and the same colour as the head, and is used to deflect attacks. Burrowing snakes that feed on other burrowing reptiles. Oviparous.

Homoroselaps Two species, *H. dorsalis* and *H. lacteus*, from southern Africa, previously placed in the Elapidae. Small. slender snakes with small heads and shiny scales. Both species are brightly coloured with yellow and orange markings. They have two hollow fangs at the front of their elongated maxilla. Burrowing species, sometimes associated with termite nests, and feeding on other small burrowing reptiles. Too small to be very dangerous to humans although bites may produce discomfort. Probably oviparous but poorly known.

Hypoptophis A single species, the African big-headed snake, *H. wilsoni*, from the Democratic Republic of the Congo. Biology unknown.

Macrelaps A monotypic genus containing only the Natal black snake, *M. microlepidotus*. A medium-sized snake with a thick, cylindrical body and smooth scales. A burrowing species that feeds on a variety of other reptiles, amphibians and small mammals. Its bite is potentially dangerous but it is normally docile. Oviparous.

Micrelaps Four species, two of which are from northeast Africa (*M. bicoloratus* and *M. vaillanti*) and two from the Middle East (*M. muelleri* and *M. tchernovi*). Small snakes with cylindrical bodies, small heads and smooth scales.

Polemon Thirteen species, including those previously assigned to *Miodon*, from West and central Africa. Small to medium-sized species with cylindrical bodies and smooth scales. Biology very poorly known.

Xenocalamus (quill-snouted snakes) Five species from central and southern Africa. Small to medium-sized snakes with unusual, pointed heads and tiny eyes. The body is cylindrical and the scales are smooth. They burrow in sandy soils, feeding only on aniphisbaenians. Oviparous, laying small clutches.

COLUBRIDAE
TYPICAL HARMLESS AND BACK-FANGED SNAKES

IN MOST PARTS OF THE WORLD, COLUBRID SNAKES ARE THE SPECIES THAT MOST READERS WILL BE FAMILIAR WITH. ALL COLUBRIDS LACK A PELVIC GIRDLE, A FUNCTIONAL LEFT LUNG AND A CORONOID BONE (A SMALL BONE IN THE LOWER JAW THAT IS FOUND IN PRIMITIVE SNAKES BUT WHICH HAS BEEN LOST IN THE MORE ADVANCED FAMILIES). THEIR HEADS ARE COVERED WITH LARGE SYMMETRICAL SCALES AND THE VERTEBRAE LACK HYPAPOPHYSES (DOWNWARD-PROJECTING SPINES) EXCEPT IN A FEW SPECIALISED SPECIES SUCH AS THOSE WITH AQUATIC HABITS AND THE EGG-EATING SNAKES, IN WHICH THE POINTED HYPAPOPHYSES OF THE OESOPHAGUS ARE USED TO SAW THROUGH THE SHELLS OF EGGS.

Other than these characters, colubrids may be almost any shape, size and colour. They have radiated widely to fill almost every ecological niche, with the exception of the ocean (although some members of the Homalopsinae, and certain races of *Nerodia fasciata*, have made a brief flirtation with the marine environment and are found in coastal and estuarine waters around Southeast Asia and the Gulf of Mexico respectively). They have an almost cosmopolitan distribution and are the dominant family in most places, although they are poorly represented in Australia.

Many of the morphological characteristics of the various species of colubrids, such as body shape, type of scales and coloration, can be accounted for by their specialisations. Variation in reproductive biology – some species are oviparous whereas others are viviparous – can likewise often be correlated with distribution and habitat. These adaptive features have caused many problems for systematists over the years because convergent evolution has brought about groups of species that look very similar even though they are not closely related, while related species may be superficially distinct from one another merely because they occupy very different niches.

The family Colubridae, as traditionally understood, contains about 1,880 species, divided into about 300 genera. In other words, three-fifths of all snakes are contained in this one huge, widespread family. It is highly unlikely that the family has a single ancestral line but it has become one of the great herpetological repositories – species that do not obviously belong in any of the other families are placed here and there is little doubt that the family will eventually be split into a number of smaller ones. Some authorities, such as Garth Underwood,[2] already recognise up to four families – Dipsadidae, Homolopsidae, Natricidae and Colubridae – within this assemblage of genera and species. Several of these are further subdivided into a number of sub-families. Several other schemes have been proposed recently.

Until there is a reasonable consensus of opinion, it seems that there is no useful purpose to be served by trying to follow one or other of these schemes. Nor is there any point in listing the various arrangements, all of which are subject to change. In the absence of any generally agreed classification, then, the best option seems to be to continue to consider all the 'colubrids' together, bearing in mind that several of the subfamilies are likely to be promoted to full family status at some time in the future.

The Colubridae, as considered here, can be divided into a number of subfamilies: up to 28 have been recognised at various times[3] but it is more common to reduce these to fewer, but larger, subfamilies. McDowell's important paper of 1987, for example,[4] lists nine and he recognises one other, the Psammophiinae. Although some subfamilies are well defined, for instance the Homalopsinae, other subfamilies consist at present of a 'core' of species that can be assigned to each, leaving a large number of species that cannot easily be slotted in. Unsatisfactory though this system is, it appears to be the best that can be followed at present. The following subfamilies may be recognised.

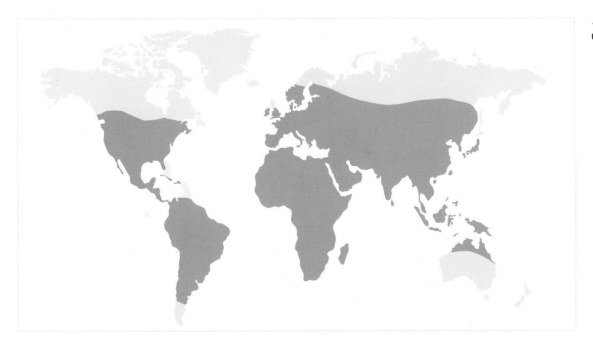

◀ **Distribution of Colubridae.**

COLUBRINAE

'Typical' snakes, with large eyes at the sides of the head, nostrils at the sides of the snout. They actively search for their prey, and strike accurately. Some species have rear fangs, e.g. *Thelotornis* and *Dispholidus*, and a number of them, including these two, are dangerous to man. Some systems of classification place these back-fanged species in a separate subfamily, the Boiginae. Examples of genera in this subfamily include many of the familiar North American, European and Asian genera, such as the whipsnakes, *Coluber*, coachwhips, *Masticophis*, smooth snakes, *Coronella*, egg-eating snakes, *Dasypeltis*, rat snakes, *Elaphe*, *Pantherophis* etc., kingsnakes, *Lampropeltis*, and gopher snakes, *Pituophis*.

HOMALOPSINAE

Aquatic snakes (freshwater and estuarine) that feed on fish, amphibians and crustaceans. Distributed throughout Southeast Asia and northern Australasia. They have valved nostrils on top of the head and their eyes are small and directed upwards. They tend to grope for their prey or ambush it. The tracheal lung is large. All have rear fangs but are regarded as harmless to man. The best known species in the subfamily is probably the fishing snake, *Erpeton tentaculatum*. This subfamily is well defined and includes ten genera: *Bitia*, *Cantoria*, *Cerberus*, *Enhydris*, *Erpeton*, *Fordonia*, *Gerarda*, *Heurnia*, *Homalopsis* and *Myron*.

XENODERMINAE

Primitive colubrids with tuberculate scales, most of which are poorly known. Only a few genera are included in this subfamily and a number of them are monotypic. They are found in Southeast Asia and include *Achalinus* and *Fimbrios*.

CALAMARIINAE

A small subfamily containing mostly small burrowing snakes. They are distributed in eastern Asia, including the Philippines, and apparently feed mostly on earthworms and other soft-bodied invertebrates. The natural history of snakes in this subfamily is poorly known and the genera include *Calamaria* and *Macrocalamus*.

PAREATINAE

Two genera of specialised slug- and snail-eating snakes from Southeast Asia. Small, slender, nocturnal snakes. This subfamily contains only two genera, *Aplopeltura*, which is monotypic, and *Pareas*.

LAMPROPHINAE
(sometimes known as Boodontinae)

African and Madagascan colubrids, including fangless and rear-fanged species. A fairly large but ill-defined subfamily that includes specialised and generalist species. Genera placed in this subfamily include the house snakes, *Lamprophis*, the African wolf snakes, *Lycophidion*, and a large number of Madagascan snakes.

PSEUDOXENODONTINAE

A small subfamily containing only two genera of poorly known Southeast Asian snakes, *Pseudoxenodon* and *Plagiopholis*.

NATRICINAE

The natricine colubrids are well-known snakes from North America, Europe and Asia. They are absent from South America and Australia. Many species are semi-aquatic and some are back-fanged. They include the North American garter snakes and water snakes, *Thamnophis* and *Nerodia*, the European water snakes, *Natrix*, as well as very many genera from Southeast Asia, such as *Sinonatrix*.

XENODONTINAE

American genera with a range of forms and lifestyles. Members of several genera have enlarged rear fangs and may produce mild effects of envenomation but none is dangerous to humans. Examples include the mussuranas, *Clelia*, ringnecked snakes, *Diadophis*, and hognose snakes, *Heterodon*, slug- and snail-eating snakes, *Sibon* and *Dipsas* (sometimes placed in a separate subfamily, the Dipsadinae) as well as a number of lesser-known South American genera.

PSAMMOPHIINAE

Mostly African but with some Asian and one European members. Characterised by greatly reduced hemipenes. Mostly active, fast moving diurnal hunters, with slender bodies and narrow heads. Rear-fanged snakes, some of which produce a fairly potent venom that can have some effects on humans. Examples of snakes in this sub-family include the sand snakes, *Psammophis*, skaapstekers, *Psammophylax*, and the Montpellier snake, *Malpolon*.

The following genera, which constitute the family Colubridae, are listed alphabetically and are not separated into subfamily groups.

Achalinus Nine species of small secretive snakes from China and Southeast Asia. Nocturnal, hiding beneath logs, etc. during the day. Thought to feed on earthworms and slugs. Oviparous.

Adelophis Two species, *A. copei* and *A. foxi*, from western Mexico. Small snakes, closely related to *Tropidoclonion*, living in damp meadows and feeding on earthworms. Viviparous, giving birth to small litters of young.

Adelphicos Six species found in Central America. Small snakes from tropical forest habitats. Their natural history is poorly known.

Aeluroglena A monotypic genus containing only *A. cucullata*, from North Africa. Related to *Coluber* but poorly known.

Afronatrix A monotypic genus containing only *A anoscopus*, from West Africa. A medium sized snake that lives in a variety of habitats from rainforest to savannah, but usually close to water. It eats frogs and, probably, fish. Reproduction unknown.

Ahaetulla (Asian vine snakes or tree snakes) Eight species found in India, Sri Lanka, China and Southeast Asia including the Indo-Australian archipelago. Formerly known as Dryophis. Medium-sized, very slender snakes that are thoroughly arboreal. Diurnal hunters that specialise in eating

NOTES
1. Stebbins, R. C. (1985), A Field Guide to the Westera Reptiles and Amphibiaas. Houghton Mifflin, Boston.
2. Underwood, G. (1966) A Contribution to the Classification of Snakes. British Museum (Natural History), London.
3. Smith, It M., Smith, R. B. and Sawin. H. L. (1977), 'A summary of snake classification', Journal of Herpetology 11(2):115-121.
4. McDowell, S. B. (1987), 'Systematics', in Snakes: Ecology and Evolutionary Biology, edited by R. A. Seigel. J. T. Collins and S. S. Novak, Macmillan Publishing Company, New York.

diurnal lizards. Their heads are elongated and pointed and their eyes are almost unique in having horizontally slit, or keyhole-shaped, pupils, giving them a high degree of binocular vision. Rear-fanged, but probably of little or no danger to humans. Viviparous.

Alluadina Two species, *A. bellyi* and *A. mocquardi*, from Madagascar. Small snakes that are poorly known.

Alsophis Fourteen species in the West Indies and several more on the South American mainland and the Galapagos Islands. Two species (*A. ater* and *A. sancticrucis*) may be extinct. Small snakes with cylindrical bodies and smooth scales. Terrestrial and diurnal, feeding mainly on lizards. Rear-fanged but unlikely to be dangerous to humans. Probably oviparous, but their biology is poorly known.

Amastridium A monotypic genus containing only *A. veliferum* from Central America. It is a small species apparently confined to tropical rain forests.

Amphiesma About 40 species of small to medium-sized water snakes found throughout much of India, Sri Lanka, China, Indo-China and Southeast Asia. Semi-aquatic, feeding on amphibians and fish. Oviparous.

Amphiesmoides A monotypic genus containing *A. ornaticeps* from China and Southeast Asia. Thought to be oviparous.

Amplorhinus A monotypic genus containing only *A. multimaculatus* from southern Africa. It is a small snake that lives in damp places, feeding on frogs and lizards. Rear-fanged but not dangerous to man. Viviparous, giving birth to four to 12 young.

Anoplohydrus A monotypic genus containing only *A. aemulans* from Sumatra. A small snake that is thought to be nocturnal and terrestrial.

Antillophis Two species, *A. andreai* from Cuba and *A. parvifrons* from Haiti and neighbouring islands. Slender, diurnal snakes that are active foragers, eating mainly *Anolis* lizards and also some *Eleutherodactylus* frogs. Probably oviparous.

Aplopeltura A monotypic genus

▲ Boie's rough-sided snake, *Aspidura brachyorrhos*, a secretive species from Sri Lanka.

containing only the Asian snail-eating snake, *A. boa*. Found throughout much of Southeast Asia, including the Philippines. A medium sized snake with a very slender, laterally compressed body and a wide, angular head. The eyes are large and the snout is blunt. Largely arboreal, this species may also be found on the ground in rainforests. It is nocturnal and feeds only on snails. Probably oviparous.

Apostolepis Up to 30 species from South America. Small, fossorial snakes with blunt snouts. Rarely seen. Thought to feed on invertebrates, small lizards and snakes. Oviparous.

Argyrogena A monotypic genus containing only *A. fasciolatus* from India. Closely related to *Coluber*. A medium-sized, slender species that is active by day. Thought to feed mainly on lizards but its natural history is poorly known.

Arizona A monotypic genus containing only the glossy snake, *A. elegans*, with a wide range over much of southern

North America. A number of subspecies are recognised. Medium-sized to large with smooth scales and a slender head. It may burrow to avoid extreme conditions but is otherwise terrestrial, feeding on rodents, lizards and other snakes. Oviparous, sometimes laying over 20 eggs in a clutch.

■ *Captivity* Most feed readily on rodents and make good captives. They have a calm disposition and hardly ever bite, even when first captured. Breeding appears to be relatively rare in captivity, probably through lack of interest. The hatchlings are rather small and may be difficult to feed.

Arrhyton Thirteen species found in the West Indies, mainly Cuba (eight species) and Jamaica (three species). Small to medium-sized, secretive snakes that have Duvernoy's glands and enlarged rear fangs. *A. exiguum* feeds on frogs, frogs' eggs (*Eleutherodactylus* species) and lizards, including geckos and *Anolis*. Large prey is held until the venom takes effect. Other species probably have similar habits but are poorly known.

Aspidura Six species from Sri Lanka. Very small to small snakes that are fossorial in habit, being found mainly in leaf litter and beneath forest debris. Nocturnal, feeding mainly on earthworms. Oviparous, laying up to 20 eggs.

Asthenodipsas Three species previously assigned to *Pareas*, the Asian slug and snail-eating snakes from Indonesia, and Malaysia. Slender arboreal snakes with broad heads, blunt snouts and large eyes. *A. vertebralis* is unusual in having dark red eyes.

Atractus A large genus of more than 80 species, found throughout most of Central and South America. Some species have been described from only single specimens and there is a high degree of endemism, with many species having very limited ranges. Very small to small snakes that can be found in forest environments, often in secretive locations such as under leaves and in rotting logs. They are thought to feed

▼ Olive keelback, *Atretium schistosum*, from India and Sri Lanka.

mainly on invertebrates. Oviparous, laying small clutches of about three eggs.

Atretium Two species found in southern India and Sri Lanka (*A. schistosum*) and southwestern China (*A. yunnanensis*). The Indian species is aquatic and lives in paddy fields, ponds, streams and rivers, feeding on fish and frogs. Oviparous. The Chinese species is apparently found in moist situations, up to altitudes of 1,500 m (5,000 ft) but is otherwise poorly known.

Balanophis A monotypic genus containing only *B. ceylonensis*, found only in Sri Lanka. A small terrestrial species that lives in moist forests. It feeds mainly on frogs and is oviparous.

Bitia A monotypic genus containing only *B. hydroides*, from Burma, Thailand and the Malayan peninsula, where it inhabits the mouths of rivers and coastal waters. It is a small snake with a narrow head and forebody, narrow ventral and subcaudal

scales and a compressed tail, and is thoroughly aquatic, probably feeding largely on fish. Viviparous.

Blythia A monotypic genus containing only *B. reticulata* from Assam (India), Tibet, Burma and southern China. A small, dark coloured snake that is probably nocturnal and semi-fossorial. Poorly known.

Bogertophis (rat snakes) Two species from North America, formerly placed in *Elaphe*. The Trans-Pecos rat snake, *B. subocularis*, is found in southern Texas and adjacent parts of northern Mexico, and the Rosalia rat snake, *B. rosaliae*, is endemic to Baja California. Both live in arid habitats but are associated with rocky gullies and arroyos where moisture may be retained locally. Medium-sized, slender but muscular snakes with keeled scales. Their heads are distinct from their necks and the eyes are large. Their scales are keeled. Very graceful in their movements. Mainly nocturnal, feeding

on lizards, birds and small mammals. Oviparous, laying clutches of up to ten eggs.

■ *Captivity* Very popular snakes with private collectors, although the Trans-Pecos rat snake is much more commonly seen than the Rosalia species. They thrive under a wide variety of conditions and will eat small rodents readily, although hatchling Rosalia rat snakes are sometimes difficult to feed at first. Breeding takes place regularly. The Trans-Pecos rat snake is unusual in mating in summer rather than the spring: the eggs hatch in the autumn or early winter.

Boiga About 20 species found in Africa, India, Sri Lanka, southern China, through-out Southeast Asia, including many island groups, and into northern Australia. They are medium-sized to large snakes with rear fangs, one of which, the mangrove snake, *B. dendrophila*, is considered slightly dangerous to man. All species apart from one are arboreal and mainly nocturnal, feeding on lizards, including nocturnal geckos and sleeping diurnal species and small mammals,

including bats. The most widespread species, the brown tree snake, *Boiga irregularis*, has been accidentally introduced to the island of Guam, where, in the absence of competition, it has caused damage to the native fauna, especially small songbirds. All the species are apparently oviparous.

■ *Captivity* A few species are occasionally kept in captivity, but there is little interest in most of them. They require tall cages and an opportunity to climb. Rodents are normally accepted. They rarely calm down sufficiently to be handled easily, however, and the keeping of the most attractive species, *Boiga dendrophila*, may be subject to restrictions on account of its venomous bite.

Boiruna Two species of obscure snakes from South America, apparently closely related to the mussuranas, *Clelia*.

Bothrolycus A monotypic genus containing only *B. ater* from central Africa. A small snake about which almost nothing appears to be known.

Bothrophthalmus A monotypic genus containing only *B. lineatus*, from West and Central Africa. A medium-sized snake that lives in moist montane forests. Natural history poorly known.

Brachyorrhos A monotypic genus containing only *B. albus*, from the Indonesian archipelago. A medium-sized snake, but very poorly known.

Brygophis A single species, *B. coulangesi*, from Madagascar, previously placed in the genus *Perinetia*, which is no longer valid. Its natural history in unknown.

Calamaria (reed snakes or worm snakes) A large genus numbering just over 50 species, several of which have been described from only a handful of specimens. Found from India and Burma, through southern and south-western China into Indo-China and Southeast Asia (19 species are known from Borneo.) Small, secretive snakes that

▼ Dog-toothed cat snake, *Boiga cynodon*, from Southeast Asia.

live in underground burrows and feed on earthworms and other soft-bodied invertebrates. Most are dark in colour, with smooth scales. Oviparous.

Calamodontophis A monotypic genus containing only *C. paucidens*, from southern Brazil. A small rear-fanged snake. Assumed to be viviparous but poorly known.

Calamorhabdium Two species from the Celebes. Very small snakes with a spine at the tip of their tails. Poorly known.

Cantoria Two species of homalopsine snakes from coastal regions of the Malaysian peninsula, the Andaman Islands, the Indonesian archipelago and India. *C. annulata* is rare and its natural history is unknown but *C. violacea* lives in tidal creeks and eats mangrove snapping prawns and perhaps other crustaceans. Viviparous.

Carphophis A monotypic genus containing only the worm snake, *C. amoenus*. This very small snake is found throughout much of eastern North America, mainly in damp situations under logs, etc. It has a small head and a barely discernible neck, and smooth shiny scales. It feeds mainly on earthworms and other soft-bodied invertebrates. Oviparous, laying one to eight eggs. The hatchlings measure only a few inches.
■ *Captivity* Not popular but easily maintained in a small vivarium containing a deep layer of moist soil or leaf litter and given a regular supply of small earthworms. Captive breeding is unknown.

Cemophora A monotypic genus containing only the scarlet snake, *C. coccinea*. This small species is found in southeastern North America and is a brightly marked 'false coral' snake. A semi-burrowing species that may also be found under bark, etc. It feeds on small lizards and snakes. Reptile eggs are also eaten. Oviparous, laying up to six elongated eggs.
■ *Captivity* A poor captive on account of its dietary habits and small size. It requires a cage with a loose substrate in which to burrow and a regular supply of small lizards to eat. Captive breeding is unknown.

Cerberus Two species found along the coasts of India and Southeast Asia, including the Philippines, Indonesian archipelago, New Guinea and northern Australia. Medium sized snakes, completely restricted to tropical estuaries, mudflats and coastal mangrove forests, where they feed on fish especially gobies. Rear-fanged but apparently harmless to man. Viviparous.

Cercaspis A monotypic genus containing only *C. carinatus*, from Sri Lanka. A medium-sized snake with a slender body, small head and distinctive coloration of white bands on a black background, closely mimicking the venomous krait, *Bungarus ceylonicus*, with which it shares its range. It prefers moist situations and eats lizards and snakes. Oviparous.

Cercophis A single species, *C. auratus*. Closely related to *Chrysopelea* and sometimes placed in that genus.

Chamaelycus Four species, *C. fasciatus* and *C. parkeri* from West and Central Africa. Small, burrowing snakes that are poorly known.

Chersodromus Two species from Mexico. Small snakes which are very poorly known.

Chilomeniscus (sand snakes) Two species of small burrowing snakes from the Sonoran Desert of southwestern North America and the Gulf of California. *C. savagei*, is restricted to Baja California and *C. stramineus* occurs in Arizona, Sonora and Baja California, incorporating the former taxa *C. cinctus* and *C. punctatissimus*, which are no longer valid. Similar to *Chionactis* but even more highly adapted to 'sand-swimming'. Sometimes found on the surface at night. They feed on invertebrates, including scorpions. Oviparous.
■ *Captivity* Easily maintained in small containers. A layer of fine, free-running sand is required. Frequent spraying is essential as these snakes will not drink from a bowl and will quickly dehydrate. They require a diet of insects and their larvae. Captive breeding unknown.

Chionactis (shovel-nosed snakes) Two species, *C. occipitalis* and *C. palarostris,* found in arid regions of southwestern North America. Small, burrowing snakes

that 'swim' through loose sand or fine gravel in search of insect larvae and other invertebrates. Both species are brightly coloured 'false coral' snakes. Oviparous.
■ *Captivity* Not widely available but easily kept alive by housing in a cage containing a few centimetres (a couple of inches) of natural sand or fine rounded pebbles in which the snakes will spend most of their time. Cultured insects such as crickets and waxworms are taken readily. The cage should be heavily sprayed occasionally as these snakes seem unable to find water if it is only available in a bowl. Breeding not known, although both species lay two or three small eggs.

Chironius Thirteen species from Central America and northern South America. Medium-sized to large species with slender bodies and very large eyes. Juveniles tend to be marked differently from adults. Mainly terrestrial but climbing occasionally, found in tropical forests. Fast-moving snakes, largely diurnal, feeding mainly on rodents and small birds. Oviparous.

Chrysopelea Five species found in India, Sri Lanka, Burma, southern China, Indo-China, the Malay peninsula, Indonesian islands and the Philippines. Medium-sized species with slender bodies and narrow, elegant heads. The eyes are large. All are arboreal and are mostly green, or green with black and red markings. They have long prehensile tails and smooth scales. These diurnal tree snakes are sometimes known as 'flying' snakes owing to their habit of launching themselves from high boughs. They break their fall by making their under-surface concave. They eat lizards, birds and small mammals. Rear-fanged but not regarded as dangerous to man. Oviparous.
■ *Captivity* Adults do quite well in captivity. They require tall cages and plenty of branches to climb and roost among. Food, consisting of small rodents, should be offered on forceps. Their temperament is unpredictable, however, and they are inclined to bite. Breeding is not regularly achieved.

Clelia (mussuranas) Eleven species from Central and South America. Large snakes with cylindrical bodies, smooth shiny scales and small eyes. Found in moist forest habitats and active by night and day. They feed mainly on snakes, including many venomous pit vipers to whose venom they appear to be immune, and rodents. They constrict their prey. Oviparous.

■ *Captivity* Occasionally kept and bred. Adults are easily fed, on rodents, but the juveniles require small reptiles.

Clonophis A monotypic genus containing only *C. kirtlandi*, Kirtland's water snake, from North America. Closely related to *Nerodia*, in which genus it was previously placed. A small species with heavily keeled dorsal scales. Found in moist places, invariably near water. It feeds on worms and slugs. Viviparous.

Coelognathus Six species of medium-sized snakes from the Oriental region, formerly assigned to *Elaphe* but actually only distantly related to them. All are medium-sized, slender, quick species that are mostly nocturnal and oviparous. They feed on lizards and small rodents.

■ *Captivity* Species such as the Radiated Rat Snake, *C. radiata*, are sometimes kept and bred in captivity but, compared with other 'rat' snakes they make nervous and unsatisfactory captives except for the dedicated specialist.

Collorhabdium A monotypic genus containing only *C. williamsoni*, from the Malaysian peninsula (Cameron Highlands). Similar to, and probably related to, the reed snakes, *Calamaria*. Only a few specimens have been collected and its natural history is poorly known.

Coluber (whipsnakes and racers) A large genus currently containing 22 or 23 species. Several species have been split off in recent years, into the genera *Dolichophis, Hemorrhois, Hierophis* and *Platyceps*. What remains includes a single wide-ranging and variable species from North America, *C. constrictor*, with ten subspecies (one of which, *C. c. mormon*, is sometimes regarded as a full species, *C. mormon*). The other species are from Africa, the Middle East and western Asia as far as northern India. They are all medium-sized to large diurnal snakes with narrow heads and large eyes. Often uniformly coloured, although juveniles frequently differ from the adults. They feed on reptiles, which they chase down, and also on small birds and mammals. Oviparous.

■ *Captivity* No often kept on account of their nervous, erratic behaviour and their tendency to bite. Some individual settle down and may accept a diet of small rodents.

Compsophis A monotypic genus containing only *C. albiventris* from Madagascar. A very small snake that may be fossorial but which is hardly known.

Coniophanes Thirteen species found from Texas, through Central America and into South America as far south as eastern Peru. Found in a variety of habitats from dry semi-desert regions to moist tropical forests. Small to medium-sized snakes with smooth, shiny scales and longitudinal stripes along their bodies. Terrestrial, diurnal snakes, feeding on a variety of small vertebrates. Rear-fanged but producing a venom that has little or no apparent effect on humans. Oviparous.

Conophis Five species of medium sized snakes from Central America, found in arid and moist habitats. Terrestrial, feeding mainly on lizards. Apparently oviparous.

Conopsis Six species from Mexico. Small, semi-burrowing snakes with stout, cylindrical bodies and smooth scales. They are found in cool montane environments but are rarely collected and little known. Viviparous.

Contia A monotypic genus containing only the sharp-tailed snake, *C. tennis*, found along part of the west coast of North America. A small, secretive, diurnal species that favours damp situations. It apparently feeds mainly on slugs. Oviparous, with small clutches of eggs.

Coronella (smooth snakes) Three species, two from Europe, North Africa and the near East and a third, *C. brachyura*, from India. Small to medium-sized snakes that have smooth scales, cylindrical bodies and a narrow head. They feed mainly on lizards, which they constrict. *C. austriaca* is viviparous, producing two to 15 young, whereas *C. girondica* and *C. brachyura* are oviparous.

Crisantophis A monotypic genus containing only *C. nevermanni*, previously included in the genus *Conophis*. A medium-sized snake with smooth scales. Found in lowland dry forests of Mexico. Biology poorly known, probably oviparous.

Crotaphopeltis Six species from Africa south of the Sahara, commonly called herald snakes. Medium-sized, rear-fanged species that are not dangerous to man. They live in marshy areas and feed on amphibians. Oviparous.

Cryophis A monotypic genus containing only *C. hailbergi*, from Mexico. Medium-sized with heavily keeled scales and large eyes. Otherwise, poorly known.

Cryptolycus A monotypic genus containing only *C. nanus*, the dwarf wolf snake from Mozambique. A small species, growing to less than 30 cm (12 in), it feeds on amphisbaenids. It lays two elongated eggs.

Cyclocorus Two species, *C. lineatus* and *C. nuchalis*, from the Philippines. Small snakes with cylindrical bodies and small eyes. Apparently fossorial species, found under logs and rotting vegetation. Said to eat other snakes but poorly known.

Cyclophiops Four species from southern China and Japan, formerly included in the North American genus *Opheodrys*. Medium sized snakes found mainly in damp situations. Green in colour. Terrestrial or semi-arboreal. Oviparous.

Darlingtonia A monotypic genus containing only *D. haetiana* from Haiti. A small terrestrial snake that appears to feed almost exclusively on the small frogs of the genus *Eleutherodactylus*. Otherwise its biology is poorly known.

Dasypeltis (egg-eating snakes) A small genus of five highly specialised snakes found throughout most of Africa. They have modified vertebrae, used for sawing through egg shells, and only rudimentary teeth. Various species are mimics of the saw-scaled viper, night adders, etc., but they are harmless. Oviparous.

■ *Captivity* Adults are among the easiest snakes to keep in captivity as they will accept the eggs of hens, pigeons, etc. Obtaining small eggs for juveniles can be a problem but they can be fed small quantities of hens egg by means of a syringe and tubing.

▲ A reddish form of the African egg-eating snake, *Dasypeltis scabra*, from the edge of the Kalahari Desert of South Africa.

Dendrelaphis About 20 species found in India, Sri Lanka, Burma, southern China, through Indo-China and Southeast Asia into northern Australia. Often known as bronze-backed snakes. Medium-sized to large, slender-bodied, arboreal snakes with large prominent eyes. They are fast-moving, diurnal species that feed mainly on lizards but may also take amphibians and even fish. May be found swimming in large lakes and rivers. Oviparous, laying clutches of up to 15 eggs.

Dendrolychus A monotypic genus containing only *D. elapoides* from West Africa. A small, arboreal snake that is thought to feed mainly on frogs. Poorly known.

Dendrophidion Eight species found from Mexico to northern South America. Medium-sized snakes with extremely slender bodies and long tails. Terrestrial and arboreal species that inhabit tropical forests and feed mainly on rodents and frogs. Oviparous.

Diadophis A monotypic genus containing only the widespread and highly variable species, *D. punctatus*. This species is found throughout much of North America, including parts of Mexico. It is a small, secretive species found in moist situations, where it feeds on earthworms, slugs and other invertebrates as well as small amphibians and reptiles, including other snakes. Oviparous, laying one to 10 eggs per clutch.
■ *Captivity* Not especially popular but an interesting captive if given a damp substrate with places to hide. The eastern forms will live indefinitely on earthworms although the larger, western forms may require a more substantial diet. Captive breeding not known and probably not attempted seriously.

Diaphorolepis Two species from Panama, Colombia and Ecuador. Medium-sized snakes with a pair of keels on each of their dorsal scales. *D. wagneri* is terrestrial, and oviparous. Poorly known.

Dinodon Seven species from Burma, southern China, northern Indo-China and Japan. Small to medium-sized snakes with thick bodies and broad heads. Found in moist forest habitats, rarely far from water. Thought to feed mainly on amphibians and fish.

Dipsadoboa Eleven species from Africa. Small, moderately slender snakes with wide heads and vertical pupils. Arboreal, nocturnal snakes that eat geckos and frogs. Rear-fanged but not dangerous to man. Oviparous.

Dipsas Thirty-three species from Mexico, through Central America as far south as Brazil and Bolivia. Also Trinidad and Tobago. Their taxonomy is rather confused at present. Medium-sized snakes with slender, laterally compressed bodies and wide, rather square heads with blunt snouts. The eyes are large and have vertical pupils. Several species are boldly marked with rings or saddles contrasting with their background colour. Nocturnal, arboreal snakes living in moist tropical forests and feeding

▶ *Drepanoides anomalus* from central South America, a secretive species and the only member of its genus.

▶ (opposite) Four-lined snake, *Elaphe quatuorlineata*, from southeastern Europe.

exclusively on snails and slugs. Oviparous.
■ *Captivity* Rarely available but interesting species that fare quite well in tall vivaria with a humid atmosphere. They require a constant supply of land snails. Captive breeding unknown and probably not achieved.

Dipsina A monotypic genus containing only the dwarf beaked snake, *D. multimaculata*, from southern and southwestern Africa. It is a small snake that feeds on small lizards and lays two to four eggs.

Dispholidus A monotypic genus containing the boomslang, *D. typus*, found throughout much of Africa south of the Sahara. The boomslang grows up to 2 m (6½ ft) in length and is notorious as one of the more dangerous rear-fanged colubrid snakes, producing a highly potent venom that can be fatal to man. Diurnal hunters of lizards, birds and mammals, with large eyes. Oviparous, laying clutches of up to 25 eggs.

Ditaxodon A monotypic genus containing only *D. taeniatus*, from Brazil. Virtually unknown.

Ditypophis A monotypic genus containing only *D. vivax* from Socotra Island. Its relationships and biology are poorly known.

Dolichophis (whipsnakes) Five species previously placed in *Coluber*. Slender, medium-sized to large snakes from eastern Europe, the Balkan region and the Caucasus.

Drepanoides A monotypic genus containing only *D. anomalus*, from South America. A small, brightly coloured snake that is terrestrial and semi-fossorial. Biology unknown.

Dromicodryas Two species, *D. berneari* and *D. quadrilineatus*, from Madagascar. Medium-sized snakes whose natural history is poorly known.

Dromophis Two species of which *D. praeornatus* is found in West Africa and *D. lineatus* has a large range covering most of tropical Africa. Slender, elongated snakes that hunt small mammals and frogs by day. Oviparous.

Drymarchon Four species, *D. corais*, the cribo, from Texas, through Mexico and Central America and into South America as far as Paraguay, *D. couperi*, the indigo snake, from southeastern North America and two additional Neotropical species, *D. caudomaculatus* and *melanurus*. Large and impressive snakes with slightly triangular cross-sections to their bodies and large shiny scales. Diurnal species that like to bask. They feed on a wide

variety of vertebrate prey, including birds, mammals, fish, amphibians and reptiles, including venomous snakes. Oviparous, laying clutches of up to 12 eggs.
■ *Captivity* The indigo snake has long been a popular species with snake fanciers. The Florida race is now rare due to habitat destruction, and is therefore protected, but captive-bred specimens are sometimes available. They make beautiful vivarium subjects although they require a large amount of space and plenty of food. Breeding is not straightforward although it is achieved on a fairly regular basis.

Drymobius (racers) Four species found from southern North America down into South America. Medium-sized, slender, cylindrical snakes with a long tail. All have large eyes associated with active diurnal hunting and they feed largely on amphibians. Occurring in a variety of habitats from semi-arid scrub to tropical moist forests. Oviparous.

Drymoluber Three species from tropical South America. Medium-sized snakes that are terrestrial or arboreal, diurnal and feed mainly on lizards. Oviparous.

Dryocalamus Six species found in India, Sri Lanka, Southeast Asia and the Philippines. Small to medium-sized arboreal snakes that are active by night.

Thought to eat invertebrates, frogs and lizards but diet, habitats and reproduction poorly known.

***Duberria* (slug-eating snakes)** Two species, one, *D. variegata*, restricted to southern Africa and the other, *D. lutrix*, extending as far north as Ethiopia. They are small, secretive snakes, which feed exclusively on slugs and snails. Viviparous, with up to 20 young per litter.

Echinanthera Six species from Brazil, previously placed in other genera such as *Dromicus* (no longer recognised) and *Liophis*.

Eirenis About 18 species found from North Africa, throughout the Middle East and into northwestern India. Small, secretive snakes that feed mainly on invertebrates. The species are difficult to separate superficially and their natural history is poorly known. Apparently all oviparous.

Elachistodon A monotypic genus containing only the Indian egg-eating snake, *E. westermanni*. This species eats only birds' eggs and closely parallels the African *Dasypeltis* species. It is rare and poorly known.

***Elaphe* (rat snakes)** Ten species from Eastern Europe, through Middle East, Asia and to Japan, where two species are endemic. Often referred to as rat snakes but including species with other common names, such as the Four-lined snake, *E. quatuorlineata*. All species are medium-sized to large, slender and agile, typically nocturnal though some are active during the evening and even at midday in cool weather. Most are good climbers though predominantly terrestrial in their habits, and they eat small rodents and lizards. They are all oviparous. Several are colourful and attractively marked and have a following among amateur snake-keepers, although not as popular as the North American rat snakes, now placed in *Pantherophis*. The genus was formerly much larger when it acted as a catch-all for species, including several from North America, now placed in other genera.

■ *Captivity* Most species do well in captivity although not all are readily available. The small species, such as the twin-spotted rat snake, *E. bimaculata* and the steppe rat snake, *E. dione*, are most easily accommodated but even the larger species, such as the four-lined snake, *E. quatuorlineata*, do well in captivity. They have similar requirements to the Corn Snake and its relatives, *Pantherophis* species, but may be slightly more demanding. For instance, they prefer large, open cages rather than enclosed boxes or drawers. Breeding is regularly achieved and all species typically mate in the spring and lay their eggs in late spring to early summer. Hatchlings of most feed readily on newborn mice but the smaller species can be difficult at times.

Elapoidis A monotypic genus, containing only *E. fusca*, from Sumatra and Java. A small, dark brown, burrowing snake that is typically found at high altitudes, where it may be very common in suitable habitats.

Elapomorphus Five species from South America. Small, cylindrical snakes with smooth, shiny scales. Burrowing species that probably feed largely on invertebrates.

Elapotinus A monotypic genus containing only *E. picteti*, from tropical Africa. Its

relationships with other snakes are unclear: it may be related to *Aparallactus* (sometimes placed in the Atractaspididae) but very poorly known.

Emmochliophis Two species, known from only a single specimen each, from Ecuador. Nothing else is known.

Enhydris Twenty-two species found from India, China, Southeast Asia, New Guinea to northern Australia. Small to medium-sized, specialised freshwater aquatic species that rarely leave the water. They have cylindrical bodies, smooth shiny scales and their eyes are directed upwards. Their diet includes fish and amphibians. Viviparous, giving birth to live young underwater.

■ *Captivity* Almost unobtainable nowadays but interesting if somewhat demanding snakes. They must be kept in an aquarium which should be heated and well covered. There should be a good growth of aquatic vegetation in which the snakes will hide, lying in wait for their prey. They require a diet of small fish.

Enuliophis A monotypic genus containing only *E. sclateri*, from Central America and northern Colombia. A small leaf-litter-dwelling species with a long, thickened tail that the snake thrashes until it breaks if threatened.

Enulius Four species from Central America to northern South America. Small, slender snakes with long tails. The rostral scale is enlarged as an adaptation for burrowing. Poorly known.

Eridiphas A monotypic genus containing only the Baja California night snake, *E. slevini*. A medium-sized nocturnal species that has a restricted range in northwestern Mexico. It appears to feed mainly on nocturnal lizards, snakes and amphibians. It is rear-fanged but harmless to man. Oviparous, laying a small clutch of elongated eggs.

Erpeton A monotypic genus containing only the tentacled snake, *Erpeton tentaculatum*, from Thailand and Indo-China. A medium-sized snake with several unusual characteristics in addition to the pair of strange appendages on its snout. Its body is almost rectangular in cross-section and its ventral scales are greatly reduced. It is thoroughly aquatic and can be found in freshwater ponds and slow-moving waters.

It feeds on fish and is viviparous, producing litters of up to 15 young.

■ *Captivity* Imported specimens are usually in poor condition and, if damaged, are susceptible to fungus infections. They require a densely planted aquarium heated to about 25°C (77°F), and a diet of small fish. Captive breeding has probably not been achieved.

Erythrolamprus (false coral snakes) Six species from Central and South America. Small to medium-sized snakes with cylindrical bodies and smooth scales. All species are brightly marked with red, black and white rings and are often claimed to mimic the coral snakes, *Micrurus* species, with whose range they overlap. Mainly diurnal, but secretive. Rear-fanged species that feed mainly on other reptiles, including venomous snakes. Not regarded as dangerous to man. Oviparous.

Etheridgeum A monotypic genus containing only *E. pulchra* from Sumatra. Biology virtually unknown.

▼ *Erythrolamprus aesculapii*, one of several 'false coral' snakes from Central and South America.

Euprepriophis Two species of medium-sized snakes formerly assigned to *Elaphe*. Both are slender with narrow heads. *E. conspicullatus* is endemic to Japan and *E. mandarina*, is from southern, northern India and Myanmar. Their natural history is not well known but both are upland species that prefer cool climates and both are oviparous.

■ *Captivity* The mandarin rat snake is a popular captive. Problems with it in the past stemmed from unhealthy, parasitised wild individuals that usually died within weeks or months of importation. Captive-bred stock, however, fares far better and breeding them is not difficult. They require similar conditions to the *Pantherophis* species but should be kept somewhat cooler. The Japanese forest rat snake is rarely available but will probably have similar requirements.

Exallodontophis A single species, *E. albignaci*, from Madagascar, previously placed in *Pararhadinaea*. Small and hardly known.

Farancia Two species, *F. abacura* and *F. erytrogramma*, found only in the southeastern corner of North America.

They are large species with smooth, glossy scales and their eyes are situated on the top of their head. *F. abacura* has a sharp pointed scale at the tip of its tail. Both species are almost totally aquatic in their habits. They feed on eels and eel-like salamanders (*Amphiuma*). Oviparous, laying large clutches of eggs in underground chambers. There is some evidence that the females coil around the eggs until they hatch.

■ *Captivity* Apparently they fare well in captivity but the problem of obtaining sufficient food of the right type would be insurmountable to most people.

Ficimia Seven species, known as hook-nosed snakes. North, Central America and northern South America. Two species are known from a single specimen only. Small, secretive, back-fanged species with an upturned rostral scale. They apparently feed largely on spiders and centipedes. Oviparous.

Fimbrios A monotypic genus containing only *F. klossi*, from Indo-China. A small snake with spinose scales on its lower jaw, the function of which is not known. Terrestrial and nocturnal in habits but otherwise poorly known.

Fordonia A monotypic genus containing only the white-bellied water snake, *F. leucobalia*. It is found wherever there is suitable habitat throughout Southeast Asia, including the Philippines and New Guinea, and along the north coast of Australia. This medium-sized snake inhabits coastal mudflats, especially those associated with mangroves. It is a highly specialised snake, feeding on small crabs, which may be constricted before being eaten piecemeal. Viviparous, with three to 13 young.

Gastropyxis A single species, the emerald snake, *G. smaragdina*, from West and Central Africa. A slender, bright green, tree snake with a prominent ridge where the belly scales meet the flanks. Prone to breaking its tail if grasped but the tail is not regenerated. Oviparous. Sometimes placed in *Hapsidophrys*.

Geagras A monotypic genus containing only *G. redimitus* from Mexico. A very small burrowing snake with a modified rostral scale. It probably feeds on invertebrates but is generally poorly known.

Geodipsas Six species from Madagascar. Small snakes that feed on frogs. Poorly known.

Geophis A large genus containing over 40 species. Found throughout Central and northern South America, in dry and moist habitats. Small, slender snakes with pointed snouts. Terrestrial species, active mainly at night. Otherwise poorly known.

Gerarda A monotypic genus containing *G. prevostiana*, which lives along the coasts of India, Burma, Sri Lanka, Perak and Thailand. Aquatic, in mangrove swamps bordering tidal rivers and estuaries. Lethargic on land. Viviparous.

Gomesophis A monotypic genus containing only *G. brasiliensis*, from Brazil. Medium-sized. Poorly known.

Gongylosoma Five species from Asia. Poorly known.

Gonionotophis Three species from West Africa. Small snakes found in rainforests. Nocturnal, probably feeding on frogs and lizards.

Gonyophis A monotypic genus containing only *G. margeritatus*, from the Malaysian peninsula and Borneo. Found mainly in hill forests. Closely related to Chrysopelea and, like members of that genus, arboreal. Rare, and poorly known.

Gonyosoma Three species from Southeast Asia, formerly included in the genus *Elaphe* (rat snakes). Medium-sized to large snakes with slender, muscular bodies and narrow, elegant heads. Usually green in colour, and highly arboreal. They feed on frogs, lizards and small mammals. Oviparous.

■ *Captivity* The red-tailed racer, *Gonyosoma oxycephalum* is moderately popular. This colourful snake requires a large cage with plenty of branches on which to climb and rest. Captive-bred animals adapt far better than wild-caught ones and usually settle down well in captivity. Not aggressive, but nervous. Adults eat small rodents without problems but the young can be difficult to feed at first. Captive breeding has occurred on several occasions but is not a regular event.

Grayia Four species from tropical West and central Africa. Medium-sized to large snakes that have aquatic tendencies. Thought to eat fish. *G. smythii* is oviparous but reproduction in the other species is unknown.

Gyalopion Two species, *G. canum* and *G. quadrangulare*, from southern North America and Mexico. The latter is brightly coloured and could be a coral snake mimic. Closely related to the *Ficimia* species, with which they share the common name of hook-nosed snakes. Small, nocturnal, back-fanged species that feed on invertebrates, especially spiders. Oviparous.

Haplocercus A monotypic genus containing only *H. ceylonensis* from Sri Lanka. A small species with a brightly coloured underside which it displays if alarmed. Semi-fossorial and nocturnal, usually found under rotting logs, etc.

Hapsidophrys A single species, *H. lineatus*, from West, Central and East Africa. A slender, green, arboreal species that is poorly known.

Helicops Fifteen species of small to medium-sized snakes from South America. Aquatic or semi-aquatic, with eyes and nostrils positioned near the top of their heads, and heavily keeled scales. Diurnal and thought to feed on fish and amphibians. Breeding habits may vary. Most species are viviparous, but *H. angulatus* appears to use either method of reproduction, depending on its location: it may lay well-developed eggs that hatch after about 16 days, or the young may be born live.

Helophis A monotypic genus containing only *H. schoutedeni*, from Zaire. Its relationships and biology are poorly known.

Hemirhagerrhis (bark snakes) Four species from Central and East Africa. Small, arboreal snakes that hide beneath loose bark by day and hunt lizards at night. Oviparous.

Hemorrhois (whipsnakes) Four species, previously placed in *Coluber*. Slender, fast-moving species that hunt mainly lizards by day but are opportunistic feeders and also take birds and small mammals. The horseshoe snake, *H. hippocrepis* occurs in southern Europe and *H. nummifer* lives on some Greek islands. *H. algirus* is North African and *H. ravergieri* lives in the Caucasus region. Oviparous.

***Heterodon* (hognose snakes)** Three species, found only in North America, including northern Mexico. Short, stocky snakes with short tails, heavily keeled scales and a prominent upturned rostral scale. May hiss, flatten their necks and make mock strikes if disturbed, or feign death. Specialist feeders on toads, which they root out of the ground with their plough-like rostral scale, although other prey may be taken. They have enlarged fangs towards the back of their mouths and there is some suspicion that they produce a venom that has a varying, but noticeable, effect on humans. Not usually considered dangerous. Oviparous, with clutches of up to 20 eggs.

■ *Captivity* Good vivarium subjects as long as they will accept rodents: most will not, but the western hognose, *H. nasicus*, usually will and is by far the best choice. Breeding this species is quite easy and the females may lay more than one clutch of eggs each year.

Heteroliodon Three species of snake from Madagascar, two of them only described in the last few years. Small,

terrestrial snakes about which little is known at present.

Heurnia A monotypic genus containing only *H. ventromaculata*, from New Guinea. A medium-sized snake closely related to *Enhydris*. Semi-aquatic, feeding mostly on fish. Viviparous.

Hierophis Three species of whipsnakes or racers previously placed in *Coluber*. Medium-sized, slender, active snakes that hunt by day. They occur in southern and eastern Europe and into Central Asia. Oviparous.

Hologerrhum Two species, *H. dermali* and *H. philippinum*, from the Philippines. Small snakes with cylindrical bodies and smooth scales. Rear-fanged but harmless to humans because of their small size.

Homalopsis A monotypic genus containing only *H. buccata*, from India, Burma, Indo-China and Southeast Asia including the Indonesian archipelago. A medium-sized snake with a stout, cylindrical body. Aquatic, found in fresh and brackish water and feeding mainly on fish. Viviparous.

Hormonotus A monotypic genus containing only *H. modestus* from West and Central Africa. A medium-sized snake that is poorly known.

Hydrablabes Two species, *H. periops* and *H. praefrontalis*, from Borneo. Small, burrowing species about which little appears to be known.

Hydraethiops Two species, *H. laevis* and *H. melanogaster*, from Central Africa. Semi-aquatic snakes related to *Afronatrix*.

Hydrodynastes Two species from South America, including the false water cobra, *H. gigas*, formerly placed in the genus *Cyclagras*, (now defunct) and *H. bicinctus*. Large, heavy-bodied snakes with smooth scales. *H. gigas* flattens its neck when disturbed, forming a hood. Young may be brightly banded but these markings are often obscured as the snake grows. Both species are found near water and have semi-aquatic lifestyles, feeding largely on frogs and toads but also taking other vertebrates, including small mammals. Oviparous, laying moderately large clutches (up to 42 eggs).

■ *Captivity* One species, *Hydrodynastes gigas*, is sometimes kept in captivity (usually under its old name of *Cyclagras*) especially in large collections in zoological gardens, etc. It settles down well and will usually adapt to a diet of rodents. It requires a large aquatic area but the cage substrate should be kept dry. Breeding has been achieved many times, and can take place at any time of the year. The young are easily reared.

Hydromorphus One to three species of semi-aquatic snakes found from Honduras to Panama in Central America. Their taxonomy is uncertain at present. Small to medium-sized species with small eyes and dull coloration. *H. concolor* is oviparous, laying clutches of about seven eggs. Biology poorly known.

Hydrops Three species, *H. caesurus*, *H. marti* and *H. triangularis*, found in northern South America, east of the Andes. Medium-sized snakes that have smooth scales and cylindrical bodies. They are brightly marked, resembling coral snakes. Highly aquatic, and active at night and by day. They feed on amphibians and fish, especially false eels, *Synbranchus*. Reproduction not known, but they are probably oviparous.

◀ **Western hognose snake,** *Heterodon nasicus*, **from North America.**

Hypoptophis A monotypic genus containing only *H. wilsoni*, from central Africa. A small snake about which little is known.

Hypsiglena (night snakes) Two species from North and Central America, *H. torquata* and *H. tanzeri*. Small snakes with prominent eyes and vertical pupils. Found in arid, rocky habitats. Nocturnal, feeding on lizards, small snakes and small mammals. Oviparous.

Hypsirhynchus A monotypic genus containing only *H. ferox*, from Haiti. A medium-sized, heavy-bodied snake. Terrestrial, feeding on Anolis lizards. Otherwise poorly known.

Ialtris Three species from Hispaniola in the West Indies. Medium-sized snakes that have rear fangs but are otherwise poorly known.

Iguanognathus A monotypic genus containing only *I. werneri* from Sumatra. A small burrowing snake that has only rarely been collected. Nothing is known of its natural history.

Imantodes Six species found in Central and South America: Medium-sized but exceedingly elongated snakes with long tails. Their heads are broad and rounded and the eyes are large and conspicuous, with vertically elliptical pupils. Totally arboreal, and capable of bridging huge distances between branches. During the day they usually coil within bromeliads and other epiphytes, and are found only in humid rainforests. They feed mainly on small lizards and frogs. Oviparous, laying small clutches of elongated eggs.

Ithycyphus Fives species from Madagascar. Medium-sized snakes with enlarged rear fangs, though not likely to be of danger to humans. Not well known. Mostly arboreal but *L goudoti* is terrestrial. They eat lizards, especially chameleons.

Lampropeltis (kingsnakes and milk snakes) Eight species. The common kingsnake, *L. getula*, has a wide range over most of North America, including northern Mexico, and several subspecies

▶ Sinaloan milk snake, *Lampropeltis triangulum sinaloae*, from Mexico.

▲ Spotted night snake, *Hypsiglena torquata*, subspecies *baueri*, from Cedros Island, Baja California.

are recognised. The milk snake, *L. triangulum* has an even larger range, from Canada well into South America and, at present, 25 subspecies have been described: several of these are of rather dubious status. Milk snakes are brightly coloured 'false coral' snakes, as are three species of mountain kingsnakes (*L. ruthveni*, *pyromelana* and *zonata*). All species are medium-sized snakes with smooth shiny scales and cylindrical bodies. They are powerful constrictors of mammals, birds and other reptiles, including venomous snakes. Most are nocturnal but they may be active during the day during cooler weather. All species are oviparous, with clutches ranging from three or four in mountain kingsnakes to over 20 in some of the large forms of the common kingsnake. A ninth species, *L. webbi*, was described in 2005 from

Mexico but there has been some doubt as to its validity.

■ *Captivity* Very popular species. All adapt very well to captive conditions without elaborate requirements. They will eat rodents readily, with the possible exception of newly hatched mountain kingsnakes, which tend to be small and may require lizards at first.

Lamprophis (house snakes) At least fourteen species with a possibility that *L. fuliginosus mentalis*, from Namaqualand, will be elevated to a full species in due course. The brown house snake, *L. fuliginosus*, is one of the most familiar snakes in southern Africa while juvenile

The grey-banded kingsnake, *Lampropeltis alterna*, is a highly variable species. This form, with wide orange and grey bands, is often known as 'Blair's form'.

semi-arid scrub to rainforests. Mainly nocturnal and arboreal. They feed on a variety of vertebrates, and some species eat the eggs of leaf-nesting frogs. Rear-fanged species which probably present no danger to humans. Oviparous.

Leptodrymus A monotypic genus containing *L. pulcherrimus* from Central America. A medium-sized snake found in rainforests up to 1,300 m (4,300 ft). Uncommon and poorly known.

Leptophis Ten species from Mexico to Argentina. Medium-sized to large snakes with slender bodies and narrow heads. Usually bright green in colour and known as 'parrot snakes'. When alarmed they hold their mouths open, displaying the bright blue interior. Arboreal, though also found on the ground. Diurnal and fast moving. Thought to feed mainly on lizards, probably also snakes, birds and small mammals. Oviparous.

Lepturophis Two species in the genus, *L. albofuscus*, and *L. borneensis*, from Indonesia and Malaysia. Medium-sized arboreal snakes.

L. aurora, are among the most colourful. All occur in Africa apart from the dubious *L. geometricus*, from Seychelles, which may be removed from the genus at some point in the future. As far as is known, they are all powerful constrictors that eat small mammals and lizards, and all are oviparous.

■ *Captivity* Several species are rare and some are unsuitable on account of their preference for lizards. The brown house snake, *L. fuliginosus*, is by far the most widely kept species. It eats small rodents quite readily and is undemanding regarding temperature. It lays up to 16 eggs per clutch and will often breed continuously throughout the year in captivity. The other species, which are not frequently bred, lay smaller clutches.
Langaha Three bizarre tree snakes from Madagascar. All species have nasal appendages, the purpose of which is probably cryptic but the shape and size varies between males and females.

Leioheterodon Three species from Madagascar. Medium-sized snakes with powerful bodies and slightly upturned snouts. Found in forested areas, where

they actively hunt for a variety of prey, including buried amphibians. Oviparous.

Leptodeira Nine species from North, Central and South America. Medium-sized snakes with slender, laterally compressed bodies, wide heads and large eyes. Found in a range of habitats, from

▼ The aurora house snake, *Lamprophis aurora*, from South Africa, and one of the most attractive members of the genus.

▲ Madagascan hognose snake, *Leioheterodon madagascariensis*.

Limnophis A monotypic genus containing only the striped swamp snake, *L. bicolor*, with a small range in southern Africa. This small species feeds on fish and amphibians and is oviparous. Otherwise poorly known.

Liochlorophis A single species, the smooth green snake, *L. vernalis*, from North America. A slender, bright green snake that rarely grows to one metre. It lives in grasslands, bogs and open woodlands and occasionally climbs into low vegetation. It eats grasshoppers, crickets, spiders, centipedes, etc. It lays eggs but these are often well developed and hatch after only 4–25 days. This species was previously in *Opheodrys*, with the rough green snake.
■ *Captivity* This species does poorly in captivity for reasons that are not fully understood and it would be better if it were not collected.

Lioheterophis A monotypic genus containing only *L. iheringi*, from Brazil. A small snake that is found in damp places and feeds on frogs. Poorly known.

Liopeltis Seven species from southern and Southeast Asia. Small to medium-sized snakes with slender bodies. Terrestrial, found in forests, usually close to water. Thought to feed on amphibians and lizards. Oviparous.

Liophidium Eight species from Madagascar and neighbouring islands. Small snakes with slender, cylindrical bodies. Found mainly in forested regions but otherwise very poorly known.

Liophis Almost 50 species from Central and South America and the West Indies, including species previously placed in the genera *Dromicus*, *Leimadophis* and *Lygophis*. Small to medium-sized snakes with cylindrical bodies and smooth scales. They are found in a variety of habitat types, including swamps, grasslands, rainforests and cloud forests. Agile and nervous snakes that bite when handled. Rear-fanged but not considered dangerous. They feed on lizards, fish, frogs and the eggs and larvae of frogs. Oviparous.

Liopholidophis Ten species from Madagascar. Small to medium-sized snakes about which little is known.

Lycodon Thirty-five species with a wide range from Pakistan, through India and Sri Lanka, Indo-China and the Philippines, to the Cook Islands, Australia. Many have gone under other names in the past. Small to medium-sized snakes, often referred to as "wolf snakes", with smooth, shiny, scales, flattened heads and small eyes. Some are banded and can be confused with the highly venomous common krait, from the same region but, although they are rear-fanged, they pose no threat to healthy humans. Secretive, terrestrial snakes. Oviparous.

Lycodonomorphus Six medium-sized species found in Central, East and southern Africa. Semi-aquatic snakes that tend to be nocturnal, feeding on frogs, tadpoles and fish. Oviparous.

Lycodryas Two species of tree snakes, *L. maculatus* and *L. sanctijohannis*, from the Comoros Islands, situated between northern Madagascar and the African mainland. Small, slender and arboreal, with large eyes and vertical pupils. Thought to be oviparous but poorly known.

Lycognathophis A monotypic genus containing only *L. seychellensis* from the Seychelles Islands. A medium-sized snake that is thought to be diurnal and terrestrial, but is otherwise the species is poorly known.

Lycophidion (African wolf snakes) Up to 18 species found in Africa south of the Sahara. Medium sized snakes that feed primarily on diurnal lizards which they catch while they are asleep at night. Oviparous.

Lystrophis Five species from South America, as far south as Argentina. Small to medium-sized snakes with thick bodies and an upturned snout, similar in build to *Heterodon*, to which they are closely related. *L. semicinctus* is a brightly banded species that may mimic coral snakes. *L. dorbignyi* is less colourful (and may mimic terrestrial pit vipers), while *L. histricus* has coral markings when young but later becomes brown. Diurnal and crepuscular snakes that feed mainly on toads. Oviparous.
■ *Captivity* Only occasionally available. Potentially interesting captives but often difficult to feed unless toads are available.

Lytorhynchus (leaf-nosed snakes) Four species from North Africa, the Middle East and central Asia. Small snakes with an enlarged rostral scale. They live in arid places, including sand dunes and gravel deserts. They are nocturnal and eat lizards, especially geckos. Rare and poorly known.

Macrocalamus Five species of mountain reed snakes from isolated mountain ranges of West Malaysia, several only recently described and some known from very few specimens. Biology poorly known but probably oviparous.

Macropisthodon Four species from India, Sri Lanka, southern China and Southeast Asia. Medium-sized, stocky snakes that are terrestrial or semi-aquatic. Rear-fanged species that mimic Asian pit vipers of the genus *Agkistrodon*. Diurnal

or nocturnal, preferring open country and feeding mainly on frogs. Oviparous.

Macroprotodon A monotypic genus containing only the false smooth snake, or cowled, snake, *M. cucullatus*, from southwestern Europe, North Africa and the Near East. The subspecies *M. c. brevis*, from Portugal and parts of Spain, is sometimes elevated to a full species. A small, secretive snake with a flattened head and small eyes. It feeds mainly on lizards which are captured at night when they are hiding, especially in old stone walls. Rear-fanged but much too small to be of any danger to man. Oviparous.

Madagascarophis Four species from Madagascar. Medium-sized, arboreal species with slender bodies, wide heads and large eyes. They apparently feed on lizards and frogs. Oviparous.

Malpolon Two species, *M. moilensis* and *M. monspessulanus*, found in southern Europe, North Africa and the Middle East. Large, fast-moving, diurnal snakes with slender bodies and a narrow head. They feed on other reptiles, small mammals and birds, especially ground-nesting and burrow-nesting species, such as bee eaters. Rear-fanged and aggressive. The effects of the venom on man vary with the severity of the bite but can produce localised swelling and nausea. Oviparous.

■ *Captivity* Rarely kept on account of their fierce temperament and tendency to damage themselves by racing around the cage and striking at the glass.

Manolepis A monotypic genus containing only *M. putnami*, from Mexico. A small, terrestrial snake about which little appears to be known.

Masticophis (coachwhips) Eight species found from southern North America down into northern South America. Fast-moving diurnal snakes with long, slender bodies and streamlined heads. They are active hunters of lizards and small mammals, often quartering the ground with their heads raised slightly. They usually attempt to escape by fleeing, but, if cornered, they bite fiercely. Oviparous, laying clutches of up to 20 eggs.
■ *Captivity* Not very suitable as captives due to their nervous and aggressive disposition. They tend to rush wildly around their cages when disturbed and frequently damage their snouts on the sides.

Mastigodryas Eleven species from Central and South America (Mexico to Argentina). Closely related to *Coluber* and *Masticophis*. Medium-sized snakes with slender bodies, narrow heads and large eyes. Rapid, diurnal hunters, feeding on amphibians, lizards, other

▲ *Liophis poecilogyrus* from the Amazon Basin.

snakes, reptile eggs, birds and small mammals. Oviparous.

Mehelya (file snakes) Ten species found throughout Africa south of the Sahara. Their body is almost triangular in cross-section and their scales are heavily keeled, hence the common name. They feed on snakes and other small vertebrates, which they constrict. Oviparous.

Meizodon A genus of five species, found in Africa. Small, secretive, diurnal snakes that feed on small lizards and frogs. Oviparous.

Micropisthodon A monotypic genus containing only *M. ochraceus* from Madagascar. A small snake about which little is known.

Mimophis A monotypic genus containing *M. mahfalensis*, from Madagascar. Closely related to the African genus *Psammophis*. A medium-sized snake with a narrow head and keeled dorsal scales. Diurnal and terrestrial. Thought to feed on lizards.

Montaspis A monotypic genus containing only *M. gilvomaculata*, from Natal, first discovered in 1990, and known only from three specimens. A small snake,

▲ *Malopolon moilensis* from Egypt.

black in colour with cream spots on the lips and a cream chin. Found near cold mountain streams at high altitude. Rear-fanged and thought to feed on frogs. Oviparous, otherwise poorly known.

Myersophis A monotypic genus containing only *M. alpestris*. This medium-sized snake is known only from Banaue, the Philippines and is rare. Its biology is completely unknown.

Myron A monotypic genus containing only Richardson's mangrove snake, *M. richardsoni*. A small snake found in New Guinea and along the northern coast of Australia, this rare species inhabits the intertidal zone on mudflats and in mangrove forests. It feeds on crabs and small fish. Viviparous but poorly known.

Natriciteres (**marsh snakes**) Three species, found in tropical Africa. Small snakes that feed on frogs and fish. Unusual among snakes in being able to break off their tail if grasped. Oviparous, laying up to eight eggs per clutch.

Natrix Four species found in Europe, North Africa and western Asia. Formerly included a great many additional species now placed in various other genera such as *Nerodia* (North America) and *Rhabdophis* (Asia). Medium-sized to large snakes that live in damp situations. Two species, *N. maura* and *N. tessellata*, are practically semi-aquatic but the grass snake, *N. natrix*, may sometimes be found away from water. All species eat amphibians, including tadpoles, and fish. The grass snake also takes small mammals and birds occasionally. Oviparous.
■ *Captivity* Quite easily maintained in

captivity on live or prepared fish, but with a rather nervous disposition. They rarely bite but may release an obnoxious fluid from their cloacal glands. Captive breeding is possible but rarely attempted.

Nerodia (**American water snakes**) Ten species found in North America: mostly in the southeast, but *N. valida* occurs on the Pacific side of northern Mexico and in Baja California. Medium-sized snakes with thick-set bodies and heavily keeled scales. Highly aquatic species that swim well and are rarely found more than a short distance away from water. They feed mainly on amphibians and fish. When captured, they often bite and invariably release a foul-smelling fluid from the cloacal glands. Viviparous, giving birth to up to 30 young (although litters of almost 100 have been recorded).
■ *Captivity* Easy to keep in captivity, and some species settle down well. Others, however, do not and remain bad tempered. They can be fed on whole or sliced fish, which should be supplemented with vitamins. Because their metabolic rate is faster than that of most other snakes, they require frequent feeding if they are to remain in good health and, especially, if they are to breed. Captive breeding takes places quite frequently and the young will often eat small pieces of fish as well as tadpoles, etc.

Ninia Nine species found in Central and northern South America, including Trinidad. Small, secretive snakes that live on the rainforest floor among leaf litter, presumed to feed on invertebrates, small lizards and small amphibians. They flatten their bodies and may raise their head and neck when alarmed. Oviparous.

Nothopsis A monotypic genus containing only *N. rugosus*, from Central America and the Pacific coastal region of northwestern South America. A small species which is found in warm, humid forests. Possibly aquatic or semi-aquatic. Nothing is known of its diet or reproduction.

Oligodon (**kukri snakes**) A very large genus, containing nearly 70 species. Small to medium-sized snakes found from Central Asia and the Middle East, India, Burma, southern China into Indo-China and Southeast Asia. May be nocturnal or diurnal and feed on invertebrates, lizards,

◄ Broad-banded water snake, *Nerodia fascita confluens*.

porphyraceus, from China and Southeast Asia. Up to seven subspecies are recognised, some of which may turn out to be full species. It is slender, with a long narrow head and is nocturnal and oviparous. Formerly assigned to *Elaphe*.

Orthriophis Four medium to large rat snakes from Asia, previously included in *Elaphe*. Large snakes, with narrow heads and slender bodies. The beauty snake, *O. taeniurus*, occurs in many subspecies, including a cave-dwelling form, *O. t. ridleyi*. Other species are Mollendorff's rat snake, *O. mollendorffi*, the eastern trinket snake, *O. cantoris*, and the poorly known *O. hodgsonii*. All are from Southeast Asia and the Far East. Mostly terrestrial although some are good climbers, and all are oviparous.

■ *Captivity* The beauty snake is widely bred in captivity and freely available, whereas the others are much rarer. Large accommodation is required for all species as they are active and often nervous. They usually feed readily on rodents but imported animals are often in poor shape and rarely thrive.

Oxybelis (vine snakes) Four species from southern Arizona to Brazil, Bolivia and Peru. Medium-sized, slender snakes, with elongated, pointed heads. Their eyes are large and have round pupils. Brown or green in colour. Highly arboreal species from moist forest habitats. Rear-fanged snakes that may open their mouths widely when threatened, sometimes biting as a last resort. Diurnal hunters that prey mainly on lizards. Oviparous.

Oxyrhabdium Two species, *O. leporinum* and *O. modestum*, endemic to the Philippines. Medium-sized snakes with cylindrical bodies and smooth scales. They have pointed snouts and burrow in rotting logs, leaf litter and forest debris. Presumably nocturnal but their habits are poorly known despite their numbers.

Oxyrhopus Thirteen species found from Mexico to South America as far south as Peru and Brazil. Medium-sized snakes with smooth scales. Brightly banded in red and black or red, white and black, like coral snakes. Terrestrial and diurnal, feeding on rodents, lizards, amphibians

---

frogs and reptile eggs. Their scales are smooth and their rostral scale is enlarged and slightly upturned. Enlarged and recurved fangs at the rear of their mouth are used to slit the shells of reptile eggs and may also help in grasping smooth or slippery prey. They are said to resemble the kukri knives used by the Gurkha troops. Some species are known to be oviparous, and the others are assumed to be. Recorded clutches tend to be small, usually six eggs or less.

■ *Captivity* Rarely available but some species appear to be quite easily cared for, eating small rodents, etc. *O. formosanus* has been bred in captivity.

Omoadiphas Two species, *O. aurula* and *O. texiguatensis*, from Honduras. Small. slender leaf-litter snakes that probably feed on earthworms and other soft-bodied invertebrates.

Oocatochus A monotypic genus containing only *O. rufodorsatus*, a species previously assigned to *Elaphe*, but never comfortable in that genus being the only semi-aquatic species and the only live-bearing one, among other differences.

Opheodrys (green snakes) A single species, the rough green snake, *O. aestivus*, from North America. A small, slender snake that is green or greyish green with keeled scales, separating it from the smooth green snake,

---

Liochlorophis vernalis, which has smooth scales. Mainly terrestrial, living in low vegetation where it feds on insects and spiders. Oviparous, laying up to 15 eggs.

■ *Captivity* The rough green snake usually does very well in a cage with plenty of cover. It should be sprayed occasionally to raise the humidity, and a constant supply of insects, including caterpillars and moth larvae should be available. Specimens have been known to live for many years and breed annually.

Opisthotropis Eleven species found in southern China, Indo-China, and on some Indonesian islands. Some species are known from very few specimens. Small to medium sized snakes which may be totally aquatic or semi-aquatic, depending on species: several are found in or around fast, clear, mountain streams. Their scales are smooth to strongly keeled. Nocturnal, feeding on fish, amphibians including tadpoles, freshwater shrimps and earthworms. Oviparous, laying clutches of eggs close to water.

Oreocalamus A monotypic genus containing only *O. hanitschi* from Borneo. A small species that has only occasionally been collected and about which little is known.

Oreophis A monotypic genus containing only the red mountain rat snake, *O.*

◄ Red mountain rat snake, *Oreophis porphyraceus*, from Southeast Asia.

and other snakes. Rear-fanged but not aggressive. Oviparous.

Pantherophis Four North American snakes previously assigned to *Elaphe* and known as rat snakes. *Pantherophis guttatus* is the Corn Snake, the most popular pet species, and *P. obsoletus* is the American rat snake, with many regional colour forms. Medium-sized, slender and agile species, all of which are mainly nocturnal and all oviparous, with clutches of six to over 20. They range from Canada to Mexico.

■ *Captivity* Among the most popular species in captivity, especially the Corn Snake, *P. guttatus*, which is bred in huge numbers for the pet trade. A variety of colour forms, including many selectively bred mutants with fanciful names are available in this species. In general all species, and many from associated genera, are very easily accommodated and bred. They are seasonal breeders, mating in the spring and laying their eggs in summer, although Baird's rat snake, *P. bairdi*, may breed a little later than the others. Although some individuals remain nervous and even aggressive, they generally calm down well in captivity and are widely considered to be among the best choices for beginners as well as advanced hobbyists.

Parahelicops A small genus, possibly monotypic, from Southeast Asia. Very poorly known.

Pararhabdophis A monotypic genus containing only *P. chapaensis*, from Indo-China. A medium-sized snake about which almost nothing is known.

Pararhadinaea One species, *P. melanogaster* from Madagascar. A small burrowing species whose history is poorly known.

Pareas Eleven species of slug-eating snakes from China, Indo-China and Southeast Asia and Borneo. Slender snakes with short, wide heads and blunt snouts. Their skulls are modified to enable them to extract snails from their shells. Three species previously included here are now referred to a separate genus, *Asthenodipsas*.

Phalotris Twelve species of small fossorial leaf-litter snakes from Brazil, sometimes assigned to *Elapomorphus*. Very poorly known; some are only recently recognised as distinct species.

Philodryas Twenty-one species of medium-sized snakes with slender, graceful bodies and narrow heads. Often called racers or whipsnakes, many are green in colour and arboreal but some, such as the Galapagos species, *P. hoodensis*, are terrestrial and brown. Diurnal in habit feeding on birds, bats, frogs, lizards and snakes. Oviparous.

Philothamnus (**green snakes and bush snakes**) Eighteen species found in Africa south of the Sahara. Slender, diurnal snakes with large eyes that feed mainly on frogs. Most species are green and live among low vegetation. Oviparous.

Phimophis Six species from Central and South America. Small to medium-sized snakes with modified rostral scales, which are turned up and overhang the lower jaw. Terrestrial and burrowing snakes that live in open situations and are thought to feed mainly on insects and their larvae. Oviparous.

Phyllorhynchus (**leaf-nosed snakes**) Two species, *P. browni* and *P. decurtatus*, from southwestern North America, including Mexico, confined mainly to the Sonoran Desert region. Small snakes in which the rostral scale is enlarged and modified and may be used to protect the snout as it is pushed into crevices in search of food, mainly lizards and their eggs.

Pituophis (**gopher, pine and bull snakes**) Pituophis (gopher, pine and bull snakes). Five species from North America. *P. deppei* and *P. lineaticollis*, are restricted to Mexico, *P. catenifer* is the gopher snake, with several subspecies across the United States (one of which, *P. c. sayi*, is known as the bull snake), *P. melanoleucus* is the pine snake also with several subspecies, and *P. ruthveni* is the endangered Louisiana pine snake. These are large, impressive, snakes with keeled scales and powerful, muscular bodies. They may hiss loudly and strike aggressively if cornered although their temperament varies. Diurnal, but nocturnal in hot weather, and feeding almost entirely on small to medium-sized mammals such as mice and rats (and therefore of great benefit to farmers and gardeners). Oviparous, laying clutches of up to 24 eggs.

■ *Captivity* Popular snakes with amateur snake keepers. They normally settle down well and feed readily although some forms can be somewhat irascible. Bred in fairly large numbers, especially several of the rarer forms. A number of colour and pattern variations are known.

Plagiopholis Five species found in China, Burma and Thailand. Small snakes, terrestrial but otherwise poorly known.

Platyceps Nine species previously placed in *Coluber*. Very slender snakes, some known as whipsnakes, from eastern Europe, North Africa and Central Asia, as far east as northern India. Diurnal, fast-moving species with large eyes. Oviparous.

Pliocercus Two species found from Mexico to the Amazon Basin. (Seven species according to some authorities.) Medium-sized snakes, some of which (or some forms of which) are bicoloured or tricoloured 'false coral' snakes. They live in tropical lowland forests and feed mainly on frogs.

Poecilopholis A monotypic genus, containing only *P. cameroensis* from Cameroon. Their relationships are unclear although they are possibly related to *Aparallactus* (Atractaspididae). Natural history poorly known.

Prosymna (shovel-snouted snakes) Thirteen species found in Africa south of the Sahara. They are small, burrowing species that live in loose soil. They feed on reptile

▼ Common mock viper, *Psammodynastes pulverulentus*, a very wide-ranging species from China, India and Southeast Asia.

eggs, which they swallow whole. Oviparous, laying a few elongated eggs.

Psammodynastes (mock vipers) Two species of small snakes from Southeast Asia, Indo-China and the Philippines. *P. pulverulentus* is a common, wide-ranging species throughout southern China, Southeast Asia and the Philippines and has been found at altitudes over 2,750 m (9,000 ft) in Malaysia. *P. pictus* is less common and has a more limited range in Malaysia, Sumatra and Java. Both have angular heads and large eyes with vertical pupils. Their scales are smooth. Mainly nocturnal, feeding on lizards and frogs. Viviparous, producing small litters.

Psammophis (sand snakes) A genus of over 20 species found throughout Africa and the Near East but *Psammophis condanarus* occurs in Burma and Thailand and *P. lineolatus* ranges into western China. A single record from Indonesia is probably in error or is based on an accidental introduction. Small to large in size, these fast-moving, diurnal snakes feed mainly on lizards, which they run down. They live on the ground, or in low vegetation, usually in arid environments. Rear-fanged and venomous, their bite may cause local swelling and pain in man. At least some species will discard their tail as a defensive measure, although it is not completely regenerated. Oviparous.

Psammophylax (skaapstekers) Three species found in central and southern Africa. Medium-sized snakes that feed on small mammals, lizards and frogs. They

▲ *Psammophis sibilans leopardinus*, from Namibia and southern Angola.

are rear-fanged but rarely bite. Although the venom is highly toxic, it is released in such small doses that skaapstekers are not considered dangerous to man. Their reproduction is variable: *P. tritaeniatus* and *P. rhombeatus* are oviparous, but *P. variabilis* may be oviparous or viviparous, depending on subspecies.

■ *Captivity* Not readily available, but good captives, they usually settle down well and feed readily on small rodents. Not widely bred in captivity and feeding the small hatchlings could be a problem.

Pseudablabes A monotypic genus containing only *P. agassisi*, from southern South America. A small burrowing snake about which hardly anything is known.

Pseudaspis A monotypic genus containing only the highly variable mole snake, *Pseudaspis cana*, which is found throughout almost the whole of the southern half of Africa. A large, bulky species, growing to over 2 m (6½ ft) in length, it feeds mainly on small mammals. Viviparous, with litters of up to 100 young.

■ *Captivity* The mole snake makes a good pet. Freshly caught snakes may be aggressive but soon calm down. Newborn young may refuse to eat rodents, preferring small lizards to start with.

Pseudoboa Five species from Central and South America, including Trinidad and Tobago. Medium-sized, terrestrial snakes that are found in rainforests, often near water. The pupils are vertically elliptical.

Nocturnal, feeding on lizards, amphisbaenians, snakes and small mammals. Rear-fanged species that nevertheless constrict their prey. Oviparous: *P. neuwiedii* sometimes lays its eggs in ant nests.

Pseudoboodon Four species, including two recently described, from the highlands of Ethiopia and Eritrea. Related to the house snakes, *Lamprophis*, but not well known. *P. lemniscatus* is viviparous but the method of reproduction in other species is unknown.

Pseudoelaphe A monotypic genus containing only the Central American rat snake, *P. flavirufa*, a slender, medium-sized snake formerly assigned to *Elaphe*. It is strictly nocturnal and oviparous.

Pseudocyclophis A monotypic genus containing only *P. persicus*, from the Middle East and into central Asia. Formerly placed in the genus *Eirenis*, from which this genus differs mainly in having a combination of 15 scale rows around its midbody and a slightly different arrangement of scales on top of its head. A small, secretive snake, which is probably oviparous but otherwise poorly known.

Pseudoeryx A monotypic genus containing only *P. plicatilis*, from Brazil and Paraguay. A medium-sized aquatic species that is thought to eat fish and amphibians. Poorly known.

Pseudoficimia A monotypic genus, containing *P. frontalis*, from Mexico. *Pseudoleptodeira* Two species, *P. latifasciata* and *P. uribei*, from Mexico. Similar to *Leptodeira*. Small, terrestrial snakes about which little is known.

Pseudorabdion Twelve species (including two formerly placed in *Idiopholis*, three in *Agrophis* and one in *Typhlogeophis*). Distributed throughout Southeast Asia and the Philippines. Small burrowing snakes with cylindrical bodies and smooth scales. Usually found among leaf litter and beneath rotting logs, coconut husks, etc. They probably eat earthworms and other soft-bodied invertebrates and are thought to be oviparous. Otherwise very poorly known and, in several cases, rarely collected.

Pseudotomodon A monotypic genus containing only *P. trigonatus*, from South America. Viviparous, otherwise very poorly known.

Pseudoxenodon (bamboo snakes) Six species from China and neighbouring regions and parts of Indonesia. The snakes are small to medium-sized. Terrestrial and nocturnal, feeding on amphibians and lizards. Their reproductive behaviour is unknown.

Pseudoxyrhopus Eleven species from Madagascar. Small to medium-sized snakes whose natural history is poorly known.

Pseustes Five species from Central and South America, including Trinidad. Medium-sized to large snakes with slender bodies and large eyes. They are terrestrial but climb occasionally and feed on birds, lizards and frogs. Oviparous.

Psomophis Three species of small ground snakes from Brazil and southeast Bolivia, previously listed under *Liophis* and *Rhadinaea*. Poorly known.

Ptyas Eight species found throughout much of central, southern and Southeast Asia. Large snakes with powerful bodies, wide heads and large eyes. Diurnal snakes that adapt to a wide range of habitats and conditions. Often found around human habitations, where they feed on rodents, although amphibians, birds, lizards and snakes may also be eaten. Oviparous, producing clutches of up to 20 large eggs. Six species previously assigned to *Zaocys* are included in this genus.

■ *Captivity* Impressive snakes for large cages, but with rather unpredictable temperaments. Wild specimens are likely to be infested with parasites but, other than this, they are hardy and adapt quite well to captivity. Captive breeding has not taken place on a regular basis.

Ptychophis A monotypic genus containing only *P. flavovirgatus*, from Brazil. A small snake with keeled dorsal scales. Rear-fanged and possibly of some danger to humans. It feeds on frogs and fish. Viviparous.

Pythonodipsas A monotypic genus containing the western keeled snake, *P. carinata*, from southwestern Africa. A small nocturnal snake with fragmented scales on the top of its head, and nostrils that are directed upwards. It lives in rocky deserts and often shelters under the prostrate leaves of the strange Welwitschia plant. Nocturnal, feeding on small lizards and rodents. Reproduction unknown.

Rabdion A monotypic genus containing only *R. forsteni*, from the Celebes. A small snake about which little is known.

Regina Four species from North America, related to the North American water snakes, *Nerodia*. Small to medium-sized species that may have smooth or heavily keeled dorsal scales. *R. alleni* and *R. rigida* are sometimes placed in a separate genus, *Liodytes*, but this is not widely accepted. Semi-aquatic snakes that are found near rivers, lakes and

◀ Spotted skaapsteker, *Psammophylax rhombeatus*, a rear-fanged colubrid from southern Africa.

swamps and feed on amphibians, fish, crayfish and aquatic invertebrates such as water snails and insect larvae. Viviparous, producing litters of up to 40 young.

Rhabdophis Nineteen species widely distributed throughout central Asia, India, China, Indo-China, Southeast Asia and Japan. Closely related to *Natrix*, with which they were formerly classified. Medium-sized, semi-aquatic snakes that feed on frogs and fish. Rear-fanged and considered dangerous to humans: at least one fatality has been recorded from *R. tigrinus*. Oviparous.

Rhabdops Two species, *R. bicolor* and *R. olivaceus*, from India, northern Indo-China and China. Small to medium-sized snakes, thought to be nocturnal and to feed on soft-bodied invertebrates. Natural history poorly known.

Rhachidelus A monotypic genus containing only *R. brazili* from Brazil and Argentina. A medium-sized, stocky snake that is diurnal and terrestrial and eats mostly birds. Oviparous.

Rhadinaea Up to 40 species, although their taxonomy is in some confusion. Widespread, as currently understood, found from North America, through Central America and into South America as far south as Argentina. Small snakes

with cylindrical bodies and smooth scales. They live in a variety of habitats but are invariably secretive species, often found among leaf litter and other debris. They eat earthworms, amphibians, including their eggs, and small reptiles. Oviparous, laying small clutches of eggs.

Rhadinophanes A monotypic genus consisting of *R. monticola*, the graceful mountain snake, from Guerrero, Mexico.

***Rhamphiophis* (beaked snakes)** A genus of three species found in Africa. Large, heavy-bodied snakes that eat a wide range of prey, including small mammals and other reptiles. Oviparous, laying up to 17 eggs per clutch.

Rhinechis A monotypic genus containing only the ladder snake, *R. scalaris*, from southwest Europe. A medium-sized, nocturnal egg-layer that feeds on rodents and nestling birds. It was previously part of *Elaphe*.
■ *Captivity* Occasionally kept and bred in captivity, with no obvious problems, although it can be aggressive and unpleasant to handle at times.

Rhinobothryum Two species, *R. bovalli* and *R. lentiginosum* from Central and South America. Medium-sized snakes with slender bodies, blunt heads and slightly keeled scales. The eyes are large and have

vertical pupils. Both species are boldly marked with red, white and black bands and look like coral snakes, especially *R. bovalli*, which is almost indistinguishable from a common species, *Micrurus alleni*. Nocturnal, arboreal snakes. Reproduction unknown.

***Rhinocheilus* (long-nosed snakes)** One or two species. *R. antoni* may be a subspecies of *R. lecontei*, the long-nosed snake, which is, in any case, variable. Medium-sized snakes from southern North America including northern Mexico, found mainly in desert or semi-desert situations. Moderately slender with a narrow head and pointed snout. The upper jaw extends further forward than the lower jaw. Brightly marked in some parts of the range, where they may mimic venomous coral snakes. Mainly nocturnal, although active by day in the cooler months of the year. Terrestrial although capable of burrowing and even climbing into low vegetation. They eat mainly lizards although small mammals, and perhaps birds, are taken by some individuals. Oviparous, laying clutches of up to 12 eggs.
■ *Captivity* Attractive and well-mannered, long-nosed snakes make good captives if they can be persuaded to accept small rodents. Unfortunately, most will not.

Rhynchocalamus A monotypic genus containing only *R. melanocephams*, from the Middle East. A small snake with a slender body, found in arid habitats. Thought to feed on invertebrates and small reptiles.

Rhynchophis A monotypic genus containing only *R. boulengeri* from China and northern Vietnam. A medium-sized snake with a slender body, pointed head and an upturned rostral appendage of unknown function. Bright green in colour and arboreal but otherwise little known.

***Salvadora* (patch-nosed snakes)** Up to eight species from North and Central

America. Medium-sized snakes with slender bodies and narrow heads. The rostral scale is enlarged. Diurnal, fast-moving hunters of lizards and snakes, although small rodents are also eaten. All species are pale in colour with a series of longitudinal lines running along their dorsal surfaces. Oviparous.

Saphenophis Five species from northwestern South America (Colombia, Ecuador and Peru). Small snakes from humid regions. Thought to be diurnal but their natural history is practically unknown.

Scaphiodontophis Two species from Central America. Small snakes with slender cylindrical bodies. *S. annulatus* is a coral snake mimic. Thought to eat lizards and other snakes. Oviparous.

Scaphiophis (shovel-nosed snakes) Two species, *S. albopunctatus* and *S. raffreyi,* with a combined range covering much of Africa. Medium-sized snakes with modified rostral scales that are thought to be used for burrowing through loose, dry soil. Oviparous. *S. raffreyi* was previously treated as a subspecies of *S. albopunctatus.*

Scolecophis A monotypic genus containing only *S. atrocinctus,* from Central America. A small, nocturnal snake, usually found among leaf litter and under forest debris. A brightly marked 'false coral' snake. It eats centipedes. Biology poorly known.

Seminatrix A monotypic genus containing only *S. pygaea,* the black swamp snake, found in the southeastern corner of North America. A small, brightly marked snake, being glossy black with a red or pink belly. It is restricted to aquatic habitats, especially where the introduced water hyacinth occurs in large quantities: the snakes like to hunt among the crowns and roots of the floating plants for their prey, consisting of small fish, tadpoles, salamanders and leeches. Viviparous, giving birth from five to 15 young.

Senticolis A monotypic genus containing only *S. triaspis,* the neotropical rat snake, formerly placed in the genus *Elaphe.* It occurs in North and Central America, and just enters the United States in southern Arizona. A medium-sized, moderately slender snake with a narrow head. It has slightly keeled scales and a long tail. A semi-arboreal species that feeds on lizards, birds and mammals. Oviparous.

Sibon (slug-eating snakes or snail suckers) Up to eighteen species, including three described this century, occurring in Mexico, Central and South America. Three species are sometimes placed in a separate genus, *Tropidodipsas.* Medium-sized but very slender arboreal snakes with laterally flattened bodies, relatively wide heads and large eyes that live in rain forests. They eat slugs and snakes and have specialised jaws for drawing snails out of their shells, paralleling the Asian *Pareas* species. *S. sartorii* is apparently terrestrial. Oviparous.

Sibynomorphus Eight species found in South America. Small to medium-sized snakes with cylindrical, moderately stout, bodies and blunt heads. Snail-eating snakes, closely related to *Sibon* but more terrestrial, found under stones in fields, etc. Presumed to be oviparous but rare and poorly known.

Sibynophis Nine species found in India, Sri Lanka, Indo-China, southern China and Southeast Asia, including the Philippines. Small to medium-sized snakes with slender bodies. Poorly known snakes that have been collected from lowland and montane rainforests. Apparently oviparous.

Simophis Two species, *S. rhmostoma* and *S. rhodei,* from Brazil and Paraguay. Small to medium-sized, slender species with smooth scales. Found in open fields and thought to feed on small mammals *S. rhinostoma* is claimed to be a false coral snake. Oviparous.

Sinonatrix Four species from China and neighbouring regions. As the name suggests, the genus is closely related to *Natrix.* The snakes are semi-aquatic and probably feed on fish and amphibians. *S. percarinata* is oviparous whereas there is some evidence that *S. annularis* is viviparous.

Siphlophis Six species of poorly known snakes from Central and South America. They have been included in a variety of other genera in the past.

Sonora (ground snakes) Three highly dimorphic species from North America. *S. semiannulata* occurs in the United States (and incorporates *S. episcopa,* which is no longer valid) whereas *S. aemula* and *S. michoacanensis* are from northern Mexico. Small, terrestrial snakes restricted to arid desert and semi-desert habitats. Some forms are brightly coloured with rings of red, black and white, whereas others are more uniform. They eat invertebrates, including spiders and scorpions. Oviparous.
■ *Captivity* Not popular, but quite easily kept in small cages with a dry substrate and some flat rocks under which the snakes can hide. A variety of cultured and collected invertebrate food can be offered, including crickets and spiders. Captive breeding has probably not been achieved, at least not intentionally.

Sordellina A monotypic genus containing only *S. punctata* from Brazil. A small snake that is found near water and apparently eats frogs and tadpoles. Oviparous.

Spalerosophis (diadem snakes) Five species of medium-sized terrestrial snakes from North Africa and the Middle East. They feed on lizards and rodents and are oviparous. Occasionally kept in captivity but not popular because they can be nervous and aggressive.

Spilotes (tiger snake, chicken snake) A monotypic genus containing only *S. pullatus,* from Mexico to Argentina. A large, powerful snake with highly variable markings. The body is flattened from side to side, the head is narrow and the eyes large. Unusual in having an even number of dorsal scale rows (also found in *Chironius*) and without a vertebral row. Found in dry scrubby habitats, often near human settlements. Arboreal, feeding on amphibians, birds (including their eggs), mammals and other reptiles. Often very aggressive. Oviparous.
■ *Captivity* Attractive specimens make impressive displays in large cages. Fairly easily maintained once they have acclimatised but rather nervous. Regular captive breeding appears not to have taken place.

Stegonotus About 10 species found throughout Southeast Asia, the Philippines, New Guinea and northern Australia. Medium-sized to large snakes with cylindrical bodies and smooth shiny scales. Found in a variety of habitats but mostly terrestrial, feeding on fish, amphibians and tadpoles, lizards, snakes and small mammals. Oviparous.

Stenophis Fifteen medium-sized snakes from Madagascar. Slender, arboreal species with broad heads and large eyes. Nocturnal. Some are boldly banded whereas others are blotched or have uniform coloration. Many species are only recently described.

Stenorrhina Two species, *S. degenhardtii* and *S. freminvillii*, from Central and northern South America. Small, cylindrical snakes with smooth scales and small heads. Nocturnal or diurnal in habits and thought to feed on spiders. Oviparous.

Stilosoma A monotypic genus containing only the short-tailed snake, *S. extenuatum*, with a very limited range in central Florida. This species is very small and slender and spends most of its time beneath the surface in dry sandy soils. It apparently eats small snakes, which it constricts. Lizards may also be taken. Oviparous but otherwise a poorly known species.

Stoliczkia Two species, *S. borneensis* from Borneo and *S. khasiensis* from India. Small snakes about which very little is known.

Storeria Two species, *S. dekayi* and *S. occipitomaculata*, found in North and Central America. Small, secretive snakes with keeled scales, usually found in damp situations, where they search for slugs, snails, earthworms and other invertebrates. Viviparous, giving birth to litters of up to 15 young.
■ *Captivity* Although there is very little interest in these small species, they will live quite well in a vivarium with a damp substrate, not too much heat and a constant supply of earthworms and slugs.

Symphimus Two species, *S. leucostomus* and *S. mayae*, from Mexico and Belize. Small snakes that prefer dry environments, thought to be burrowers and feeding mainly on lizards.

Sympholis A monotypic genus containing only *S. lippiens*, from Mexico. A small species of 'false coral' snake, with yellow and black bands on its body.

Fossorial and secretive. Its biology is poorly known.

Synophis Four species from Colombia and Ecuador. Small to medium-sized snakes with slender bodies, narrow heads and large eyes. Terrestrial and diurnal, often found in damp habitats and thought to feed on amphibians and small lizards. Oviparous.

Tachymenis Seven species from western and northern South America. Small snakes that are found in dry habitats, sometimes at moderate altitudes. Terrestrial species, thought to feed mainly on lizards. Viviparous.

Taeniophallus (forest snakes) Eight species of slender terrestrial snakes from South America. Poorly known, thought to be oviparous.

Tantalophis A monotypic genus containing only *T. discolor* from Mexico. A small, terrestrial snake that is poorly known.

Tantilla (black-headed snakes or crowned snakes) A large genus of about 60 similar species found from southern North America to Argentina. Very small, secretive snakes, with cylindrical bodies and smooth scales. They are characterized by a black patch on the top of their heads. Found in a wide variety of habitats, and usually nocturnal. They feed on insects and larvae and in some cases, apparently, small fish. The Rim Rock black-headed snake, *T. oolitica*, is classed as endangered and several other species have very small ranges. Oviparous, laying small clutches of up to three eggs.

Tantillita Three species from Central America. Closely related to the black-headed snakes, *Tantilla*, which it resembles in most respects.

Telescopus (tiger snakes and cat snakes) Twelve species distributed throughout Africa, southeastern Europe and the Near East, mainly in arid situations. Slender, nocturnal snakes with large, prominent eyes and vertical pupils. They feed mainly on diurnal lizards, which they seek out in crevices while they are sleeping, but also take birds and small mammals. Rear-fanged but not dangerous to man. Oviparous.
■ *Captivity* A few species are occasionally kept in captivity, where they usually fare

quite well. Small individuals of some species can be difficult to feed but adults usually take mice. Probably not bred with any degree of regularity.

Tetralepis A monotypic genus containing only *T. fruhstorferi* from east Java. A small snake, found only at high altitudes with a cool, seasonal climate. Natural history poorly known.

Thamnodynastes Six species from South America (but under revision). Small to medium-sized snakes with stocky bodies, wide heads and large eyes that have vertically elliptical pupils. Terrestrial and arboreal snakes that tend to be nocturnal. Thought to eat small lizards. Rear-fanged species whose bite may produce local pain and swelling in humans. Viviparous.

Thamnophis (garter snakes and ribbon snakes) Up to 31 species, including several recently described from Mexico. Some, such as *T. sirtalis*, are divided into a number of subspecies. Small to medium-sized snakes with slender bodies and heavily keeled scales. Most species are marked with a series of longitudinal lines running the length of their bodies. Diurnal species invariably found near water or in damp situations. They feed largely upon amphibians although some also take earthworms, fish and small mammals. Viviparous, with litters ranging in size from less than 10 to almost 100, depending on species. The San Francisco garter snake, *T. sirtalis tetrataenia*, is one of the rarest snakes in North America and is legally protected.
■ *Captivity* Attractive snakes that have long been popular with enthusiasts although not always as easy to keep in good health as is often thought. Due to their rapid metabolism, they require frequent feeding and, if fish is used, vitamin and mineral supplements are advisable. If rodents are accepted, these form a better diet. Breeding takes place regularly in captivity and the young are easily reared on a diet of earthworms at first, later graduating to slices of fish. Ribbon snakes (three species) make less satisfactory captives as they prefer amphibians and often refuse to eat fish.

Thelotornis (bird or twig snakes) Three species, *T. kirtlandii*, *T. capensis* and *T. usambaricus*, recently described, found in tropical and southern Africa. Extremely slender arboreal snakes with long pointed heads growing to over 1 m (3 ft 4 in) in length. Their eyes have horizontal pupils, shaped like keyholes and they feed on lizards and small birds, relying on their cryptic coloration to ambush their prey. Rear-fanged and potentially dangerous to man. Oviparous, laying narrow, elongated eggs.

Thermophis A monotypic genus containing only *T. baileyi*, from Tibet. Natural history poorly known.

Thrasops Four species from tropical Africa. Large snakes with elegant heads. Black or green in colour with large black eyes. Arboreal, feeding on lizards, frogs and small mammals. Oviparous.
■ *Captivity* Good captives provided they are given a large cage with plenty of branches on which to climb and rest. Rodents are usually accepted in captivity. Breeding has taken place but only occasionally.

Tomodon Two species from southeastern South America. Small snakes that are thought to be terrestrial or semi-arboreal, feeding on lizards and small rodents. Viviparous.

Trachischium Five species from northern India and neighbouring countries. Small snakes that are terrestrial and probably nocturnal. Poorly known.

Tretanorhinus Four species from Mexico to northwestern South America, Cuba and some smaller West Indian islands. Small snakes that are totally aquatic. Nocturnal, feeding on small fish. Oviparous. Poorly known.

Trimetopon Ten species from Central America. Small snakes that live in rainforest habitats but which are otherwise poorly known.

Trimorphodon (lyre snakes) Two species but often divided into several subspecies, some of which are treated as full species occasionally. Medium-sized snakes with slender bodies, wide heads and large eyes. The pupils are vertical and they are nocturnal, feeding on lizards, snakes and small mammals. Terrestrial, usually found in rocky places, and oviparous.

Tripanurgos A monotypic genus containing only *T. compressus*, with a wide range in Central and South America, including Trinidad. Sometimes placed in the genus *Siphlophis*. A medium-sized but very slender snake with laterally compressed body. The head is wide and flattened, and the large eyes have vertical pupils and are red in juveniles. A nocturnal and arboreal snake that feeds mainly on frogs. Oviparous.

Tropidoclonion A monotypic genus containing only the lined snake, *T. lineatum* from North America. A small species, similar to a miniature garter snake. Often found around houses and in parks but also in open woodland and agricultural situations. Thought to feed mainly on earthworms. Viviparous.

Tropidodryas Two species found in southeastern Brazil. Small snakes that are semi-arboreal and probably diurnal. They feed on frogs, lizards, birds and rodents. Biology poorly known.

Tropidonophis Nineteen species from Indonesia and Australasia, including five species formerly placed in the genus *Macropophis*. Medium-sized to large species with heavily keeled scales. Semi-aquatic species invariably found near water, including streams, rivers and

swamps. Diurnal snakes that feed mostly on amphibians. Oviparous.

Umbrivaga Two species from northern South America. Small, terrestrial snakes that feed on small amphibians and reptiles. Natural history poorly known.

Uromacer Four species from Hispaniola and its surrounding islands. Medium-sized to large snakes, three with extremely slender bodies and narrow, pointed heads and the other, *U. catesbyi*, heavy bodied with a blunt snout. Diurnal and semi-arboreal, feeding almost entirely on terrestrial and arboreal lizards.

Uromacerina A monotypic genus containing only *U. ricardini* from Brazil. Related to *Uromacer* and similar to the members of that genus. A rare, arboreal species that eats lizards. Poorly known.

Urotheca Nine species from Central and South America, previously included in other genera such as *Dromicus* and *Rhadinaea*. Agile, terrestrial species, mostly diurnal and oviparous as far as is known.

Virginia Two species of earth snakes, *V. striatula* and *V. valeriae*, from North

▼ Namib tiger snake, *Telescopus beetzi*.

America. Small, secretive snakes that are found under rocks and debris. They like moist situations and feed largely on earthworms. Viviparous, producing small litters of young.

Waglerophis A monotypic genus, containing only *W. merremi*, from South America, sometimes placed in the genus *Xenodon*. A medium-sized, thickset snake, resembling a terrestrial pit viper. A terrestrial species that may be active by night and by day. It lives in damp habitats, near water, and feeds mainly on amphibians. When threatened it flattens its head and neck and raises them off the ground. A very aggressive species with enlarged rear fangs, thought to be used to puncture the bodies of toads. The effects of its bite on humans are not known. Oviparous.

Xenelaphis Two species, *X. ellipsifer* and *X. hexagonotus*, found in Thailand, Malaysia, Borneo and Java. Large snakes, semi-aquatic, feeding mostly on frogs.

Xenochrophis (keelbacks) Ten species, *X. piscator* has a large range, from Afghanistan right through to Southeast Asia and the Indonesian Archipelago. The other species have more limited ranges within the same region. Medium-sized snakes, closely related to *Natrix*, that live near water and feed mainly on fish. May be very numerous in suitable habitats. Rear-fanged species that may give a painful, though probably not dangerous, bite.
■ *Captivity* One species, *Xenochrophis piscator*, is often imported as 'Asian garter snakes'. Not very suitable for captivity as they often fail to feed properly.

Xenodermus A monotypic genus containing only *X. javanicus* from Burma, Thailand, the Malaysia peninsula, the Indonesian archipelago and Borneo. A small snake with three rows of tubercules running down its back. The remaining dorsal scales are keeled and those on the head are small and granular. This species often burrows and is always found near water. It is thought to feed mainly on frogs. Oviparous.

Xenodon (false vipers) Seven species found from Mexico to Argentina. Medium-sized to large, heavy-bodied snakes with broad heads. Their markings

and behaviour are similar to several species of terrestrial pit vipers, *Bothrops* and *Porthidium* species, which share their range. Sedentary rainforest species that live on the banks of rivers and feed mainly on toads. Rear-fanged and belligerent; not thought to be particularly dangerous to man but capable of giving a painful bite. Oviparous.

Xenopholis One or, possibly, two species, which are not well known. *X. scalaris* is from the Amazon Basin, and northern South America. It is a small, slender species, diurnal in habits and found in damp forests. It feeds mainly on small frogs. Reproduction unknown.

Xenoxybelis Two species of slender, elongated vine snakes from South America. Closely related to *Oxybelis* and sometimes placed in that genera. *X. argenteus* is a widespread and common species whereas *X. boulengeri* has only recently been recognised as a separate species.

Xyelodontophis A monotypic genus containing only *X. uluguruensis*, the dog-toothed vine snake, described in 2002 from the Uluguru Mountains, Tanzania. An arboreal species, similar to *Thelotornis* but lacking the characteristic horizontal pupil of members of that genus.

Xylophis Two species from southern India. Small snakes that are probably semi-fossorial but whose natural history is almost unknown.

Zamenis Five small to medium-sized European and Middle Eastern snakes previously assigned to *Elaphe*. All are slender, oviparous and mostly nocturnal. The Leopard Snake, *Z. situla*, is arguably the most colourful European snake and occurs in striped and spotted forms. *Z. lineatus*, the Italian Aesculapian snake was only recently separated from the Aesculapian snake, *Z. longissima*. The other two species are *Z. hohenackeri* and *Z. persicus* from western Asia.
■ *Captivity* The species that are generally available make good captives where they are legally available. The Leopard Snake is the most popular but all can be kept in a similar fashion to the *Pantherophis* species with which they used to be classified within *Elaphe*. *Zamenis* species, however, prefer slightly lower temperatures and, being generally smaller, are not as prolific as their North American counterparts, usually laying three to six eggs.

▼ The Transcaucasian rat snake, *Zamenis hohenackeri*, occurs on rocky mountain slopes between the Black Sea and the Caspian Sea and at lower altitudes in parts of Turkey, Lebanon and Israel. It is secretive and rarely seen.

ELAPIDAE
CORAL SNAKES, COBRAS, KRAITS, MAMBAS AND SEA SNAKES

THE ELAPIDAE INCLUDES SOME OF THE BEST KNOWN, NOT TO SAY NOTORIOUS, SNAKES. IT ALSO INCLUDES A LARGE NUMBER OF SMALL, GENERALLY INOFFENSIVE SPECIES, AND THE SEA SNAKES, WHICH ARE SOMETIMES REGARDED AS MEMBERS OF A FAMILY IN THEIR OWN RIGHT (OCCASIONALLY TWO FAMILIES), BUT ARE HERE PLACED IN TWO SEPARATE SUBFAMILIES.

Members of the Elapidae share the same general body form and scalation as the colubrids, to which they are undoubtedly very closely related and there is some dissent as to which family is the more primitive of the two. The conservative view is that the elapids evolved from colubrids or colubrid-like species and this arrangement is maintained here.

The elapids have an almost global distribution but are better represented in the southern hemisphere than the northern. They occur in southern North America, Central and South America, most of Africa excluding the most arid parts of the Sahara Desert, the whole of southern and Southeast Asia, and Australia, but are absent from the mainland of Madagascar. Marine elapids (sea snakes) are present to some extent in most tropical oceans but are absent from the Atlantic Ocean and the Caribbean. With one exception, they are most commonly found in coastal waters.

Differences between the colubrids and the elapids are limited to the arrangement of the teeth. The elapids have a pair of fixed fangs attached to the maxillary bone at the front of their upper jaw. There are no maxillary teeth immediately behind the fangs although there are teeth on the posterior part of the maxilla in most genera. The fangs are hollow, and venom can be forced through the central canal.

Like the colubrids, members of this family have radiated into many ecological niches, including the marine environment. This has led to the evolution of a varied set of characteristics in size, shape and colour. Most notable has been the convergent evolution of certain Australian forms to fill the niche left vacant by the absence of vipers on that continent: some Australian species are so viper-like that they are commonly known as 'adders'.

There are a number of schemes for subdividing this family (or families, as some authorities recognise up to three different ones). Changes within this group (or groups) of snakes are very likely in the coming years.

▼ Distribution of Elapidae I (terrestrial).

System 1 (three subfamilies or families)
a) the terrestrial species – Elapinae (or Elapidae)
b) the sea kraits – Laticaudinae (or Laticaudidae)
c) the sea snakes – Hydrophiinae (or Hydrophiidae)

System 2 (two subfamilies or families)
a) all the terrestrial species – Elapinae (or Elapidae)
b) the sea snakes and the sea kraits – Hydrophiinae (or Hydrophiidae)

System 3 (two subfamilies or families)
a) species from the Americas, Africa and Asia – Elapinae (or Elapidae)
b) the sea snakes and the sea kraits and Australasian terrestrial species – Hydrophiinae (or Hydrophiidae)

Many authorities think that the latter system most accurately reflects evolutionary history of the group and this is, broadly speaking, the scheme followed here, even though it is the least intuitive. I have retained all the species in a single family and shall deal first with the non-Australasian terrestrial species ("Elapinae") followed by the Australasian terrestrial species, the sea kraits and finally the sea snakes ("Hydrophiinae").

BUNGARINAE
Typical African and Asian elapids, including most of the well-known species such as the cobras, mambas and kraits.

Aspidelaps Two species from Africa. Short, stocky snakes with enlarged rostral scales. One species, *A. lubricus*, is a brightly marked 'coral' snake whereas the other, *A. scutatus*, is a camouflaged, burrowing species. Nocturnal, feeding mainly on other reptiles. Moderately dangerous to man. Oviparous.

Boulengerina (water cobras) Two species from Central Africa. Medium-sized snakes with moderately heavy bodies. They are unusual among elapids (except the sea snakes) in being largely aquatic in habits and feeding on fish. Potentially dangerous to humans but not normally aggressive. Oviparous.

Bungarus (kraits) Thirteen species from India; Sri Lanka, China, Indo-China and other parts of Southeast Asia. Medium-sized to large snakes with large shiny scales. Their bodies are slender and many are characteristically triangular in cross-section. Other species, though, are cylindrical or laterally compressed. The vertebral scales (those running down the centre of the dorsal surface) are large and hexagonal in shape. Most species are boldly banded in black and white or black and yellow but some are more uniformly coloured. Kraits are nocturnal and terrestrial snakes that occupy a variety of habitats. They feed almost exclusively on other snakes and are often found around human settlements. Their venom is very toxic and potentially fatal to humans. Oviparous.

Calliophis Eleven species, including those previously included in *Maticora* (coral snakes). Found from India to Indonesia. Small snakes with narrow heads and small eyes. Mostly nocturnal species that live in forests and feed on other reptiles, including burrowing snakes. Known species are oviparous. Several species have hugely elongated venom glands that extend up to one-third of the way down their body. Usually inoffensive though potentially dangerous to humans.

Dendroaspis (mambas) Four species found throughout tropical and southern Africa. Medium-sized to large snakes (occasionally over 4 m (13 ft) in the case of the black mamba, *D. polylepis*) with narrow heads. The black mamba is terrestrial but the other three species are arboreal and green in colour. Fast-moving, diurnal hunters which run down their prey, consisting of birds and small mammals. Extremely dangerous to man. Oviparous.

Elapsoidea (garter snakes) Eight species found throughout Africa south of the Sahara, including Somalia. Small, burrowing species that are often brightly coloured as juveniles. Nocturnal, feeding mainly on other reptiles. Potentially dangerous to man but unlikely to be fatal. Oviparous.

Hemachatus A monotypic genus containing only *H. haemachatus*, the rinkhals or spitting cobra. A medium-sized, stocky snake that may be plain or brightly banded. It is nocturnal and feeds on a wide range of vertebrates, especially toads. Its bite is potentially fatal to man,

▲ Western green mamba, *Dendroaspis viridis*.

and venom sprayed into the eyes causes intense pain and sometimes blindness. Viviparous, with litters occasionally numbering 50 or more.

Hemibungarus Three species. They are found in Southeast Asia and the Philippines. Small snakes with narrow heads. The body of *H. calligaster* is boldly marked with pale rings on its back and it is locally known as a 'coral' snake. Secretive species found in rotting logs and other debris in forested areas. Thought to be oviparous and to feed on other small reptiles but biology poorly known.

Micruroides A monotypic genus containing only the Sonoran coral snake, *M. euryxanthus*, from the southwestern United States and northwestern Mexico. A small snake with typical 'coral' coloration of black-white-red-white-black bands around its body. It differs from the *Micrurus* species in minor details of scalation. A secretive, nocturnal snake, often found in river washes. It feeds on lizards and other snakes and is generally inoffensive to humans. There are no recorded fatalities from its bite. Oviparous, laying small clutches of eggs.

Micrurus (coral snakes) Sixty-eight species from southern United States, through Central America and into South America as far south as central Argentina. A variety of habitats are used, from deserts to tropical rainforests. Small to medium-sized snakes with moderately slender bodies and small heads. Most

coral snakes are brightly marked, typically with rings of red, black and yellow (or white). The sequence of the rings varies somewhat and a few species have red and black rings only. Coral snakes may be active by night or by day, although diurnal species tend to be restricted to areas with plenty of cover, or they are active only during the early morning or late evening, or after heavy rain. They feed largely on other reptiles and some specialise in eating the various species of burrowing amphisbaenians that share much of their range. Although their fangs are short, coral snakes produce a potent venom. Bites from some species can be fatal to humans unless antivenom is available. Oviparous.

Naja (cobras) About 21 species, nine of which occur in Africa. The wide-ranging Asiatic cobra, formerly *N. naja*, has now been separated into at least seven distinct species. Medium-sized to large snakes with stocky, cylindrical bodies. Their heads are narrow and elegant but the most characteristic feature is the area immediately behind the head, which can be spread to form a wide hood that is almost unique among snakes. Cobras are terrestrial hunters, and may be nocturnal or diurnal. They feed on birds, small mammals and other reptiles. Some species from Africa and from Asia spit venom as a method of defence. All species are potentially dangerous to man. Oviparous: egg-guarding has been observed in some species.

Ophiophagus A monotypic genus containing only the king cobra, *O. hannah*, found from India, through Indo-

China to Southeast Asia and the Philippines. The world's largest venomous snake, at a maximum recorded length of over 5 m (16½ ft). Most specimens, however, are under 4 m (13 ft). The body is moderately slender, the head narrow. A narrow hood is spread when the snake rears up. Normally found in wooded, humid habitats but also on occasion near human settlements. The king cobra feeds only on other snakes, especially other cobras and knits. It is exceedingly dangerous to humans, though not especially aggressive unless disturbed. Oviparous, laying large clutches of up to 40 eggs in a nest of dead leaves and other debris. Both sexes remain in the vicinity of their eggs and guard them until they hatch.

Paranaja A monotypic genus containing only *P. multifasciata*, from West Africa. A medium-sized, slender snake· which is mainly terrestrial. Its biology is poorly known.

Parapistocalamus A monotypic genus containing only *P. hedigeri* from New Guinea and Bougainville in the Solomon Islands. A small snake with a slender body. It occurs in moist forests and is secretive, living under rotting logs and leaf mould. It is rare and its biology is very poorly known although it is thought to feed on the eggs of large land snails.

Pseudohaje Two species from West and Central Africa. Large cobras with slender bodies, large eyes and narrow hoods. Apparently arboreal but habits and biology very poorly known.

◄ Black Indian cobra, *Naja naja*.

▼ Red-headed krait, *Bungarus flaviceps*.

Walterinnesia A monotypic genus containing only the desert cobra, *W. aegyptia*. It is found in Egypt, the Middle East and the Arabian Peninsula, especially near oases and human settlements. A medium-sized, fairly stout snake with glossy black scales. It has no hood, nor does it rear up when disturbed. It feeds largely upon lizards, especially *Uromastyx* species, in whose burrows it sometimes lives. Dangerous to humans but bites are rare.

HYDROPHIINAE

The Hydrophiinae are, traditionally, the sea snakes and in the past they have been regarded as a separate family. Although there is still some doubt about their true relationships, it is generally accepted nowadays that the differences between them and certain terrestrial elapids (those from Australasia) are coincidental to their specialised lifestyles, i.e. they are adaptive. Therefore, the more recent view is that the Australasian terrestrial species and the sea snakes (and sea kraits) are all more closely related to each other than they are to elapids from other parts of the world.

I will deal first with the terrestrial members of the subfamily, followed by the sea kraits and ending with the sea snakes.

1. Australasian terrestrial species

Acanthophis (**death adders**) Four species found in Australia and New Guinea. Medium sized but very bulky snakes, with heavily keeled scales, that are counterparts of the vipers (which are absent from the region). They are found in a variety of habitats and eat lizards, birds and small mammals, which may be lured within range by means of the brightly coloured tail tip. Potentially dangerous to man: fatalities have occurred. Viviparous, with up to 30 young per litter, depending on species.

Aspidomorphus Three species from New Guinea and neighbouring islands. Small snakes with rounded snouts and small eyes. Nocturnal, burrowing species about which almost nothing is known.

Austrelaps (**copperheads**) Three species of medium-sized snakes restricted to Australia, including Tasmania. Cylindrical snakes that may flatten their heads when cornered. Diurnal, favouring moist situations and feeding mainly on small lizards and frogs. Viviparous, producing litters of three up to 32 young, depending on species. They are potentially dangerous to man: fatalities have occurred.

▲ Copperhead, *Austrelaps superbus*, from southeastern Australia.

Cacophis (**crowned snakes**) Four species found only along the eastern coastal zone of Australia. Small to medium-sized cylindrical snakes with a characteristic dark cap on top of their heads. Their main food is lizards, especially skinks, which are hunted at night while they are asleep. Their bite is not considered especially dangerous to man. Viviparous.

Demansia (**whipsnakes**) Eight species found in Australia and southern New Guinea. Small to medium-sized snakes with long, slender bodies, narrow heads and large eyes. They look superficially like the European and North American whipsnakes and coachwhips, and have a similar lifestyle, feeding on diurnal lizards, which they run down. Some species also eat frogs, and reptile eggs have also been found in the stomachs of two species. Oviparous, laying clutches of up to 12 eggs. A communal nest of the yellow-faced whipsnake, *D. psammophis*, has been found, containing about 600 eggs. Reluctant to bite but potentially dangerous to man.

Denisonia Five species found only in Australia. Small to medium-sized snakes

which may be slender or moderately stout. The scales are smooth but coloration varies and their eyes are large and have vertical pupils. Nocturnal, terrestrial snakes that feed mostly on frogs and lizards. Viviparous, producing litters of three to seven young. Large specimens are potentially dangerous to man.

Drysdalia Two species from southern Australia, sometimes placed in the genus *Elapognathus*. Small snakes with cylindrical bodies and narrow heads. Secretive species that live beneath debris and feed on lizards, which they hunt mainly during the day. Inoffensive and effectively harmless to humans. Viviparous, with small litters of up to 10 young.

Echiopsis Two species, the bardick, *E. curta*, and the Lake Cronin snake, *E. atriceps*. Small, fairly stout snakes from Australia. Nocturnal or crepuscular, feeding mainly on frogs and lizards but also taking small mammals and birds. When cornered, the bardick flattens its body and will bite if provoked. It is potentially dangerous to man though probably not fatal. Viviparous, with clutches of up to 14 young. The Lake Cronin snake is rare and poorly known.

Elapognathus Two species found around the southern coasts of Australia, including one species in Tasmania. Small snakes with cylindrical bodies and smooth scales. Terrestrial snakes that may be diurnal, crepuscular or nocturnal, depending on temperature. They feed mainly on lizards but may also take frogs. Not considered dangerous to man. Viviparous, producing small litters of up to 10 young. In cooler regions, females may breed every second or third year.

Furina Five species, the red-naped snake, *F. diadema*, and the orange-naped snake, *F. ornata*, from Australia. Small snakes with cylindrical bodies and smooth, glossy scales. Young specimens are brightly coloured with distinctive coloured patches on the tops of their heads. Nocturnal species that feed on lizards, especially skinks, which are caught while in their night-time retreats. Not considered to be dangerous to man on account of their small size. Oviparous, laying small clutches of one to six eggs.

Hemiaspis Two species found in eastern Australia. Small to medium-sized snakes with cylindrical bodies and smooth, shiny scales. Terrestrial species that may be crepuscular or nocturnal. *H. damelii* feeds almost exclusively on frogs whereas the other species, *H. signata*, eats frogs and lizards. Their bites may be painful but are not considered dangerous to man. Viviparous, producing litters of three to 20 young.

Hoplocephalus Three species restricted to eastern Australia. Medium-sized snakes with elongated bodies and broad heads. The ventral scales have a ridge along either side to assist in climbing. specialised snakes that may be arboreal (*H. bitorquatus*), saxicolous (*H. bungaroides*) or both (*H. stephensii*). They feed mainly on lizards but frogs, birds and small mammals (including bats) are also taken. Potentially dangerous to man. Viviparous, producing litters of two to 12 young every other year.

Loveridgelaps A monotypic genus containing only *L. elapoides*, from the Solomon Islands. A medium-sized snake with a slender, cylindrical body and bright 'coral snake' coloration consisting of white and black bands. The dorsal parts of the white bands are suffused with bright yellow. A very rare snake that occurs in forested areas, especially near streams. It is nocturnal and secretive and feeds on lizards, blind snakes and, probably, frogs. Possibly dangerous to humans but not aggressive. Reproductive habits unknown.

Micropechis (small-eyed snake) A monotypic genus containing only *M. ikaheka*, from New Guinea and some neighbouring islands. A medium-sized to large snake with a stocky body. The eye is very small. A secretive species that lives beneath forest debris in rainforests, swamps and other moist habitats. Largely nocturnal, probably feeding on other reptiles, frogs and small mammals. A dangerously venomous species whose bites can produce symptoms similar to those of sea snakes (myotoxic).

Notechis (tiger snakes) Two variable species, *N. ater* and *N. scutatus* with restricted ranges along southern Australia. Forms of the black tiger snake, *N. ater*, also occur on Tasmania and several small offshore islands. Medium-sized to large snakes with powerful bodies and smooth, shiny scales. Variable in coloration but with a tendency to become melanistic, especially in cooler localities. When disturbed, they inflate and deflate their bodies, while giving a loud hiss. The neck and front part of the body is flattened to a considerable degree and the snake may strike repeatedly. They are terrestrial and diurnal for most of the year, becoming nocturnal during hot weather. Their diet consists of fish, frogs, lizards, birds and small mammals – in fact almost anything that will fit into their mouths. Very dangerous to man: fatalities have occurred.

▲ Inland taipan, or fierce snake,
Oxyuranus microlepidotus, from the arid
centre of Australia.

Ogmodon A monotypic genus containing only the Fijian species *O. vitianus*. A small snake, rarely collected and found only on the island of Vitu Levi. It is a secretive, fossorial species that lives in mountain valleys. There is evidence that it eats earthworms and other soft-bodied invertebrates.

Oxyuranus (taipans) Two species, the inland taipan, *O. microlepidotus*, found in central Australia and the Taipan, *O. scutellatus*, from northern Australia and southern New Guinea. Large, moderately slender snakes with large heads and prominent eyes. Mainly diurnal but becoming nocturnal in hot weather. Taipans of both species feed on mammals including rodents and bandicoots. Large prey is bitten then released, to be tracked down later, but small prey may be held while the venom takes effect. Extremely dangerous to man, although rarely encountered. The inland taipan produces the most powerful venom of any land snake in the world. Oviparous, laying clutches of up to 22 eggs.

Pseudechis Six species found in Australia (five species) and New Guinea (one or two species). Large, moderately slender snakes with smooth glossy or matt scales and variable coloration. They all flatten their neck when cornered. Terrestrial snakes that may be diurnal, crepuscular or nocturnal, depending on the weather. A wide range of prey is taken, including frogs, lizards, other snakes, birds and small mammals. Not normally aggressive but potentially very dangerous to man. Reproduction variable: *P. porphyriacus* is viviparous, but the others are oviparous, with clutches of up to 19 eggs.

Pseudonaja (brown snakes) Seven species found throughout Australia (although some have limited ranges) and with one species ranging into eastern New Guinea. The western brown snake, *P. nuchalis*, occurs in several forms, some

of which may later be described as distinct species. Small, medium-sized or large snakes with moderately slender bodies and smooth scales. They have small heads but their eyes are fairly large. Terrestrial species that are active mainly in the day, chasing and running down their prey of lizards, birds and small mammals. Irritable and aggressive snakes that may flatten their necks when annoyed. Potentially dangerous to man. Oviparous, sometimes laying clutches of over 30 eggs (larger species) but usually somewhat less.

Rhinoplocephalus Six species as currently recognised although species have been shuffled between this genus and *Cryptophis* in the past. Species previously known as *Unechis* are also included here. Found in desert or semi-desert regions in

◀ Mulga, or king brown, snake, *Pseudechis australis*, found throughout Australia.

Suta Ten species, including several previously placed in *Denisonia*, *Unechis* and others. Small snakes with small heads and smooth scales. Mostly uniform in colour although several have black patches on the tops of their heads and some have a dark vertebral line. Shy, nocturnal snakes that occupy a variety of habitats but which are most often associated with mist woods and grasslands. Their prey consists almost entirely of small skinks. Viviparous, with litters of one to 11 young.

Toxicocalamus About nine species found only in New Guinea and neighbouring islands. Small to medium-sized snakes with small eyes. They live in rainforests and montane forests and are nocturnal and perhaps semi-burrowing. Otherwise their biology is poorly known.

Tropidechis A monotypic genus containing only the rough-scaled snake, *T. carinatus*, restricted to a small area of southeastern Australia. A medium-sized snake with a moderately slender body and heavily keeled scales. The snake is nocturnal and partially arboreal, feeding on tree frogs and arboreal mammals, but it may also descend to the ground to forage. Potentially dangerous to man. Viviparous, producing up to 18 relatively large young.

various parts of Australia. Small snakes with stout, cylindrical bodies, short tails and small, flattened heads. The scales are smooth and shiny. They are active at night, foraging in crevices and undergrowth for small sleeping lizards. Not considered dangerous to man on account of their small size. Viviparous, producing small litters of relatively large young. The biology of some species is poorly known.

Salomonelaps A monotypic genus containing only *S. par*, from the Solomon Islands. A medium-sized snake with variable coloration and markings. It is found in forested areas and is mainly diurnal, feeding on frogs and small reptiles. Potentially dangerous to humans, though it is not normally aggressive. Reproduction unknown.

Simoselaps Fourteen species found throughout Australia, restricted mainly to the arid parts. Small, burrowing snakes that move beneath the surface, swimming rapidly through loose sand or soil. Their scales are smooth and highly polished and a number of species have shovel-shaped snouts to aid with digging and burrowing (and are therefore known as shovel-nosed snakes). Several species are brightly marked with transverse body bands or annuli. In many of these features they parallel the habits and appearance of snakes of the North American genera *Chilomeniscus* and *Chionactis*. They come up to the surface at night. Some species eat small lizards (skinks) while others eat reptile eggs. A few species eat both. Some, probably all, species are oviparous, laying clutches of three to five eggs.

Vermicella (bandy-bandies) Two species found in Australia. Both are regarded as rare, and have suffered from habitat destruction, especially through agricultural practices. Small to medium-sized snakes with slender, cylindrical bodies, smooth, shiny scales and small eyes. Both species are boldly marked with white rings around an otherwise black body. Burrowing species that appear on the surface only at night in warm damp weather, in search of blind snakes (*Ramphotyphlops* species), on which they appear to feed exclusively. Not regarded as particularly dangerous to man, although bites have occurred. Oviparous, with clutches of up to 13 eggs.

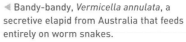
◄ Bandy-bandy, *Vermicella annulata*, a secretive elapid from Australia that feeds entirely on worm snakes.

2. Sea kraits

Laticauda Seven species, including two recently described (2005). Primarily marine snakes although one species, *L. crockeri*, is found only in the land-locked Lake Te-Nggano, Rennell Island, in the Solomon Islands, where the water is brackish. They are found around the shores of Southeast Asia, including those of the many large and small islands in the southwestern Pacific. Two species reach the northern Australian coast. Medium-sized snakes with cylindrical bodies and a flattened tail. All species are distinctively banded in black (or dark brown) and white, but *L. crockeri* is inclined to become melanistic and may be uniformly dark brown in colour. Apart from *L. crockeri*, the sea kraits are found in shallow water over coral reefs and outcrops. Access to exposed land appears to be a necessity, for shedding, drinking and egg laying. They feed on fish, especially eels. Oviparous, laying clutches of up to 20 eggs in crevices in exposed coral and rocky outcrops. There is some doubt surrounding the reproduction of *L. colubrina* and *L. crockeri*: there are unconfirmed reports of live-bearing in these two species. *L. colubrina*, however, lays eggs in at least parts of its range.

3. Sea snakes

Acalyptophis A monotypic genus containing the horned sea snake, *A. peronii* from offshore waters around northern Australia, Indonesia and adjacent parts of Southeast Asia. A medium-sized snake with a slender forebody and stout hindbody. The head is small and the tail is laterally flattened. It prefers seas with sandy beds and coral reefs and apparently feeds on small fish such as gobies. Viviparous, producing 4 to 10 young.

Aipysurus Eight species found in shallow waters between the northern Australian coast, Indonesia and New Guinea. Three species have slightly more extensive ranges into the South China Sea. Small to large (mostly medium-sized) snakes with quite stout bodies and laterally flattened tails. They are found in the vicinity of reefs and most species eat small fish. *A. laevis* also takes crustaceans and fish eggs, while *A. eydouxii* seems to eat only fish eggs and its venom apparatus is not well developed. Viviparous, producing small litters of young.

Astrotia A monotypic genus containing only Stokes' sea snake, *A. stokesii*. This species has a large range, from the seas around India, through Southeast Asia as far as northern Australian waters. A large, heavy-bodied sea snake with a deeply flattened tail and a keel-like row of ventral scales. It feeds on slow-moving fish and may be aggressive to humans. Fatalities have resulted from attacks by this species. Viviparous, producing one to five large young.

Disteira Four species, one of which, *D. kingii*, comes from northern Australia, whereas the others are from India, the Malayan peninsula and Southeast Asia. Similar to *Hyarophis*, in which genus they are included by some authorities.

Emydocephalus Two species of sea snakes, *E. annulatus* from the seas around northern Australia, and *E. ijimae*, from the region of Taiwan and the Ryukyu Islands, Japan. Medium-sized snakes with slender bodies and only moderately flattened tails. Their heads are short, rounded and covered with large scales. The rostral scale is conical in shape and the general appearance has led to the common name of 'turtle-headed sea snakes'. Both species feed exclusively on the eggs of fish. Their venom apparatus is poorly developed and they do not pose a threat to humans. Viviparous.

Enhydrina Two species, *E. zweifeli* and *E. schistosa*, sometimes placed in the genus Disteira. They are distinguished by a specialised scale at the front of their chin,

◄ Yellow-lipped sea krait, *Laticauda colubrina*, from Indian, Southeast Asian and northeast Australian waters.

thought to be an adaptation to their diet of catfish and puffer fish. *E. schistosa* is a widespread species, living in shallow waters, especially those of estuaries and tidal bays, from the Persian Gulf to the South China Sea and northern Australia: *E. zweifeli* is restricted to the coasts of New Guinea. Medium-sized snakes with elongated bodies. Because of its habitat preference, *E. schistosa* is sometimes trodden on in shallow water. It bites when provoked and is the cause of most sea snake mortalities. Viviparous, producing litters of up to 34 young.

Ephalophis A monotypic genus containing only *E. greyi*, found around the north-west coast of Australia. A small species with cylindrical body and flattened tail. It lives only among the tidal mangrove creeks and flats, where it feeds on gobies in shallow water. This species is relatively agile when out of the water and may remain in the intertidal zone at low water. The effects of its venom on humans are unknown. Probably viviparous.

Hydrelaps A monotypic genus containing the Port Darwin seasnake *H. darwiniensis*, from the coasts of northwestern Australia. A small species, similar in shape and habits to *Ephalophis greyi*, foraging in shallow water for small fish living in crab burrows of the intertidal zone. Inoffensive but potentially dangerous to humans. Presumed to be viviparous.

Hydrophis Thirty species, and therefore the largest genus of sea snakes. Found from the Persian Gulf to the western Pacific and northern shores of Australia. One species, *H. semperi*, is unique among hydropheine snakes: it is found only in the freshwater Lake Taal on Luzon Island, the Philippines. Small, medium-sized or, occasionally, large snakes, with small heads and relatively slender bodies, although the hindpart becomes progressively bulkier in some species. Apart from the freshwater species mentioned above, the members of this genus are found in shallow seas and coastal waters although they have also been recorded at great depths. They feed mostly on eels, although some species eat fish eggs. Their venom is potent and human fatalities have occurred. Viviparous.

Kerilia A monotypic genus containing only *K. jerdoni*, from Southeast Asia.

Medium-sized with a compressed body and tail. Biology poorly known. Assumed to be viviparous.

Kolpophis A monotypic genus containing only *K. annandalei*, found in the coastal waters from Thailand to Indonesia. Further details of this newly described species are lacking.

Lapemis Two species, *L. curtus* and *L. hardwickii*, with a wide distribution from the Persian Gulf to the north coast of Australia. Stout species with large heads. The body scales become progressively more keeled towards the middle of the belly and are spiny in adult males. (But note these are not the ventral scales, which are greatly reduced in size in these and all sea snakes.) They live in coastal waters, especially in and around estuaries and river mouths where the water is turbid, and feed on small fish. They bite readily if handled and human fatalities have occurred. Viviparous, producing small litters of young.

Parahydrophis A monotypic genus containing only *P. mertoni*, found around the northern coasts of Australia and the southern coasts of New Guinea and neighbouring islands. A small species with moderately slender, cylindrical body and smooth scales. It is found in tidal estuarine waters, among mangroves and feeds on small fish. Potentially dangerous to humans. Viviparous, producing small litters of young.

Pelamis A monotypic genus containing the pelagic sea snake, *P. platurus*. This species has a range larger than that of any other snake. It is pelagic and is found in the surface waters off eastern Africa, southern Asia as far north as Japan, and northern Australasia, reaching round to Tasmania in the south. In addition, it can be found along the Pacific coast of Central and northern South America. Its body is slender and the head is long and narrow. Its coloration is variable but is normally some combination of bluish black and yellow. Entirely yellow individuals are also known. Hundreds, if not thousands, of individuals sometimes join forces to form huge 'slicks' extending over great areas. The shelter afforded by these aggregations may attract the fish on which they feed. Liable to bite, although fishermen often handle them with apparent impunity though their venom is very toxic. In tropical waters, reproduction probably occurs throughout the year. Litters of two to six young.

Thalassophina A monotypic genus containing only *T. viperina*, previously assigned to the genus *Praescutata*, among others. It is found from the Persian Gulf, through the South China Sea as far as Indonesia. A medium-sized species with very rough scales. Viviparous.

Thalassophis A monotypic genus containing only *T. anomoms*, found in the coastal waters of Thailand and Indonesia.

▼ Distribution of Elapidae II (sea snakes).

BIBLIOGRAPHY

Nearly all the books here deal exclusively with snakes. I have included a few reptile, or reptile and amphibian guides, however, either because they have especially good sections on snakes or because they deal with parts of the world that are not otherwise covered.

Snake Natural History and Biology

Burton, John A., *Snakes: An Illustrated Guide.* Blandford Press, London, 1991.

Cobom, John., *The Atlas of Snakes of the World,* TFH Publications, New Jersey, USA.

Greene, H. W., *Snakes, The Evolution of Mystery in Nature,* University of California Press, Berkeley, 1997.

Mattison, C., *Snake,* Dorling Kindersley, 1999.

Mehrtens, John., *Living Snakes of the World,* Sterling Publishing Co., New York, and Blandford Press. London, 1987.

Parker, H. W. and Grandison, A. G. C., *Snakes — A Natural History,* British Museum (Natural History), London, 1977.

Porter, *Herpetology.* W. B. Saunders Company, 1972.

Seigel, Richard A., Collins, Joseph T. and Novak, Susan S., *Snakes: Ecology and Evolutionary Biology.* Macmillan Publishing Company, New York, 1987.

Seigel, Richard A. and Collins, Joseph T., Snakes: *Ecology and Behaviour,* McGraw-Hill, New York, 1993.

Regional Accounts and Identification Guides

WORLDWIDE

The EMBL Reptile Database. An invaluable CD, suitable for recent Mac and Windows operating systems, listing every known species of reptile, including synonyms, distribution and references. Available from Peter Uetz (visit the website www.reptile-database.org for methods of ordering).

NORTH AMERICA

Behler. John L. and Wayne King, F., *The Audubon Society Field Guide to North American Reptiles and Amphibians,* Alfred A. Knopf, New York, 1979.

Ashton, Ray E. and Ashton, Patricia S., *Handbook of Reptiles and Amphibians of Florida. Part 1: The Snakes,* Windward Publishing, Inc., Miami, Florida, 1981. (Of more general interest than its title suggests because Florida has such a rich snake fauna.)

Conant, Roger, *A Field Guide to the Reptiles and Amphibians of Eastern and Central North America,* Houghton Mifflin Company, Boston, third edition, 1998.

Ernst, C. H. and Ernst, E. M., *Snakes of the United States and Canada,* Smithsonian Books, Washington, 2003.

Grismer, L. L., *Amphibians and Reptiles of Baja California,* University of California Press, Berkeley, 2002.

Stebbins, Robert C., *A Field Guide to Western Reptiles and Amphibians,* Houghton Mifflin Company, Boston, second edition, 1985.

Tennant, Alan, *The Snakes of Texas.* Texas Monthly Press, Austin, Texas. 1984. (Of general interest because Texas has such a rich snake fauna. Also available in an abridged form as *A Field Guide to the Snakes of Texas,* 1985.)

Wright, A. H. and Wright. A. A., *Handbook of Snakes,* two volumes, Comstock Publishing Associates. Ithaca, 1957. (The standard work on the snakes of North America.)

SOUTH AND CENTRAL AMERICA

Amaral, Afrânio do, *Serpentes do Brasil* (Brazilian Snakes: A Color Iconography), Ministry of Education and Culture, São Paulo, Brazil, 1977. (In Portuguese and English. Rather dated in its treatment and layout but still the most complete account of the snakes of this herpetologically important country.)

Cei, J. M., *Reptile del Centro, Centro-oeste y Sur de la Argentina,* Museo Regionale di Scienze Naturali, Turin, 1986. (In Spanish.)

Chippaux, Jean-Philippe, *Les Serpents de la Guyane Française* (The snakes of French Guiana), Institut Français de recherche scientifique pour le développement en coopération. Collection Faune Tropicale No. XXVII, Paris, 1986. (In French.)

Henderson, Robert W. and Schwartz, Albert, *A Guide to the Identification of the Amphibians and Reptiles of Hispaniola,* Milwaukee Public Museum, Special Publications in Biology and Geology Number 4, 1984.

Perez-Santos, Carlos and Moreno, Ana G., *Ofidios de Colombia,* Museo Regionale di Scienze Naturali, Turin, 1988. (In Spanish.)

Perez-Santos, Carlos and Moreno, Ana G., *Serpientes do Ecuador* (Snakes of Ecuador), Museo Regionale di Scienze Naturali, Turin, 1991. (In Spanish.)

Rivero, J. A., *The Amphibians and Reptiles of Puerto Rico,* Universidad de Puerto Rico.

Rose, Janis A., *La Taxonomia y Zoogeographia de los Ofidios de Venezuela,* Universidad Central de Venezuela, Caracas, 1966. (In Spanish.)

Savage, J. M., *The Amphibians and Reptiles of Costa Rica,* University of Chicago Press, Chicago, 2002.

Schwartz, Albert and Henderson, Robert W., *A Guide to the Identification of the Amphibians and Reptiles of the West Indies Exclusive of Hispaniola,* Milwaukee Public Museum, 1985.

Wilson, Larry D. and Meyer, John R., *The Snakes of Honduras,* Milwaukee Public Museum, 1985.

EUROPE

Appleby, L., *British Snakes,* Baker, 1971.

Arnold, E. N. and Burton, J. A., *A Field Guide to the Reptiles and Amphibians of Britain and Europe,* Collins. London, 1978.

Boulenger, G. A., *The Snakes of Europe,* Methuen and Company, Ltd., London, 1913. (Hopelcssly out of date taxonomically, but the first book to deal with the European snakes in a readable style. A collectors' item.)

Dimitropoulos, A., *Snakes in the Cyclades,* (In Greek with English summaries.)

Frazer, D., *Reptiles and Amphibians in Britain,* Collins, London, 1989.

Steward, J. W., *The Snakes of Europe,* David and Charles, Newton Abbot, England, 1971.

ASIA AND THE MIDDLE EAST

Alcala, A. C., *Guide to Philippine Flora and Fauna. Volume X: Amphibians and Reptiles,* Natural Resources Management Centre. Ministry of Natural Resources and University of the Philippines, 1986.

Cox, M. J., *The Snakes of Thailand and their Husbandry,* Krieger, Malabar. Florida, 1991.

Goris, R. C. and Maeda, N., *Guide to the Amphibians and Reptiles of Japan,* Krieger, Florida, 2004.

Latifi, M., *The Snakes of Iran,* Society for the Study of Amphibians and Reptiles. Oxford, Ohio, 1991.

Leviton, A. E., Anderson, S. C., Adler, Kraig and Minton, S. A., *Handbook to Middle East Amphibians and Reptiles,* Society for the Study of Reptiles and Amphibians, Oxford, Ohio, 1992. (Covers part of the Arabian peninsula, Kuwait, Iraq and a small part of Iran.)

Lim, K. K. P. and Lim, F. L. K., *A Guide to the Amphibians and Reptiles of Singapore,* Singapore Science Centre, 1992. (A small but useful book with excellent colour photographs of the most common species found in Singapore.)

Maki, M. A., *Monograph of the Snakes of Japan,* 3 volumes, Dai-ichi Shobo, Tokyo, 1931. (In Japanese. A valuable collectors' item.)

O'Shea, M., *A Guide to the Snakes of Papua New Guinea,* Independent Publishing, Port Moresby, Papua New Guinea, 1996.

de Silva, A., *Colour Guide to the Snakes of Sri Lanka,* R & A Publishing Limited, Avon. England, 1990.

Steubing, R. B. and Inger, R. F., *A Field Guide to the Snakes of Borneo,* Natural History Publications (Borneo), Kota Kinabalu, Malaysia, 1999.

Tweedie, M. F. W., *The Snakes of Malaya,* Government Printing Office, Singapore, 1953. (Becoming rather out of date now but still the most detailed account of the snakes of the Malaysian Peninsula and Singapore.)

Wall, Colonel F., *Ophidia Taprobanica or The Snakes of Ceylon*, Government Printing Office, Colombo. Ceylon (Sri Lanka). 1921. (Rather out of date taxonomically but very valuable owing to the wealth of first-hand observations reported here. A collectors' item.)

Whitaker, R. and Captain, A, *Snakes of India*, Draco Books, Chennai, India, 2004.

Zhao, Er-mi and Adler, Kraig, *Herpetology of China*, Society for the Study of Amphibians and Reptiles, Oxford, Ohio, 1993.

AUSTRALASIA

Cogger, H. G., *Reptiles and Amphibians of Australia (6th edition)*, A. H. and A. W. Reed Pty Ltd., Sydney, 2000.

Ehmann. H., *Encyclopedia of Australian Animals: Reptiles*, Angus and Robertson, Pymble, New South Wales, 1992.

Glasby, C. J., Ross, G. J. B., and Beesley, P. L. (eds). *Fauna of Australia. Vol 2A Amphibia and Reptilia*, Australian Government Publishing Service, Canberra, 1993.

Gow, G. F., *Complete Guide to Australian Snakes*, Angus and Robertson, Sydney, 1989.

McCoy, M., *Reptiles of the Solomon Islands*, Wau Ecology Institute Handbook No. 7, Wan, Papua New Guinea, 1980.

O'Shea, M., *A Guide to the Snakes of Papua New Guinea*, Independent Publishing, Port Moresby, Papua New Guinea (in press).

Shine, R., *Australian Snakes: A Natural History*, Reed Books, Balgowlah., NSW. (Describes the natural history of the rich Australian snake fauna. Not an identification guide.)

Weigel, J., *Snakes of South-East Australia* (Australian Reptiles Park's Guide to), Australian Reptile Park, Gosford, NSW, 1990.

AFRICA

Branch, B., *Field Guide to the Snakes and other Reptiles of Southern Africa*, New Holland, London, 1988.

Buys, P. J. and Buys. P. J. C., *Snakes of South West Africa*, Gamsburg Publishers, Windhock, no date (1980s).

Broadley, D. G., *FitzSimon's Snakes of Southern Africa*, Delta Books. 1983. (A revised version of the original book by Vivian FitzSimons, which is hard to obtain now.)

Broadley, D. G. and Cock. E.V., *Snakes of Rhodesia*, Longman, Rhodesia (Zimbabwe), 1975.

FitzSimons, V. F. M., *Snakes of Southern Africa*, Purnell and Sons, Cape Town, 1962. (Becoming rather dated but still of value owing to the great amount of detail.)

Glaw, F. and Vences, M., *A Fieldguide to the Reptiles and Amphibians of Madagascar*, Published by the authors, Germany, 1994.

Isemonger, R. M., *Snakes of Africa, Southern, Central and East*, Nelson, 1962.

Morais, J., *A Complete Guide to the Snakes of Southern Africa*, Southern Book Publishers (Pty) Ltd., South Africa, 1992, and Blandford Press, London, 1993.

Patterson R., *Reptiles of Southern Africa*, C. Struik, Cape Town, 1987.

Pitman, C. R. S., *A Guide to the Snakes of Uganda*, Wheldon and Wesley. Hertfordshire, 1974.

Spawls, S. and Branch, B., *The Dangerous Snakes of Africa*, Blandford Press, London, 1995.

Spawls, S., Howell, K., Drewes, R. and Ashe, J., *A Field Guide to the Reptiles of East Africa*, Academic Press, London, 2002.

Accounts of Families and Groups of Species

Armstrong, B. L. and Murphy, J. B., *The Natural History of Mexican Rattlesnakes*, University of Kansas, Lawrence, 1979.

Brodman, P., *Die Giftschlangen Europas und die Gattung* Vipera *in Afrika und Asien* (The poisonous snakes of Europe and the genus *Vipera* in Africa and Asia), Kümmerley and Frey, Bern, 1987. (In German.)

Campbell, J. A. and Lamar, W. W., *The Venomous Reptiles of Latin America*, Comstock Publishing Associates, Cornell University Press, Ithaca, 1989.

Campbell, J. A. and Brodie, E. D (eds), *Biology of the Pitvipers*, Selva, Tyler, Texas, 1992.

Gloyd, H. K. and Conant, R., *Snakes of the Agkistrodon Complex: A Monographic Review*, Society for the Study of Amphibians and Reptiles, 1990.

Heatwole, H., *Sea Snakes*, second edition, Kreiger, Florida, 1999.

Klauber, L. M., *Rattlesnakes: Their Habits, Life Histories and Influence on Mankind*, two volumes, University of California Press, third edition, 1997.

Lowe, C. H., Schwalbe, C. R. and Johnson, T. B., *The Venomous Reptiles of Arizona*, Arizona Fish and Game Department. 1986.

Mallow, D., Ludwig, D. and Nilson, G, *True Vipers: Natural History and Toxicology of Old World Vipers*, Krieger, Florida, 2003.

Mao, Shou-Hsian and Chen, Been-Yuan, *Sea Snakes of Taiwan*, NSC special publication number 4, The National Science Council, Taipei, Taiwan, 1980.

Mattison, C., *Rattler!*, Cassell, London, 1996.

Phelps, T., *Poisonous Snakes*. Blandford Press, London, revised edition 1989.

Pope, C., H., *The Giant Snakes*. Routledge and Kegan Paul, London, 1961. (A popular account of the six largest species of snakes.)

Schulz, K-D, *A Monograph of the Colubrid Snakes of the Genus Elaphe*, Koeltz Scientific Books, Würselen, Germany, 1996. (Deals with all the species formerly previously in Elaphe, including all those that have now been moved to various other genera.)

Sweeney, R., *Garter Snakes: Their Natural History and Care in Captivity*, Blandford, London, 1992.

Thorpe, R. S., Wüster, W. and Malhorra, A. (eds), *Venomous Snakes: Ecology, Evolution and Snakebite*, Clarendon Press, Oxford, 1997.

Tolson, P. J. and Henderson. R. W., *The Natural History of West Indian Boas*, R & A Publishing Limited, Taunton, Somerset, 1993.

Williams, K. L. and Wallach, V., *Snakes of the World, Volume 1. Synopsis of Snake Generic Names*, Krieger Publishing Company, Malabar, Florida, 1989.

Williams. K. L., *Systematics and Natural History of the American Milk Snake*, Lampropeltis triangulum, Milwaukee Public Museum, second edition, 1988.

Websites

Websites come and go and trying to list all those that deal with snakes would be futile. The following handful are those that I have found most useful and reliable. Several of them provide links for further research.

www.reptile-database.org. The EMBL reptile database.

en.wikipedia.org/wiki/List_of_Serpentes_familes. Wikipedia list of Serpentes families.

biology.bangor.ac.uk/~bss166/. A site maintained by Wolfgang Wüster at the University of Bangor, Wales.

www.kingsnake.com. A huge resource aimed mainly at the amateur snake keeper and breeder, complete with forums.

ebeltz.net/herps/etymain.html#Snakes. An explanation of the scientific names of U.S. snakes and other reptiles and amphibians.

www.iucnredlist.org/. IUCN list of threatened species, including snakes.

Snake Hunting

Kauffeld, Carl, Snakes: *The Keeper and the Kept*, Doubleday and Company, Inc., New York, 1969. (Snake hunting in the United States, with some notes on keeping snakes in captivity.)

Wykes, A., *Snake Man: The Story of C. J. P. Ionides*, Hamish Hamilton, London, 1960. (A biographical account of an eccentric and fascinating snake catcher.)

Snakes in Captivity

Mattison, Chris, *Keeping and Breeding Snakes*, Blandford Press, London, 1988.

Ross, Richard A. and Marzac, Gerald, *The Reproductive Husbandry of Pythons and Boas*, Institute for Herpetological Research, Stanford, California, 1990.

Note: There are dozens of books and booklets dealing with the care and breeding of snakes in captivity but there is not room to list them all.

INDEX

ACKNOWLEDGEMENTS

Such a large project as this book is never possible without the help of a number of individuals. People who helped by supplying specific information relating to their research, providing copies of papers they have written, or helped in other ways include the following (in alphabetical order):

Dr Claes Andren (University of Goteborg); Dr E. N. Arnold (British Museum (Natural History), London); Dr W. R. Branch (Port Elizabeth Museum, South Africa); Richard Clark; Richard Gibson (Herpetology Department, Zoological Society of London); Matt Goetz (Herpetology Department, Durrell Wildlife Conservation Trust, Jersey Zoo); Dr L. Lee Grismer (La Sierra State University, California); Dr Robert Henderson (Milwaukee Public Museum, Wisconsin); Dr Colin McCarthy (British Museum (Natural History), London); Professor S. McDowell (Rutgers University, New Jersey); Dr Goran Nilson (University of Goteborg); Dr Nikolai Orlov (Russian Academy of Sciences, St Petersburg); Paul Orange; Mark O'Shea; Dr R. D. G. Theakston (Liverpool School of Tropical Medicine).

Literature searches were carried out at the libraries of the Universities of Nottingham and Sheffield.

Special thanks to Richard Trant, who loaned several volumes of rare books from his collection and also helped with the bibliography; to Mark O'Shea for access to parts of the manuscript of his then unpublished book A Guide to the Snakes of Papua New Guinea; to Frank Schofield, Adam and April Wright, and several other friends for locating or providing specimens for photography; to the photographers, listed on page 249, who gave permission for photographs to be used; and to the artist, Alan Rollason, for his excellent work on the line drawings. Gretchen Davison helped to check sections of the manuscript and assisted in many other ways.

For the second edition, I owe the same debt of gratitude to all the people listed above, many of whom have provided yet more help in preparing the second edition. For responding to specific enquiries this time around, I am grateful to Rainer Günther (Zoologisches Museum, Universität Humboldt, Berlin); Robert Henderson (Milwaukee Public Museum, Milwaukee); Robin Lawson (California Academy of Sciences, San Francisco); Peter Uetz (The Institute for Genomic Research, Rockville, Maryland) and Wolfgang Wüster (University of Wales at Bangor).

Additional acknowledgements for help with photography, specifically for the revised edition, include Philippe Blais, Alan Francis, Daniel Fitter, Nick Garbutt, Gretchen Mattison, John Pickett, Paul Rowley (Liverpool School of Tropical Medicine), Anslem da Silva (University of Peradeniya, Sri Lanka), Sean Thomas, Martin Withers, and a number of local guides and helpers in far-flung places. All these people have given their time and help willingly and with good humour, contributing to the book's content but in no way responsible for its inadequacies. At Cassell Illustrated I would like to thank the editor, Laura Price, and the designer, Philip Gilderdale, who stepped in at the eleventh hour to put more time and effort into the book's completion than could reasonably have been expected.

PHOTOGRAPHIC CREDITS

Photographs have been provided by a number of photographers, who are credited below. Since the value of a natural history book is often judged by its visual appeal, their contributions are gratefully acknowledged here. My own photographs have been taken with the help of numerous people who have loaned or located specimens for me over the years. Many others have accompanied me on field trips to a variety of places on several continents. Their help has. always been given freely and cheerfully and their company has greatly added to my enjoyment of snakes and my determination to find out all that I can about them.

William R. Branch: 26 (top), 33, 43, 64, 78 (bottom), 95, 100 (top), 101, 103 (bottom), 104, 107, 122 (top and bottom left), 129 (top left), 136, 151 (bottom), 156 (bottom), 218 (bottom), 227, 236, 248 (top), 249, 250, 253

Nick Garbutt: 22 (bottom),194-195, 213, 232, 248 (bottom)

Koert Langeveld: 169

William B. Love: 37 (top), 79 (right), 85 (top), 91, 124 (right), 128 (top), 129 (bottom left), 130 (middle), 133 (top right and left), 135, 153, 161 (bottom), 164, 222

Chris Mattison: 1, 2-3, 8-9, 10, 12-13, 16-17, 18-19, 20, 21, 22 (top), 23, 24, 25, 26 (bottom), 27, 28, 29 30, 31, 32, 34, 35, 36, 37 (middle, bottom left and bottom right) 38, 40, 42, 44, 45, 46, 47, 48, 50, 53, 54, 55, 56-57, 59 (top) 60, 62, 67, 68, 71, 72-73, 74, 75, 76, 77, 78 (top and bottom left), 79, 80, 81, 82, 83, 84 (top), 85 (bottom), 87, 89, 94, 96-97, 99, 100 (bottom), 109, 110, 111, 112, 113 (left bottom) 114, 116, 117, 118, 120-121, 122 (bottom right) 123, 125, 126, 127, 129 (top right), 130 (bottom left and right), 131, 132, 133 (middle and bottom), 134, 135 (top right and bottom), 137 (left), 138-139, 142, 143, 144, 145, 146, 149, 151 (top), 152 (top), 154, 155, 156 (middle), 157, 159, 160, 162, 166-167, 168 (top and middle), 171, 175, 176, 177, 180, 182, 184, 185, 186, 189, 190, 193, 198, 200, 201, 204, 207, 210 (top), 211, 214, 219, 220, 223 (bottom), 224, 230, 231, 235, 237, 240, 241, 242, 243, 246, 247, 254, 256

William B. Montgomery: 129 (bottom right)

Mark O'Shea: 4, 78 (bottom right), 84 (bottom), 93, 113 (top left, right), 115, 124 (top right), 128 (bottom right), 130 (top), 137 (right), 158, 161 (top), 174, 181, 199, 210 (bottom), 223 (top), 238, 244, 245, 262 (bottom)

James Savage: 128 (bottom left)

John Tashjian: 124 (bottom), 129 (bottom left), 147, 216, 217, 218 (top), 221, 225, 226

Geoff Trinder: 148

John Weigel: 59 (bottom), 61, 66, 71, 79 (left), 102, 103 (top), 106, 113 (left top), 141, 152 (bottom), 156 (top), 168 (bottom), 172, 179, 206, 209, 258, 259, 260, 261, 262 (top)